hymns
for
the
living
church

hope PUBLISHING COMPANY
CAROL STREAM, ILLINOIS 60188

2003

Foreword

Throughout the history of the Christian church each period of spiritual renewal has been accompanied by an outburst of new Christian song. If we keep this fact in mind, a look at the contemporary scene is encouraging. The many new hymns in various styles that adorn today's burgeoning religious activity remind us that the church of Jesus Christ is indeed alive and thriving. The Hope Publishing Company, in keeping with its century-long tradition as a publisher of evangelical hymnbooks, is pleased to include many of these fresh expressions of our faith in this new collection, *Hymns for the Living Church.*

To meet present needs, a hymnal needs to be large and truly eclectic. While retaining a major part of the material that has characterized recent Hope hymnals, this book has added a great number of worship hymns from all periods as well as many songs by today's gifted writers. Included are new and historic sacred folk songs, hymns and spirituals of European and American heritage.

Hymns for the Living Church also reflects the theological thought of our day. We have tried to choose those hymns that support the preaching and teaching emphases of the "living church" in this last half of the 20th century. Of course, the central theme is the gospel and the believer's personal experience of salvation in Christ. There is also a strong emphasis on Christian growth and maturity. Current trends in evangelism and missions are supported by a number of new lyrics. Today's eschatological awareness is reflected in the many and varied selections about heaven, the coming kingdom, and Christ's second advent. Finally, the enlarged section under the caption "social concern" is indicative of the social conscience of God's people today.

In keeping with worship reform in our time, we have made an effort to update the words of hymns. Vague and obsolete imagery has been eliminated. Whenever possible, "thee" and "thine" (referring to human beings) have been changed to "you" and "yours." Since many older hymns have undergone frequent changes during their long usage, only major alterations are listed in the author credits.

From a musical point of view, we are convinced that *Hymns for the Living Church* is outstandingly singable. We have endeavored to select the best of the folk hymns and newer songs now in wide use. In choosing material from earlier periods, we have selected those tunes that are "strong" and "bright," which should be easily learned and long remembered. We have also considered the range of each melody, in order to encourage full participation in congregational singing. Many hymn tunes are offered in two or more keys, so that the director and organist will have a choice.

Our goal has been to maintain a strong biblical emphasis throughout the hymnal. The central message of each hymn is evident in the scripture passage quoted underneath the title line. In addition, we have provided a list of scriptural allusions and quotations in hymns. Ministers will find that this index can be of immense help in correlating the singing with other parts of the service.

Because we have shortened many of the traditional Scripture Readings (Nos. 592-671), it has been possible to include a larger number of selections, with several new topics. In a day when so many versions of the Bible are in vogue and no single one seems to be "authorized" or "standard," we have used a variety of translations and paraphrases. For each individual passage, we have selected the version we judge to be best for corporate reading in regular worship.

In editing this volume, we have tried to provide complete indexes with information that is accurate and up-to-date. In addition to listing birth and death dates of authors, translators, composers and arrangers, we have for the first time attempted to pinpoint the origin of each poem and hymn tune. The dates given above each hymn indicate the year of writing or of the first publishing of that particular text and musical setting. We have also endeavored to acknowledge the ownership of all copyrights, and to secure proper permission for their use. Any unintentional omission will be corrected in a subsequent edition.

The editorial committee expresses its thanks to the hundreds of ministers and musicians from leading churches who have helped us choose the contents of this hymnal. It is our hope that *Hymns for the Living Church* will make a significant contribution to the renewal and the growth of these churches, and of many others as well.

Donald P. Hustad
Editor

Contents

THE HYMNS

THE SCRIPTURE READINGS

THE INDEXES

Holy, Holy, Holy! Lord God Almighty   1

They rest not day and night, saying, Holy, holy, holy, Lord God almighty. Rev. 4:8

NICAEA 11 12 12 10

Reginald Heber, 1826

John B. Dykes, 1861

1. Ho - ly, ho - ly, ho - ly! Lord God Al - might - y!
2. Ho - ly, ho - ly, ho - ly! all the saints a - dore Thee,
3. Ho - ly, ho - ly, ho - ly! though the dark - ness hide Thee,
4. Ho - ly, ho - ly, ho - ly! Lord God Al - might - y!

Ear - ly in the morn - ing our song shall rise to Thee;
Cast - ing down their gold - en crowns a - round the glass - y sea;
Though the eye of sin - ful man Thy glo - ry may not see,
All Thy works shall praise Thy name, in earth, and sky, and sea;

Ho - ly, ho - ly, ho - ly! mer - ci - ful and might - y!
Cher - u - bim and ser - a - phim fall - ing down be - fore Thee,
On - ly Thou art ho - ly; there is none be - side Thee,
Ho - ly, ho - ly, ho - ly! mer - ci - ful and might - y!

God in three per - sons, bless - ed Trin - i - ty!
Which wert and art, and ev - er - more shalt be.
Per - fect in pow'r, in love, and pu - ri - ty.
God in three per - sons, bless - ed Trin - i - ty! A - men.

THE TRINITY

2 Almighty Father, Strong to Save

See the works of the Lord, and His wonders in the deep. Psa. 107:24

Hymnal 1940 version
A Missionary Service Book, 1937
St. 1, 4, William Whiting, 1860

MELITA 888888
John B. Dykes, 1861

1. Al-might-y Fa-ther, strong to save, Whose arm hath bound the
2. O Christ, the Lord of hill and plain O'er which our traf-fic
3. O Spir-it, whom the Fa-ther sent To spread a-broad the
4. O Trin-i-ty of love and power, Our breth-ren shield in

rest-less wave, Who bidd'st the might-y o-cean deep Its
runs a-main By moun-tain pass or val-ley low; Wher-
firm-a-ment; O Wind of heav-en, by Thy might Save
dan-ger's hour; From rock and tem-pest, fire and foe, Pro-

own ap-point-ed lim-its keep: O hear us when we
ev-er, Lord, Thy breth-ren go, Pro-tect them by Thy
all who dare the ea-gle's flight, And keep them by Thy
tect them where-so-e'er they go; Thus ev-er-more shall

cry to Thee For those in per-il on the sea.
guard-ing hand From ev-ery per-il on the land.
watch-ful care From ev-ery per-il in the air.
rise to Thee Glad praise from air and land and sea. A-men.

By permission of the Church Pension Fund.

THE TRINITY

God, Our Father, We Adore Thee 3

Ye have received the Spirit of adoption, whereby we cry, Abba, Father. Rom. 8:15

George W. Frazer, 1904
St. 3, Alfred S. Loizeaux, 1952

BEECHER 8 7 8 7 D.
John Zundel, 1870

1. God, our Fa-ther, we a-dore Thee! We, Thy chil-dren, bless Thy name!
2. Son E-ter-nal, we a-dore Thee! Lamb up-on the throne on high!
3. Ho-ly Spir-it, we a-dore Thee! Par-a-clete and heav'n-ly guest!
4. Fa-ther, Son, and Ho-ly Spir-it—Three in One! we give Thee praise!

Cho-sen in the Christ be-fore Thee, We are "ho-ly with-out blame."
Lamb of God, we bow be-fore Thee, Thou hast brought Thy peo-ple nigh!
Sent from God and from the Sav-ior, Thou hast led us in-to rest.
For the rich-es we in-her-it, Heart and voice to Thee we raise!

We a-dore Thee! we a-dore Thee! Ab-ba's prais-es we pro-claim!
We a-dore Thee! we a-dore Thee! Son of God, who came to die!
We a-dore Thee! we a-dore Thee! By Thy grace for-ev-er blest:
We a-dore Thee! we a-dore Thee! Thee we bless, thro' end-less days!

We a-dore Thee! we a-dore Thee! Ab-ba's prais-es we pro-claim!
We a-dore Thee! we a-dore Thee! Son of God, who came to die!
We a-dore Thee! we a-dore Thee! By Thy grace for-ev-er blest!
We a-dore Thee! we a-dore Thee! Thee we bless, thro' end-less days! A-men.

This tune in a lower key, No. 75

THE TRINITY

4 Come, Thou Almighty King

Give unto the Lord the glory due unto His name . . . Psa. 29:2

Source unknown, c. 1757

ITALIAN HYMN 6 6 4 6 6 6 4
Felice de Giardini, 1769

1. Come, Thou Al - might - y King, Help us Thy name to sing, Help us to praise: Fa - ther, all glo - ri - ous, O'er all vic - to - ri - ous, Come, and reign o - ver us, An - cient of Days.
2. Come, Thou In - car - nate Word, Gird on Thy might - y sword, Our prayer at - tend: Come, and Thy peo - ple bless, And give Thy word suc - cess: Spir - it of ho - li - ness, On us de - scend.
3. Come, Ho - ly Com - fort - er, Thy sa - cred wit - ness bear In this glad hour: Thou who al - might - y art, Now rule in ev - ery heart, And ne'er from us de - part, Spir - it of pow'r.
4. To Thee, great One in Three, E - ter - nal prais - es be Hence, ev - er - more! Thy sov - ereign maj - es - ty May we in glo - ry see, And to e - ter - ni - ty Love and a - dore! A - men.

This tune in a lower key, No. 74

5 Father of Heaven, Whose Love Profound

. . . The Father, the Word, and the Holy Ghost: and these three are one. I John 5:7

QUEBEC L.M.

Edward Cooper, 1805

Henry Baker, 1854

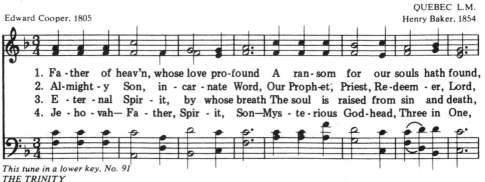

1. Fa - ther of heav'n, whose love pro - found A ran - som for our souls hath found,
2. Al - might - y Son, in - car - nate Word, Our Proph - et, Priest, Re - deem - er, Lord,
3. E - ter - nal Spir - it, by whose breath The soul is raised from sin and death,
4. Je - ho - vah— Fa - ther, Spir - it, Son—Mys - te - rious God - head, Three in One,

This tune in a lower key, No. 91
THE TRINITY

Be - fore Thy throne we hum - bly bend; To us Thy par - d'ning love ex - tend.
Be - fore Thy throne we hum - bly bend; To us Thy sav - ing grace ex - tend.
Be - fore Thy throne we hum - bly bend; To us Thy quick - 'ning pow'r ex - tend.
Be - fore Thy throne we hum - bly bend; Grace, par - don, life to us ex - tend. A - men.

Holy Father, Great Creator 6

Blessed be God . . . the Father of mercies and the God of all comfort. II Cor. 1:3

REGENT SQUARE 878787

Alexander V. Griswold, 1835

Henry T. Smart, 1867

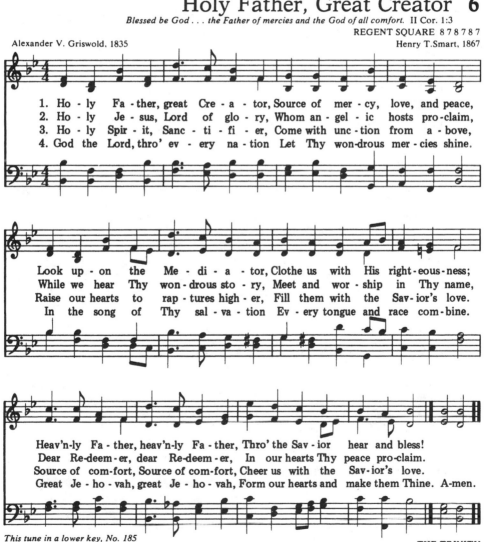

1. Ho - ly Fa - ther, great Cre - a - tor, Source of mer - cy, love, and peace,
2. Ho - ly Je - sus, Lord of glo - ry, Whom an - gel - ic hosts pro - claim,
3. Ho - ly Spir - it, Sanc - ti - fi - er, Come with unc - tion from a - bove,
4. God the Lord, thro' ev - ery na - tion Let Thy won - drous mer - cies shine.

Look up - on the Me - di - a - tor, Clothe us with His right - eous - ness;
While we hear Thy won - drous sto - ry, Meet and wor - ship in Thy name,
Raise our hearts to rap - tures high - er, Fill them with the Sav - ior's love.
In the song of Thy sal - va - tion Ev - ery tongue and race com - bine.

Heav'n - ly Fa - ther, heav'n - ly Fa - ther, Thro' the Sav - ior hear and bless!
Dear Re - deem - er, dear Re - deem - er, In our hearts Thy peace pro - claim.
Source of com - fort, Source of com - fort, Cheer us with the Sav - ior's love.
Great Je - ho - vah, great Je - ho - vah, Form our hearts and make them Thine. A - men.

This tune in a lower key, No. 185

THE TRINITY

7 Praise Ye the Father

I will . . . praise Thy name for Thy lovingkindness. Psa. 138:2

FLEMMING 11 11 11 6

Elizabeth R. Charles, c. 1859

Friedrich F. Flemming, 1811

1. Praise ye the Fa - ther! for His lov - ing kind - ness, Ten - der - ly
2. Praise ye the Sav - ior! great is His com - pas - sion, Gra - cious - ly
3. Praise ye the Spir - it! Com - fort - er of Is - rael, Sent of the

cares He for His err - ing chil - dren; Praise Him, ye an - gels,
cares He for His cho - sen peo - ple; Young men and maid - ens,
Fa - ther and the Son to bless us; Praise ye the Fa - ther,

praise Him in the heav - ens, Praise ye Je - ho - vah!
ye old men and chil - dren, Praise ye the Sav - ior!
Son and Ho - ly Spir - it, Praise ye the tri - une God! A - men.

8 Glory Be to God the Father

To Him be glory and dominion for ever and ever. Rev. 1:6

FREUEN WIR UNS ALLE 8 7 8 7

Horatius Bonar, 1866

Michael Weisse, c. 1480-1534

Unison

1. Glo - ry be to God the Fa - ther! Glo - ry be to God the Son!
2. Glo - ry be to Him who loved us, Washed us from each spot and stain!
3. Glo - ry to the King of an - gels! Glo - ry to the Church - 's King!
4. Glo - ry, bless - ing, praise e - ter - nal! Thus the choir of an - gels sings,

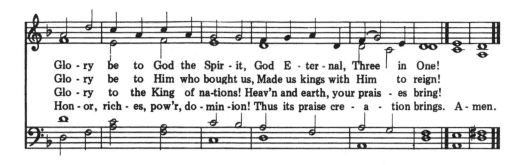

Glo - ry be to God the Spir - it, God E - ter - nal, Three in One!
Glo - ry be to Him who bought us, Made us kings with Him to reign!
Glo - ry to the King of na-tions! Heav'n and earth, your prais - es bring!
Hon - or, rich - es, pow'r, do - min -ion! Thus its praise cre - a - tion brings. A - men.

Holy God, We Praise Thy Name 9

Holy, Holy, Holy is the Lord of hosts. Isa. 6:3

Attr. to Ignace Franz, c. 1774
Trans. by Clarence A. Walworth, 1853
Based on *Te Deum*, c. 4th century

GROSSER GOTT, WIR LOBEN DICH 7 8 7 8 7 7
Katholisches Gesangbuch, Vienna, c. 1774

1. Ho - ly God, we praise Thy name; Lord of all, we bow be - fore Thee;
2. Hark, the loud ce - les - tial hymn An - gel choirs a - bove are rais - ing;
3. Lo! the ap - os - tol - ic train Join Thy sa - cred name to hal - low;
4. Ho - ly Fa - ther, Ho - ly Son, Ho - ly Spir - it, Three we name Thee;

All on earth Thy scep - ter claim, All in heav'n a - bove a - dore Thee.
Cher - u - bim and ser - a - phim In un - ceas - ing cho - rus prais - ing,
Proph - ets swell the glad re - frain, And the white-robed mar - tyrs fol - low;
While in es - sence on - ly One, Un - di - vid - ed God we claim Thee,

In - fi - nite Thy vast do-main, Ev - er - last - ing is Thy reign.
Fill the heav'ns with sweet ac - cord: Ho - ly, ho - ly, ho - ly Lord.
And from morn to set of sun, Through the Church the song goes on.
And a - dor - ing bend the knee, While we sing our praise to Thee. A - men.

THE TRINITY

10 All Glory Be to God on High

Glory to God in the highest, and on earth peace, good will toward men. Luke 2:14

Nicolaus Decius, 1522
Based on *Gloria in Excelsis*
Trans. by Catherine Winkworth, 1863

ALLEIN GOTT IN DER HÖH 8 7 8 7 8 8 7
Nicolaus Decius, 1522
Geistliche Lieder, 1539

1. All glo-ry be to God on high, Who hath our race be-friend-ed. To us no harm shall now come nigh; The strife at last is end-ed. God show-eth His good will to men, And peace shall reign on earth a-gain: O thank Him for His good-ness!

2. We praise, we wor-ship Thee, we trust, And give Thee thanks for-ev-er, O Fa-ther, that Thy rule is just, And wise, and chang-es nev-er. Thy bound-less pow'r o'er all things reigns, Thou dost what-e'er Thy will or-dains. 'Tis well Thou art our Rul-er!

3. O Je-sus Christ, our God and Lord, Be-got-ten of the Fa-ther, Who hast our fal-len race re-stored And stray-ing sheep dost gath-er; Thou Lamb of God, en-throned on high, Be-hold our need, and hear our cry: Have mer-cy on us, Je-sus!

4. O Ho-ly Spir-it, pre-cious Gift, Thou Com-fort-er un-fail-ing, Do Thou our trou-bled souls up-lift, A-gainst the foe pre-vail-ing; Since Christ for us His blood hath shed, A-vert our woes and calm our dread; We trust in Thee to help us! A-men.

THE TRINITY

A Mighty Fortress Is Our God   11

God is our refuge and strength. Psa. 46:1

Psalm 46
Martin Luther, 1529
Trans. by Frederick H. Hedge, 1852

EIN' FESTE BURG 8 7 8 7 6 6 6 6 7
Martin Luther, 1529

1. A might-y for-tress is our God, A bul-wark nev-er fail-ing;
2. Did we in our own strength con-fide, Our striv-ing would be los-ing,
3. And though this world, with dev-ils filled, Should threat-en to un-do us,
4. That word a-bove all earth-ly powers, No thanks to them, a-bid-eth;

Our help-er He, a-mid the flood Of mor-tal ills pre-vail-ing:
Were not the right Man on our side, The man of God's own choos-ing:
We will not fear, for God hath willed His truth to tri-umph through us:
The Spir-it and the gifts are ours Through him who with us sid-eth:

For still our an-cient foe Doth seek to work us woe; His craft and power are
Dost ask who that may be? Christ Je-sus, it is He; Lord Sab-a-oth His
The Prince of Dark-ness grim, We trem-ble not for him; His rage we can en-
Let goods and kin-dred go, This mor-tal life al-so; The bod-y they may

great, And, armed with cru-el hate, On earth is not his e-qual.
name, From age to age the same, And He must win the bat-tle.
dure, For lo, his doom is sure; One lit-tle word shall fell him.
kill: God's truth a-bid-eth still; His king-dom is for-ev-er. A-men.

GOD THE FATHER: HIS PRAISE

12 Praise the Lord, His Glories Show

Bless ye the Lord . . . ye ministers of His, that do His pleasure. Psa. 103:21

Psalm 148
Henry F. Lyte, 1834

GWALCHMAI 7 7 7 7 Alleluias
Joseph D. Jones, 1868

1. Praise the Lord, His glo - ries show, Al - le - lu - ia!
2. Earth to heav'n and heav'n to earth, Al - le - lu - ia!
3. Praise the Lord, His mer - cies trace, Al - le - lu - ia!

Saints with - in His courts be - low, Al - le - lu - ia!
Tell His won - ders, sing His worth, Al - le - lu - ia!
Praise His prov - i - dence and grace, Al - le - lu - ia!

An - gels round His throne a - bove, Al - le - lu - ia!
Age to age and shore to shore, Al - le - lu - ia!
All that He for man hath done, Al - le - lu - ia!

All that see and share His love, Al - le - lu - ia!
Praise Him, praise Him ev - er - more! Al - le - lu - ia!
All He sends us through His Son. Al - le - lu - ia! A-men.

GOD THE FATHER

Sing Praise to God Who Reigns Above 13

The Lord reigneth; let the earth rejoice . . . Psa. 97:1

Johann J. Schütz, 1675
Trans. by Frances E. Cox, 1864

MIT FREUDEN ZART 8 7 8 7 8 8 7
Bohemian Brethren's *Kirchengesänge*, Berlin, 1566

1. Sing praise to God who reigns a - bove, The God of all cre - a - tion, The God of pow'r, the God of love, The God of our sal - va - tion; With heal - ing balm my soul He fills, And ev - ery faith - less mur-mur stills: To God all praise and glo - ry.

2. What God's al - might - y pow'r hath made His gra-cious mer - cy keep-eth; By morn-ing glow or eve-ning shade His watch-ful eye ne'er sleep - eth; With - in the king - dom of His might, Lo! all is just and all is right: To God all praise and glo - ry.

3. The Lord is nev - er far a - way, But, through all grief dis - tress-ing, An ev - er - pres - ent help and stay, Our peace, and joy, and bless - ing; As with a moth - er's ten - der hand, He leads His own, His cho-sen band: To God all praise and glo - ry.

4. Thus, all my glad - some way a - long, I sing a - loud Thy prais - es, That men may hear the grate-ful song My voice un - wea - ried rais - es, Be joy - ful in the Lord, my heart, Both soul and bod - y bear your part: To God all praise and glo - ry. A - men.

HIS PRAISE

14 Rejoice, Ye Pure in Heart

Rejoice in the Lord, O ye righteous . . . , Psa. 33:1

Edward H. Plumptre, 1865

MARION S.M. Ref.
Arthur H. Messiter, 1883

1. Re - joice, ye pure in heart, Re - joice, give thanks, and sing;
2. Bright youth and snow-crowned age, Strong men and maid - ens fair,
3. With all the an - gel choirs, With all the saints on earth,
4. Yes, on through life's long path, Still chant - ing as ye go;
5. Still lift your stand - ard high, Still march in firm ar - ray;

Your fes - tal ban - ner wave on high, The cross of Christ your King.
Raise high your free, ex - ult - ing song, God's won - drous praise de - clare.
Pour out the strains of joy and bliss, True rap - ture, no - blest mirth!
From youth to age, by night and day, In glad - ness and in woe.
As war - riors through the dark - ness toil Till dawns the gold - en day.

Refrain

Re - joice, re - joice, Re - joice, give thanks, and sing! A - men.
Re - joice, re - joice,

15 Begin, My Tongue, Some Heavenly Theme

My tongue shall speak of Thy righteousness . . . Psa. 35:28

Isaac Watts, 1707

LAND OF REST C.M.
Traditional American melody
Arr. by Annabel M. Buchanan, 1938

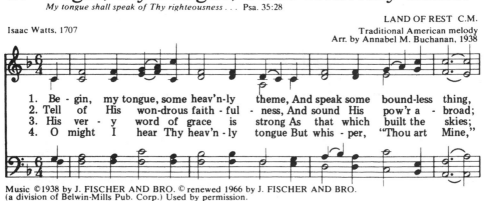

1. Be - gin, my tongue, some heav'n - ly theme, And speak some bound - less thing,
2. Tell of His won - drous faith - ful - ness, And sound His pow'r a - broad;
3. His ver - y word of grace is strong As that which built the skies;
4. O might I hear Thy heav'n - ly tongue But whis - per, "Thou art Mine,"

GOD THE FATHER

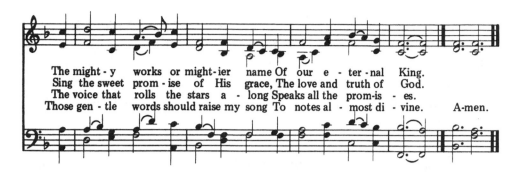

The might-y works or might-ier name Of our e-ter-nal King.
Sing the sweet prom-ise of His grace, The love and truth of God.
The voice that rolls the stars a-long Speaks all the prom-is-es.
Those gen-tle words should raise my song To notes al-most di-vine. A-men.

O Splendor of God's Glory Bright 16

That was the true Light, which lighteth every man . . . John 1:9

WINCHESTER NEW L.M.

St. Ambrose of Milan, c. 340-397
Trans. composite

Georg Rebenlein's *Musicalisch Handbuch*, Hamburg, 1690
Arr. by William H. Havergal, 1847

1. O Splen-dor of God's glo-ry bright, From light e-
2. Come, ver-y Sun of heav-en's love, In last-ing
3. Con-firm our will to do the right, And keep our
4. All praise to God the Fa-ther be, All praise, e-

ter-nal bring-ing light, Thou Light of light, light's
ra-diance from a-bove, And pour the Ho-ly
hearts from en-vy's blight; Let faith her ea-ger
ter-nal Son, to Thee, Whom with the Spir-it

liv-ing Spring, True Day, all days il-lu-min-ing:
Spir-it's ray On all we think or do to-day.
fires re-new, And hate the false, and love the true.
we a-dore For-ev-er and for-ev-er-more. A-men.

17 Praise the Lord! Ye Heavens, Adore Him

Praise ye the Lord from the heavens: praise Him in the heights. Psa. 148:1

Psalm 148
Foundling Hospital Collection, 1796
St. 3, Edward Osler, 1836

AUSTRIAN HYMN 8 7 8 7 D.
Franz Joseph Haydn, 1797

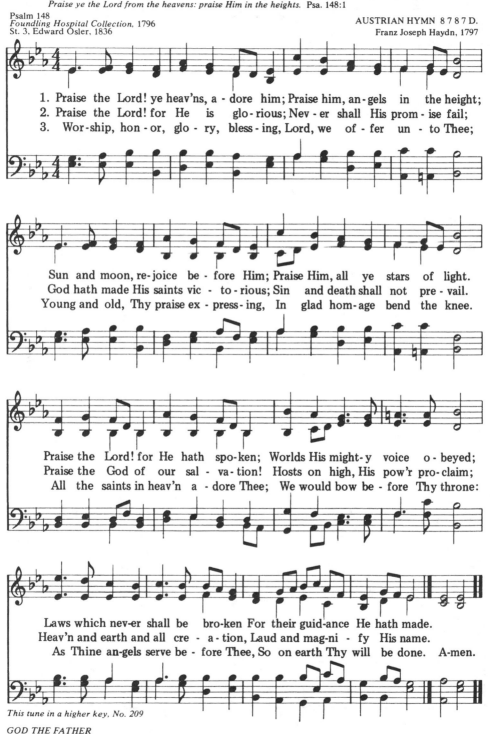

1. Praise the Lord! ye heav'ns, a - dore him; Praise him, an - gels in the height;
2. Praise the Lord! for He is glo - rious; Nev - er shall His prom - ise fail;
3. Wor - ship, hon - or, glo - ry, bless - ing, Lord, we of - fer un - to Thee;

Sun and moon, re-joice be - fore Him; Praise Him, all ye stars of light.
God hath made His saints vic - to - rious; Sin and death shall not pre - vail.
Young and old, Thy praise ex - press - ing, In glad hom-age bend the knee.

Praise the Lord! for He hath spo-ken; Worlds His might-y voice o - beyed;
Praise the God of our sal - va - tion! Hosts on high, His pow'r pro-claim;
All the saints in heav'n a - dore Thee; We would bow be - fore Thy throne:

Laws which nev-er shall be bro-ken For their guid-ance He hath made.
Heav'n and earth and all cre - a - tion, Laud and mag-ni - fy His name.
As Thine an-gels serve be - fore Thee, So on earth Thy will be done. A-men.

This tune in a higher key, No. 209

GOD THE FATHER

Praise the Lord Who Reigns Above **18**

Praise God in His sanctuary: praise Him in the firmament of His power. Psa. 150:1

Psalm 150
Charles Wesley, 1743

AMSTERDAM 7 6 7 6 7 7 7 6
Foundery Collection, 1742

1. Praise the Lord who reigns a - bove And keeps His court be - low;
2. Cel - e - brate th'e - ter - nal God With harp and psal - ter - y,
3. Him, in whom they move and live, Let ev - ery crea - ture sing,

Praise the ho - ly God of love, And all His great - ness show;
Tim - brels soft and cym - bals loud In His high praise a - gree;
Glo - ry to their Mak - er give, And hom - age to their King.

Praise Him for His no - ble deeds, Praise Him for His match - less pow'r;
Praise Him ev - ery tune - ful string; All the reach of heav'n - ly art,
Hallow-ed be His name be - neath, As in heav'n on earth a - dored;

Him from whom all good pro-ceeds Let earth and heav'n a - dore.
All the pow'rs of mu - sic bring, The mu - sic of the heart.
Praise the Lord in ev - ery breath, Let all things praise the Lord. A - men.

HIS PRAISE

19 Ye Servants of God, Your Master Proclaim

Salvation, and glory, and honor, and power, unto the Lord our God. Rev. 19:1

HANOVER 10 10 11 11

Charles Wesley, 1744

William Croft, 1708

1. Ye serv-ants of God, your Mas-ter pro-claim, And pub-lish a-
2. God rul-eth on high, al-might-y to save; And still He is
3. Sal-va-tion to God who sits on the throne, Let all cry a-
4. Then let us a-dore and give Him His right, All glo-ry and

broad His won-der-ful name; The name all vic-to-rious of
nigh— His pres-ence we have; The great con-gre-ga-tion His
loud, and hon-or the Son; The prais-es of Je-sus the
pow'r, all wis-dom and might; All hon-or and bless-ing, with

Je-sus ex-tol; His king-dom is glo-rious, He rules o-ver all.
tri-umph shall sing, As-crib-ing sal-va-tion to Je-sus our King.
an-gels pro-claim, Fall down on their fac-es and wor-ship the Lamb.
an-gels a-bove, And thanks nev-er ceas-ing, and in-fi-nite love. A-men.

20 All People That on Earth Do Dwell

Make a joyful noise unto the Lord, all ye lands. Psa. 100:1

OLD HUNDREDTH L.M.

Psalm 100
William Kethe, 1561

Genevan Psalter, 1551
Louis Bourgeois, c. 1510-c. 1561

1. All peo-ple that on earth do dwell, Sing to the Lord with cheer-ful voice;
2. The Lord, ye know, is God in-deed; With-out our aid He did us make;
3. O en-ter then His gates with praise, Ap-proach with joy His courts un-to;
4. For why? The Lord our God is good, His mer-cy is for-ev-er sure;

This tune in another rhythm, No. 572

GOD THE FATHER

Him serve with fear, His praise forth tell, Come ye be-fore Him and re - joice.
We are His flock, He doth us feed, And for His sheep He doth us take.
Praise, laud, and bless His name al-ways, For it is seem-ly so to do.
His truth at all times firm-ly stood, And shall from age to age en - dure. A - men.

O Worship the King, All Glorious Above 21

O Lord my God, . . . Thou art clothed with honor and majesty. Psa. 104:1

Psalm 104
William Kethe, 1561
Adapt. by Robert Grant, 1833

LYONS 10 10 11 11
William Gardiner's *Sacred Melodies*, 1815
Arr. from Johann M. Haydn, 1737-1806

1. O wor - ship the King, all glo - rious a - bove, O grate - ful - ly
2. O tell of His might, O sing of His grace, Whose robe is the
3. Thy boun - ti - ful care what tongue can re - cite? It breathes in the
4. Frail chil - dren of dust, and fee - ble as frail, In Thee do we

sing His pow'r and His love; Our Shield and De - fend - er, the An - cient of
light, whose can - o - py space. His char - iots of wrath the deep thun - der clouds
air, it shines in the light; It streams from the hills, it de - scends to the
trust, nor find Thee to fail; Thy mer - cies how ten - der! how firm to the

Days, Pa - vil - ioned in splen - dor and gird - ed with praise.
form, And dark is His path on the wings of the storm.
plain, And sweet - ly dis - tills in the dew and the rain.
end! Our Mak - er, De - fend - er, Re - deem - er and Friend. A - men.

22 Stand Up and Bless the Lord

Stand up and bless the Lord your God, for ever and ever. Neh. 9:5

James Montgomery, 1824

ST. MICHAEL S.M.
Genevan Psalter, 1551
Arr. by William Crotch, 1836

1. Stand up and bless the Lord, Ye peo - ple of His
2. Though high a - bove all praise, A - bove all bless - ing
3. O for the liv - ing flame From His own al - tar
4. God is our strength and song, And His sal - va - tion
5. Stand up and bless the Lord, The Lord your God a -

choice; Stand up and bless the Lord your God
high, Who would not bless fear His Lord ho - ly name,
brought, To touch our lips, our minds in - spire,
ours; Then be His love in Christ pro - claimed
dore; Stand up and bless His glo - rious name,

With heart and soul and voice.
And laud and mag - ni - fy?
And wing to heav'n our thought!
With all our ran - somed pow'rs.
Hence - forth for - ev - er - more. A - men.

23 Come, We That Love the Lord

Praise the Lord! Sing to the Lord a new song . . . Psa. 149:1

Isaac Watts, 1707

ST. THOMAS S.M.
Aaron Williams, 1763

1. Come, we that love the Lord, And let our joys be known; Join
2. Let those re - fuse to sing Who nev - er knew our God; But
3. The men of grace have found Glo - ry be - gun be - low; Ce -
4. The hill of Zi - on yields A thou - sand sa - cred sweets Be -
5. Then let our songs a - bound, And ev - ery tear be dry; We're

Alternate tune with refrain, MARCHING TO ZION, No. 275
GOD THE FATHER

in a song with sweet ac - cord, And thus sur - round the throne.
chil - dren of the heav'n - ly King May speak their joys a - broad.
les - tial fruit on earth - ly ground From faith and hope may grow.
fore we reach the heav'n - ly fields, Or walk the gold - en streets.
march - ing thro' Em - man - uel's ground To fair - er worlds on high. A-men.

Let All the World in Every Corner Sing 24

Sing unto the Lord, all the earth. Psa. 96:1

ALL THE WORLD 14 12 12 14

George Herbert, 1633

Robert G. McCutchan, 1934

Unison

1. Let all the world in ev - ery cor - ner sing: My God and King!
2. Let all the world in ev - ery cor - ner sing: My God and King!

The heav'ns are not too high, His praise may thith - er fly; The
The church with psalms must shout, No door can keep them out; But,

earth is not too low, His prais - es there may grow. Let
more than all, the heart Must bear the long - est part. Let

all the world in ev - ery cor - ner sing: My God and King!
all the world in ev - ery cor - ner sing: My God and King! A - men.

HIS PRAISE

25 Joyful, Joyful, We Adore Thee

All Thy works shall praise Thee, O Lord . . . Psa. 145:10

Henry Van Dyke, 1907

HYMN TO JOY 8 7 8 7 D.
Ludwig van Beethoven, 1824

1. Joy-ful, joy-ful, we a-dore Thee, God of glo-ry, Lord of love;
2. All Thy works with joy sur-round Thee, Earth and heav'n re-flect Thy rays,
3. Thou art giv-ing and for-giv-ing, Ev-er bless-ing, ev-er blest,
4. Mor-tals join the might-y cho-rus Which the morn-ing stars be-gan;

Hearts un-fold like flow'rs be-fore Thee, Open-ing to the sun a-bove.
Stars and an-gels sing a-round Thee, Cen-ter of un-bro-ken praise.
Well-spring of the joy of liv-ing, O-cean-depth of hap-py rest!
Fa-ther love is reign-ing o'er us, Broth-er love binds man to man.

Melt the clouds of sin and sad-ness; Drive the dark of doubt a-way;
Field and for-est, vale and moun-tain, Flow-ery mead-ow, flash-ing sea,
Thou our Fa-ther, Christ our Broth-er— All who live in love are Thine;
Ev-er sing-ing, march we on-ward, Vic-tors in the midst of strife;

Giv-er of im-mor-tal glad-ness, Fill us with the light of day!
Chant-ing bird and flow-ing foun-tain Call us to re-joice in Thee.
Teach us how to love each oth-er, Lift us to the joy di-vine.
Joy-ful mu-sic leads us sun-ward In the tri-umph song of life. A-men.

GOD THE FATHER

Praise, My Soul, the King of Heaven 26

Bless the Lord, O my soul, and forget not all His benefits. Psa. 103:2

Psalm 103
Henry F. Lyte, 1834

LAUDA ANIMA 8 7 8 7 8 7
John Goss, 1869

1. Praise, my soul, the King of heav - en, To His feet your
2. Praise Him for His grace and fa - vor To our fa - thers
3. Fa - ther - like, He tends and spares us; Well our fee - ble
4. An - gels in the height, a - dore Him, You be - hold Him

trib - ute bring; Ran - somed, healed, re - stored, for - giv - en,
in dis - tress; Praise Him, still the same as ev - er,
frame He knows, In His hands He gen - tly bears us,
face to face; Saints tri - um - phant, bow be - fore Him;

Ev - er - more His prais - es sing. Al - le - lu - ia!
Slow to chide and swift to bless. Al - le - lu - ia!
Res - cues us from all our foes. Al - le - lu - ia!
Gath - ered in from ev - ery race. Al - le - lu - ia!

Al - le - lu - ia! Praise the ev - er - last - ing King!
Al - le - lu - ia! Glo - rious in His faith - ful - ness!
Al - le - lu - ia! Wide - ly yet His mer - cy flows!
Al - le - lu - ia! Praise with us the God of grace! A - men.

HIS PRAISE

27 Let the Whole Creation Cry

Let them praise . . . for He commanded, and they were created. Psa. 148:5

Psalm 148
Stopford A. Brooke, 1881

LLANFAIR 7 7 7 7 Alleluias
Robert Williams, 1817

1. Let the whole cre - a - tion cry Al - le - lu - ia!
2. Praise Him, all ye hosts a - bove, Al - le - lu - ia!
3. War - riors fight - ing for the Lord, Al - le - lu - ia!
4. Men and wom - en, young and old, Al - le - lu - ia!

Glo - ry to the Lord on high! Al - le - lu - ia!
Ev - er bright and fair in love! Al - le - lu - ia!
Proph - ets burn - ing with His Word, Al - le - lu - ia!
Raise the an - them man - i - fold; Al - le - lu - ia!

Heav'n and earth, a - wake and sing, Al - le - lu - ia!
Sun and moon, lift up your voice, Al - le - lu - ia!
Those to whom the arts be - long, Al - le - lu - ia!
And let chil - dren's hap - py hearts, Al - le - lu - ia!

God is God and there - fore King, Al - le - lu - ia!
Night and stars in God re - joice, Al - le - lu - ia!
Add their voic - es to the song, Al - le - lu - ia!
In this wor - ship bear their parts: Al - le - lu - ia! A - men.

GOD THE FATHER

Come, Thou Fount of Every Blessing 28

Blessed be the Lord, who daily loadeth us with benefits. Psa. 68:19

NETTLETON 8 7 8 7 D.

Robert Robinson, 1758
Adapt. by E. Margaret Clarkson, 1973

Traditional American melody
John Wyeth's *Repository of Sacred Music*, 1813

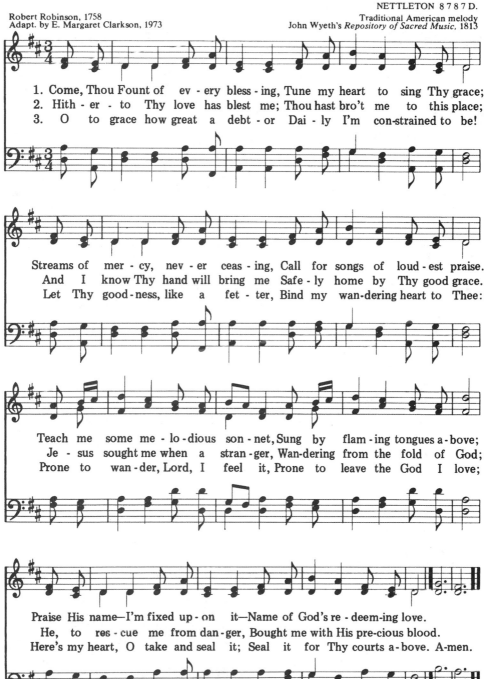

1. Come, Thou Fount of ev - ery bless - ing, Tune my heart to sing Thy grace;
2. Hith - er - to Thy love has blest me; Thou hast bro't me to this place;
3. O to grace how great a debt - or Dai - ly I'm con-strained to be!

Streams of mer - cy, nev - er ceas - ing, Call for songs of loud - est praise.
And I know Thy hand will bring me Safe - ly home by Thy good grace.
Let Thy good - ness, like a fet - ter, Bind my wan-dering heart to Thee:

Teach me some me - lo - dious son - net, Sung by flam - ing tongues a - bove;
Je - sus sought me when a stran - ger, Wan-dering from the fold of God;
Prone to wan - der, Lord, I feel it, Prone to leave the God I love;

Praise His name—I'm fixed up - on it—Name of God's re - deem-ing love.
He, to res - cue me from dan - ger, Bought me with His pre-cious blood.
Here's my heart, O take and seal it; Seal it for Thy courts a - bove. A-men.

HIS PRAISE

29 Give to Our God Immortal Praise

For His mercy endureth forever. Psa. 136:1

Psalm 136
Isaac Watts, 1719

WARRINGTON L.M.
Ralph Harrison, 1784

1. Give to our God im - mor - tal praise; Mer - cy and
2. He built the earth, He spread the sky, And fixed the
3. He fills the sun with morn - ing light; He bids the
4. He sent His Son with pow'r to save From guilt and
5. Through this vast world He guides our feet, And leads us

truth are all His ways: Won - ders of grace to God be -
star - ry lights on high: Won - ders of grace to God be -
moon di - rect the night: His mer - cies ev - er shall en -
dark - ness and the grave: Won - ders of grace to God be -
to His heav'n - ly seat: His mer - cies ev - er shall en -

long; Re - peat His mer - cies in your song.
long; Re - peat His mer - cies in your song.
dure, When suns and moons shall shine no more.
long; Re - peat His mer - cies in your song.
dure, When this our world shall be no more. A - men.

30 Lord of All Being, Throned Afar

For in Him we live, and move, and have our being. Acts 17:28

MENDON L.M.
Traditional German melody
Samuel Dyer's *Third Edition of Sacred Music,* 1824

Oliver W. Holmes, 1848

1. Lord of all be - ing, throned a - far, Thy glo - ry flames from sun and star;
2. Sun of our life, Thy quick-'ning ray Sheds on our path the glow of day;
3. Our mid-night is Thy smile with-drawn; Our noon-tide is Thy gra-cious dawn,
4. Grant us Thy truth to make us free, And kin-dling hearts that burn for Thee;

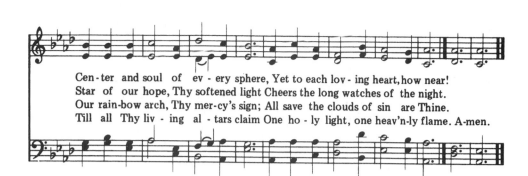

Cen-ter and soul of ev-ery sphere, Yet to each lov-ing heart, how near!
Star of our hope, Thy softened light Cheers the long watches of the night.
Our rain-bow arch, Thy mer-cy's sign; All save the clouds of sin are Thine.
Till all Thy liv-ing al-tars claim One ho-ly light, one heav'n-ly flame. A-men.

Praise Him, O Praise Him 31

Enter into His gates with thanksgiving . . . Psa. 100:4

Mary Lou Reynolds. 1970

PASCHALL Irreg.
William J. Reynolds. 1970

1. Praise Him, O praise Him, Praise the Lord for all His bless-ings;
2. Bless Him, O bless Him, Bless the Lord for all His mer-cy;
3. Glo-ry and hon-or, Glo-ry be to God the Fa-ther;

Praise Him, O praise Him, Sing a joy-ful song be-fore Him;
Bless Him, O bless Him, Let the trum-pet sound His glo-ry;
Glo-ry and hon-or To the Son and Ho-ly Spir-it;

Praise Him, O praise Him, Sing a joy-ful, ju-bi-lant song. A-men.

32 How Great Thou Art

Great is the Lord. and greatly to be praised. Psa. 48:1

O STORE GUD 11 10 11 10 Ref.

Carl Boberg, c. 1885
Trans. by Stuart K. Hine, 1949

Swedish Folk melody
Arr. by Stuart K. Hine, 1949

1. O Lord my God, when I in awe-some won-der Con-sid-er
2. When thro' the woods and for-est glades I wan-der And hear the
3. And when I think that God, His Son not spar-ing, Sent Him to
4. When Christ shall come with shout of ac-cla-ma-tion And take me

all the worlds Thy hands have made, I see the stars, I hear the roll-ing
birds sing sweet-ly in the trees, When I look down from loft-y moun-tain
die, I scarce can take it in, That on the cross, my bur-den glad-ly
home, what joy shall fill my heart! Then I shall bow in hum-ble ad-o-

Refrain

thun-der, Thy pow'r thro'-out the u-ni-verse dis-played.
gran-deur, And hear the brook and feel the gen-tle breeze.
bear-ing, He bled and died to take a-way my sin.
ra-tion, And there pro-claim, my God, how great Thou art.

Then sings my

soul, my Sav-ior God, to Thee; How great Thou art, how great Thou art! Then sings my

soul, my Sav-ior God, to Thee: How great Thou art, how great Thou art!

*Translator's original words are "works" and "mighty."

GOD THE FATHER: HIS PRAISE

My God, How Wonderful Thou Art 33

I dwell in the high and holy place, with him also that is of a . . . humble spirit. Isa. 57:15

DUNDEE C.M.

Frederick W. Faber, 1849

Thomas Ravenscroft's *Psalmes,* 1621

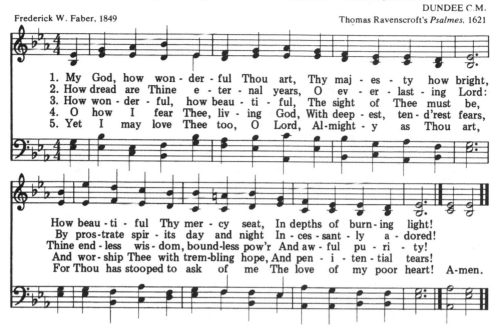

1. My God, how won - der - ful Thou art, Thy maj - es - ty how bright,
2. How dread are Thine e - ter - nal years, O ev - er - last - ing Lord:
3. How won - der - ful, how beau - ti - ful, The sight of Thee must be,
4. O how I fear Thee, liv - ing God, With deep - est, ten - d'rest fears,
5. Yet I may love Thee too, O Lord, Al-might - y as Thou art,

How beau - ti - ful Thy mer - cy seat, In depths of burn - ing light!
By pros-trate spir - its day and night In - ces - sant - ly a - dored!
Thine end - less wis - dom, bound-less pow'r And aw - ful pu - ri - ty!
And wor - ship Thee with trem-bling hope, And pen - i - ten - tial tears!
For Thou has stooped to ask of me The love of my poor heart! A - men.

God, My King, Thy Might Confessing 34

I will extol Thee, my God, O King; and I will bless Thy name . . . Psa. 145:1

STUTTGART 8 7 8 7

Richard Mant, 1824
Based on Psalm 145

C. Friedrich Witt, 1715
Arr. by Henry J. Gauntlett, 1861

1. God, my King, Thy might con - fess - ing, Ev - er will I bless Thy name;
2. Hon - or great our God be - fit - teth; Who His ma - jes - ty can reach?
3. They shall talk of all Thy glo - ry, On Thy might and great - ness dwell,
4. Full of kind - ness and com - pas - sion, Slow to an - ger, vast in love,
5. All Thy works, O Lord, shall bless Thee; Thee shall all Thy saints a - dore:

Day by day Thy throne ad-dress-ing, Still will I Thy praise pro-claim.
Age to age His works trans-mit-teth, Age to age His pow'r shall teach.
Speak of Thy dread acts the sto - ry, And Thy deeds of won - der tell.
God is good to all cre - a - tion; All His works His good - ness prove.
King su-preme shall they con - fess Thee, And pro-claim Thy sov' - reign pow'r. A - men.

HIS ATTRIBUTES

35 Immortal, Invisible, God Only Wise

Unto the King eternal, immortal, invisible, the only wise God, be honor and glory . . . I Tim. 1:17

ST. DENIO 11 11 11 11

Walter C. Smith, 1867

Traditional Welsh hymn melody

1. Im - mor - tal, in - vis - i - ble, God on - ly wise,
2. Un - rest - ing, un - hast - ing, and si - lent as light,
3. To all, life Thou giv - est, to both great and small,
4. Great Fa - ther of glo - ry, pure Fa - ther of light,

In light in - ac - ces - si - ble hid from our eyes,
Nor want - ing, nor wast - ing, Thou rul - est in might;
In all life Thou liv - est, the true life of all.
Thine an - gels a - dore Thee, all veil - ing their sight;

Most bless - ed, most glo - rious, the An - cient of Days,
Thy jus - tice like moun - tains high soar - ing a - bove
We blos - som and flour - ish as leaves on the tree,
All praise we would ren - der; O help us to see

Al - might - y, vic - to - rious, Thy great name we praise.
Thy clouds, which are foun - tains of good - ness and love.
And with - er and per - ish— but naught chang - eth Thee.
'Tis on - ly the splen - dor of light hid - eth Thee! A - men.

GOD THE FATHER

The God of Abraham Praise 36

And God said unto Moses, I AM THAT I AM. Exo. 3:14

LEONI 6 6 8 4 D.

Thomas Olivers, 1770
Based on Jewish *Doxology*

Synagogue melody
Arr. by Meyer Lyon, 1770

1. The God of A-braham praise, Who reigns en-throned a-bove;
2. He by Him-self hath sworn, I on His oath de-pend;
3. The God who reigns on high The great arch-an-gels sing,
4. The whole tri-um-phant host Give thanks to God on high;

An-cient of ev-er-last-ing days, And God of love.
I shall, on ea-gles' wings up-borne, To heav'n as-cend;
And "Ho-ly, ho-ly, ho-ly" cry, "Al-might-y King!"
"Hail, Fa-ther, Son and Ho-ly Ghost!" They ev-er cry.

Je-ho-vah, great I AM, By earth and heav'n con-fessed:
I shall be-hold His face, I shall His pow'r a-dore,
Who was and is the same, And ev-er-more shall be:
Hail, A-braham's God and mine! I join the heav'n-ly lays;

I bow and bless the sa-cred name For-ev-er blest.
And sing the won-ders of His grace For-ev-er-more.
Je-ho-vah, Fa-ther, great I AM, We wor-ship Thee.
All might and maj-es-ty are Thine, And end-less praise. A-men.

37 Great Is Thy Faithfulness

His compassions fail not. They are new every morning. Lam. 3:22,23

Thomas O. Chisholm, 1923

FAITHFULNESS 11 10 11 10 Ref.
William M. Runyan, 1923

1. Great is Thy faith-ful-ness, O God my Fa-ther, There is no shad-ow of
2. Sum-mer and win-ter, and springtime and har-vest, Sun, moon and stars in their
3. Par-don for sin and a peace that en-dur-eth, Thy own dear pres-ence to

turn-ing with Thee; Thou chang-est not, Thy com-pas-sions they fail not;
cours-es a-bove Join with all na-ture in man-i-fold wit-ness
cheer and to guide; Strength for to-day and bright hope for to-mor-row,

Refrain

As Thou hast been Thou for-ev-er wilt be.
To Thy great faith-ful-ness, mer-cy and love. Great is Thy faith-ful-ness!
Bless-ings all mine, with ten thou-sand be-side!

Great is Thy faith-ful-ness! Morn-ing by morn-ing new mer-cies I see; All I have

need-ed Thy hand hath pro-vid-ed—Great is Thy faith-ful-ness, Lord, un-to me!

GOD THE FATHER

When All Thy Mercies, O My God 38

I will sing of the mercies of the Lord forever . . . Psa. 89:1

BELMONT C.M.

Joseph Addison, 1712

William Gardiner's *Sacred Melodies*, 1812

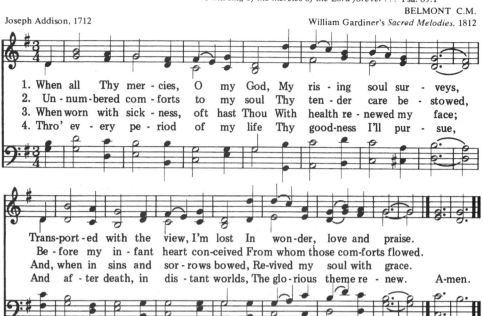

1. When all Thy mer - cies, O my God, My ris - ing soul sur - veys,
2. Un - num - bered com - forts to my soul Thy ten - der care be - stowed,
3. When worn with sick - ness, oft hast Thou With health re - newed my face;
4. Thro' ev - ery pe - riod of my life Thy good - ness I'll pur - sue,

Trans - port - ed with the view, I'm lost In won - der, love and praise.
Be - fore my in - fant heart con - ceived From whom those com - forts flowed.
And, when in sins and sor - rows bowed, Re - vived my soul with grace.
And af - ter death, in dis - tant worlds, The glo - rious theme re - new. A - men.

God Is Love; His Mercy Brightens 39

O the depth of the riches . . . of the wisdom and knowledge of God! Rom. 11:33

CROSS OF JESUS 8 7 8 7

John Bowring, 1825

John Stainer, 1887

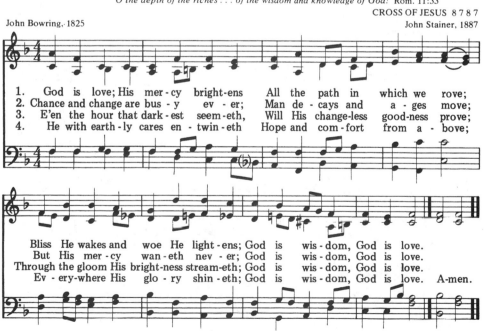

1. God is love; His mer - cy bright - ens All the path in which we rove;
2. Chance and change are bus - y ev - er; Man de - cays and a - ges move;
3. E'en the hour that dark - est seem - eth, Will His change - less good - ness prove;
4. He with earth - ly cares en - twin - eth Hope and com - fort from a - bove;

Bliss He wakes and woe He light - ens; God is wis - dom, God is love.
But His mer - cy wan - eth nev - er; God is wis - dom, God is love.
Through the gloom His bright - ness stream - eth; God is wis - dom, God is love.
Ev - ery - where His glo - ry shin - eth; God is wis - dom, God is love. A - men.

40 To God Be the Glory

Give unto the Lord the glory due unto His name. Psa. 29:2

TO GOD BE THE GLORY 11 11 11 11 Ref.

Fanny J. Crosby, 1875

William H. Doane, 1875

1. To God be the glo - ry, great things He hath done, So loved He the world that He
2. O per - fect re - demp-tion, the pur-chase of blood, To ev - ery be - liev - er the
3. Great things He hath taught us, great things He hath done, And great our re-joic - ing thro'

gave us His Son, Who yield-ed His life an a - tone-ment for sin, And o-pened the
prom - ise of God; The vil - est of - fend - er who tru - ly be-lieves, That mo-ment from
Je - sus the Son; But pur - er, and high-er, and great - er will be Our won-der, our

Refrain

Life-gate that all may go in.
Je - sus a par-don re-ceives. Praise the Lord, praise the Lord, Let the earth hear His
trans-port, when Je - sus we see.

voice! Praise the Lord, praise the Lord, Let the peo - ple re - joice! O come to the

Fa-ther thro' Je - sus the Son, And give Him the glo - ry, great things He hath done.

GOD THE FATHER

Children of the Heavenly Father 41

As a father pitieth his children, so the Lord pitieth . . . Psa. 103:13

Carolina Sandell Berg. 1858
Trans. by Ernest W. Olson. 1925

TRYGGARE KAN INGEN VARA L.M.
Traditional Swedish melody

1. Chil - dren of the heav'n - ly Fa - ther Safe - ly in His bos - om gath - er;
2. God His own doth tend and nour - ish; In His ho - ly courts they flour - ish.
3. Nei - ther life nor death shall ev - er From the Lord His chil - dren sev - er;
4. Though He giv - eth or He tak - eth, God His chil - dren ne'er for - sak - eth;

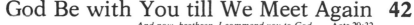

Nest - ling bird nor star in heav - en Such a ref - uge e'er was giv - en.
From all e - vil things He spares them; In His might - y arms He bears them.
Un - to them His grace He show - eth, And their sor - rows all He know - eth.
His the lov - ing pur - pose sole - ly To pre - serve them pure and ho - ly.

God Be with You till We Meet Again 42

And now. brethren. I commend you to God . . . Acts 20:32

Jeremiah E. Rankin, 1880

GOD BE WITH YOU Irreg.
William G. Tomer, 1880

1. God be with you till we meet a - gain; By His coun-sels guide, up-hold you,
2. God be with you till we meet a - gain; 'Neath His wings pro-tect-ing hide you,
3. God be with you till we meet a - gain; When life's per-ils thick con-found you,
4. God be with you till we meet a - gain; Keep love's ban-ner float-ing o'er you,

With His sheep se - cure - ly fold you; God be with you till we meet a - gain.
Dai - ly man - na still pro-vide you; God be with you till we meet a - gain.
Put His arms un - fail - ing round you; God be with you till we meet a - gain.
Smite death's threat'ning wave before you; God be with you till we meet a - gain.

43 Praise to the Lord, the Almighty

For then shalt thou have thy delight in the Almighty. Job 22:26

Joachim Neander, 1680
Trans. by Catherine Winkworth, 1863

LOBE DEN HERREN 14 14 4 7 8
Stralsund Gesangbuch, 1665

1. Praise to the Lord, the Al-might-y, the King of cre-a-tion! O my soul, praise Him, for He is thy health and sal-va-tion! All ye who hear, Now to His tem-ple draw near; Join me in glad ad-o-ra-tion!

2. Praise to the Lord, who o'er all things so won-drous-ly reign-eth, Shel-ters thee un-der His wings, yea, so gen-tly sus-tain-eth! Hast thou not seen How thy de-sires e'er have been Grant-ed in what He or-dain-eth?

3. Praise to the Lord, who doth pros-per thy work and de-fend thee; Sure-ly His good-ness and mer-cy here dai-ly at-tend thee. Pon-der a-new What the Al-might-y can do, If with His love He be-friend thee.

4. Praise to the Lord! O let all that is in me a-dore Him! All that hath life and breath, come now with prais-es be-fore Him! Let the A-men Sound from His peo-ple a-gain: Glad-ly for aye we a-dore Him. A-men.

Unto the Hills Around 44

I will lift up mine eyes unto the hills. Psa. 121:1

Psalm 121
John D. S. Campbell, 1877

SANDON 10 4 10 4 10 10
Charles H. Purday, 1860

1. Un - to the hills a - round do I lift up My long - ing eyes;
2. He will not suf - fer that thy foot be moved: Safe shalt thou be.
3. Je - ho - vah is Him - self thy keep - er true, Thy change-less shade;
4. From ev - ery e - vil shall He keep thy soul, From ev - ery sin;

O whence for me shall my sal - va - tion come, From whence a - rise?
No care - less slum - ber shall His eye - lids close, Who keep - eth thee.
Je - ho - vah thy de - fense on thy right hand Him - self hath made.
Je - ho - vah shall pre - serve thy go - ing out, Thy com - ing in.

From God the Lord doth come my cer - tain aid,
Be - hold our God the Lord, He slum - bereth ne'er,
And thee no sun by day shall ev - er smite;
A - bove thee watch - ing, He whom we a - dore

From God the Lord who heav'n and earth hath made.
Who keep - eth Is - rael in His ho - ly care.
No moon shall harm thee in the si - lent night.
Shall keep thee hence - forth, yea, for - ev - er - more. A-men.

45 The Lord's My Shepherd, I'll Not Want

The Lord is my shepherd; I shall not want. Psa. 23:1

Psalm 23
Scottish Psalter, 1650
William Whittingham and others

CRIMOND C.M.
Jessie S. Irvine, 1871
Arr. by David Grant, 1872

1. The Lord's my Shep - herd, I'll not want; He makes me down to lie
2. My soul He doth re - store a - gain; And me to walk doth make
3. Yea, though I walk through death's dark vale, Yet will I fear no ill;
4. My ta - ble Thou hast fur - nish - ed In pres - ence of my foes;
5. Good-ness and mer - cy all my life Shall sure - ly fol - low me;

In pas - tures green; He lead - eth me The qui - et wa - ters by.
With - in the paths of right-eous - ness, E'en for His own name's sake.
For Thou art with me, and Thy rod And staff me com - fort still.
My head Thou dost with oil a - noint, And my cup o - ver-flows.
And in God's house for - ev - er - more My dwell-ing place shall be. A-men.

46 The King of Love My Shepherd Is

I am the good shepherd . . . I lay down My life for the sheep. John 10:14, 15

Henry W. Baker, 1868
Based on Psalm 23

DOMINUS REGIT ME 8 7 8 7
John B. Dykes, 1868

1. The King of love my Shep-herd is, Whose good - ness fail - eth nev - er;
2. Where streams of liv - ing wa - ter flow My ran-somed soul He lead - eth,
3. Per-verse and fool - ish oft I strayed But yet 'in love He sought me,
4. In death's dark vale I fear no ill With Thee, dear Lord, be - side me;
5. And so through all the length of days Thy good - ness fail - eth nev - er:

I noth - ing lack if I am His And He is mine for - ev - er.
And, where the ver - dant pas - tures grow, With food ce - les - tial feed - eth.
And on His shoul-der gen - tly laid, And home re - joic - ing brought me.
Thy rod and staff my com - fort still, Thy cross be - fore to guide me.
Good Shep-herd, may I sing Thy praise With - in Thy house for - ev - er. A-men.

GOD THE FATHER

God Moves in a Mysterious Way 47

What I do thou knowest not now; but thou shalt know hereafter. John 13:7

William Cowper, 1774

DUNDEE C.M.
Thomas Ravenscroft's *Psalmes*, 1621

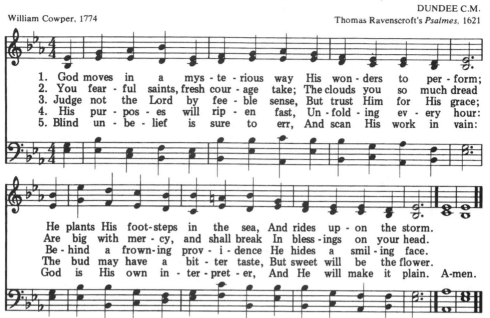

1. God moves in a mys - te - rious way His won - ders to per - form;
2. You fear - ful saints, fresh cour - age take; The clouds you so much dread
3. Judge not the Lord by fee - ble sense, But trust Him for His grace;
4. His pur - pos - es will rip - en fast, Un - fold - ing ev - ery hour:
5. Blind un - be - lief is sure to err, And scan His work in vain:

He plants His foot-steps in the sea, And rides up - on the storm.
Are big with mer - cy, and shall break In bless - ings on your head.
Be - hind a frown-ing prov - i - dence He hides a smil - ing face.
The bud may have a bit - ter taste, But sweet will be the flower.
God is His own in - ter - pret - er, And He will make it plain. A - men.

O God, Our Help in Ages Past 48

Lord, thou hast been our dwelling place in all generations. Psa. 90:1

Psalm 90
Isaac Watts, 1719

ST. ANNE C.M.
William Croft, 1708

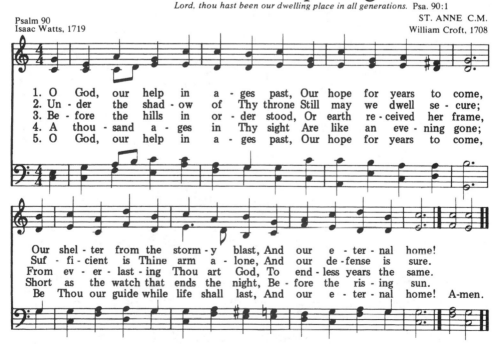

1. O God, our help in a - ges past, Our hope for years to come,
2. Un - der the shad - ow of Thy throne Still may we dwell se - cure;
3. Be - fore the hills in or - der stood, Or earth re - ceived her frame,
4. A thou - sand a - ges in Thy sight Are like an eve - ning gone;
5. O God, our help in a - ges past, Our hope for years to come,

Our shel - ter from the storm - y blast, And our e - ter - nal home!
Suf - fi - cient is Thine arm a - lone, And our de - fense is sure.
From ev - er - last - ing Thou art God, To end - less years the same.
Short as the watch that ends the night, Be - fore the ris - ing sun.
Be Thou our guide while life shall last, And our e - ter - nal home! A - men.

HIS PROVIDENCE AND CARE

49 A Pilgrim Was I and A-wandering

Surely goodness and mercy shall follow me all the days of my life. Psa. 23:6

John W. Peterson and
Alfred B. Smith, 1958
Based on Psalm 23

SURELY GOODNESS AND MERCY Irreg. Ref.
John W. Peterson and
Alfred B. Smith, 1958

1. A pil-grim was I and a-wan-d'ring, In the cold night of
2. He re-stor-eth my soul when I'm wea-ry, He giv-eth me
3. When I walk thro' the dark lone-some val-ley, My Sav-ior will

sin I did roam, When Je-sus the kind Shep-herd found me, And
strength day by day; He leads me be-side the still wa-ters, He
walk with me there; And safe-ly His great hand will lead me To the

Refrain

now I am on my way home.
guards me each step of the way. Sure-ly good-ness and mer-cy shall
man-sions He's gone to pre-pare.

fol-low me All the days, all the days of my life; Sure-ly good-ness

and mer-cy shall fol-low me All the days, all the days of my life.

GOD THE FATHER

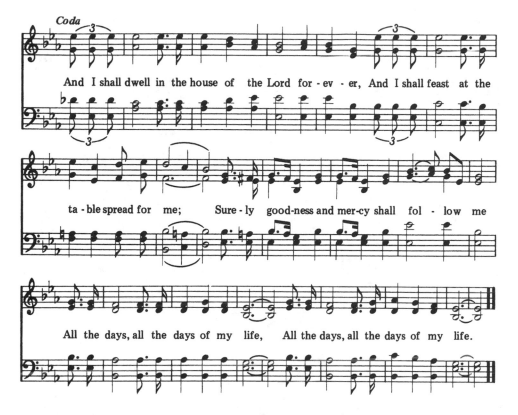

And I shall dwell in the house of the Lord for-ev-er, And I shall feast at the

ta-ble spread for me; Sure-ly good-ness and mer-cy shall fol-low me

All the days, all the days of my life, All the days, all the days of my life.

Let Us, with a Gladsome Mind 50

O give thanks unto the Lord, for He is good . . . Psa. 136:1

MONKLAND 7 7 7 7

Psalm 136
John Milton, 1623

John Antes, 1740-1811
Arr. by John B. Wilkes, 1861

1. Let us, with a glad-some mind, Praise the Lord for He is kind:
2. Let us sound His Name a-broad, For of gods He is the God:
3. He with all-com-mand-ing might Filled the new-made world with light:
4. All things liv-ing He doth feed; His full hand sup-plies their need:
5. Let us then with glad-some mind, Praise the Lord for He is kind:

Refrain

For His mer-cies shall en-dure, Ev-er faith-ful, ev-er sure. A-men.

51 I Will Sing of the Mercies of the Lord

I will sing of the mercies of the Lord forever . . . Psa. 89:1

Psalm 89:1

MERCIES Irreg.
Source unknown

I will sing of the mer-cies of the Lord for-ev-er, I will sing, I will sing, I will sing of the mer-cies of the Lord for-ev-er, I will sing of the mer-cies of the Lord. With my mouth will I make known Thy faith-ful-ness, Thy faith-ful-ness, With my mouth will I make known Thy

God of Concrete, God of Steel 52

The earth is the Lord's and the fulness thereof . . . Psa. 24:1

NEW HORIZONS 7 7 7 7 7 7

Richard G. Jones, 1969

Francis Westbrook, 1969

Unison

1. God of con - crete, God of steel, God of pis - ton and of wheel,
2. Lord of ca - ble, Lord of rail, Lord of mo - tor - way and mail,
3. Lord of sci - ence, Lord of art, God of map and graph and chart,
4. God whose glo - ry fills the earth, Gave the u - ni - verse its birth,

God of py - lon, God of steam, God of gird - er and of beam,
Lord of rock - et, Lord of flight, Lord of soar - ing sat - el - lite,
Lord of phys - ics and re - search, Word of Bi - ble, faith of Church,
Loosed the Christ with East - er's might, Saves the world from e - vil's blight,

God of at - om, God of mine, All the world of pow'r is Thine!
Lord of light - ning's liv - id line, All the world of speed is Thine!
Lord of se - quence and de - sign, All the world of truth is Thine!
Claims man - kind by grace di - vine, All the world of love is Thine! A - men.

HIS WORKS IN CREATION

53 All Things Bright and Beautiful

All things were made by Him . . . John 1:3

Cecil F. Alexander, 1848

ROYAL OAK 7 6 7 6 D.
Traditional English melody

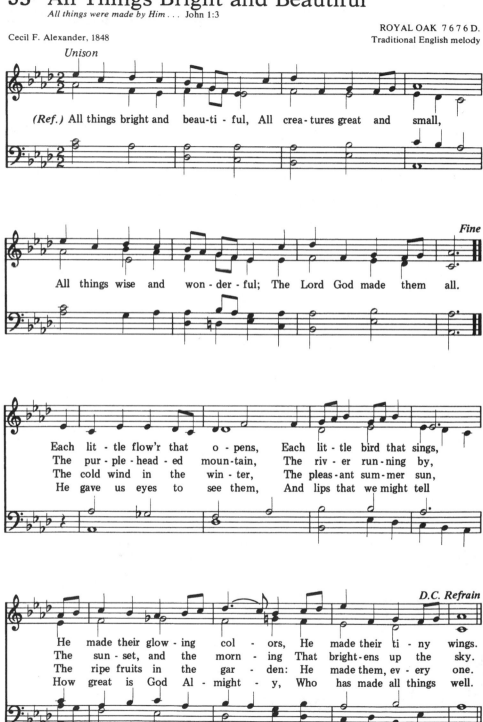

Unison

(Ref.) All things bright and beau-ti-ful, All crea-tures great and small,

Fine

All things wise and won-der-ful; The Lord God made them all.

Each lit-tle flow'r that o-pens, Each lit-tle bird that sings,
The pur-ple-head-ed moun-tain, The riv-er run-ning by,
The cold wind in the win-ter, The pleas-ant sum-mer sun,
He gave us eyes to see them, And lips that we might tell

D.C. Refrain

He made their glow-ing col-ors, He made their ti-ny wings.
The sun-set, and the morn-ing That bright-ens up the sky.
The ripe fruits in the gar-den: He made them, ev-ery one.
How great is God Al-might-y, Who has made all things well.

GOD THE FATHER

The Spacious Firmament on High 54

The heavens declare the glory of God, and the firmament showeth His handiwork. Psa. 19:1

Psalm 19
Joseph Addison, 1712

CREATION L.M.D.
Franz Joseph Haydn, 1798

1. The spa-cious fir-ma-ment on high, With all the blue e-the-real
2. Soon as the eve-ning shades pre-vail, The moon takes up the won-drous
3. What though in sol-emn si-lence all Move round the dark ter-res-trial

sky, And span-gled heav'ns, a shin-ing frame, Their great O-rig-i-nal pro-
tale; And night-ly to the lis-tening earth Re-peats the sto-ry of her
ball? What though no re-al voice nor sound A-mid their ra-diant orbs be

claim. Th'unwearied sun, from day to day, Does his Cre-a-tor's pow'r dis-play; And
birth; While all the stars that round her burn, And all the plan-ets in their turn, Con-
found? In rea-son's ear they all re-joice, And ut-ter forth a glo-rious voice For-

pub-lish-es to ev-ery land The work of an al-might-y hand.
firm the ti-dings as they roll, And spread the truth from pole to pole.
ev-er sing-ing as they shine, "The hand that made us is di-vine." A-men.

HIS WORKS IN CREATION

55 For the Beauty of the Earth

Every good gift and every perfect gift is from above. James 1:17

DIX 777777

Folliott S. Pierpoint, 1864

Conrad Kocher, 1838
Arr. by William H. Monk, 1861

1. For the beau - ty of the earth, For the glo - ry
2. For the beau - ty of each hour Of the day and
3. For the joy of ear and eye, For the heart and
4. For the joy of hu - man love, Broth - er, sis - ter,
5. For each per - fect gift of Thine To our race so

of the skies, For the love which from our birth
of the night, Hill and vale, and tree, and flow'r,
mind's de - light, For the mys - tic har - mo - ny
par - ent, child, Friends on earth and friends a - bove,
free - ly giv'n, Grac - es hu - man and di - vine,

O - ver and a - round us lies, Lord of all, to
Sun and moon and stars of light, Lord of all, to
Link - ing sense to sound and sight, Lord of all, to
For all gen - tle thoughts and mild, Lord of all, to
Flow'rs of earth and buds of heav'n, Lord of all, to

Thee we raise This our hymn of grate - ful praise.
Thee we raise This our hymn of grate - ful praise.
Thee we raise This our hymn of grate - ful praise.
Thee we raise This our hymn of grate - ful praise.
Thee we raise This our hymn of grate - ful praise. A - men.

GOD THE FATHER

God of Everlasting Glory 56

The glory of the Lord shall endure forever. Psa. 104:31

BRETON ROAD 8 5 8 5 D.

John W. Peterson, 1965

John W. Peterson, 1965

1. God of ev-er-last-ing glo-ry, Fill-ing earth and sky,
2. As we push man's fron-tiers for-ward In-to out-er space,
3. In the o-pen book of na-ture Faith re-mains un-moved—
4. Through the course of hu-man his-t'ry Has Thy pur-pose run,

Ev-ery-where Thy won-ders o-pen To our search-ing eye:
Reach-ing for the stars and plan-ets, Still Thy hand we trace;
Pat-terns of the Mas-ter Build-er By each fact are proved;
And in sub-stance have we seen Thee In Thy glo-rious Son:

In our tel-e-scop-ic prob-ing—Light years from our world,
In the lab-'ra-to-ry's si-lence, Where Thy se-crets hide,
So with rev-'rent hearts we pon-der All the grand de-sign
He it was who came to save us And our hopes to raise—

In the at-om's theo-ried struc-ture Sci-ence has un-furled.
There the mar-vels of cre-a-tion Are for us sup-plied.
Of the u-ni-verse a-round us, Wrought by hands di-vine.
God of ev-er-last-ing glo-ry, Thy great name we praise! A-men.

HIS WORKS IN CREATION

57 I Sing the Almighty Power of God

O come, let us worship . . . let us kneel before the Lord our maker. Psa. 95:6

FOREST GREEN C.M.D.
Traditional English melody
Arr. by Ralph Vaughan Williams, 1906

Isaac Watts, 1715

1. I sing th'al-might-y pow'r of God That made the moun-tains rise,
2. I sing the good-ness of the Lord That filled the earth with food;
3. There's not a plant or flow'r be-low But makes Thy glo-ries known;

That spread the flow-ing seas a-broad And built the loft-y skies.
He formed the crea-tures with His word And then pro-nounced them good.
And clouds a-rise and tem-pests blow By or-der from Thy throne;

I sing the wis-dom that or-dained The sun to rule the day;
Lord, how Thy won-ders are dis-played Where-e'er I turn my eye,
While all that bor-rows life from Thee Is ev-er in Thy care,

The moon shines full at His com-mand And all the stars o-bey.
If I sur-vey the ground I tread Or gaze up-on the sky!
And ev-ery-where that man can be, Thou, God, art pres-ent there. A-men.

Music from "The English Hymnal" by permission of Oxford University Press, London.

GOD THE FATHER

This Is My Father's World 58

The morning stars sang together, and all the sons of God shouted for joy. Job 38:7

TERRA BEATA S.M.D.

Maltbie D. Babcock, 1901

Franklin L. Sheppard, 1915

1. This is my Fa-ther's world, And to my lis-tening ears All
2. This is my Fa-ther's world, The birds their car - ols raise, The
3. This is my Fa-ther's world, O let me ne'er for - get That

na - ture sings, and round me rings The mu-sic of the spheres.
morn-ing light, the lil - y white, De-clare their Mak-er's praise.
though the wrong seems oft so strong, God is the Rul - er yet.

This is my Fa-ther's world: I rest me in the thought Of
This is my Fa-ther's world: He shines in all that's fair; In the
This is my Fa-ther's world: Why should my heart be sad? The

rocks and trees, of skies and seas—His hand the won-ders wrought.
rus - tling grass I hear Him pass, He speaks to me ev-ery-where.
Lord is King: let the heav - ens ring! God reigns: let earth be glad! A-men.

HIS WORKS IN CREATION

59 All Creatures of Our God and King

All Thy works shall praise Thee, O Lord. Psa. 145:10

St. Francis of Assisi, 1225
Trans. by William H. Draper, 1926

LASST UNS ERFREUEN L.M. Alleluias
Geistliche Kirchengesäng, Cologne, 1623

1. All crea-tures of our God and King, Lift up your voice and with us sing
2. Thou rush-ing wind that art so strong, Ye clouds that sail in heav'n a - long,
3. Thou flow-ing wa - ter, pure and clear, Make mu-sic for thy Lord to hear,
4. And all ye men of ten-der heart, For-giv - ing oth - ers, take your part,
5. Let all things their Cre-a - tor bless, And wor-ship Him in hum-ble - ness,

Al-le - lu - ia, Al-le - lu - ia! Thou burn-ing sun with gold - en beam,
O praise Him, Al-le - lu - ia! Thou ris - ing morn in praise re - joice,
Al-le - lu - ia, Al-le - lu - ia! Thou fire so mas-ter - ful and bright,
O sing ye, Al-le - lu - ia! Ye who long pain and sor - row bear,
O praise Him, Al-le - lu - ia! Praise, praise the Fa - ther, praise the Son,

Thou sil - ver moon with soft - er gleam, O praise Him, O praise Him,
Ye lights of eve - ning, find a voice, O praise Him, O praise Him,
That giv - est man both warmth and light, O praise Him, O praise Him,
Praise God and on Him cast your care, O praise Him, O praise Him,
And praise the Spir - it, three in one, O praise Him, O praise Him,

Al-le - lu - ia, al - le - lu - ia, al - le - lu - ia!
Al-le - lu - ia, al - le - lu - ia, al - le - lu - ia!
Al-le - lu - ia, al - le - lu - ia, al - le - lu - ia!
Al-le - lu - ia, al - le - lu - ia, al - le - lu - ia!
Al-le - lu - ia, al - le - lu - ia, al - le - lu - ia! A - men.

This tune in a unison setting, No. 166
Words copyright by J. Curwen & Sons. Used by permission.
GOD THE FATHER: HIS WORKS IN CREATION

Come, Christians, Join to Sing 60

O come, let us sing unto the Lord. Psa. 95:1

MADRID 6 6 6 6 D.

Traditional Spanish melody
Arr. by David Evans, 1927

Christian H. Bateman, 1843

1. Come, Chris-tians, join to sing Al - le - lu - ia! A - men!
2. Come, lift your hearts on high, Al - le - lu - ia! A - men!
3. Praise yet our Christ a - gain, Al - le - lu - ia! A - men!

Loud praise to Christ our King; Al - le - lu - ia! A - men!
Let prais - es fill the sky; Al - le - lu - ia! A - men!
Life shall not end the strain; Al - le - lu - ia! A - men!

Let all, with heart and voice, Be - fore His throne re - joice;
He is our Guide and Friend; To us He'll con - de - scend;
On heav - en's bliss - ful shore His good - ness we'll a - dore,

Praise is His gra - cious choice: Al - le - lu - ia! A - men!
His love shall nev - er end: Al - le - lu - ia! A - men!
Sing - ing for - ev - er - more, "Al - le - lu - ia! A - men!"

JESUS CHRIST: HIS PRAISE

61 At the Name of Jesus

That at the name of Jesus every knee should bow . . . Phil. 2:10

Caroline M. Noel, 1870
Based on Philippians 2:5-11

KING'S WESTON 6 5 6 5 D.
Ralph Vaughan Williams, 1925

1. At the name of Je - sus Ev - ery knee shall bow,
2. At His voice cre - a - tion Sprang at once to sight,
3. Hum - bled for a sea - son, To re - ceive a name
4. In your hearts en - throne Him; There let Him sub - due
5. Broth - ers, this Lord Je - sus Shall re - turn a - gain,

Ev - ery tongue con - fess Him King of Glo - ry now;
All the an - gel fac - es, All the hosts of light,
From the lips of sin - ners, Un - to whom He came,
All that is not ho - ly, All that is not true:
With His Fa - ther's glo - ry O'er the earth to reign;

'Tis the Fa - ther's pleas - ure We should call Him Lord,
Thrones and dom - i - na - tions, Stars up - on their way,
Faith - ful - ly He bore it Spot - less to the last,
Crown Him as your Cap - tain In temp - ta - tion's hour;
For all wreaths of em - pire Meet up - on His brow,

Who from the be - gin - ning Was the might - y Word.
All the heav'n - ly or - ders In their great ar - ray.
Brought it back vic - to - rious, When from death He passed.
Let His will en - fold you In its light and power.
And our hearts con - fess Him King of Glo - ry now. A - men.

Music from "Enlarged Songs of Praise" by permission of Oxford University Press.

JESUS CHRIST

All Hail the Power of Jesus' Name 62

He hath . . . a name written, King of Kings, and Lord of Lords. Rev. 19:16

Edward Perronet, 1779
Adapt. by John Rippon, 1787

DIADEM C.M. Ref.
James Ellor, 1838

1. All hail the pow'r of Je-sus' name! Let an-gels pros-trate
2. Ye cho-sen seed of Is-rael's race, Ye ran-somed of the
3. Let ev-ery kin-dred, ev-ery tribe, On this ter-res-trial
4. O that with yon-der sa-cred throng We at His feet may

fall, Let an-gels pros-trate fall; Bring forth the roy-al di-a-
fall, Ye ran-somed of the fall; Hail Him who saves you by His
ball, On this ter-res-trial ball; To Him all maj-es-ty as-
fall, We at His feet may fall! We'll join the ev-er-last-ing

dem,
grace, And crown Him, crown Him,
cribe,
song, And crown Him, crown Him, crown Him, crown Him, crown Him,

crown

crown Him, crown Him, And crown Him Lord of all. A-men.

Him, And crown Him

Alternate tunes, CORONATION and MILES LANE, No. 63

HIS PRAISE

63 All Hail the Power of Jesus' Name

He hath . . . a name written, King of Kings, and Lord of Lords. Rev. 19:16

Edward Perronet, 1779
Adapt. by John Rippon, 1787

CORONATION C.M. Repeats
Oliver Holden, 1792

1. All hail the power of Je - sus' name! Let an - gels pros - trate fall;
2. Ye cho - sen seed of Is - rael's race, Ye ran - somed from the fall,
3. Let ev - ery kin - dred, ev - ery tribe, On this ter - res - trial ball,
4. O that with yon - der sa - cred throng We at His feet may fall!

Bring forth the roy - al di - a - dem, And crown Him Lord of all;
Hail Him who saves you by His grace, And crown Him Lord of all;
To Him all maj - es - ty as - cribe, And crown Him Lord of all;
We'll join the ev - er - last - ing song, And crown Him Lord of all;

Bring forth the roy - al di - a - dem, And crown Him Lord of all!
Hail Him who saves you by His grace, And crown Him Lord of all!
To Him all maj - es - ty as - cribe, And crown Him Lord of all!
We'll join the ev - er - last - ing song, And crown Him Lord of all!

MILES LANE C.M. Repeats
William Shrubsole, 1779

(Second Tune)

1. All hail the power of Je-sus' name! Let angels pros-trate fall; Bring forth the roy - al

di - a - dem, And crown Him, crown Him, crown Him, Crown Him Lord of all!

Alternate tune, DIADEM, No. 62
JESUS CHRIST

In Thee Is Gladness **64**

My spirit hath rejoiced in God my Savior. Luke 1:47

Johann Lindemann, 1598
Trans. by Catherine Winkworth, 1858 and 1863

IN DIR IST FREUDE 5 5 7 D. 5 5 5 5 9 D.
Giovanni Gastoldi, 1591

1. In Thee is glad-ness a - mid all sad - ness, Je - sus, sun - shine of my heart!
2. If He is ours we fear no pow - ers, Not of earth; nor sin, nor death!

By Thee are giv - en the gifts of heav - en, Thou the true Re-deem - er art!
He sees and bless - es in worst dis-tress - es, He can change them with a breath!

Our souls Thou wak - est, our bonds Thou break-est, Who trusts Thee sure - ly
Our hearts are pin - ing to see Thy shin - ing, Dy - ing or liv - ing,
Where-fore the sto - ry tell of His glo - ry With heart and voic - es;
We shout for glad - ness, tri - umph o'er sad - ness, Love Him and praise Him

hath built se - cure - ly, He stands for - ev - er: Al - le - lu - ia!
to Thee are cleav - ing, Naught can us sev - er: Al - le - lu - ia!
all heav'n re - joic - es In Him for - ev - er: Al - le - lu - ia!
and still shall raise Him Glad hymns for - ev - er: Al - le - lu - ia!

HIS PRAISE

65 O Could I Speak the Matchless Worth

And we beheld His glory . . . full of grace and truth. John 1:14

ARIEL 8 8 6 8 8 6 6

Source unknown
Arr. by Lowell Mason, 1836

Samuel Medley, 1789

1. O could I speak the match - less worth, O
2. I'd sing the char - ac - ters He bears, And
3. Soon the de - light - ful day will come When

could I sound the glo - ries forth Which in my Sav - ior shine, I'd
all the forms of love He wears, Ex - alt - ed on His throne: In
my dear Lord will bring me home, And I shall see His face; Then

sing His glo - rious right-eous-ness, And mag - ni - fy the won-drous grace
loft - iest songs of sweet-est praise, I would to ev - er - last - ing days
with my Sav - ior, Broth - er, Friend, A blest e - ter - ni - ty I'll spend,

Which made sal - va - tion mine, Which made sal - va - tion mine.
Make all His glo - ries known, Make all His glo - ries known.
Tri - um-phant in His grace, Tri - um-phant in His grace. A - men.

JESUS CHRIST

Take the Name of Jesus with You 66

. . . Do all in the name of the Lord Jesus. Col. 3:17

PRECIOUS NAME 8 7 8 7 Ref.

Lydia Baxter, 1870

William H. Doane, 1871

1. Take the name of Je - sus with you, Child of sor - row and of
2. Take the name of Je - sus ev - er, As a shield from ev - ery
3. O the pre - cious name of Je - sus! How it thrills our souls with
4. At the name of Je - sus bow - ing, Fall - ing pros - trate at His

woe; It will joy and com - fort give you, Take it,
snare; If temp - ta - tions 'round you gath - er, Breathe that
joy, When His lov - ing arms re - ceive us, And His
feet, King of kings in heav'n we'll crown Him, When our

Refrain

then, wher - e'er you go.
ho - ly name in prayer. Pre - cious name, O how
songs our tongues em - ploy. Pre - cious name,
jour - ney is com - plete.

sweet! Hope of earth and joy of heav'n; Pre - cious
O how sweet!

name, O how sweet! Hope of earth and joy of heav'n.
Pre-cious name, O how sweet, how sweet!

HIS PRAISE

67 Fairest Lord Jesus

Thou art fairer than the children of men . . . Psa. 45:2

CRUSADER'S HYMN 5 6 8 5 5 8

Gesangbuch, Münster, 1677
Trans. anonymous, 1850
St. 4, trans. by Joseph A. Seiss, 1873

H. A. Hoffmann von Fallersleben's
Schlesische Volkslieder, 1842
Arr. by Richard S. Willis, 1850

1. Fair - est Lord Je - sus! Ru - ler of all na - ture,
2. Fair are the mead - ows, Fair - er still the wood - lands,
3. Fair is the sun - shine, Fair - er still the moon - light,
4. Beau - ti - ful Sav - ior! Lord of the na - tions!

O Thou of God and man the Son! Thee will I cher - ish,
Robed in the bloom - ing garb of spring: Je - sus is fair - er,
And all the twink - ling star - ry host: Je - sus shines bright - er,
Son of God and Son of Man! Glo - ry and hon - or,

Thee will I hon - or, Thou, my soul's glo - ry, joy, and crown!
Je - sus is pur - er, Who makes the woe-ful heart to sing.
Je - sus shines pur - er, Than all the an - gels heav'n can boast.
Praise, ad - o - ra - tion, Now and for - ev - er - more be Thine! A - men.

68 How Sweet the Name of Jesus Sounds

Unto you therefore which believe He is precious . . . I Pet. 2:7

ST. PETER C.M.

John Newton, 1779

Alexander R. Reinagle, c. 1836

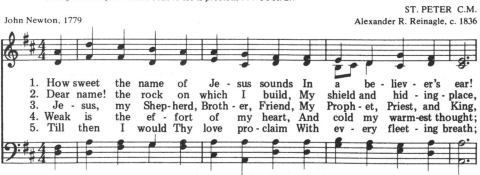

1. How sweet the name of Je - sus sounds In a be - liev - er's ear!
2. Dear name! the rock on which I build, My shield and hid - ing - place,
3. Je - sus, my Shep - herd, Broth - er, Friend, My Proph - et, Priest, and King,
4. Weak is the ef - fort of my heart, And cold my warm-est thought;
5. Till then I would Thy love pro - claim With ev - ery fleet - ing breath;

JESUS CHRIST

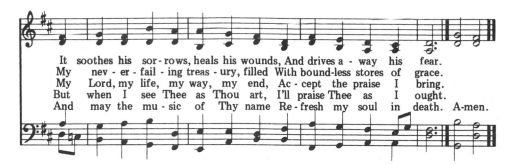

It soothes his sor-rows, heals his wounds, And drives a-way his fear.
My nev-er-fail-ing treas-ury, filled With bound-less stores of grace.
My Lord, my life, my way, my end, Ac-cept the praise I bring.
But when I see Thee as Thou art, I'll praise Thee as I ought.
And may the mu-sic of Thy name Re-fresh my soul in death. A-men.

All Glory to Jesus, Begotten of God 69

Thou art My Son; this day have I begotten Thee. Psa. 2:7

RIDGEMOOR 11 6 11 6

John W. Peterson, 1957

John W. Peterson, 1957

1. All glo-ry to Je-sus, be-got-ten of God, The great I
2. To think that the guard-ian of plan-ets in space, The Shep-herd
3. The King of all kings and the Lord of all lords, He reigns in

AM is He; Cre-a-tor, sus-tain-er—but won-der of all,
of the stars, Is ten-der-ly lead-ing the church of His love,
glo-ry now; Some day He is com-ing earth's king-dom to claim,

CODA after last verse

The Lamb of Cal-va-ry!
By hands with crim-son scars!
And ev-ery knee shall bow! And ev-ery knee shall bow!

HIS PRAISE

70 Join All the Glorious Names

Far above . . . every name that is named. Eph. 1:21

Isaac Watts, 1707

DARWALL 666688
John Darwall, 1770

1. Join all the glo - rious names Of wis - dom, love, and pow'r,
2. Great Proph - et of my God, My tongue would bless Thy name:
3. Je - sus, my great High Priest, Of - fered His blood, and died;
4. Thou art my Coun - sel - or, My Pat - tern, and my Guide,
5. My Sav - ior and my Lord, My Con - qu'ror and my King,

That ev - er mor - tals knew, That an - gels
By Thee the joy - ful news Of our sal -
My guilt - y con - science seeks No sac - ri -
And Thou my Shep - herd art; O, keep me
Thy scep - tre and Thy sword, Thy reign - ing

ev - er bore: All are too poor to speak His worth,
va - tion came, The joy - ful news of sins for - giv'n,
fice be - side: His pow'r - ful blood did once a - tone
near Thy side; Nor let my feet e'er turn a - stray
grace, I sing: Thine is the pow'r; be - hold I sit

Too poor to set my Sav - ior forth.
Of hell sub - dued and peace with heav'n.
And now it pleads be - fore the throne.
To wan - der in the crook - ed way.
In will - ing bonds be - neath Thy feet. A - men.

This tune in a lower key, No. 79

JESUS CHRIST

The Great Physician Now Is Near 71

He hath sent Me to heal the broken-hearted . . . Luke 4:18

GREAT PHYSICIAN 8 7 8 7 Ref.

William Hunter, 1859

John H. Stockton, 1869

1. The great Phy - si - cian now is near—The sym - pa - thiz - ing Je - sus;
2. Your man - y sins are all for - giv'n— O hear the voice of Je - sus;
3. All glo - ry to the dy - ing Lamb—I now be - lieve in Je - sus;
4. And when to that bright world a - bove We rise to be with Je - sus,

He speaks the droop-ing heart to cheer—O hear the voice of Je - sus!
Go on your way in peace to heav'n And wear a crown with Je - sus.
I love the bless - ed Sav - ior's name, I love the name of Je - sus.
We'll sing a - round the throne of love His name, the name of Je - sus.

Refrain

Sweet-est note in ser - aph song, Sweet-est name on mor - tal tongue,

Sweet - est car - ol ev - er sung— Je - sus, bless - ed Je - sus!

HIS PRAISE

72 My Jesus, I Love Thee

We love Him because He first loved us. I John 4:19

William R. Featherstone, c. 1862

GORDON 11 11 11 11
Adoniram J. Gordon, 1876

1. My Je - sus, I love Thee, I know Thou art mine; For Thee all the
2. I love Thee, be - cause Thou hast first lov - ed me, And pur - chased my
3. I'll love Thee in life, I will love Thee in death, And praise Thee as
4. In man - sions of glo - ry and end - less de - light, I'll ev - er a -

fol - lies of sin I re - sign; My gra - cious Re - deem - er, my Sav - ior art
par - don on Cal - va - ry's tree; I love Thee for wear - ing the thorns on Thy
long as Thou lend - est me breath; And say when the death - dew lies cold on my
dore Thee in heav - en so bright; I'll sing with the glit - ter - ing crown on my

Thou; If ev - er I loved Thee, my Je - sus, 'tis now.
brow; If ev - er I loved Thee, my Je - sus, 'tis now.
brow; If ev - er I loved Thee, my Je - sus, 'tis now.
brow; If ev - er I loved Thee, my Je - sus, 'tis now. A - men.

73 O Jesus, King Most Wonderful

I will extol Thee, my God, O King . . . Psa. 145:1

Attr. to Bernard of Clairvaux, 1091-1153
Trans. by Edward Caswall, 1849

SERENITY C.M.
William V. Wallace, 1856
Arr. by Uzziah C. Burnap, 1878

1. O Je - sus, King most won - der - ful! Thou Con - quer - or re - nowned!
2. When once Thou vis - it - est the heart, Then truth be - gins to shine,
3. O Je - sus! Light of all be - low, Thou Fount of liv - ing fire!
4. Thy won - drous mer - cies are un - told Thro' each re - turn - ing day;
5. Thee may our tongues for - ev - er bless; Thee may we love a - lone;

This tune in a higher key, No. 216

JESUS CHRIST

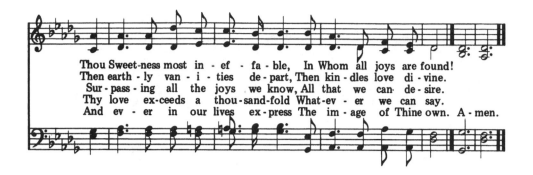

Thou Sweet-ness most in-ef-fa-ble, In Whom all joys are found!
Then earth-ly van-i-ties de-part, Then kin-dles love di-vine.
Sur-pass-ing all the joys we know, All that we can de-sire.
Thy love ex-ceeds a thou-sand-fold What-ev-er we can say.
And ev-er in our lives ex-press The im-age of Thine own. A-men.

Shepherd of Eager Youth 74

. . . Our Lord Jesus, that great shepherd of the sheep . . . Heb. 13:20

Clement of Alexandria, c. 200
Trans. by Henry M. Dexter, 1846

ITALIAN HYMN 6 6 4 6 6 6 4
Felice de Giardini, 1769

1. Shep-herd of ea-ger youth, Guid-ing in love and truth, Through de-vious ways; Christ our tri-um-phant King, We come Thy name to sing, Hith-er our chil-dren bring To shout Thy praise.
2. Thou art our ho-ly Lord, The all-sub-du-ing Word, Heal-er of strife; Thou didst Thy-self a-base, That from sin's deep dis-grace Thou might-est save our race, And give us life.
3. Thou art the great High Priest; Thou hast pre-pared the feast Of heav'n-ly love; While in our mor-tal pain None calls on Thee in vain; Help Thou dost not dis-dain, Help from a-bove.
4. Ev-er be Thou our Guide, Our Shep-herd and our Pride, Our Staff and Song; Je-sus, Thou Christ of God, By Thy e-ter-nal word, Lead us where Thou hast trod, Make our faith strong.
5. So now and till we die Sound we Thy prais-es high, And joy-ful sing; Let all the ho-ly throng, Who to Thy Church be-long, U-nite to swell the song To Christ our King! A-men.

This tune in a higher key, No. 4

HIS PRAISE

75 Love Divine, All Loves Excelling

Above all these things put on charity, which is the bond of perfectness. Col. 3:14

BEECHER 8 7 8 7 D.

Charles Wesley, 1747

John Zundel, 1870

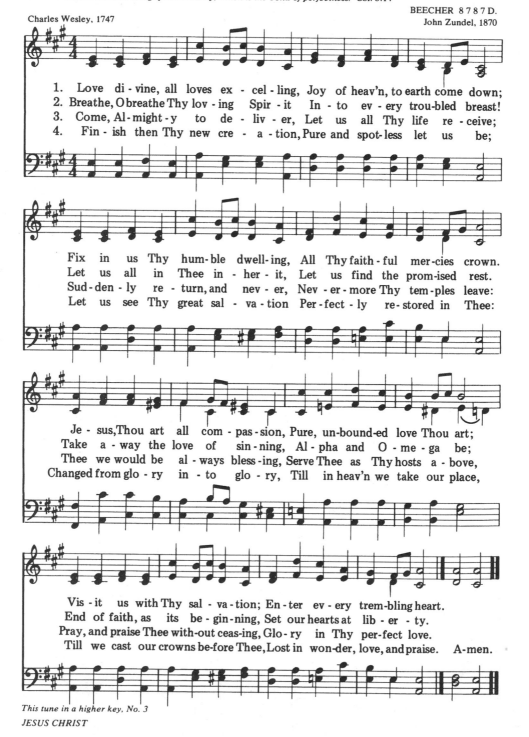

1. Love di - vine, all loves ex - cel - ling, Joy of heav'n, to earth come down;
2. Breathe, O breathe Thy lov - ing Spir - it In - to ev - ery trou-bled breast!
3. Come, Al - might - y to de - liv - er, Let us all Thy life re - ceive;
4. Fin - ish then Thy new cre - a - tion, Pure and spot-less let us be;

Fix in us Thy hum - ble dwell - ing, All Thy faith - ful mer - cies crown.
Let us all in Thee in - her - it, Let us find the prom-ised rest.
Sud - den - ly re - turn, and nev - er, Nev - er - more Thy tem - ples leave:
Let us see Thy great sal - va - tion Per - fect - ly re - stored in Thee:

Je - sus, Thou art all com - pas - sion, Pure, un - bound - ed love Thou art;
Take a - way the love of sin - ning, Al - pha and O - me - ga be;
Thee we would be al - ways bless - ing, Serve Thee as Thy hosts a - bove,
Changed from glo - ry in - to glo - ry, Till in heav'n we take our place,

Vis - it us with Thy sal - va - tion; En - ter ev - ery trem-bling heart.
End of faith, as its be - gin - ning, Set our hearts at lib - er - ty.
Pray, and praise Thee with-out ceas-ing, Glo - ry in Thy per-fect love.
Till we cast our crowns be-fore Thee, Lost in won-der, love, and praise. A-men.

This tune in a higher key, No. 3

JESUS CHRIST

We Sing the Boundless Praise 76

Worthy is the Lamb that was slain . . . Rev. 5:12

BOUNDLESS PRAISE S.M.D.

Joseph C. Macaulay, 1957

Harry D. Loes, 1957

1. We sing the bound-less praise Of Him who reigns on high,
2. Thy pre-cious blood a-lone, O Christ, has brought us near;
3. All hail! Re-deem-er, King, Thou Lamb of Cal-va-ry!

And of His glo-rious Son, the Lamb Who brought sal-va-tion nigh.
No long-er stran-gers, God in love Calls us His chil-dren dear.
Let ran-somed sin-ners sing Thy name Thro' all e-ter-ni-ty.

Thine ev-er-last-ing pow'r And maj-es-ty we sing,
The ti-tle of the Lamb Thou bear-est still in heav'n,
When stand the ran-somed throng Be-fore the great I Am,

But with our songs of sov-'reign grace We'll make heav'n's arch-es ring.
Me-mo-rial of Thy sac-ri-fice, And love to sin-ners giv'n.
This shall their end-less an-them be, "All wor-thy is the Lamb!" A-men.

HIS PRAISE

77 Awake, My Soul, to Joyful Lays

I will . . . praise Thy name for Thy lovingkindness. Psa. 138:2

Samuel Medley, 1782

LOVINGKINDNESS L.M. Repeats
William Caldwell, 1837

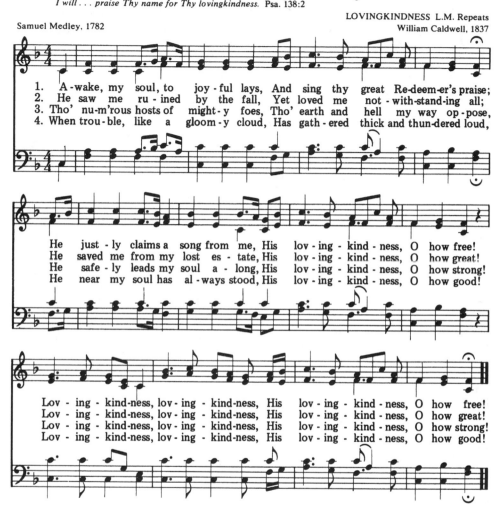

1. A-wake, my soul, to joy-ful lays, And sing thy great Re-deem-er's praise;
2. He saw me ru-ined by the fall, Yet loved me not-with-stand-ing all;
3. Tho' nu-m'rous hosts of might-y foes, Tho' earth and hell my way op-pose,
4. When trou-ble, like a gloom-y cloud, Has gath-ered thick and thun-dered loud,

He just-ly claims a song from me, His lov-ing-kind-ness, O how free!
He saved me from my lost es-tate, His lov-ing-kind-ness, O how great!
He safe-ly leads my soul a-long, His lov-ing-kind-ness, O how strong!
He near my soul has al-ways stood, His lov-ing-kind-ness, O how good!

Lov-ing-kind-ness, lov-ing-kind-ness, His lov-ing-kind-ness, O how free!
Lov-ing-kind-ness, lov-ing-kind-ness, His lov-ing-kind-ness, O how great!
Lov-ing-kind-ness, lov-ing-kind-ness, His lov-ing-kind-ness, O how strong!
Lov-ing-kind-ness, lov-ing-kind-ness, His lov-ing-kind-ness, O how good!

78 Praise the Savior, Ye Who Know Him

Jesus Christ the same yesterday, and today, and forever. Heb. 13:8

Thomas Kelly, 1806

ACCLAIM 8 8 8 5
Traditional German melody

1. Praise the Sav-ior, ye who know Him! Who can tell how much we owe Him?
2. Je-sus is the name that charms us; He for con-flict fits and arms us;
3. Trust in Him, ye saints, for-ev-er; He is faith-ful, chang-ing nev-er;
4. Keep us, Lord, O keep us cleav-ing To Thy-self and still be-liev-ing,
5. Then we shall be where we would be, Then we shall be what we should be;

Glad - ly let us ren - der to Him All we are and have.
Noth - ing moves and noth - ing harms us While we trust in Him.
Nei - ther force nor guile can sev - er Those He loves from Him.
Till the hour of our re - ceiv - ing Prom - ised joys with Thee.
Things that are not now, nor could be, Soon shall be our own. A - men.

We Come, O Christ, to Thee 79

I am the way, the truth, and the life . . . John 14:6

DARWALL 6 6 6 6 8 8

E. Margaret Clarkson, 1947

John Darwall, 1770

1. We come, O Christ, to Thee, True Son of God and man, By Whom all things con-
2. Thou art the Way to God, Thy blood our ran - som paid; In Thee we face our
3. Thou art the liv - ing Truth! All wis - dom dwells in Thee, Thou Source of ev - ery
4. Thou on - ly art true Life, To know Thee is to live The more a - bund - ant
5. We wor-ship Thee, Lord Christ, Our Sav - ior and our King, To Thee our youth and

sist, In Whom all life be - gan: In Thee a - lone we
Judge And Mak - er un - a - fraid. Be - fore the throne ab -
skill, E - ter - nal Ver - i - ty! Thou great I Am! In
life That earth can nev - er give: O ris - en Lord! We
strength A - dor - ing - ly we bring: So fill our hearts, that

live and move, And have our be - ing in Thy love.
solved we stand, Thy love has met Thy law's de - mand.
Thee we rest, True an - swer to our ev - ery quest.
live in Thee, And Thou in us e - ter - nal - ly.
men may see Thy life in us, and turn to Thee. A - men.

This tune in a higher key, No. 70

HIS PRAISE

80 I Greet Thee, Who My Sure Redeemer Art

For there is none other name . . . whereby we must be saved. Acts 4:12

John Calvin, 1545
Trans. by Elizabeth L. Smith, 1868

TOULON 10 10 10 10
Genevan Psalter, 1551

1. I greet Thee, who my sure Re - deem - er art,
2. Thou art the King of mer - cy and of grace,
3. Thou art the life, by which a - lone we live,
4. Our hope is in no oth - er save in Thee;

My on - ly Trust and Sav - ior of my heart,
Reign - ing om - nip - o - tent in ev - ery place:
And all our sub - stance and our strength re - ceive;
Our faith is built up - on Thy prom - ise free;

Who pain didst un - der - go for my poor sake;
So come, O King, and our whole be - ing sway;
Sus - tain us by Thy faith and by Thy pow'r,
Lord, give us peace, and make us calm and sure,

I pray Thee from our hearts all cares to take.
Shine on us with the light of Thy pure day.
And give us strength in ev - ery try - ing hour.
That in Thy strength we ev - er - more en - dure. A - men.

JESUS CHRIST

All Praise to Him Who Reigns Above 81

Blessed be the name of the Lord. Job 1:21

BLESSED NAME L.M. Ref.

William H. Clark, 19th century
Refrain, Ralph E. Hudson, 1887

Source unknown
Arr. by Ralph E. Hudson, 1887, and
William J. Kirkpatrick, 1888

1. All praise to Him who reigns a - bove In maj - es - ty su - preme,
2. His name a - bove all names shall stand, Ex - alt - ed more and more,
3. Re - deem - er, Sav - ior, Friend of man Once ru - ined by the fall,
4. His name shall be the Coun - sel - or, The might - y Prince of Peace,

Who gave His Son for man to die, That He might man re - deem!
At God the Fa - ther's own right hand, Where an - gel hosts a - dore.
Thou hast de - vised sal - va - tion's plan, For Thou hast died for all.
Of all earth's king - doms Con - quer - or, Whose reign shall nev - er cease.

Refrain

Bless - ed be the name, bless - ed be the name, Bless - ed be the name of the Lord;

Bless - ed be the name, bless - ed be the name, Bless - ed be the name of the Lord.

HIS PRAISE

82 Friends All Around Us Are Trying to Find

Of His fulness have all we received, and grace for grace. John 1:16

OKMULGEE 10 10 10 10 Ref.

Harry D. Loes, 1915

Harry D. Loes, 1915

1. Friends all a-round us are try-ing to find What the heart yearns for, by
2. Some car-ry bur-dens whose weight has for years Crushed them with sor-row and
3. No oth-er name stirs the joy chords with-in, And thro' none else is re-
4. Je-sus is all this sad world needs to-day; Blind-ly men strive, for sin

sin un-der-mined; I have the se-cret, I know where 'tis found:
blind-ed with tears; Yet One stands read-y to help them just now,
mis-sion of sin; He knows the pain of the heart sore-ly tried,
dark-ens the way. O to draw back the grim cur-tains of night—

Refrain

On-ly in Je-sus true pleas-ures a-bound.
If they with faith and in pen-i-tence bow. All that I want is in
All of its needs will in Him be sup-plied.
One glimpse of Je-sus, and all will be bright.

Je - sus; He sat-is-fies, joy He sup-plies;
Je-sus, in Je-sus; with the free-ly;

Life would be worth-less with-out Him, All things in Je-sus I find.
with-out Him, with-out Him,

JESUS CHRIST

Jesus, the Very Thought of Thee 83

In whom, though now ye see Him not . . . ye rejoice. I Pet. 1:8

Attr. to Bernard of Clairvaux, c. 1150
Trans. by Edward Caswall, 1849

ST. AGNES C.M.
John B. Dykes, 1866

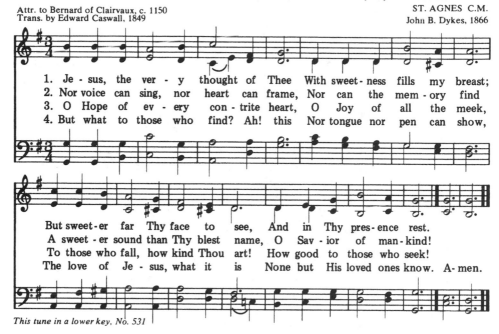

1. Je - sus, the ver - y thought of Thee With sweet - ness fills my breast;
2. Nor voice can sing, nor heart can frame, Nor can the mem - ory find
3. O Hope of ev - ery con - trite heart, O Joy of all the meek,
4. But what to those who find? Ah! this Nor tongue nor pen can show,

But sweet - er far Thy face to see, And in Thy pres - ence rest.
A sweet - er sound than Thy blest name, O Sav - ior of man - kind!
To those who fall, how kind Thou art! How good to those who seek!
The love of Je - sus, what it is None but His loved ones know. A - men.

This tune in a lower key, No. 531

Come and Praise the Lord Our King 84

Unto Him that loved us, and washed us from our sins . . . be glory. Rev. 1:5, 6

Source unknown

MICHAEL'S BOAT 7 4 7 4
Traditional melody

Unison

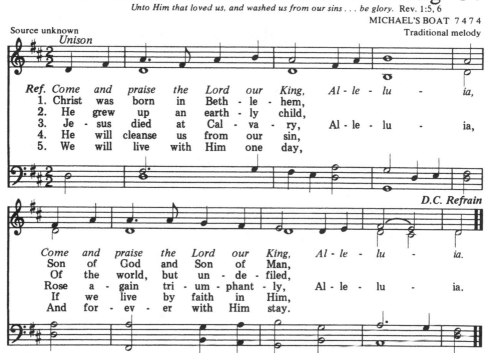

Ref. Come and praise the Lord our King, Al - le - lu - ia,
1. Christ was born in Beth - le - hem,
2. He grew up an earth - ly child,
3. Je - sus died at Cal - va - ry, Al - le - lu - ia,
4. He will cleanse us from our sin,
5. We will live with Him one day,

D.C. Refrain

Come and praise the Lord our King, Al - le - lu - ia.
Son of God and Son of Man,
Of the world, but un - de - filed,
Rose a - gain tri - um - phant - ly, Al - le - lu - ia.
If we live by faith in Him,
And for - ev - er with Him stay.

HIS PRAISE

85 Crown Him with Many Crowns

...And on His head were many crowns... Rev. 19:12

Matthew Bridges, 1851, and
Godfrey Thring, 1874

DIADEMATA S.M.D.
George J. Elvey, 1868

1. Crown Him with man - y crowns, The Lamb up - on His throne;
2. Crown Him the Son of God Be - fore the worlds be - gan,
3. Crown Him the Lord of life, Who tri - umphed o'er the grave,
4. Crown Him the Lord of love! Be - hold His hands and side,

Hark! how the heav'n - ly an - them drowns All mu - sic but its own!
And ye, who tread where He hath trod, Crown Him the Son of Man;
And rose vic - to - rious in the strife For those He came to save;
Those wounds, yet vis - i - ble a - bove, In beau - ty glo - ri - fied:

A - wake, my soul, and sing Of Him who died for thee, And
Who ev - ery grief hath known That wrings the hu - man breast, And
His glo - ries now we sing, Who died and rose on high, Who
All hail, Re - deem - er, hail! For Thou hast died for me: Thy

hail Him as thy match-less King Thro' all e - ter - ni - ty.
takes and bears them for His own, That all in Him may rest.
died e - ter - nal life to bring, And lives that death may die.
praise and glo - ry shall not fail Thro'- out e - ter - ni - ty. A - men.

This tune in a higher key, No. 422

JESUS CHRIST

Christ Has for Sin Atonement Made 86

. . . And know that this is indeed the Christ, the Savior of the world. John 4:42

BENTON HARBOR 8 7 8 7 Ref.

Elisha A. Hoffman, 1891

Elisha A. Hoffman, 1891

1. Christ has for sin a-tone-ment made, What a won-der-ful Sav-ior!
2. I praise Him for the cleans-ing blood, What a won-der-ful Sav-ior!
3. He cleansed my heart from all its sin, What a won-der-ful Sav-ior!
4. He walks be-side me in the way, What a won-der-ful Sav-ior!

We are re-deemed! the price is paid! What a won-der-ful Sav-ior!
That rec-on-ciled my soul to God; What a won-der-ful Sav-ior!
And now He reigns and rules there-in; What a won-der-ful Sav-ior!
And keeps me faith-ful day by day, What a won-der-ful Sav-ior!

Refrain

What a won-der-ful Sav-ior is Je-sus, my Je-sus!

What a won-der-ful Sav-ior is Je-sus, my Lord!

HIS PRAISE

87 I Love Thee, I Love Thee

O love the Lord, all ye His saints. Psa. 31:23

Source unknown

I LOVE THEE 11 11 11 11
Ingalls' *Christian Harmony*, 1805

1. I love Thee, I love Thee, I love Thee, my Lord;
I love Thee, my Savior, I love Thee, my God;
I love Thee, I love Thee, and that Thou dost know;
But how much I love Thee my ac-tions will show.

2. I'm hap-py, I'm hap-py, O won-drous ac-count!
My joys are im-mor-tal, I stand on the mount;
I gaze on my treas-ure and long to be there,
With Je-sus and an-gels and kin-dred so dear.

3. O Je-sus, my Sav-ior, with Thee I am blest,
My life and sal-va-tion, my joy and my rest;
Thy name be my theme, and Thy love be my song;
Thy grace shall in-spire both my heart and my tongue.

4. O, who's like my Sav-ior? He's Sa-lem's bright King;
He smiles and He loves me and helps me to sing;
I'll praise Him, I'll praise Him with notes loud and clear,
While riv-ers of pleas-ure my spir-it shall cheer. A-men.

JESUS CHRIST

I've Found a Friend 88

Greater love hath no man than this, that a man lay down his life for his friends. John 15:13

FRIEND 8 7 8 7 D.

James G. Small, 1863

George C. Stebbins, 1878

1. I've found a Friend, O such a Friend! He loved me ere I knew Him;
2. I've found a Friend, O such a Friend! He bled, He died to save me;
3. I've found a Friend, O such a Friend! So kind and true and ten - der,

He drew me with the cords of love, And thus He bound me to Him.
And not a - lone the gift of life, But His own self He gave me.
So wise a Coun - sel - or and Guide, So might - y a De - fend - er!

And round my heart still close - ly twine Those ties which naught can sev - er,
Naught that I have my own I call, I hold it for the Giv - er;
From Him who loves me now so well, What pow'r my soul can sev - er?

For I am His and He is mine, For - ev - er and for - ev - er.
My heart, my strength, my life, my all Are His, and His for - ev - er.
Shall life or death, or earth or hell? No! I am His for - ev - er.

HIS PRAISE

89 Majestic Sweetness Sits Enthroned

But we see Jesus . . . crowned with glory and honor. Heb. 2:9

Samuel Stennett, 1787

ORTONVILLE C.M. Repeats
Thomas Hastings, 1837

1. Ma - jes - tic sweet - ness sits en - throned Up - on the Sav - ior's
2. No mor - tal can with Him com - pare, A - mong the sons of
3. He saw me plunged in deep dis - tress, He flew to my re -
4. To Him I owe my life and breath, And all the joys I
5. Since from His boun - ty I re - ceive Such proofs of love di -

brow; His head with ra - diant glo - ries crowned, His
men; Fair - er is He than all the fair That
lief; For me He bore the shame - ful cross And
have; He makes me tri - umph o - ver death, And
vine, Had I a thou - sand hearts to give, Lord,

lips with grace o'er - flow, His lips with grace o'er - flow.
fill the heav'n - ly train, That fill the heav'n - ly train.
car - ried all my grief, And car - ried all my grief.
saves me from the grave, And saves me from the grave.
they should all be Thine, Lord, they should all be Thine. A - men.

90 O for a Thousand Tongues to Sing

My tongue shall speak of Thy . . . praise all the day long. Psa. 35:28

Charles Wesley, 1739

AZMON C.M.
Carl G. Gläser, 1784-1829
Arr. by Lowell Mason, 1839

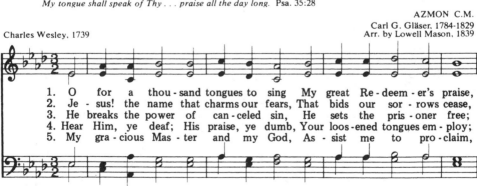

1. O for a thou - sand tongues to sing My great Re - deem - er's praise,
2. Je - sus! the name that charms our fears, That bids our sor - rows cease,
3. He breaks the power of can - celed sin, He sets the pris - oner free;
4. Hear Him, ye deaf; His praise, ye dumb, Your loos - ened tongues em - ploy;
5. My gra - cious Mas - ter and my God, As - sist me to pro - claim,

This tune in a lower key, No. 346

JESUS CHRIST

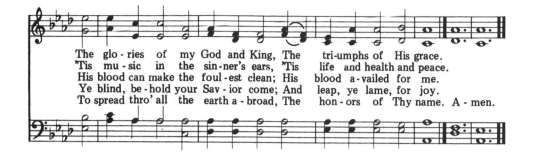

The glo-ries of my God and King, The tri-umphs of His grace.
'Tis mu-sic in the sin-ner's ears, 'Tis life and health and peace.
His blood can make the foul-est clean; His blood a-vailed for me.
Ye blind, be-hold your Sav-ior come; And leap, ye lame, for joy.
To spread thro' all the earth a-broad, The hon-ors of Thy name. A-men.

Jesus, Thou Joy of Loving Hearts 91

He . . . filleth the hungry soul with goodness. Psa. 107:9

Attr. to Bernard of Clairvaux, c. 1150
Trans. by Ray Palmer, 1858

QUEBEC L.M.
Henry Baker, 1854

1. Je - sus, Thou Joy of lov - ing hearts, Thou Fount of
2. Thy truth un - changed hath ev - er stood; Thou sav - est
3. We taste Thee, O Thou liv - ing Bread, And long to
4. Our rest - less spir - its yearn for Thee, Where - e'er our
5. O Je - sus, ev - er with us stay, Make all our

life, Thou Light of men, From the best bliss that earth im - part,
those that on Thee call; To them that seek Thee, Thou art
feast up - on Thee still; We drink of Thee, the Foun - tain -
change - ful lot is cast; Glad, when Thy gra - cious smile we
mo - ments calm and bright; Chase the dark night of sin a -

parts, We turn un - filled to Thee a - gain.
good, To them that find Thee, all in all.
head, And thirst our souls from Thee to fill.
see, Blest, when our faith can hold Thee fast.
way, Shed o'er the world Thy ho - ly light. A - men.

This tune in a higher key, No. 5

92 I Know of a Name

Thou shalt call His name Jesus: for He shall save His people . . . Matt. 1:21

THAT BEAUTIFUL NAME 10 7 10 7 Ref.

Jean Perry, 1916

Mabel J. Camp, 1916

1. I know of a Name, a beau-ti-ful Name, That an-gels brought
2. I know of a Name, a beau-ti-ful Name, That un-to a
3. The One of that Name my Sav-ior be-came, My Sav-ior of
4. I love that blest Name, that won-der-ful Name, Made high-er than

down to earth; They whis-pered it low one night long a - go,
Babe was giv'n; The stars glit-tered bright through-out that glad night,
Cal - va - ry; My sins nailed Him there, my bur-dens He bare,
all in heav'n; 'Twas whis-pered, I know, in my heart long a - go—

Refrain

To a maid-en of low-ly birth.
And an-gels praised God in heav'n.
He suf-fered all this for me. That beau-ti-ful Name, that
To Je-sus my life I've giv'n.

beau-ti-ful Name, From sin has pow'r to free us! That beau-ti-ful

Name, that won-der-ful Name, That match-less Name is Je - sus!

JESUS CHRIST

Deep in My Heart There's a Gladness 93

Therefore my heart greatly rejoiceth: and with my song will I praise Him. Psa. 28:7

KETCHUM 8 7 8 7 Ref.

Albert A. Ketchum, 1923

Albert A. Ketchum, 1923

1. Deep in my heart there's a glad - ness, Je - sus has saved me from
2. On - ly a glimpse of His good - ness, That was suf - fi - cient for
3. He is the fair - est of fair ones, He is the Lil - y, the

sin! Praise to His name—what a Sav - ior! Cleans - ing with-
me; On - ly one look at the Sav - ior, Then was my
Rose; Riv - ers of mer - cy sur - round Him, Grace, love and

Refrain — Unison or Two Parts

out and with - in.
spir - it set free. Why do I sing a - bout Je - sus?
pit - y He shows.

Why is He pre-cious to me? He is my Lord and my

Sav - ior, Dy - ing! He set me free!
(set me free!)

HIS PRAISE

94 Worthy Is the Lamb

Worthy is the Lamb that was slain . . . Rev. 5:12

Stephen Leddy, 1967

WORTHY LAMB Irreg.
Stephen Leddy, 1967

Unison

1. Wor - thy is the Lamb who died in awe - some grief;
2. Wor - thy is the Lamb who paid the price of death;
3. Wor - thy is the Lamb, though dead all else should be;
4. Wor - thy is the Lamb to live my life a - lone;

Wor - thy is the Lamb who saved a dy - ing thief.
Wor - thy is the Lamb who gave my soul its breath;
Wor - thy is the Lamb to live in you and me;
Wor - thy is the Lamb to make my soul His own,

Wor - thy is the Lamb to make up for my fall; Yes,
Wor - thy is the Lamb to grant my life the call; Yes,
Wor - thy is the Lamb to take our bit - ter gall; Yes,
Wor - thy is the Lamb to change our lives, like Paul; Yes,

wor - thy is the Lamb, praise God, He is all!
wor - thy is the Lamb, praise God, He is all!
wor - thy is the Lamb, praise God, He is all!
wor - thy is the Lamb, praise God, He is all!

JESUS CHRIST

Hail, Thou Once Despised Jesus 95

He is despised and rejected of men . . . Isa. 53:3

IN BABILONE 8 7 8 7 D.

Attr. to John Bakewell, 1757
Prob. alt. by Martin Madan, 1760

Traditional Netherlands melody
Arr. by Julius Röntgen, c. 1906

1. Hail, Thou once de-spis-ed Je-sus! Hail, Thou Gal-i-le-an King!
2. Pas-chal Lamb, by God ap-point-ed, All our sins on Thee were laid;
3. Je-sus, hail! en-throned in glo-ry, There for-ev-er to a-bide;
4. Wor-ship, hon-or, pow'r and bless-ing Thou art wor-thy to re-ceive;

Thou didst suf-fer to re-lease us; Thou didst free sal-va-tion bring.
By al-might-y love ap-point-ed, Thou hast full a-tone-ment made.
All the heav'n-ly hosts a-dore Thee, Seat-ed at Thy Fa-ther's side.
Loud-est prais-es, with-out ceas-ing, Meet it is for us to give.

Hail, Thou pa-tient Friend and Sav-ior, Bear-er of our sin and shame!
All Thy peo-ple are for-giv-en Through the vir-tue of Thy blood;
There for sin-ners Thou art plead-ing; There Thou dost our place pre-pare;
Help, ye bright an-gel-ic spir-its, Bring your sweet-est, no-blest lays;

By Thy mer-its we find fa-vor; Life is giv-en through Thy name.
O-pened is the gate of heav-en; Peace is made 'twixt man and God.
Ev-er for us in-ter-ced-ing Till in glo-ry we ap-pear.
Help to sing our Sav-ior's mer-its, Help to chant Em-man-uel's praise! A-men.

HIS PRAISE

96 Praise Him! Praise Him!

Praise Him according to His excellent greatness. Psa. 150:2

Fanny J. Crosby, 1869

JOYFUL SONG Irreg. Ref.
Chester G. Allen, 1869

1. Praise Him! praise Him! Je - sus, our bless - ed Re - deem - er! Sing, O Earth, His
2. Praise Him! praise Him! Je - sus, our bless - ed Re - deem - er! For our sins He
3. Praise Him! praise Him! Je - sus, our bless - ed Re - deem - er! Heav'n - ly por - tals

won-der -ful love pro - claim! Hail Him! hail Him! high-est arch-an - gels in glo - ry;
suf-fered, and bled and died; He our Rock, our hope of e - ter - nal sal - va - tion,
loud with ho - san - nas ring! Je - sus, Sav - ior, reign-eth for - ev - er and ev - er;

Strength and hon - or give to His ho - ly name! Like a shep-herd Je - sus will
Hail Him! hail Him! Je - sus the Cru - ci - fied. Sound His prais - es! Je - sus who
Crown Him! crown Him! Proph-et and Priest and King! Christ is com - ing! o - ver the

Refrain

guard His chil-dren, In His arms He car-ries them all day long:
bore our sor - rows; Love un-bound-ed, won-der-ful, deep and strong: Praise Him! praise Him!
world vic - to - rious, Pow'r and glo - ry un - to the Lord be - long:

JESUS CHRIST

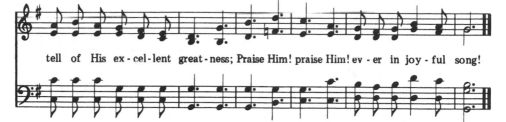

tell of His ex-cel-lent great-ness; Praise Him! praise Him! ev-er in joy-ful song!

There Is No Name So Sweet on Earth 97

Wherefore God also hath . . . given Him a name which is above every name. Phil. 2:9

THE SWEETEST NAME 8 7 8 7 Ref.

George W. Bethune, 1858

William B. Bradbury, 1861

1. There is no name so sweet on earth, No name so sweet in heav - en,
2. And when He hung up - on the tree, They wrote this name a - bove Him;
3. So now, up - on His Fa - ther's throne, Al - might - y to re - lease us
4. O Je - sus, by that match-less name, Thy grace shall fail us nev - er;

The name, be - fore His won-drous birth To Christ the Sav - ior giv - en.
That all might see the rea - son we For - ev - er - more must love Him.
From sin and pain, He glad - ly reigns, The Prince and Sav - ior, Je - sus.
To - day as yes - ter - day the same, Thou art the same for - ev - er.

Refrain

We love to sing of Christ our King, And hail Him, bless - ed Je - sus;

For there's no word ear ev - er heard So dear, so sweet as "Je - sus."

HIS PRAISE

98 O Savior, Precious Savior

Whom having not seen, ye love . . . I Pet. 1:8

MUNICH 7 6 7 6 D.
Neuvermehrtes Gesangbuch, Meiningen, 1693
Arr. by Felix Mendelssohn, 1847

Frances R. Havergal, 1870

1. O Sav - ior, pre - cious Sav - ior, Whom yet un - seen we love,
2. O bring - er of sal - va - tion, Who won - drous - ly hast wrought,
3. In Thee all ful - ness dwell - eth, All grace and pow'r di - vine;
4. O grant the con - sum - ma - tion Of this our song a - bove,

O Name of might and fa - vor, All oth - er names a - bove!
Thy - self the rev - e - la - tion Of love be - yond our thought,
The glo - ry that ex - cel - leth, O Son of God, is Thine;
In end - less ad - o - ra - tion, And ev - er - last - ing love;

We wor - ship Thee, we bless Thee, To Thee, O Christ, we sing;
We wor - ship Thee, we bless Thee, To Thee, O Christ, we sing;
We wor - ship Thee, we bless Thee, To Thee, O Christ, we sing;
Then shall we praise and bless Thee, Where per - fect prais - es ring,

We praise Thee, and con - fess Thee, Our ho - ly Lord and King.
We praise Thee, and con - fess Thee, Our gra - cious Lord and King.
We praise Thee, and con - fess Thee, Our glo - rious Lord and King.
And ev - er - more con - fess Thee, Our Sav - ior and 'our King. A - men.

JESUS CHRIST

Jesus! What a Friend for Sinners 99

Behold . . . a friend of publicans and sinners! Luke 7:34

HYFRYDOL 8 7 8 7 D.

J. Wilbur Chapman, 1910

Rowland H. Prichard, c. 1830
Arr. by Robert Harkness, 1910

1. Je - sus! what a Friend for sin - ners! Je - sus! Lov - er of my soul;
2. Je - sus! what a Strength in weak - ness! Let me hide my - self in Him;
3. Je - sus! what a Help in sor - row! While the bil - lows o'er me roll,
4. Je - sus! what a Guide and Keep - er! While the tem - pest still is high,
5. Je - sus! I do now re - ceive Him, More than all in Him I find,

Friends may fail me, foes as - sail me, He, my Sav - ior, makes me whole.
Tempt - ed, tried, and some - times fail - ing, He, my Strength, my vic - t'ry wins.
E - ven when my heart is break - ing, He, my Com - fort, helps my soul.
Storms a - bout me, night o'er - takes me, He, my Pi - lot, hears my cry.
He hath grant - ed me for - give - ness, I am His, and He is mine.

Refrain

Hal - le - lu - jah! what a Sav - ior! Hal - le - lu - jah! what a Friend!

Sav - ing, help - ing, keep - ing, lov - ing, He is with me to the end.

HIS PRAISE

100 O Come, O Come, Emmanuel

Behold a virgin shall . . . bear a son, and shall call His name Immanuel. Isa. 7:14

Latin hymn.
Trans. by John M. Neale, 1851
St. 5. Henry Sloane Coffin, 1916

VENI EMMANUEL 8 8 8 8 8 8
Thomas Helmore, 1854
Based on plainsong phrases

Unison

1. O come, O come, Em - man - u - el, And ran - som cap - tive
2. O come, Thou Rod of Jes - se, free Thine own from Sa - tan's
3. O come, Thou Day-spring, come and cheer Our spir - its by Thine
4. O come, Thou Key of Da - vid, come, And o - pen wide our
5. O come, De - sire of na - tions, bind All peo - ples in one

Is - ra - el, That mourns in lone - ly ex - ile here
tyr - an - ny; From depths of hell Thy peo - ple save
ad - vent here; And drive a - way the shades of night,
heav'n - ly home; Make safe the way that leads on high,
heart and mind; Bid en - vy, strife and quar - rels cease;

Un - til the Son of God ap - pear.
And give them vic - t'ry o'er the grave.
And pierce the clouds and bring us light! Re - joice! re - joice! Em-
And close the path to mis - er - y.
Fill all the world with heav - en's peace.

man - u - el Shall come to thee, O Is - ra - el! A - men.

JESUS CHRIST

Let All Mortal Flesh Keep Silence 101

Let all the earth keep silence . . . Hab. 2:20

PICARDY 878787

Liturgy of St. James, 5th century
Adapt. by Gerard Moultrie, 1864

Traditional French melody, 17th century
Hymn version, 1906

Unison

1. Let all mor-tal flesh keep si-lence, And with fear and
2. King of kings, yet born of Ma-ry, As of old on
3. Rank on rank the host of heav-en Spreads its van-guard
4. At his feet the six-winged Ser-aph, Cher-u-bim, with

trem-bling stand; Pon-der noth-ing earth-ly mind-ed,
earth He stood, Lord of lords, in hu-man ves-ture,
on the way, As the Light of light de-scend-eth
sleep-less eye, Veil their fac-es to the pres-ence,

For with bless-ing in His hand, Christ our God to
In the bod-y and the blood, He will give to
From the realms of end-less day, That the pow'rs of
As with cease-less voice they cry, Al-le-lu-ia,

earth de-scend-eth, Our full hom-age to de-mand.
all the faith-ful His own self for heav'n-ly food.
hell may van-ish As the dark-ness clears a-way.
Al-le-lu-ia, Al-le-lu-ia, Lord most high! A-men.

HIS ADVENT

102 Come, Thou Long Expected Jesus

The desire of all nations shall come . . . Haggai 2:7

HYFRYDOL 8 7 8 7 D.
Rowland H. Prichard, c. 1830
Arr. by Ralph Vaughan Williams, 1906

Charles Wesley, 1744

1. Come, Thou long ex-pect-ed Je-sus, Born to set Thy peo-ple free;
2. Born Thy peo-ple to de-liv-er, Born a child and yet a king.

From our fears and sins re-lease us; Let us find our rest in Thee.
Born to reign in us for-ev-er, Now Thy gra-cious king-dom bring.

Is-rael's strength and con-so-la-tion, Hope of all the earth Thou art;
By Thine own e-ter-nal Spir-it Rule in all our hearts a-lone;

Dear De-sire of ev-ery na-tion, Joy of ev-ery long-ing heart.
By Thine all suf-fi-cient mer-it, Raise us to Thy glo-rious throne. A-men.

Music from "The English Hymnal;" used by permission of Oxford University Press.

JESUS CHRIST: HIS ADVENT

O Come, All Ye Faithful **103**

Let us now go even unto Bethlehem . . . Luke 2:15

Latin hymn
Attr. to John F. Wade, 1751
Trans. by Frederick Oakeley, 1841, and others

ADESTE FIDELES Irreg. Ref.
John F. Wade's *Cantus Diversi*, 1751

1. O come, all ye faith-ful, joy-ful and tri-um-phant,
2. God of God, and Light of Light be-got-ten,
3. Sing, choirs of an-gels, sing in ex-ul-ta-tion!
4. Yea, Lord, we greet Thee, born this hap-py morn-ing,

O come ye, O come ye to Beth-le-hem!
Lo, He ab-hors not the Vir-gin's womb;
O sing, all ye cit-i-zens of heav'n a-bove;
Je-sus, to Thee be all glo-ry giv'n;

Come and be-hold Him, born the King of an-gels;
Ver-y God, be-got-ten, not cre-a-ted,
Glo-ry to God, all glo-ry in the high-est;
Word of the Fa-ther, now in flesh ap-pear-ing;

Refrain

O come, let us a-dore Him, O come, let us a-dore Him,

O come, let us a-dore Him, Christ the Lord. A-men.

HIS BIRTH

104 It Came upon the Midnight Clear

Glory to God in the highest, and on earth peace . . . Luke 2:14

Edmund H. Sears, 1849

CAROL C.M.D.
Richard S. Willis, 1850

1. It came up - on the mid - night clear, That glo - rious song of old,
2. Still through the clo - ven skies they come, With peace - ful wings un - furled,
3. And ye, be - neath life's crush - ing load, Whose forms are bend - ing low,
4. For lo, the days are has - tening on, By proph - et seen of old,

From an - gels bend - ing near the earth To touch their harps of gold:
And still their heav'n - ly mu - sic floats O'er all the wea - ry world:
Who toil a - long the climb - ing way With pain - ful steps and slow,
When, with the ev - er - cir - cling years, Shall come the time fore - told,

"Peace on the earth, good - will to men, From heav'n's all - gra - cious King": The
A - bove its sad and low - ly plains They bend on hov - ering wing: And
Look now! for glad and gold - en hours Come swift - ly on the wing: O
When the new heav'n and earth shall own The Prince of Peace their King, And

world in sol - emn still - ness lay To hear the an - gels sing.
ev - er o'er its Ba - bel sounds The bless - ed an - gels sing.
rest be - side the wea - ry road, And hear the an - gels sing.
the whole world send back the song Which now the an - gels sing.

JESUS CHRIST

What Child Is This, Who, Laid to Rest 105

Where is He that is born King of the Jews? Matt. 2:2

GREENSLEEVES 8 7 8 7 Ref.

William C. Dix, c. 1865

Traditional English melody, 16th century

1. What Child is this, who, laid to rest, On Ma-ry's lap is sleep-ing?
2. Why lies He in such mean es-tate Where ox and ass are feed-ing?
3. So bring Him in-cense, gold and myrrh, Come, peas-ant, king, to own Him;

Whom an-gels greet with an-thems sweet, While shep-herds watch are keep-ing?
Good Chris-tian, fear; for sin-ners here The si-lent Word is plead-ing.
The King of kings sal-va-tion brings, Let lov-ing hearts en-throne Him.

Refrain

This, this is Christ the King, Whom shep-herds guard and an-gels sing:

This, this is Christ the King, The babe, the Son of Ma-ry.

HIS BIRTH

106 Hark! the Herald Angels Sing

And suddenly there was . . . a multitude of the heavenly host praising God . . . Luke 2:13

MENDELSSOHN 7 7 7 7 D. Ref.
Felix Mendelssohn, 1840
Arr. by William H. Cummings, 1856

Charles Wesley, 1739

1. Hark! the her - ald an - gels sing, "Glo - ry to the new - born King:
2. Christ, by high - est heav'n a - dored; Christ, the ev - er - last - ing Lord!
3. Hail the heav'n - born Prince of Peace! Hail the Sun of Right - eous - ness!

Peace on earth, and mer - cy mild, God and sin - ners rec - on - ciled!"
Late in time be - hold Him come, Off - spring of the Vir - gin's womb:
Light and life to all He brings, Ris'n with heal - ing in His wings.

Joy - ful, all ye na - tions, rise, Join the tri - umph of the skies;
Veiled in flesh the God - head see; Hail th'in - car - nate De - i - ty,
Mild He lays His glo - ry by, Born that man no more may die,

With th'an - gel - ic host pro - claim, "Christ is born in Beth - le - hem!"
Pleased as man with men to dwell, Je - sus, our Em - man - u - el.
Born to raise the sons of earth, Born to give them sec - ond birth.

Hark! the her - ald an - gels sing, "Glo - ry to the new - born King." A - men.

JESUS CHRIST

Gentle Mary Laid Her Child 107

And she brought forth her firstborn son . . . and laid Him in a manger. Luke 2:7

TEMPUS ADEST FLORIDUM 7 6 7 6 D.

Piae Cantiones, 1582
Arr. by Ernest Macmillan, 1930

Joseph S. Cook, 1919

1. Gen - tle Ma - ry laid her Child Low - ly in a man - ger;
2. An - gels sang a - bout His birth; Wise Men sought and found Him;
3. Gen - tle Ma - ry laid her Child Low - ly in a man - ger;

There He lay, the un - de - filed, To the world a stran - ger:
Heav - en's star shone bright - ly forth, Glo - ry all a - round Him:
He is still the un - de - filed, But no more a stran - ger:

Such a Babe in such a place, Can He be the Sav - ior?
Shep - herds saw the won - drous sight, Heard the an - gels sing - ing;
Son of God, of hum - ble birth, Beau - ti - ful the sto - ry;

Ask the saved of all the race Who have found His fa - vor.
All the plains were lit that night, All the hills were ring - ing.
Praise His name in all the earth, Hail the King of glo - ry!

HIS BIRTH

108 The First Noel, the Angel Did Say

And there were in the same country shepherds abiding in the field . . . Luke 2:8

THE FIRST NOEL Irreg. Ref.

Traditional English carol

W. Sandys' *Christmas Carols*, 1833
Arr. by John Stainer, 1871

1. The first No - el, the an-gel did say, Was to cer-tain poor shepherds in
2. They look - ed up and saw a star Shin-ing in the east, be-
3. And by the light of that same star Three wise men came from
4. This star drew nigh to the north-west, O'er Beth - le - hem it
5. Then en - tered in those wise men three, Full rev - 'rent-ly up-
6. Then let us all with one ac - cord Sing prais - es to our

fields as they lay; In fields where they lay keep-ing their sheep, On a
yond them far, And to the earth it gave great light, And
coun - try far; To seek for a king was their in - tent, And to
took its rest, And there it did both stop and stay, Right
on their knee, And of - fered there in His pres - ence Their
heav'n - ly Lord, That hath made heav'n and earth of naught, And

Refrain

cold win-ter's night that was so deep.
so it con - tin - ued both day and night.
fol - low the star wher - ev - er it went. No - el, No - el, No-
o - ver the place where Je - sus lay.
gold, and myrrh, and frank - in -cense.
with His blood man - kind hath bought.

el, No - el, Born is the King of Is - ra - el.

JESUS CHRIST

Once in Royal David's City 109

Unto you is born this day in the city of David a Savior . . . Luke 2:11

IRBY 878777

Cecil F. Alexander, 1848

Henry J. Gauntlett, 1849

1. Once in roy - al Da - vid's cit - y Stood a low - ly cat - tle
2. He came down to earth from heav - en Who is God and Lord of
3. Je - sus is our child-hood's pat - tern, Day by day like us He
4. And our eyes at last shall see Him, Thro' His own re-deem - ing

shed, Where a moth - er laid her ba - by In a
all, And His shel - ter was a sta - ble, And His
grew; He was lit - tle, weak, and help - less, Tears and
love; For that child so dear and gen - tle Is our

man - ger for His bed: Ma - ry was that moth - er
cra - dle was a stall: With the poor, and mean, and
smiles like us He knew: And He feel - eth for our
Lord in heav'n a - bove, And He leads his chil - dren

mild, Je - sus Christ her lit - tle child.
low - ly Lived on earth, our Sav - ior ho - ly.
sad - ness, And He shar - eth in our glad-ness.
on To the place where He is gone.

HIS BIRTH

110 Angels from the Realms of Glory

We . . . are come to worship Him. Matt. 2:2

REGENT SQUARE 878787

James Montgomery, 1816

Henry T. Smart, 1867

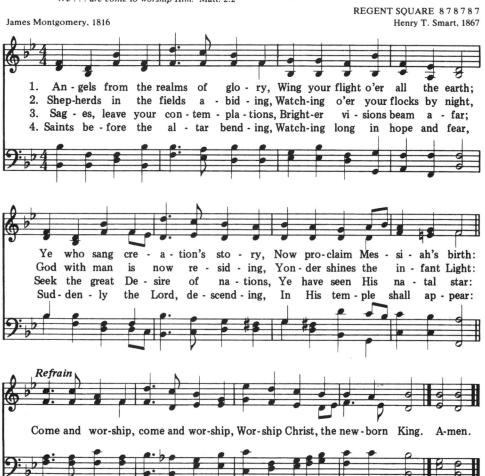

1. An - gels from the realms of glo - ry, Wing your flight o'er all the earth;
2. Shep-herds in the fields a - bid - ing, Watch-ing o'er your flocks by night,
3. Sag - es, leave your con - tem - pla - tions, Bright-er vi - sions beam a - far;
4. Saints be - fore the al - tar bend - ing, Watch-ing long in hope and fear,

Ye who sang cre - a - tion's sto - ry, Now pro-claim Mes - si - ah's birth:
God with man is now re - sid - ing, Yon - der shines the in - fant Light:
Seek the great De - sire of na - tions, Ye have seen His na - tal star:
Sud - den - ly the Lord, de - scend - ing, In His tem - ple shall ap - pear:

Refrain

Come and wor-ship, come and wor-ship, Wor-ship Christ, the new - born King. A-men.

This tune in a lower key, No. 185

111 From Heaven Above to Earth I Come

I bring you good tidings of great joy . . . Luke 2:10

VOM HIMMEL HOCH L.M.

Martin Luther, 1535
Trans. by Catherine Winkworth, 1855

Geystliche Lieder, Leipzig, 1539

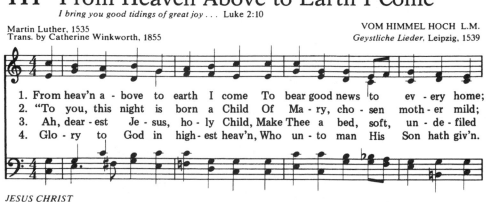

1. From heav'n a - bove to earth I come To bear good news to ev - ery home;
2. "To you, this night is born a Child Of Ma - ry, cho - sen moth - er mild;
3. Ah, dear - est Je - sus, ho - ly Child, Make Thee a bed, soft, un - de - filed
4. Glo - ry to God in high - est heav'n, Who un - to man His Son hath giv'n.

JESUS CHRIST

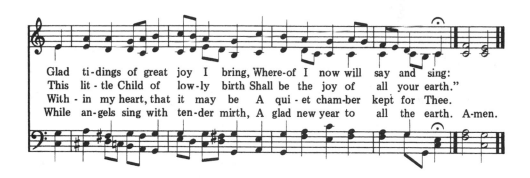

Glad ti-dings of great joy I bring, Where-of I now will say and sing:
This lit-tle Child of low-ly birth Shall be the joy of all your earth."
With-in my heart, that it may be A qui-et cham-ber kept for Thee.
While an-gels sing with ten-der mirth, A glad new year to all the earth. A-men.

Away in a Manger 112

She brought forth her firstborn son . . . and laid Him in a manger. Luke 2:7

CRADLE SONG 11 11 11 11
William J. Kirkpatrick, 1895

Source unknown, c. 1885

Unison

1. A - way in a man - ger, no crib for a bed, The lit - tle Lord
2. The cat - tle are low - ing, the Ba - by a - wakes, But lit - tle Lord
3. Be near me, Lord Je - sus; I ask Thee to stay Close by me for-

Je - sus laid down His sweet head; The stars in the bright sky looked
Je - sus, no cry - ing He makes. I love Thee, Lord Je - sus, look
ev - er, and love me, I pray. Bless all the dear chil - dren in

down where He lay, The lit - tle Lord Je - sus a - sleep on the hay.
down from the sky, And stay by my cra - dle till morn - ing is nigh.
Thy ten - der care, And fit us for heav - en, to live with Thee there.

HIS BIRTH

113 Angels We Have Heard on High

Glory to God in the highest and on earth peace . . . Luke 2:14

GLORIA 7 7 7 7 Ref.

Traditional French carol

Traditional French melody

1. An - gels we have heard on high, Sweet - ly sing - ing o'er the plains,
2. Shepherds, why this ju - bi - lee? Why your joy - ous strains pro - long?
3. Come to Beth - le - hem, and see Him whose birth the an - gels sing;
4. See with - in a man - ger laid Je - sus, Lord of heav'n and earth!

And the moun-tains in re - ply Ech - o back their joy - ous strains.
Say what may the ti - dings be, Which in - spire your heav'n - ly song?
Come, a - dore on bend - ed knee Christ the Lord, the new - born King.
Ma - ry, Jo - seph, lend your aid, With us sing our Sav - ior's birth.

Refrain

Glo - ri - a in ex-cel-sis De - o,

Glo - ri - a in ex-cel-sis De - o.

JESUS CHRIST

As with Gladness Men of Old 114

When they saw the star, they rejoiced . . . Matt. 2:10

DIX 7 7 7 7 7 7

William C. Dix, 1858

Conrad Kocher, 1838

1. As with glad - ness men of old Did the guid - ing star be - hold; As with joy they hailed its light, Lead - ing on - ward, beam - ing bright, So, most gra - cious Lord, may we Ev - er - more be led to Thee.

2. As with joy - ful steps they sped To that low - ly man - ger bed, There to bend the knee be - fore Him Whom heav'n and earth a - dore, So, may we with will - ing feet Ev - er seek the mer - cy seat.

3. As they of - fered gifts most rare At that man - ger rude and bare, So may we with ho - ly joy, Pure and free from sin's al - loy, All our cost - liest treas - ures bring, Christ, to Thee our heav'n - ly King.

4. Ho - ly Je - sus, ev - ery day Keep us in the nar - row way; And when earth - ly things are past, Bring our ran - somed souls at last Where they need no star to guide, Where no clouds Thy glo - ry hide. A - men.

HIS BIRTH

115 Go, Tell It on the Mountain

. . . They made known abroad the saying . . . concerning this child. Luke 2:17

John W. Work, II, 1907

GO TELL IT Irreg.
Traditional Spiritual

Unison

(Ref.) Go, tell it on the moun-tain, O-ver the hills and ev-ery-where;

Fine

Go, tell it on the moun - tain That Je-sus Christ is born.

1. While shep-herds kept their watch-ing O'er si - lent flocks by night, Be-
2. The shep-herds feared and trem-bled When, lo! a - bove the earth Rang
3. Down in a low - ly man-ger Our hum - ble Christ was born, And

D.C.

hold, through-out the heav - ens There shone a ho - ly light.
out the an - gel cho - rus That hailed our Sav - ior's birth.
God sent us sal - va - tion That bless - ed Christ-mas morn.

Words used by permission of Mrs. John W. Work, III.

JESUS CHRIST

Good Christian Men, Rejoice 116

Unto you is born this day . . . a Savior, which is Christ the Lord. Luke 2:11

Latin carol, 14th century
Trans. by John M. Neale, 1853

IN DULCI JUBILO Irreg.
Traditional German melody

1. Good Chris-tian men, re - joice With heart and soul and voice!
2. Good Chris-tian men, re - joice With heart and soul and voice!
3. Good Chris-tian men, re - joice With heart and soul and voice!

Give ye heed to what we say: Je - sus Christ is born to - day;
Now ye hear of end - less bliss; Je - sus Christ was born for this!
Now ye need not fear the grave; Je - sus Christ was born to save!

Ox and ass be - fore Him bow, And He is in the man-ger now.
He hath oped the heav'n - ly door, And man is blest for - ev - er - more.
Calls you one and calls you all To gain His ev - er - last - ing hall.

Christ is born to - day! Christ is born to - day!
Christ was born for this! Christ was born for this!
Christ was born to save! Christ was born to save!

HIS BIRTH

117 Silent Night! Holy Night!

And they . . . found Mary, and Joseph, and the babe lying in a manger. Luke 2:16

Joseph Mohr, 1818
Trans. by John F. Young, 1863

STILLE NACHT Irreg.
Franz Grüber, 1818

1. Si - lent night! ho - ly night! All is calm, all is bright
2. Si - lent night! ho - ly night! Shep-herds quake at the sight,
3. Si - lent night! ho - ly night! Son of God, love's pure light,

'Round yon vir - gin moth-er and Child, Ho - ly In-fant so ten-der and mild,
Glo - ries stream from heav-en a - far, Heav'n-ly hosts sing Al - le - lu - ia;
Ra - diant beams from Thy ho - ly face, With the dawn of re - deem - ing grace,

Sleep in heav - en - ly peace, Sleep in heav - en - ly peace.
Christ the Sav - ior is born, Christ the Sav - ior is born.
Je - sus, Lord, at Thy birth, Je - sus, Lord, at Thy birth. A-men.

118 Shepherds Came, Their Praises Bringing

Sing praises unto our King. Psa. 47:6

QUEM PASTORES LAUDAVERE 8 8 8 7

German-Latin, c. 1410
Trans. by George B. Caird, 1944

Traditional German melody
Arr. by Ralph Vaughan Williams, 1906

1. Shep-herds came, their prais-es bring - ing, Who had heard the an - gels sing - ing,
2. Sag - es whom a star had guid - ed, In - cense, gold and myrrh pro - vid - ed,
3. Je - sus, born the King of heav - en, Un - to us in mer - cy giv - en,

Music from "The English Hymnal" by permission of Oxford University Press.

JESUS CHRIST

"Far from you be fear un - ru - ly, Christ is King of glo - ry born."
Made their sac - ri - fic - es du - ly To the King of glo - ry born.
Be un - to Thy mer - it tru - ly Hon - or, praise and glo - ry done. A - men.

While Shepherds Watched Their Flocks 119

There were shepherds abiding in the field, keeping watch over their flocks . . . Luke 2:8

CHRISTMAS C.M. Repeats
George Frederick Handel, 1728
Arr. in Weyman's *Melodia Sacra*, 1815

Nahum Tate, 1700

1. While shep-herds watched their flocks by night, All seat - ed on the
2. "Fear not!" said he; for might - y dread Had seized their troub - led
3. "To you, in Da - vid's town this day, Is born of Da - vid's
4. "The heav'n-ly Babe you there shall find To hu - man view dis -
5. "All glo - ry be to God on high, And to the earth be

ground, The an - gel of the Lord came down, And glo - ry shone a - round, And glo - ry shone a - round.
mind, "Glad ti - dings of great joy I bring To you and all man - kind, To you and all man - kind.
line, The Sav - ior who is Christ the Lord, And this shall be the sign: And this shall be the sign:
played, All mean - ly wrapped in swath - ing bands, And in a man - ger laid; And in a man - ger laid.
peace: Good will hence - forth from heav'n to men, Be - gin and nev - er cease, Be - gin and nev - er cease." A - men.

This tune in a higher key, No. 454

HIS BIRTH

120 Joy to the World! The Lord Is Come

Make a joyful noise unto the Lord, all the earth . . . Psa. 98:4

ANTIOCH C.M.

Isaac Watts, 1719
Based on Psalm 98

George Frederick Handel, 1742
Arr. by Lowell Mason, 1839

1. Joy to the world! the Lord is come; Let earth re-
2. Joy to the earth! the Sav - ior reigns; Let men their
3. No more let sins and sor - rows grow, Nor thorns in-
4. He rules the world with truth and grace, And makes the

ceive her King; Let ev - ery heart pre - pare Him room,
songs em - ploy; While fields and floods, rocks, hills, and plains
fest the ground; He comes to make His bless - ings flow
na - tions prove The glo - ries of His right - eous - ness,

And heav'n and na - ture sing, And heav'n and na - ture
Re - peat the sound - ing joy, Re - peat the sound - ing
Far as the curse is found, Far as the curse is
And won - ders of His love, And won - ders of His

1. And heav'n and na - ture sing,

1. And

sing, And heav'n, and heav'n and na - ture sing.
joy, Re - peat, re - peat the sound - ing joy.
found, Far as, far as the curse is found.
love, And won - ders, won - ders of His love.

heav'n and na - ture sing,

JESUS CHRIST

O Little Town of Bethlehem 121

Thou, Bethlehem . . . though thou be little . . . out of thee shall He come. Micah 5:2

ST. LOUIS 8 6 8 6 7 6 8 6

Phillips Brooks, 1868

Lewis H. Redner, 1868

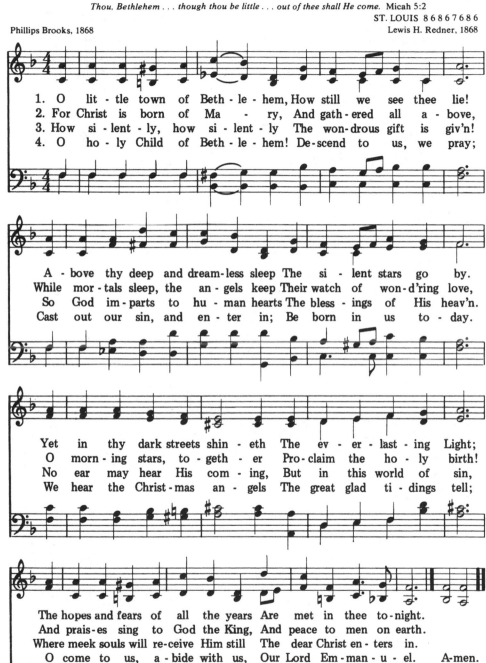

1. O lit - tle town of Beth - le - hem, How still we see thee lie!
2. For Christ is born of Ma - ry, And gath - ered all a - bove,
3. How si - lent - ly, how si - lent - ly The won - drous gift is giv'n!
4. O ho - ly Child of Beth - le - hem! De - scend to us, we pray;

A - bove thy deep and dream-less sleep The si - lent stars go by.
While mor - tals sleep, the an - gels keep Their watch of won - d'ring love,
So God im - parts to hu - man hearts The bless - ings of His heav'n.
Cast out our sin, and en - ter in; Be born in us to - day.

Yet in thy dark streets shin - eth The ev - er - last - ing Light;
O morn - ing stars, to - geth - er Pro - claim the ho - ly birth!
No ear may hear His com - ing, But in this world of sin,
We hear the Christ - mas an - gels The great glad ti - dings tell;

The hopes and fears of all the years Are met in thee to - night.
And prais - es sing to God the King, And peace to men on earth.
Where meek souls will re - ceive Him still The dear Christ en - ters in.
O come to us, a - bide with us, Our Lord Em - man - u - el. A - men.

HIS BIRTH

122 Of the Father's Love Begotten

In the beginning was the Word . . . and the Word was God. John 1:1

Aurelius C. Prudentius, 4th century
Trans. by John M. Neale, 1854, and
Henry W. Baker, 1859

DIVINUM MYSTERIUM 8 7 8 7 8 7 7
Plainsong, 13th century
Arr. by C. Winfred Douglas, 1916

1. Of the Fa - ther's love be - got - ten, Ere the worlds be - gan to be,
2. O that birth for - ev - er bless - ed, When the Vir - gin, full of grace,
3. O ye heights of heav'n, a - dore Him; An - gel hosts, His prais - es sing,
4. Christ, to Thee with God the Fa - ther, And, O Ho - ly Ghost, to Thee,

He is Al - pha and O - me - ga, He the Source, the End - ing He,
By the Ho - ly Ghost con - ceiv - ing, Bare the Sav - ior of our race;
Pow'rs, do - min - ions, bow be - fore Him, And ex - tol our God and King;
Hymn and chant and high thanks-giv - ing And un - wea - ried prais - es be:

Of the things that are, that have been, And that fu - ture
And the Babe, the world's Re - deem - er, First re - vealed His
Let no tongue on earth be si - lent, Ev - ery voice in
Hon - or, glo - ry, and do - min - ion, And e - ter - nal

years shall see, Ev - er - more and ev - er - more!
sa - cred face, Ev - er - more and ev - er - more!
con - cert ring, Ev - er - more and ev - er - more!
vic - to - ry, Ev - er - more and ev - er - more! A - men.

Little Baby Jesus, Born in Bethlehem 123

. . . *Call His name Jesus, for He shall save His people from their sins.* Matt. 1:21

YULE SPIRITUAL Irreg.

Blaine H. Allen, 1969

Blaine H. Allen, 1969

Unison

1. Lit - tle Ba - by Je - sus, born in Beth - le - hem;
2. Lit - tle Ba - by Je - sus, born in Beth - le - hem;
3. Lit - tle Ba - by Je - sus, born in a sta - ble bare;
4. Lit - tle Ba - by Je - sus, born in Beth - le - hem;

Lit - tle Ba - by Je - sus, born in Beth - le - hem;
Lit - tle Ba - by Je - sus, born in Beth - le - hem;
Lit - tle Ba - by Je - sus, ly - ing in a man - ger there;
Lit - tle Ba - by Je - sus, born in Beth - le - hem;

Lit - tle Ba - by Je - sus, born to be The Sa - vior of the world for
Lit - tle Ba - by Je - sus, born to die, To suf - fer on the cross for
Lit - tle Ba - by Je - sus, King to be, The mas - ter of the earth, the
Lit - tle Ba - by Je - sus, do come in, Come right in - to my heart and

you and me; Lit - tle Ba - by Je - sus, born in Beth-le - hem.
you and I; Lit - tle Ba - by Je - sus, born in Beth-le - hem.
sky and sea; Lit - tle Ba - by Je - sus, born in Beth-le - hem.
save me from sin! Lit - tle Ba - by Je - sus, born in Beth-le - hem.

HIS BIRTH

124 Thou Didst Leave Thy Throne

He came unto His own and His own received Him not. John 1:11

Emily E. S. Elliott, 1864

MARGARET Irreg.
Timothy R. Matthews, 1876

1. Thou didst leave Thy throne and Thy king-ly crown When Thou cam-est to earth for me; But in Beth-le-hem's home there was found no room For Thy ho-ly na-tiv-i-ty:
2. Heav-en's arch-es rang when the an-gels sang, Pro-claim-ing Thy roy-al de-gree; But in low-ly birth Thou didst come to earth, And in great hu-mil-i-ty:
3. The fox-es found rest and the birds their nest In the shade of the for-est tree; But thy couch was the sod, O Thou Son of God, In the des-ert of Gal-i-lee:
4. Thou cam-est, O Lord, with the liv-ing Word That should set Thy peo-ple free; But with mock-ing scorn, and with crown of thorn, They bore Thee to Cal-va-ry:
5. When the heav-ens shall ring, and the an-gels sing, At Thy com-ing to vic-to-ry, Let Thy voice call me home, say-ing, "Yet there is room, There is room at My side for thee:"

Refrain

1-4. O come to my heart, Lord Je-sus! There is room in my heart for Thee.
5. My heart shall re-joice, Lord Je-sus! When Thou com-est and call-est for me. A-men.

JESUS CHRIST

We Would See Jesus; Lo! His Star 125

. . . Sir, we would see Jesus. John 12:21

HENLEY 11 10 11 10

J. Edgar Park, 1913

Lowell Mason, 1854

1. We would see Je - sus; lo! His star is shin - ing
2. We would see Je - sus, Ma - ry's son most ho - ly,
3. We would see Je - sus, on the moun - tain teach - ing,
4. We would see Je - sus, in His work of heal - ing,
5. We would see Je - sus; in the ear - ly morn - ing

A - bove the sta - ble while the an - gels sing;
Light of the vil - lage life from day to day;
With all the lis - t'ning peo - ple gath - ered round;
At e - ven - tide be - fore the sun was set;
Still as of old He call - eth, "Fol - low me";

There in a man - ger on the hay re - clin - ing;
Shin - ing re - vealed through ev - ery task most low - ly,
While birds and flow'rs and sky a - bove are preach - ing
Di - vine and hu - man, in His deep re - veal - ing,
Let us a - rise, all mean - er ser - vice scorn - ing:

Haste, let us lay our gifts be - fore the King.
The Christ of God, the Life, the Truth, the Way.
The bless - ed - ness which sim - ple trust has found.
Of God and man in lov - ing ser - vice met.
Lord, we are Thine, we give our - selves to Thee. A-men.

HIS LIFE AND MINISTRY

126 Amen, Amen!

And the Word was made flesh and dwelt among us . . . John 1:14

AMEN Irreg.

Traditional Spiritual
Adapt. by John F. Wilson, 1970

Traditional Spiritual
Arr. by John F. Wilson, 1970

A - men, A - men, A -

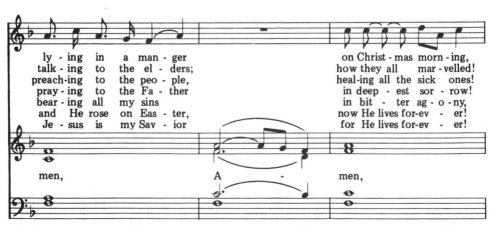

men, A - men, A - men! A -

Solo

1. See the lit - tle ba - by
2. See Him in the tem - ple
3. See Him at the sea - shore
4. See Him in the gar - den
5. See Him on the cross
6. Yes, He died to save us
7. Al - le - lu - ia!

ly - ing in a man - ger   on Christ-mas morn - ing,
talk - ing to the el - ders;   how they all mar - velled!
preach-ing to the peo - ple,   heal-ing all the sick ones!
pray - ing to the Fa - ther   in deep - est sor - row!
bear - ing all my sins   in bit - ter ag - o - ny,
and He rose on Eas - ter,   now He lives for-ev - er!
Je - sus is my Sav - ior   for He lives for-ev - er!

men, A - men,

JESUS CHRIST

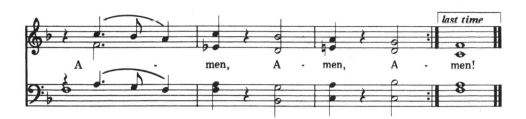

A - men, A - men, A - men!

Who Is He in Yonder Stall? 127

He is Lord of lords and King of kings. Rev. 17:14

LOWLINESS 7 7 Ref.

Benjamin R. Hanby, 1866

Benjamin R. Hanby, 1866

1. Who is He in yon-der stall, At whose feet the shep-herds fall?
2. Who is He the peo - ple bless For His words of gen - tle - ness?
3. Who is He that stands and weeps At the grave where Laz - arus sleeps?
4. Lo! at mid - night, who is He Prays in dark Geth-sem - a - ne?
5. Who is He that from the grave Comes to heal and help and save?

Who is He in deep dis - tress, Fast - ing in the wil - der - ness?
Who is He to whom they bring All the sick and sor - row - ing?
Who is He the gath - 'ring throng Greet with loud tri - um - phant song?
Who is He on yon - der tree Dies in grief and ag - o - ny?
Who is He that from His throne Rules through all the world a - lone?

Refrain

'Tis the Lord! O won-drous sto - ry! 'Tis the Lord! the King of glo - ry! At His feet we hum - bly fall, Crown Him! crown Him, Lord of all!

128 One Day When Heaven Was Filled

When the fulness of the time was come, God sent forth His Son . . . Gal. 4:4

CHAPMAN 11 10 11 10 Ref.

J. Wilbur Chapman, 1910

Charles H. Marsh, 1910

1. One day when heav-en was filled with His prais-es, One day when
2. One day they led Him up Cal-va-ry's moun-tain, One day they
3. One day they left Him a-lone in the gar-den, One day He
4. One day the grave could con-ceal Him no long-er, One day the
5. One day the trum-pet will sound for His com-ing, One day the

sin was as black as could be, Je-sus came forth to be
nailed Him to die on the tree; Suf-fer-ing an-guish, de-
rest-ed, from suf-fer-ing free; An-gels came down o'er His
stone rolled a-way from the door; Then He a-rose, o-ver
skies with His glo-ry will shine; Won-der-ful day, my be-

born of a vir-gin, Dwelt a-mong men, my ex-am-ple is He!
spised and re-ject-ed, Bear-ing our sins, my Re-deem-er is He!
tomb to keep vig-il; Hope of the hope-less, my Sav-ior is He!
death He has con-quered; Now is as-cend-ed, my Lord ev-er-more!
lov-ed ones bring-ing; Glo-ri-ous Sav-ior, this Je-sus is mine!

Refrain

Liv-ing, He loved me; dy-ing, He saved me; Bur-ied, He

car-ried my sins far a-way; Ris-ing, He jus-ti-fied

JESUS CHRIST

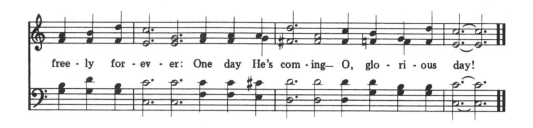

freely forever: One day He's coming— O, glorious day!

Who Is This Boy? 129

Thou art the Christ, the Son of the living God. Matt. 16:16

St. 1, Source unknown
St. 2, 3, John F. Wilson, 1967

MOUNTAIN VIEW Irreg.
John F. Wilson, 1967

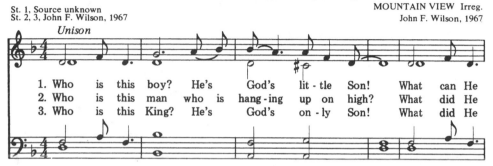

Unison

1. Who is this boy? He's God's little Son! What can He
2. Who is this man who is hanging up on high? What did He
3. Who is this King? He's God's only Son! What did He

do? Save everyone! What does He bring? Peace and
do? Why do they crucify? What does He bring? Hope and
do? Rise for everyone! What does He bring? Life and

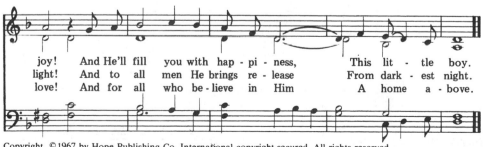

joy! And He'll fill you with happiness, This little boy.
light! And to all men He brings release From darkest night.
love! And for all who believe in Him A home above.

HIS LIFE AND MINISTRY

130 Tell Me the Story of Jesus

He expounded unto them . . . the things concerning Himself. Luke 24:27

STORY OF JESUS 8 7 8 7 D. Ref.

Fanny J. Crosby, 1880

John R. Sweney, 1880

1. Tell me the sto - ry of Je - sus, Write on my heart ev - ery word;
2. Fast - ing a - lone in the des - ert, Tell of the days that are past,
3. Tell of the cross where they nailed Him, Writhing in an - guish and pain;
Ref. Tell me the sto - ry of Je - sus, Write on my heart ev - ery word;

Fine

Tell me the sto - ry most pre - cious, Sweet-est that ev - er was heard.
How for our sins He was tempt - ed, Yet was tri - um-phant at last.
Tell of the grave where they laid Him, Tell how He liv - eth a - gain.
Tell me the sto - ry most pre - cious, Sweet-est that ev - er was heard.

Tell how the an - gels in cho - rus Sang as they wel - comed His birth,
Tell of the years of His la - bor, Tell of the sor - row He bore,
Love in that sto - ry so ten - der Clear - er than ev - er I see:

D.C. for Refrain

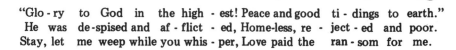

"Glo - ry to God in the high - est! Peace and good ti - dings to earth."
He was de-spised and af - flict - ed, Home-less, re - ject - ed and poor.
Stay, let me weep while you whis - per, Love paid the ran - som for me.

JESUS CHRIST: HIS LIFE AND MINISTRY

All Glory, Laud and Honor 131

Blessed is the King of Israel that cometh in the name of the Lord. John 12:13

Theodulph of Orleans, c. 800
Trans. by John M. Neale, 1854

ST. THEODULPH 7 6 7 6 D.
Melchior Teschner, c. 1613

1. All glo-ry, laud and hon - or To Thee, Re-deem-er, King,
2. The com-pa-ny of an - gels Are prais-ing Thee on high,
3. To Thee, be-fore Thy pas - sion, They sang their hymns of praise;

To whom the lips of chil - dren Made sweet ho-san-nas ring:
And mor-tal men and all things Cre - at-ed make re - ply:
To Thee, now high ex - alt - ed, Our mel-o-dy we raise:

Thou art the King of Is - rael, Thou Da - vid's roy-al Son,
The peo-ple of the He - brews With palms be-fore Thee went:
Thou didst ac-cept their prais - es— Ac-cept the praise we bring,

Who in the Lord's name com - est, The King and bless-ed One!
Our praise and prayer and an - thems Be-fore Thee we pre - sent.
Who in all good de - light - est, Thou good and gra-cious King! A-men.

HIS TRIUMPHAL ENTRY

132 Ride On! Ride On in Majesty

Behold, thy King cometh unto thee, meek, and sitting upon an ass. Matt. 21:5

WINCHESTER NEW L.M.

Henry H. Milman, 1827

Georg Rebenlein's *Musicalisch Handbuch*, Hamburg, 1690
Arr. by William H. Havergal, 1847

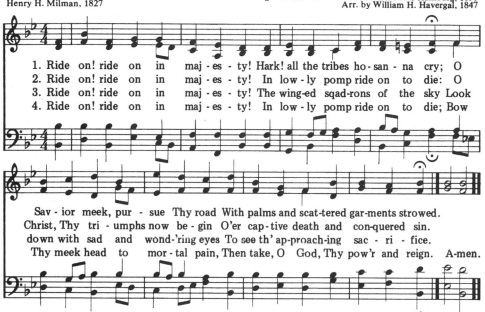

1. Ride on! ride on in maj-es-ty! Hark! all the tribes ho-san-na cry; O
2. Ride on! ride on in maj-es-ty! In low-ly pomp ride on to die: O
3. Ride on! ride on in maj-es-ty! The wing-ed sqad-rons of the sky Look
4. Ride on! ride on in maj-es-ty! In low-ly pomp ride on to die; Bow

Sav-ior meek, pur-sue Thy road With palms and scat-tered gar-ments strowed.
Christ, Thy tri-umphs now be-gin O'er cap-tive death and con-quered sin.
down with sad and wond'ring eyes To see th' ap-proach-ing sac-ri-fice.
Thy meek head to mor-tal pain, Then take, O God, Thy pow'r and reign. A-men.

133 Alone Thou Goest Forth, O Lord

Is it nothing to you, all ye that pass by? Lam. 1:12

Peter Abelard, c. 1100
Trans. by F. Bland Tucker, 1938

BANGOR C.M.
William Tans'ur, 1734

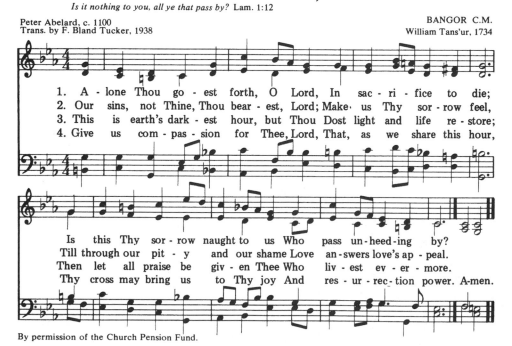

1. A-lone Thou go-est forth, O Lord, In sac-ri-fice to die;
2. Our sins, not Thine, Thou bear-est, Lord; Make us Thy sor-row feel,
3. This is earth's dark-est hour, but Thou Dost light and life re-store;
4. Give us com-pas-sion for Thee, Lord, That, as we share this hour,

Is this Thy sor-row naught to us Who pass un-heed-ing by?
Till through our pit-y and our shame Love an-swers love's ap-peal.
Then let all praise be giv-en Thee Who liv-est ev-er-more.
Thy cross may bring us to Thy joy And res-ur-rec-tion power. A-men.

By permission of the Church Pension Fund.

JESUS CHRIST

Hosanna, Loud Hosanna 134

Hosanna; Blessed is He that cometh in the name of the Lord. Mark 11:9

ELLACOMBE 7 6 7 6 D.

Jennette Threlfall, 1873

Gesangbuch, Wirtemberg, 1784

1. Ho - san - na, loud ho - san - na The lit - tle chil - dren sang;
2. From Ol - i - vet they fol - lowed 'Mid an ex - ult - ant crowd,
3. "Ho - san - na in the high - est!" That an - cient song we sing,

Through pil - lared court and tem - ple The love - ly an - them rang;
The vic - tor palm branch wav - ing, And chant - ing clear and loud;
For Christ is our Re - deem - er, The Lord of heav'n, our King;

To Je - sus, who had blessed them Close fold - ed to His breast,
The Lord of men and an - gels Rode on in low - ly state,
O may we ev - er praise Him With heart and life and voice,

The chil - dren sang their prais - es, The sim - plest and the best.
Nor scorned that lit - tle chil - dren Should on His bid - ding wait.
And in His bliss - ful pres - ence E - ter - nal - ly re - joice! A-men.

HIS TRIUMPHAL ENTRY

135 He Was Wounded for Our Transgressions

He was wounded for our transgressions. . . Isa. 53:5

Thomas O. Chisholm, 1941

OAK PARK Irreg.
Merrill Dunlop, 1941

1. He was wound-ed for our trans - gress - ions, He bore our
2. He was num-bered a - mong trans - gress - ors, We did es-
3. We had wan-dered, we all had wan - dered Far from the
4. Who can num - ber His gen - er - a - tion? Who shall de-

sins in His bod - y on the tree; For our guilt He
teem Him for - sak - en by His God; As our sac - ri-
fold of "the Shep - herd of the sheep;" But He sought us
clare all the tri - umphs of His cross? Mil - lions dead now

gave us peace, From our bond-age gave re - lease, And with His
fice He died, That the law be sat - is - fied, And all our
where we were, On the moun-tains bleak and bare, And brought us
live a - gain, Myr - iads fol - low in His train! Vic - to - rious

stripes, and with His stripes, And with His stripes our souls are healed.
sin, and all our sin, And all our sin was laid on Him.
home, and brought us home, And brought us safe - ly home to God.
Lord, vic - to - rious Lord, Vic - to - rious Lord and com - ing King!

JESUS CHRIST

O Sacred Head, Now Wounded 136

When they had platted a crown of thorns, they put it upon His head . . . Matt. 27:29

Attr. to Bernard of Clairvaux, 12th century
Trans. (German) by Paul Gerhardt, 1656
Trans. (English) by James W. Alexander, 1830

PASSION CHORALE 7 6 7 6 D.

Hans Leo Hassler, 1601
Arr. by J. S. Bach, 1729

1. O sa-cred Head, now wound-ed, With grief and shame weighed down,
2. What Thou, my Lord, hast suf-fered Was all for sin-ners' gain;
3. What lan-guage shall I bor-row To thank Thee, dear-est friend,

Now scorn-ful-ly sur-round-ed With thorns, Thine on-ly crown:
Mine, mine was the trans-gres-sion, But Thine the dead-ly pain.
For this Thy dy-ing sor-row, Thy pit-y with-out end?

O sa-cred Head, what glo-ry, What bliss till now was Thine!
Lo, here I fall, my Sav-ior! 'Tis I de-serve Thy place;
O make me Thine for-ev-er; And should I faint-ing be,

Yet, though de-spised and go-ry, I joy to call Thee mine.
Look on me with Thy fa-vor, Vouch-safe to me Thy grace.
Lord, let me nev-er, nev-er Out-live my love to Thee. A-men.

HIS SUFFERING AND DEATH

137 What Wondrous Love Is This

What manner of love the Father hath bestowed upon us . . . I John 3:1

American folk hymn

WONDROUS LOVE 12 9 12 9
Southern Harmony, 1835

1. What won-drous love is this, O my soul, O my soul, What
2. To God and to the Lamb I will sing, I will sing, To
3. And when from death I'm free, I'll sing on, I'll sing on, And

won-drous love is this, O my soul! What won-drous love is
God and to the Lamb I will sing; To God and to the
when from death I'm free, I'll sing on; And when from death I'm

this that caused the Lord of bliss To bear the dread-ful curse for my
Lamb, who is the great "I Am," While mil-lions join the theme, I will
free, I'll sing and joy-ful be, And through e-ter-ni-ty I'll sing

soul, for my soul, To bear the dread-ful curse for my soul!
sing, I will sing, While mil-lions join the theme, I will sing!
on, I'll sing on, And through e-ter-ni-ty I'll sing on!

JESUS CHRIST

There Is a Green Hill Far Away 138

Wherefore Jesus also . . . suffered without the gate. Heb. 13:12

GREEN HILL C.M. Ref.

Cecil F. Alexander, 1848

George C. Stebbins, 1878

1. There is a green hill far a - way, Out-side a cit - y wall,
2. We may not know, we can - not tell What pains He had to bear;
3. He died that we might be for-giv'n, He died to make us good,
4. There was no oth - er good e - nough To pay the price of sin;

Where the dear Lord was cru - ci - fied, Who died to save us all.
But we be - lieve it was for us He hung and suf - fered there.
That we might go at last to heav'n, Saved by His pre-cious blood.
He on - ly could un-lock the gate Of heav'n and let us in.

Refrain

O dear - ly, dear - ly has He loved, And we must love Him too;

And trust in His re - deem - ing blood, And try His works to do.

139 'Tis Midnight; and on Olive's Brow

. . . They went out into the mount of Olives. Matt. 26:30

William B. Tappan, 1822

OLIVE'S BROW L.M.
William B. Bradbury, 1853

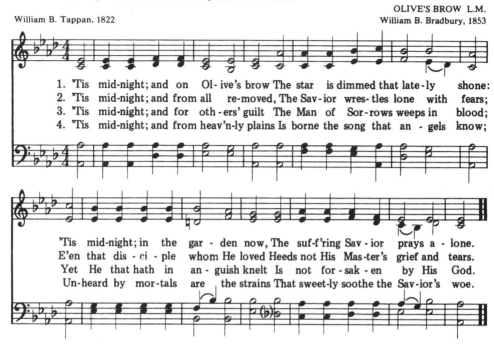

1. 'Tis mid-night; and on Ol-ive's brow The star is dimmed that late-ly shone:
2. 'Tis mid-night; and from all re-moved, The Sav-ior wres-tles lone with fears;
3. 'Tis mid-night; and for oth-ers' guilt The Man of Sor-rows weeps in blood;
4. 'Tis mid-night; and from heav'n-ly plains Is borne the song that an-gels know;

'Tis mid-night; in the gar-den now, The suf-f'ring Sav-ior prays a-lone.
E'en that dis-ci-ple whom He loved Heeds not His Mas-ter's grief and tears.
Yet He that hath in an-guish knelt Is not for-sak-en by His God.
Un-heard by mor-tals are the strains That sweet-ly soothe the Sav-ior's woe.

140 In the Cross of Christ I Glory

God forbid that I should glory, save in the cross . . . Gal. 6:14

John Bowring, 1825

RATHBUN 8 7 8 7
Ithamar Conkey, 1849

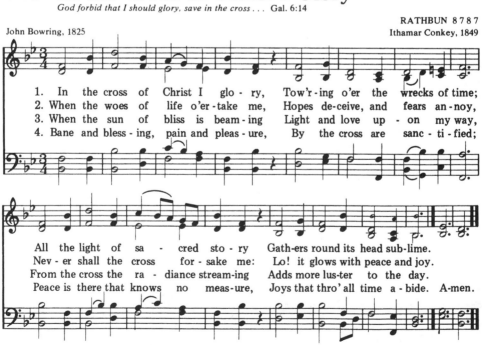

1. In the cross of Christ I glo-ry, Tow'r-ing o'er the wrecks of time;
2. When the woes of life o'er-take me, Hopes de-ceive, and fears an-noy,
3. When the sun of bliss is beam-ing Light and love up-on my way,
4. Bane and bless-ing, pain and pleas-ure, By the cross are sanc-ti-fied;

All the light of sa-cred sto-ry Gath-ers round its head sub-lime.
Nev-er shall the cross for-sake me: Lo! it glows with peace and joy.
From the cross the ra-diance stream-ing Adds more lus-ter to the day.
Peace is there that knows no meas-ure, Joys that thro' all time a-bide. A-men.

Lift High the Cross 141

I, if I be lifted up from the earth, will draw all men unto Me. John 12:32

George W. Kitchin and
Michael R. Newbolt, 1916

CRUCIFER Irreg. Ref.
Sydney H. Nicholson, 1916

(Ref.) Lift high the Cross, the love of Christ pro-claim, Till all the world a-dore His sa-cred name.

1. Come, breth-ren, fol-low where our Sav-ior trod, Our King vic-to-rious, Christ, the Son of God.
2. Led on their way by this tri-um-phant sign, The hosts of God in con-qu'ring ranks com-bine.
3. O Lord, once lift-ed on the glo-rious Tree, As Thou hast prom-ised, draw men un-to Thee.
4. Set up Thy throne, that earth's de-spair may cease Be-neath the shad-ow of its heal-ing peace.
5. For Thy blest Cross which doth for all a-tone, Cre-a-tion's prais-es rise be-fore Thy throne.

Music by permission of the Proprietors of Hymns Ancient & Modern.

HIS SUFFERING AND DEATH

142 Deep Were His Wounds, and Red

. . . And with His stripes we are healed. Isa. 53:5

William Johnson, 1958

MARLEE 6 6 6 6 8 8
Leland B. Sateren, 1958

Unison

1. Deep were His wounds, and red, On cru-el Cal-va-ry,
2. He suf-fered shame and scorn, And wretch-ed, dire dis-grace;
3. His life, His all He gave When He was cru-ci-fied;

As on the cross He bled In bit-ter ag-o-ny; But they, whom
For-sak-en and for-lorn, He hung there in our place. But such as
Our bur-dened souls to save, What fear-ful death He died! But each of

sin has wound-ed sore, Find heal-ing in the wounds He bore.
would from sin be free, Look to His Cross for vic-to-ry.
us, though dead in sin, Through Him e-ter-nal life may win. A-men.

143 Glory Be to Jesus

The blood of Jesus Christ . . . cleanseth us from all sin. I John 1:7

Italian hymn, 18th century
Trans. by Edward Caswall, 1857

WEM IN LEIDENSTAGEN 6 5 6 5
Friedrich Filitz, 1847

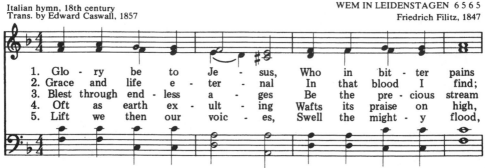

1. Glo-ry be to Je-sus, Who in bit-ter pains
2. Grace and life e-ter-nal In that blood I find;
3. Blest through end-less a-ges Be the pre-cious stream
4. Oft as earth ex-ult-ing Wafts its praise on high,
5. Lift we then our voic-es, Swell the might-y flood,

JESUS CHRIST

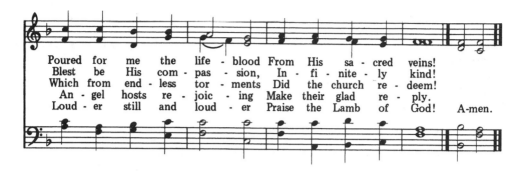

Poured for me the life - blood From His sa - cred veins!
Blest be His com - pas - sion, In - fi - nite - ly kind!
Which from end - less tor - ments Did the church re - deem!
An - gel hosts re - joic - ing Make their glad re - ply.
Loud - er still and loud - er Praise the Lamb of God! A - men.

Ask Ye What Great Thing I Know 144

I determined not to know anything . . . save Jesus Christ, and Him crucified. I Cor. 2:2

Johann C. Schwedler, 1741
Trans. by Benjamin H. Kennedy, 1863

HENDON 7 7 7 7 7
Henri A. César Malan, 1827

1. Ask ye what great thing I know That de - lights and
2. Who de - feats my fierc - est foes? Who con - soles my
3. Who is life in life to me? Who the death of
4. This is that great thing I know; This de - lights and

stirs me so? What the high re - ward I win? Whose the name I
sad - dest woes? Who re - vives my faint - ing heart, Heal - ing all its
death will be? Who will place me on His right With the count - less
stirs me so: Faith in Him who died to save, Him who tri - umphed

glo - ry in? Je - sus Christ, the Cru - ci - fied.
hid - den smart? Je - sus Christ, the Cru - ci - fied.
hosts of light? Je - sus Christ, the Cru - ci - fied.
o'er the grave, Je - sus Christ, the Cru - ci - fied. A - men.

HIS SUFFERING AND DEATH

145 Were You There?

It was the third hour, and they crucified Him. Mark 15:25

Traditional Spiritual

WERE YOU THERE? Irreg.
Traditional Spiritual

1. Were you there when they cru-ci-fied my Lord? (Were you there?)
2. Were you there when they nailed Him to the tree? (Were you there?)
3. Were you there when they pierced Him in the side? (Were you there?)
4. Were you there when they laid Him in the tomb? (Were you there?)
5. Were you there when He rose up from the dead? (Were you there?)

Were you there when they cru-ci-fied my Lord? (Were you there?)
Were you there when they nailed Him to the tree? (Were you there?)
Were you there when they pierced Him in the side? (Were you there?)
Were you there when they laid Him in the tomb? (Were you there?)
Were you there when He rose up from the dead? (Were you there?)

Oh!

Some-times it caus-es me to trem-ble, trem-ble,
(5. Some-times I feel like shout-ing glo-ry, glo-ry,)

trem-ble, Were you there when they cru-ci-fied my Lord? (Were you there?)
trem-ble, Were you there when they nailed Him to the tree? (Were you there?)
trem-ble, Were you there when they pierced Him in the side? (Were you there?)
trem-ble, Were you there when they laid Him in the tomb? (Were you there?)
glo-ry! Were you there when He rose up from the dead? (Were you there?)

JESUS CHRIST

I Saw Onc Hanging on a Tree 146

Who . . . bare our sins in His own body on the tree. I Pet. 2:24

John Newton, 1779

EXCELL C.M. Ref.
Edwin O. Excell, 1917

1. I saw One hang - ing on a tree, In ag - o - ny and blood;
2. Sure, nev - er till my lat - est breath, Can I for - get that look;
3. My con-science felt and owned the guilt, And plunged me in de - spair;
4. A sec - ond look He gave, which said, "I free - ly all for - give:

He fixed His lov - ing eyes on me, As near His cross I stood.
It seemed to charge me with His death, Though not a word He spoke.
I saw my sins His blood had spilt And helped to nail Him there.
This blood is for your ran - som paid, I die that you may live."

Refrain

O, can it be, up - on a tree The Sav - ior died for me?

My soul is thrilled, my heart is filled, To think He died for me!

HIS SUFFERING AND DEATH

147 Go to Dark Gethsemane

Then cometh Jesus with them unto a place called Gethsemane . . . Matt. 26:36

James Montgomery, 1825

REDHEAD 777777
Richard Redhead, 1853

1. Go to dark Geth-sem-a-ne, Ye that feel the tempt-er's pow'r;
2. Fol-low to the judg-ment hall; View the Lord of life ar-raigned.
3. Cal-v'ry's mourn-ful moun-tain climb; There, a-dor-ing at His feet,
4. Ear-ly has-ten to the tomb Where they laid His breath-less clay;

Your Re-deem-er's con-flict see; Watch with Him one bit-ter hour;
O the worm-wood and the gall! O the pangs His soul sus-tained!
Mark that mir-a-cle of time, God's own sac-ri-fice com-plete:
All is sol-i-tude and gloom, Who hath tak-en Him a-way?

Turn not from His griefs a-way; Learn of Je-sus Christ to pray.
Shun not suf-f'ring, shame, or loss; Learn of Him to bear the cross.
"It is fin-ished!" hear the cry; Learn of Je-sus Christ to die.
Christ is ris'n! He meets our eyes. Sav-ior, teach us so to rise. A-men.

148 When I Survey the Wondrous Cross

What things were gain to me, those I counted loss for Christ. Phil. 3:7

HAMBURG L.M.
Lowell Mason, 1824
Based on plainsong melody

Isaac Watts, 1707

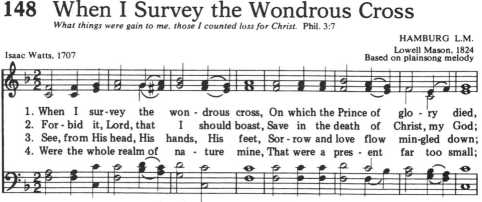

1. When I sur-vey the won-drous cross, On which the Prince of glo-ry died,
2. For-bid it, Lord, that I should boast, Save in the death of Christ, my God;
3. See, from His head, His hands, His feet, Sor-row and love flow min-gled down;
4. Were the whole realm of na-ture mine, That were a pres-ent far too small;

JESUS CHRIST

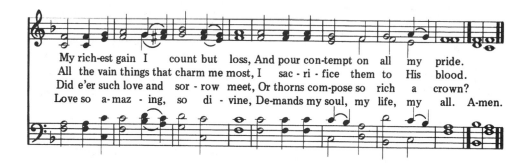

My rich-est gain I count but loss, And pour con-tempt on all my pride.
All the vain things that charm me most, I sac - ri - fice them to His blood.
Did e'er such love and sor - row meet, Or thorns com-pose so rich a crown?
Love so a-maz - ing, so di - vine, De-mands my soul, my life, my all. A-men.

Rock of Ages, Cleft for Me 149

I will put thee in a clift of the rock, and will cover thee . . . Exo. 33:22

TOPLADY 7 7 7 7 7 7

Augustus M. Toplady, 1776

Thomas Hastings, 1830

1. Rock of A - ges, cleft for me, Let me hide my - self in Thee;
2. Not the la - bors of my hands Can ful - fill Thy law's de - mands;
3. Noth - ing in my hand I bring, Sim - ply to Thy cross I cling;
4. While I draw this fleet - ing breath, When my eyes shall close in death,

Let the wa - ter and the blood, From Thy riv - en side which flowed,
Could my zeal no res - pite know, Could my tears for - ev - er flow,
Na - ked, come to Thee for dress, Help-less, look to Thee for grace;
When I soar to worlds un - known, See Thee on Thy judg - ment throne,

Be of sin the dou - ble cure, Cleanse me from its guilt and pow'r.
All for sin could not a - tone; Thou must save and Thou a - lone.
Foul, I to the foun - tain fly, Wash me, Sav - ior, or I die!
Rock of A - ges, cleft for me, Let me hide my - self in Thee. A-men.

Alternate tune, REDHEAD, No. 147

HIS SUFFERING AND DEATH

150 My Lord Has Garments So Wondrous Fine

. . . Out of the ivory palaces, whereby they have made thee glad. Psa. 45:8

MONTREAT 9 6 9 6 Ref.

Henry Barraclough, 1915

Henry Barraclough, 1915

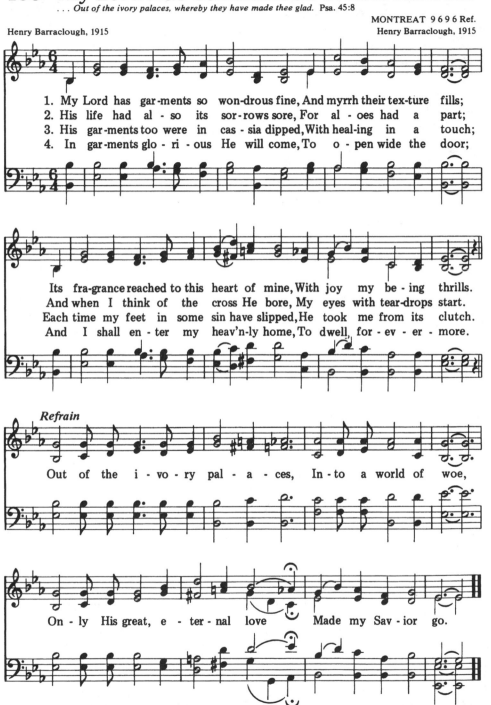

1. My Lord has gar-ments so won-drous fine, And myrrh their tex-ture fills;
2. His life had al - so its sor-rows sore, For al - oes had a part;
3. His gar-ments too were in cas - sia dipped, With heal-ing in a touch;
4. In gar-ments glo - ri - ous He will come, To o - pen wide the door;

Its fra-grance reached to this heart of mine, With joy my be - ing thrills.
And when I think of the cross He bore, My eyes with tear-drops start.
Each time my feet in some sin have slipped, He took me from its clutch.
And I shall en - ter my heav'n-ly home, To dwell for - ev - er-more.

Refrain

Out of the i - vo - ry pal - a - ces, In - to a world of woe,

On - ly His great, e - ter - nal love Made my Sav - ior go.

JESUS CHRIST

Beneath the Cross of Jesus 151

Now there stood by the cross of Jesus . . . John 19:25

ST. CHRISTOPHER 7 6 8 6 8 6 8 6

Elizabeth C. Clephane, 1872

Frederick C. Maker, 1881

1. Be - neath the cross of Je - sus I fain would take my stand—
2. Up - on that cross of Je - sus Mine eye at times can see
3. I take, O cross, thy shad - ow For my a - bid - ing place;

The shad - ow of a might - y Rock With - in a wea - ry land;
The ver - y dy - ing form of One Who suf - fered there for me;
I ask no oth - er sun - shine than The sun - shine of His face;

A home with - in the wil - der - ness, A rest up - on the way,
And from my smit - ten heart with tears Two won - ders I con - fess—
Con - tent to let the world go by, To know no gain nor loss,

From the burn - ing of. the noon - tide heat, And the bur - den of the day.
The won - ders of re - deem - ing love And my un - wor - thi - ness.
My sin - ful self my on - ly shame, My glo - ry all the cross. A - men.

Music by courtesy of the Psalms & Hymns Trust, London.

HIS SUFFERING AND DEATH

152 Ah, Holy Jesus, How Hast Thou Offended?

He is despised and rejected of men . . . Isa. 53:3

Johann Heermann, c. 1630
Trans. by Robert S. Bridges, 1899
Based on Jean de Fecamp, d. 1078

HERZLIEBSTER JESU 11 11 11 5
Johann Crüger, 1640

1. Ah, ho-ly Je-sus, how hast Thou of-fend-ed,
2. Who was the guilt-y? Who brought this up-on Thee?
3. For me, kind Je-sus, was Thy in-car-na-tion,
4. There-fore, kind Je-sus, since I can-not pay Thee,

That man to judge Thee hath in hate pre-tend-ed? By foes de-
A-las, my trea-son, Je-sus, hath un-done Thee! 'Twas I, Lord
Thy mor-tal sor-row, and Thy life's ob-la-tion; Thy death of
I do a-dore Thee, and will ev-er pray Thee, Think on Thy

rid-ed, by Thine own re-ject-ed, O most af-flict-ed!
Je-sus, I it was de-nied Thee; I cru-ci-fied Thee.
an-guish and Thy bit-ter pas-sion, For my sal-va-tion.
pit-y and Thy love un-swerv-ing, Not my de-serv-ing. A-men.

Words from "The Yattendon Hymnal" (edited by Robert Bridges and H. Ellis Wooldridge) by permission of Oxford University Press.

153 Cross of Jesus, Cross of Sorrow

Christ also . . . suffered for sins, the just for the unjust. I Pet. 3:18

CROSS OF JESUS 8 7 8 7

William J. Sparrow-Simpson, 1887

John Stainer, 1887

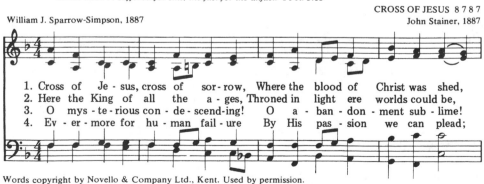

1. Cross of Je-sus, cross of sor-row, Where the blood of Christ was shed,
2. Here the King of all the a-ges, Throned in light ere worlds could be,
3. O mys-te-rious con-de-scend-ing! O a-ban-don-ment sub-lime!
4. Ev-er-more for hu-man fail-ure By His pas-sion we can plead;

JESUS CHRIST

Per-fect man on thee did suf-fer, Per-fect God on thee has bled!
Robed in mor-tal flesh is dy-ing, Cru-ci-fied by sin for me.
Ver-y God Him-self is bear-ing All the suf-fer-ings of time!
God has borne all mor-tal an-guish, Sure-ly He will know our need. A-men.

King of My Life, I Crown Thee Now 154

Consider Him that endured such contradiction of sinners against Himself. Heb. 12:3

Jennie E. Hussey, 1921

DUNCANNON C.M. Ref.
William J. Kirkpatrick, 1921

1. King of my life, I crown Thee now, Thine shall the glo-ry be;
2. Show me the tomb where Thou wast laid, Ten-der-ly mourned and wept;
3. Let me, like Ma-ry thro' the gloom, Come with a gift to Thee;
4. May I be will-ing, Lord, to bear Dai-ly my cross for Thee;

Lest I for-get Thy thorn-crowned brow, Lead me to Cal-va-ry.
An-gels in robes of light ar-rayed Guard-ed Thee whilst Thou slept.
Show to me now the emp-ty tomb, Lead me to Cal-va-ry.
E-ven Thy cup of grief to share, Thou hast borne all for me.

Refrain

Lest I for-get Geth-sem-a-ne; Lest I for-get Thine ag-o-ny;

Lest I for-get Thy love for me, Lead me to Cal-va-ry.

HIS SUFFERING AND DEATH

155 "Man of Sorrows," What a Name

A man of sorrows and acquainted with grief . . . Isa. 53:3

HALLELUJAH! WHAT A SAVIOR! 7 7 7 8

Philip P. Bliss, 1875

Philip P. Bliss, 1875

1. "Man of Sor - rows," what a name For the Son of God who came
2. Bear - ing shame and scoff - ing rude, In my place con-demned He stood;
3. Guilt - y, vile and help - less, we; Spot - less Lamb of God was He;
4. Lift - ed up was He to die, "It is fin - ished," was His cry;
5. When He comes, our glo - rious King, All His ran - somed home to bring,

Ru - ined sin - ners to re - claim! Hal - le - lu - jah! what a Sav - ior!
Sealed my par - don with His blood; Hal - le - lu - jah! what a Sav - ior!
"Full a - tone - ment" can it be? Hal - le - lu - jah! what a Sav - ior!
Now in heav'n ex - alt - ed high; Hal - le - lu - jah! what a Sav - ior!
Then a - new this song we'll sing: Hal - le - lu - jah! what a Sav - ior!

156 Alas! and Did My Savior Bleed?

. . . He was bruised for our iniquities. Isa. 53:5

MARTYRDOM C.M.

Isaac Watts, 1707

Hugh Wilson, c. 1800

1. A - las! and did my Sav - ior bleed, And did my Sov - 'reign die? Would
2. Was it for crimes that I have done, He groaned up - on the tree? A-
3. Well might the sun in dark - ness hide And shut his glo - ries in, When
4. But drops of grief can ne'er re - pay The debt of love I owe; Here,

He de - vote that sa - cred head For sin - ners such as I?
maz - ing pit - y! grace un - known! And love be - yond de - gree!
God, the might - y Mak - er, died For man the crea - ture's sin.
Lord, I give my - self a - way; 'Tis all that I can do. A-men.

Alternate tune with refrain, HUDSON, No. 279
JESUS CHRIST: HIS SUFFERING AND DEATH

I Know That My Redeemer Liveth 157

. . . My Redeemer liveth, and . . . He shall stand at the latter day upon the earth. Job 19:25

Jessie B. Pounds, 1893

HANNAH 9 8 9 8 Ref.
James H. Fillmore, 1893

1. I know that my Re-deem-er liv - eth, And on the earth a - gain shall stand; I know e - ter - nal life He giv - eth, That grace and pow'r are in His hand.
2. I know His prom-ise nev - er fail - eth, The word He speaks, it can - not die; Tho' cru - el death my flesh as - sail - eth, Yet I shall see Him by and by.
3. I know my man-sion He pre - par - eth, That where He is there I may be; O won-drous thought, for me He car - eth, And He at last will come for me.

1. And on the earth
1. That
grace and pow'r

Refrain

I know, I know that Je - sus liv - eth, And on the earth a - gain shall stand. I know, I know that life He giv - eth, That grace and pow'r are in His hand.

I know, I know
And on the earth
I know, I
know, I know
I

158 I Serve a Risen Savior

. . . That I may know Him, and the power of His resurrection. Phil. 3:10

Alfred H. Ackley, 1933

ACKLEY Irreg. Ref.
Alfred H. Ackley, 1933

1. I serve a ris-en Sav-ior, He's in the world to-day; I know that He is
2. In all the world a-round me I see His lov-ing care, And tho' my heart grows
3. Re-joice, re-joice, O Christ-ian, lift up your voice and sing E-ter-nal hal-le-

liv-ing, what-ev-er men may say; I see His hand of mer-cy, I
wea-ry, I nev-er will de-spair; I know that He is lead-ing thro'
lu-jahs to Je-sus Christ the King! The Hope of all who seek Him, the

hear His voice of cheer, And just the time I need Him He's al-ways ne૨.
all the storm-y blast, The day of His ap-pear-ing will come at last
Help of all who find, None oth-er is so lov-ing, so good and kin૦

Refrain

He lives, He lives, Christ Je-sus lives to-day! He walks with me and
He lives, He lives,

talks with me a-long life's nar-row way. He lives, He lives, sal-
He lives, He lives,

JESUS CHRIST

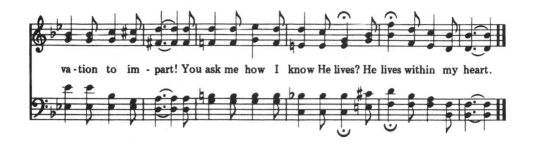

va - tion to im - part! You ask me how I know He lives? He lives within my heart.

Jesus Lives and So Shall I 159

O Death, where is thy sting? I Cor. 15:55

Christian F. Gellert, 1757
Trans. by J. D. Lang, 1826

ZUVERSICHT 787877
Johann Crüger, 1653

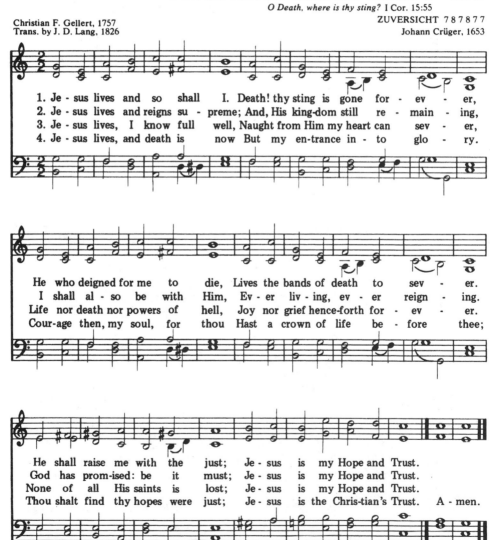

1. Je - sus lives and so shall I. Death! thy sting is gone for - ev - er,
2. Je - sus lives and reigns su - preme; And, His king-dom still re - main - ing,
3. Je - sus lives, I know full well, Naught from Him my heart can sev - er,
4. Je - sus lives, and death is now But my en-trance in - to glo - ry.

He who deigned for me to die, Lives the bands of death to sev - er.
I shall al - so be with Him, Ev - er liv - ing, ev - er reign - ing.
Life nor death nor powers of hell, Joy nor grief hence-forth for - ev - er.
Cour-age then, my soul, for thou Hast a crown of life be - fore thee;

He shall raise me with the just; Je - sus is my Hope and Trust.
God has prom-ised: be it must; Je - sus is my Hope and Trust.
None of all His saints is lost; Je - sus is my Hope and Trust.
Thou shalt find thy hopes were just; Je - sus is the Chris-tian's Trust. A - men.

HIS RESURRECTION

160 O Sons and Daughters, Let Us Sing

He is not here, but is risen . . . Luke 24:6

Jean Tisserand, c. 1490
Trans. by John M. Neale, 1851

O FILII ET FILIAE 8 8 8 Alleluias
Traditional French melody, 17th century

1. O sons and daugh-ters, let us sing! The King of
2. That Eas-ter morn at break of day, The faith-ful
3. An an-gel clad in white they see, Who sat and
4. How blest are they who have not seen, And yet whose
5. On this most ho-ly day of days, Our hearts and

heav'n, the glo-rious King, O'er death to-day rose tri-umph-ing,
wom-en went their way To seek the tomb where Je-sus lay,
spake un-to the three, "Your Lord doth go to Gal-i-lee,"
faith hath con-stant been; For they e-ter-nal life shall win,
voic-es, Lord, we raise To Thee, in ju-bi-lee and praise,

Al-le-lu-ia! Al-le-lu-ia! A-men.

161 The Strife Is O'er, the Battle Done

Death is swallowed up in victory. I Cor. 15:54

Latin hymn, c. 1695
Trans. by Francis Pott, 1859

VICTORY 8 8 8 4 Alleluias
Giovanni P. da Palestrina, 1591
Arr. by William H. Monk, 1861

1. The strife is o'er, the bat-tle done; The vic-to-ry of life is
2. The pow'rs of death have done their worst, But Christ their le-gions hath dis-
3. The three sad days have quick-ly sped; He ris-es glo-rious from the
4. He closed the yawn-ing gates of hell; The bars from heav'n's high por-tals
5. Lord, by the stripes which wound-ed Thee, From death's dread sting Thy serv-ants

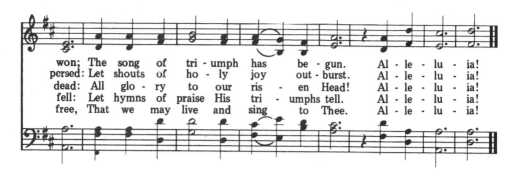

won; The song of tri - umph has be - gun. Al - le - lu - ia!
persed: Let shouts of ho - ly joy out - burst. Al - le - lu - ia!
dead: All glo - ry to our ris - en Head! Al - le - lu - ia!
fell: Let hymns of praise His tri - umphs tell. Al - le - lu - ia!
free, That we may live and sing to Thee. Al - le - lu - ia!

Now the Green Blade Riseth 162

. . . A corn of wheat . . . if it die, it bringeth forth much fruit. John 12:24

FRENCH CAROL 11 11 10 11

John M. C. Crum, 1928

Traditional French melody
Arr. by Martin Shaw, 1928

1. Now the green blade ris - eth from the bur - ied grain, Wheat that in
2. In the grave they laid Him, Love whom men had slain, Think - ing that
3. Forth he came at Eas - ter, like the ris - en grain, He that for
4. When our hearts are win - try, griev - ing, or in pain, Thy touch can

dark earth man - y days has lain; Love lives a - gain, that
nev - er He would wake a - gain, Laid in the earth like
three days in the grave had lain; Quick from the dead my
call us back to life a - gain, Fields of our hearts that

Refrain

with the dead has been:
grain that sleeps un - seen:
ris - en Lord is seen: Love is come a - gain like wheat that spring-eth green.
dead and bare have been:

From "The Oxford Book of Carols" by permission of the Oxford University Press.

HIS RESURRECTION

163 Christ the Lord Is Risen Today

Now is Christ risen . . . and become the first fruits of them that slept. I Cor. 15:20

Charles Wesley, 1739

EASTER HYMN 7 7 7 7 Alleluias
Arr. from *Lyra Davidica*, London, 1708

1. Christ the Lord is risen to-day, Al - le - lu - ia!
2. Lives a - gain our glo - rious King; Al - le - lu - ia!
3. Love's re - deem-ing work is done, Al - le - lu - ia!
4. Soar we now where Christ has led, Al - le - lu - ia!

Sons of men and an - gels say: Al - le - lu - ia!
Where, O death, is now thy sting? Al - le - lu - ia!
Fought the fight, the bat - tle won; Al - le - lu - ia!
Fol-lowing our ex - alt - ed Head; Al - le - lu - ia!

Raise your joys and tri - umphs high, Al - le - lu - ia!
Dy - ing once, He all doth save: Al - le - lu - ia!
Death in vain for - bids Him rise; Al - le - lu - ia!
Made like Him, like Him we rise; Al - le - lu - ia!

Sing, ye heav'ns, and earth re - ply, Al - le - lu - ia!
Where thy vic - to - ry, O grave? Al - le - lu - ia!
Christ has o-pened Par - a - dise. Al - le - lu - ia!
Ours the cross, the grave, the skies. Al - le - lu - ia! A-men.

JESUS CHRIST

Come, Ye Faithful, Raise the Strain 164

Thou hast ascended on high, thou hast led captivity captive. Psa. 68:18

ST. KEVIN 7 6 7 6 D.

John of Damascus, 8th century
Trans. by John M. Neale, 1859

Arthur S. Sullivan, 1872

1. Come, ye faith - ful, raise the strain Of tri - um - phant glad - ness;
2. 'Tis the spring of souls to - day, Christ hath burst His pris - on,
3. "Al - le - lu - ia!" now we cry To our King Im - mor - tal,

God hath brought His peo - ple forth In - to joy from sad - ness.
And from three day's sleep in death As a sun hath ris - en.
Who, tri - um - phant, burst the bars Of the tomb's dark por - tal;

Now re - joice, Je - ru - sa - lem, And with true af - fec - tion
All the win - ter of our sins, Long and dark, is fly - ing
"Al - le - lu - ia!" with the Son, God the Fa - ther prais - ing;

Wel - come in un - wea - ried strains Je - sus' res - ur - rec - tion.
From His light, to whom we give Laud and praise un - dy - ing.
"Al - le - lu - ia!" yet a - gain To the Spir - it rais - ing. A-men.

HIS RESURRECTION

165 Low in the Grave He Lay

The angel of the Lord . . . rolled back the stone from the door. Matt. 28:2

Robert Lowry, 1874

CHRIST AROSE 6 5 6 4 Ref.
Robert Lowry, 1874

1. Low in the grave He lay—Je - sus my Sav - ior! Wait-ing the com-ing day—
2. Vain - ly they watch His bed—Je - sus my Sav - ior! Vain - ly they seal the dead—
3. Death can-not keep his prey—Je - sus my Sav - ior! He tore the bars a - way—

Refrain

Je - sus my Lord!
Je - sus my Lord! Up from the grave He a - rose, With a
Je - sus my Lord! He a - rose,

might - y tri-umph o'er His foes; He a - rose a vic - tor from the
He a-rose!

dark do-main, And He lives for - ev - er with His saints to reign. He a -

rose! He a-rose!
He a - rose! He a - rose! Hal - le - lu - jah! Christ a - rose!

JESUS CHRIST

I Know That My Redeemer Lives 166

I know that my Redeemer liveth . . . Job 19:25

LASST UNS ERFREUEN 8 8 4 4 8 8 Alleluias

Samuel Medley, 1775

Geistliche Kirchengesäng, Cologne, 1623
Arr. by Ralph Vaughan Williams, 1906

1. I know that my Re-deem-er lives; O the sweet joy this sen-tence gives! Al-le-lu - ia! Al-le-lu - ia! He lives, He lives, who once was dead; He lives, my ev-er-last-ing Head. Al-le-lu - ia! Al-le-lu - ia! Al-le-lu - ia! Al-le-lu - ia! A-men.

2. He lives to bless me with His love, And still He pleads for me a-bove; Al-le-lu - ia! Al-le-lu - ia! He lives to raise me from the grave, And me e-ter-nal-ly to save.

3. He lives, my kind, wise, con-stant Friend; Who still will keep me to the end; Al-le-lu - ia! Al-le-lu - ia! He lives, and while He lives I'll sing, Je - sus, my Proph-et, Priest and King.

4. He lives my man-sion to pre - pare, And He will bring me safe-ly there; Al-le-lu - ia! Al-le-lu - ia! He lives, all glo - ry to His name, Je - sus, un-change-a-bly the same.

This tune in a four-part setting, No. 59
Music from "The English Hymnal" by permission of Oxford University Press.

HIS RESURRECTION

167 Jesus Christ Has Triumphed Now

He is not here; for He has risen. Matt. 28:6

RESURRECTION Irreg.
John F. Wilson, 1974

John F. Wilson, 1974

1. Je - sus Christ has tri - umphed now! Res - ur - rec-tion!
He has con - quered death some - how! Res - ur - rec - tion!
2. God has raised Him from the dead! Res - ur - rec-tion!
Ris - en our vic - to - rious Head! Res - ur - rec - tion!
3. Je - sus Christ now lives a - gain! Res - ur - rec-tion!
Of - fer - ing new life to men! Res - ur - rec - tion!

Now see the tomb lay bare; Res - ur - rec - tion! Death could not
Death could not end His reign; Res - ur - rec - tion! God's will was

hold Him there; Res - ur - rec-tion! Al - le - lu - ia! Comes the res - ur-
then made plain; Res - ur - rec-tion! Al - le - lu - ia! Comes the res - ur-

rec - tion; Al - le - lu - ia! Comes the res - ur - rec - tion!
rec - tion; Al - le - lu - ia! Comes the res - ur - rec - tion!

JESUS CHRIST

The Day of Resurrection 168

Jesus met them, saying, All hail. Matt. 28:9

John of Damascus, 8th century
Trans. by John M. Neale, 1862

LANCASHIRE 7 6 7 6 D.
Henry T. Smart, 1835

1. The day of res-ur-rec-tion! Earth, tell it out a-broad;
2. Our hearts be pure from e-vil, That we may see a-right
3. Now let the heav'ns be joy-ful! Let earth her song be-gin!

The Pass-o-ver of glad-ness, The Pass-o-ver of God.
The Lord in rays e-ter-nal Of res-ur-rec-tion light;
The world re-sound in tri-umph, And all that is there-in;

From death to life e-ter-nal, From earth un-to the sky,
And, lis-t'ning to His ac-cents, May hear, so calm and plain,
Let all things seen and un-seen Their notes of glad-ness blend;

Our Christ hath brought us o-ver With hymns of vic-to-ry.
His own "All hail!" and, hear-ing, May raise the vic-tor strain.
For Christ the Lord hath ris-en, Our Joy that hath no end. A-men.

This tune in a lower key, No. 517

HIS RESURRECTION

169 "Welcome, Happy Morning!"

Thanks be to God who giveth us the victory... I Cor. 15:57

Venantius H. C. Fortunatus, 6th century
Trans. by John Ellerton, 1868

HERMAS 6 5 6 5 D. Ref.
Frances R. Havergal, 1871

1. "Wel - come, hap - py morn - ing!" Age to age shall say;
2. Mak - er and Re - deem - er, Life and health of all,
3. Thou, of life the Auth - or, Death didst un - der - go,
4. Loose the souls long pris - oned, Bound with Sa - tan's chain;

Hell to - day is van - quished! Heav'n is won to - day!
Thou from heav'n be - hold - ing Hu - man na - ture's fall,
Tread the path of dark - ness, Sav - ing strength to show;
All that now are fall - en Raise to life a - gain;

Lo! the Dead is liv - ing, God for - ev - er - more,
Of the Fa - ther's God - head True and on - ly Son,
Come then, True and Faith - ful, Now ful - fill Thy Word,
Show Thy face in bright - ness, Bid the na - tions see;

Him, their true Cre - a - tor, All His work a - dore;
Man - hood to de - liv - er, Man - hood didst put on.
'Tis Thine own third morn - ing; Rise, O bur - ied Lord!
Bring a - gain our day - light; Day re - turns with Thee!

JESUS CHRIST

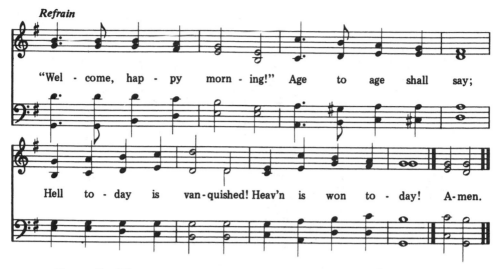

Refrain

"Wel - come, hap - py morn - ing!" Age to age shall say;

Hell to - day is van-quished! Heav'n is won to - day! A-men.

Good Christian Men, Rejoice and Sing 170

With great power gave the apostles witness of the resurrection . . . Acts 4:33

GELOBT SEI GOTT 8 8 8 Alleluias

Cyril A. Alington, 1931

Melchior Vulpius, 1609

1. Good Chris - tian men, re - joice and sing! Now is the tri - umph
2. The Lord of life is ris'n for aye; Bring flow'rs of song to
3. Praise we in songs of vic - to - ry That love, that life which
4. Thy name we bless, O ris - en Lord, And sing to - day with

of our King! To all the world glad news we bring:
strew His way; Let all man - kind re - joice and say:
can - not die, And sing with hearts up - lift - ed high:
one ac - cord The life laid down, the life re - stored:

Refrain

Al - le - lu - ia! Al - le - lu - ia! Al - le - lu - ia!

Words by permission of the Proprietors of Hymns Ancient & Modern.

HIS RESURRECTION

171 Thine Is the Glory, Risen, Conquering Son

O grave, where is thy victory? I Cor. 15:55

Edmond L. Budry, 1884
Trans. by Richard B. Hoyle, 1923

MACCABEUS 10 11 11 11 Ref.
George Frederick Handel, 1746

1. Thine is the glo - ry, Ris - en, con-qu'ring Son; End - less is the
2. Lo! Je - sus meets us, Ris - en, from the tomb; Lov - ing - ly He
3. No more we doubt Thee, Glo-rious Prince of Life! Life is naught with-

vic - t'ry Thou o'er death hast won. An - gels in bright rai - ment
greets us, Scat - ters fear and gloom; Let His church with glad - ness
out Thee; Aid us in our strife; Make us more than con-qu'rors,

Rolled the stone a - way, Kept the fold - ed grave - clothes
Hymns of tri - umph sing, For her Lord now liv - eth;
Through Thy death - less love; Bring us safe through Jor - dan

Refrain

Where Thy bod - y lay.
Death hath lost its sting. Thine is the glo - ry, Ris - en, con-qu'ring Son;
To Thy home a - bove.

End - less is the vic - t'ry Thou o'er death hast won. A - men.

Words from "Cantate Domino" by permission of the World Student Christian Federation, Geneva.

JESUS CHRIST: HIS RESURRECTION

Hark! Ten Thousand Harps and Voices 172

Worthy is the Lamb that was slain . . . Rev. 5:12

HARWELL 878777 Alleluias

Thomas Kelly, 1806

Lowell Mason, 1840

1. Hark! ten thou-sand harps and voic - es Sound the note of praise a - bove;
2. Sing how Je - sus came from heav - en, How He bore the cross be - low,
3. Je - sus, hail! Thy glo - ry bright-ens All a - bove and gives it worth;
4. King of glo - ry, reign for - ev — er! Thine an ev - er - last-ing crown.
5. Sav - ior, has - ten Thine ap - pear - ing; Bring, O bring the glo - rious day,

Je - sus reigns and heav'n re - joic - es, Je - sus reigns, the God of love.
How all pow'r to Him is giv - en, How He reigns in glo - ry now.
Lord of life, Thy smile en - light - ens, Cheers and charms Thy saints on earth.
Noth-ing from Thy love shall sev - er Those whom Thou hast made Thine own:
When, the aw - ful sum-mons hear - ing, Heav'n and earth shall pass a - way.

See, He sits on yon - der throne: Je - sus rules the world a - lone.
'Tis a great and end - less theme— O, 'tis sweet to sing of Him.
When we think of love like Thine, Lord, we own it love di - vine.
Hap - py ob - jects of Thy grace, Des - tined to be - hold Thy face.
Then with gold - en harps we'll sing, "Glo - ry, glo - ry to our King!"

Refrain

Al - le - lu - ia! Al - le - lu - ia! Al - le - lu - ia! A - men.

HIS ASCENSION AND REIGN

173 Hail the Day That Sees Him Rise

Lift up your heads, O ye gates . . . and the King of glory shall come in. Psa. 24:7

Charles Wesley, 1739

LLANFAIR 7 7 7 7 Alleluias
Welsh hymn melody
Arr. by John Roberts, 1837

1. Hail the day that sees Him rise, Al - le - lu - ia!
2. There for Him high tri - umph waits; Al - le - lu - ia!
3. See, He lifts His hands a - bove! Al - le - lu - ia!
4. Lord, be - yond our mor - tal sight, Al - le - lu - ia!

To His throne a - bove the skies; Al - le - lu - ia!
Lift your heads, e - ter - nal gates, Al - le - lu - ia!
See, He shows the prints of love! Al - le - lu - ia!
Raise our hearts to reach Thy height, Al - le - lu - ia!

Christ, the Lamb for sin - ners giv'n, Al - le - lu - ia!
He hath con - quered death and sin, Al - le - lu - ia!
Hark! His gra - cious lips be - stow, Al - le - lu - ia!
There Thy face un - cloud - ed see, Al - le - lu - ia!

En - ters now the high - est heav'n. Al - le - lu - ia!
Take the King of glo - ry in! Al - le - lu - ia!
Bless - ings on His church be - low. Al - le - lu - ia!
Find our heav'n of heav'ns in Thee! Al - le - lu - ia! A - men.

Alleluia! Sing to Jesus 174

Alleluia; Salvation, and glory, and honor, and power, unto the Lord our God . . . Rev. 19:1

HYFRYDOL 8 7 8 7 D.

William C. Dix, 1866

Rowland H. Prichard, c. 1830
Arr. by Ralph Vaughan Williams, 1906

1. Al - le - lu - ia! sing to Je - sus, His the scep - tre, His the throne;
2. Al - le - lu - ia! not as or - phans Are we left in sor - row now;
3. Al - le - lu - ia! Bread of Heav - en, Thou on earth our food and stay;

Al - le - lu - ia! His the tri - umph, His the vic - to - ry a - lone.
Al - le - lu - ia! He is near us, Faith be - lieves, nor ques - tions how;
Al - le - lu - ia! here the sin - ful Flee to Thee from day to day;

Hark! the songs of peace - ful Zi - on Thun - der like a might - y flood,
Though the cloud from sight re - ceived Him When the for - ty days were o'er,
In - ter - ces - sor, friend of sin - ners, Earth's Re - deem - er, plead for me,

"Je - sus, out of ev - ery na - tion, Hath re - deemed us by His blood."
Shall our hearts for - get His prom - ise, "I am with you ev - er - more"?
Where the songs of all the sin - less Sweep a - cross the crys - tal sea. A - men.

Music from "The English Hymnal" by permission of Oxford University Press.

HIS ASCENSION AND REIGN

175 Look, Ye Saints! the Sight Is Glorious

God hath made that same Jesus . . . both Lord and Christ. Acts 2:36

. REGENT SQUARE 878787

Thomas Kelly, 1809

Henry T. Smart, 1867

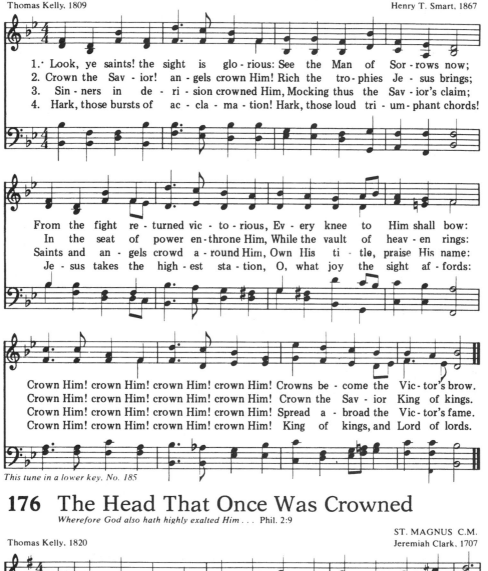

1. Look, ye saints! the sight is glo - rious: See the Man of Sor - rows now;
2. Crown the Sav - ior! an - gels crown Him! Rich the tro - phies Je - sus brings;
3. Sin - ners in de - ri - sion crowned Him, Mocking thus the Sav - ior's claim;
4. Hark, those bursts of ac - cla - ma - tion! Hark, those loud tri - um - phant chords!

From the fight re - turned vic - to - rious, Ev - ery knee to Him shall bow:
In the seat of power en - throne Him, While the vault of heav - en rings:
Saints and an - gels crowd a - round Him, Own His ti - tle, praise His name:
Je - sus takes the high - est sta - tion, O, what joy the sight af - fords:

Crown Him! crown Him! crown Him! crown Him! Crowns be - come the Vic - tor's brow.
Crown Him! crown Him! crown Him! crown Him! Crown the Sav - ior King of kings.
Crown Him! crown Him! crown Him! crown Him! Spread a - broad the Vic - tor's fame.
Crown Him! crown Him! crown Him! crown Him! King of kings, and Lord of lords.

This tune in a lower key. No. 185

176 The Head That Once Was Crowned

Wherefore God also hath highly exalted Him . . . Phil. 2:9

ST. MAGNUS C.M.

Thomas Kelly, 1820

Jeremiah Clark, 1707

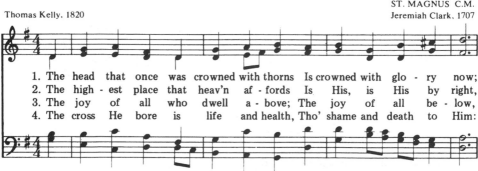

1. The head that once was crowned with thorns Is crowned with glo - ry now;
2. The high - est place that heav'n af - fords Is His, is His by right,
3. The joy of all who dwell a - bove; The joy of all be - low,
4. The cross He bore is life and health, Tho' shame and death to Him:

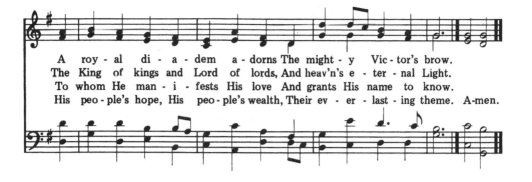

A roy - al di - a - dem a - dorns The might - y Vic - tor's brow.
The King of kings and Lord of lords, And heav'n's e - ter - nal Light.
To whom He man - i - fests His love And grants His name to know.
His peo - ple's hope, His peo - ple's wealth, Their ev - er - last - ing theme. A - men.

Rejoice, the Lord Is King 177

But we see Jesus . . . crowned with glory and honor. Heb. 2:9

Charles Wesley, 1746

DARWALL 6 6 6 6 8 8
John Darwall, 1770

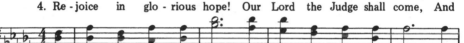

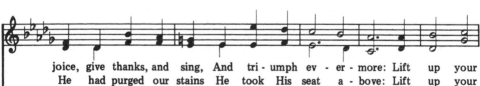

1. Re - joice, the Lord is King: Your Lord and King a - dore! Re -
2. Je - sus the Sav - ior reigns, The God of truth and love; When
3. His king - dom can - not fail, He rules o'er earth and heav'n; The
4. Re - joice in glo - rious hope! Our Lord the Judge shall come, And

joice, give thanks, and sing, And tri - umph ev - er - more: Lift up your
He had purged our stains He took His seat a - bove: Lift up your
keys of death and hell Are to our Je - sus giv'n: Lift up your
take his serv - ants up To their e - ter - nal home. Lift up your

heart, lift up your voice! Re - joice, a - gain I say, re - joice!
heart, lift up your voice! Re - joice, a - gain I say, re - joice!
heart, lift up your voice! Re - joice, a - gain I say, re - joice!
heart, lift up your voice! Re - joice, a - gain I say, re - joice! A - men.

This tune in a lower key, No. 79

HIS ASCENSION AND REIGN

178 It May Be at Morn

Ye shall see the Son of man . . . coming in the clouds of heaven. Mark 14:62

H. L. Turner, 1878

CHRIST RETURNETH Irreg. Ref.
James McGranahan, 1878

1. It may be at morn, when the day is a - wak - ing, When
2. It may be at mid - day, it may be at twi - light, It
3. While hosts cry Ho - san - na, from heav - en de - scend - ing, With
4. O joy! O de - light! should we go with - out dy - ing, No

sun - light through dark-ness and shad - ow is break - ing, That Je - sus will
may be, per-chance, that the black-ness of mid-night Will burst in - to
glo - ri - fied saints and the an - gels at - tend - ing, With grace on His
sick - ness, no sad - ness, no dread and no cry - ing, Caught up through the

come in the full - ness of glo - ry, To re - ceive from the world His own.
light in the blaze of His glo - ry, When Je - sus re - ceives His own.
brow, like a ha - lo of glo - ry, Will Je - sus re - ceive His own.
clouds with our Lord in - to glo - ry, When Je - sus re - ceives His own.

Refrain

O Lord Je - sus, how long, how long Ere we shout the glad song, Christ re -

turn-eth! Hal - le - lu - jah! hal - le - lu - jah! A - men, Hal - le - lu - jah! A - men.

JESUS CHRIST

Jesus May Come Today 179

Unto them that look for Him shall He appear the second time . . . Heb. 9:28

CROWNING DAY Irreg. Ref.

Henry Ostrom, 1910

Charles H. Marsh, 1910

1. Je - sus may come to - day, Glad day! Glad day! And I would
2. I may go home to - day, Glad day! Glad day! Seem - eth I
3. Why should I anx - ious be? Glad day! Glad day! Lights ap - pear
4. Faith - ful I'll be to - day, Glad day! Glad day! And I will

see my Friend; Dan - gers and trou - bles would end If
hear their song; Hail to the ra - di - ant throng! If
on the shore, Storms will af - fright nev - er - more, For
free - ly tell Why I should love Him so well, For

Refrain

Je - sus should come to - day.
I should go home to - day.
He is "at hand" to - day.
He is my all to - day.

Glad day! Glad day! Is it the crown-ing

day? I'll live for to - day, nor anx - ious be, Je - sus my Lord I

soon shall see; Glad day! Glad day! Is it the crown - ing day?

HIS COMING IN GLORY

180 Jesus Is Coming to Earth Again

The Lord Himself shall descend from heaven with a shout . . . I Thess. 4:16

SECOND COMING Irreg. Ref.

Lelia N. Morris, 1912

Lelia N. Morris, 1912

1. Je - sus is com - ing to earth a - gain, What if it were to - day?
2. Sa - tan's do - min - ion will soon be o'er, O, that it were to - day!
3. Faith - ful and true would He find us here, If He should come to - day?

Com - ing in pow - er and love to reign, What if it were to - day?
Sor - row and sigh - ing shall be no more, O, that it were to - day!
Watch - ing in glad - ness and not in fear, If He should come to - day?

Com - ing to claim His cho - sen Bride, All the re - deemed and pu - ri - fied,
Then shall the dead in Christ a - rise, Caught up to meet Him in the skies,
Signs of His com - ing mul - ti - ply, Morn-ing light breaks in east - ern sky,

O - ver this whole earth scat-tered wide, What if it were to - day?
When shall these glo - ries meet our eyes? What if it were to - day?
Watch, for that time is draw - ing nigh, What if it were to - day?

Refrain

Glo - ry, glo - ry! Joy to my heart 'twill bring;
Joy to my heart 'twill bring;

JESUS CHRIST

Glo - ry, glo - ry! When we shall crown Him King;
When we shall crown Him King;

Glo - ry, glo - ry! Haste to pre - pare the way;
Haste to pre - pare the way;

Glo - ry, glo - ry! Je - sus will come some day.

The King Shall Come 181

Surely I come quickly . . . Even so, come, Lord Jesus. Rev. 22:20

KENTUCKY HARMONY C.M.

Early Greek hymn
Trans. by John Brownlie, 1907

Traditional American melody
Kentucky Harmony, 1816

Unison

1. The King shall come when morn - ing dawns And light tri - um-phant breaks, When
2. Not as of old a lit - tle child To bear and fight and die, But
3. O bright-er than the ris - ing morn When He, vic - to-rious, rose And
4. O bright-er than that glo - rious morn Shall this fair morn - ing be, When
5. The King shall come when morn - ing dawns And light and beau - ty brings. Hail,

beau - ty gilds the east - ern hills And life to joy a - wakes.
crowned with glo - ry like the sun That lights the morn-ing sky.
left the lone-some place of death, De - spite the rage of foes:
Christ our King in beau - ty comes And we His face shall see!
Christ the Lord! Thy peo - ple pray: Come quick-ly, King of kings! A - men.

HIS COMING IN GLORY

182 Marvelous Message We Bring

Watch therefore, for ye know neither the day nor the hour . . . Matt. 25:13

COMING AGAIN 7 7 7 7 Ref.

John W. Peterson, 1957

John W. Peterson, 1957

1. Mar - vel - ous mes - sage we bring, Glo - ri - ous car - ol we sing,
2. For - est and flow - er ex - claim, Moun - tain and mead - ow the same,
3. Stand - ing be - fore Him at last, Tri - al and trou - ble all past,

Won - der - ful word of the King— Je - sus is com - ing a - gain! (a-gain!)
All earth and heav - en pro - claim— Je - sus is com - ing a - gain! (a-gain!)
Crowns at His feet we will cast— Je - sus is com - ing a - gain! (a-gain!)

Refrain — Unison

Com - ing a - gain, Com - ing a -

gain; May - be morn - ing, may - be noon,

May - be eve - ning and may - be soon! Com - ing a -

JESUS CHRIST

gain, Com - ing a - gain;

O what a won-der-ful day it will be— Je-sus is com-ing a gain!

Christ Is Coming! Let Creation 183

Looking for that blessed hope, and the glorious appearing of . . . Jesus Christ. Titus 2:13

John R. Macduff, 1853

UNSER HERRSCHER 8 7 8 7 8 7

Joachim Neander, 1680

1. Christ is com-ing! let cre-a-tion From her groans and tra-vail cease;
2. Earth can now but tell the sto-ry Of Thy bit-ter cross and pain;
3. Long Thine ex-iles have been pin-ing, Far from rest, and home, and Thee:
4. With that bless-ed hope be-fore us, Let no harp re-main un-strung;

Let the glo-rious proc-la-ma-tion Hope re-store and faith in-crease:
She shall yet be-hold Thy glo-ry, When Thou com-est back to reign:
But in heav'n-ly ves-tures shin-ing, They their lov-ing Lord shall see:
Let the might-y ad-vent cho-rus On-ward roll from tongue to tongue:

Christ is com-ing! Christ is com-ing! Come, Thou bless-ed Prince of Peace.
Christ is com-ing! Christ is com-ing! Let each heart re-peat the strain.
Christ is com-ing! Christ is com-ing! Haste the joy-ous ju-bi-lee.
Christ is com-ing! Christ is com-ing! Come, Lord Je-sus, quick-ly come! A-men.

HIS COMING IN GLORY

184 Lift Up Your Heads, Pilgrims A-weary

Then shall they see the Son of man coming . . . with power and great glory. Luke 21:27

CAMP Irreg. Ref.

Mabel J. Camp, 1913

Mabel J. Camp, 1913

1. Lift up your heads, pil-grims a-wea-ry, See day's ap-proach now
2. Dark was the night, sin warred a-gainst us; Heav-y the load of
3. O bless-ed hope! O bliss-ful prom-ise! Fill-ing our hearts with
4. E-ven so come, pre-cious Lord Je-sus; Cre-a-tion waits re-

crim-son the sky; Night shad-ows flee, and your Be-lov-ed,
sor-row we bore; But now we see signs of His com-ing;
rap-ture di-vine; O day of days! hail Thy ap-pear-ing!
demp-tion to see; Caught up in clouds, soon we shall meet Thee;

A-wait-ed with long-ing, at last draw-eth nigh.
Our hearts glow with-in us, joy's cup run-neth o'er!
Thy tran-scen-dent glo-ry for-ev-er shall shine!
O bless-ed as-sur-ance, for-ev-er with Thee!

Refrain

He is com-ing a-gain, He is com-ing a-gain, The ver-y same

Je-sus, re-ject-ed of men; He is com-ing a-gain, He is com-ing a-gain,

JESUS CHRIST

With pow'r and great glo-ry, He is com-ing a-gain!
is com-ing a-gain!

Lo, He Comes with Clouds Descending 185

Behold, He cometh with clouds; and every eye shall see Him. Rev. 1:7

Charles Wesley, 1758, and
Martin Madan, 1760
Based on John Cennick, 1752

REGENT SQUARE 8 7 8 7 8 7
Henry T. Smart, 1867

1. Lo, He comes with clouds de-scend-ing, Once for fa-vored sin-ners slain;
2. Ev-ery eye shall now be-hold Him, Robed in dread-ful maj-es-ty;
3. Now re-demp-tion, long ex-pect-ed, See in sol-emn pomp ap-pear:
4. Yea, A-men! let all a-dore Thee, High on Thine e-ter-nal throne;

Thou-sand thou-sand saints at-tend-ing Swell the tri-umph of His train:
Those who set at naught and sold Him, Pierced and nailed Him to the tree,
All His saints, by men re-ject-ed, Now shall meet Him in the air:
Sav-ior, take the pow'r and glo-ry, Claim the king-dom for Thine own:

Al-le-lu-ia! al-le-lu-ia! God ap-pears on earth to reign.
Deep-ly wail-ing, deep-ly wail-ing, Shall the true Mes-si-ah see.
Al-le-lu-ia! al-le-lu-ia! See the day of God ap-pear.
O, come quick-ly, O, come quick-ly! Ev-er-last-ing God, come down. A-men.

This tune in a higher key, No. 110

HIS COMING IN GLORY

186 In the Glow of Early Morning

Be ye also patient . . . for the coming of the Lord draweth nigh. James 5:8

Winfield Macomber, 1888

MACOMBER 8 7 8 7 D.
Winfield Macomber, 1888

1. In the glow of ear - ly morn-ing, In the sol - emn hush of night,
2. Oft me-thinks I hear His foot-steps Steal-ing down the paths of time;
3. Long we've wait - ed, blest Re - deem - er, Wait - ed for the first bright ray

Down from heav - en's o - pen por - tals Steals a mes - sen - ger of light,
And the fu - ture, dark with shad - ows, Bright-ens with this hope sub - lime.
Of the morn when sin and sor - row At Thy pres-ence flee a - way.

Whis-p'ring sweet - ly to my spir - it, While the hosts of heav - en sing:
Sound the soul - in - spir - ing an - them; An - gel hosts, your harps at - tune;
But our vig - il's near - ly o - ver; Hope of heav'n, O price - less boon!

This the won - drous thrill - ing sto - ry—Christ is com - ing, Christ my King.
Earth's long night is al - most o - ver—Christ is com - ing, com - ing soon.
In the east the glow ap - pear - ing—Christ is com - ing, com - ing soon.

This the won-drous thrill - ing sto - ry — Christ is com - ing, Christ my King.
Earth's long night is al - most o - ver—Christ is com - ing, com - ing soon.
In the east the glow ap - pear - ing—Christ is com - ing, com - ing soon.

JESUS CHRIST: HIS COMING IN GLORY

Breathe on Me, Breath of God 187

He breathed on them, and saith, Receive ye the Holy Ghost. John 20:22

Edwin Hatch, 1878

TRENTHAM S.M.
Robert Jackson, 1888

1. Breathe on me, Breath of God, Fill me with life a - new, That I may
2. Breathe on me, Breath of God, Un - til my heart is pure, Un - til my
3. Breathe on me, Breath of God, Till I am whol - ly Thine, Un - til this
4. Breathe on me, Breath of God, So shall I nev - er die, But live with

love what Thou dost love, And do what Thou wouldst do.
will is one with Thine, To do and to en - dure.
earth - ly part of me Glows with Thy fire di - vine.
Thee the per - fect life Of Thine e - ter - ni - ty. A-men.

Come, Holy Ghost, Our Souls Inspire 188

. . . The love of God is shed abroad in our hearts by the Holy Ghost . . . Rom. 5:5

Attr. to Rabanus Maurus, c. 776-856
Trans. by John Cosin, 1627

MENDON L.M.
Traditional German melody
Arr. by Samuel Dyer, 1824

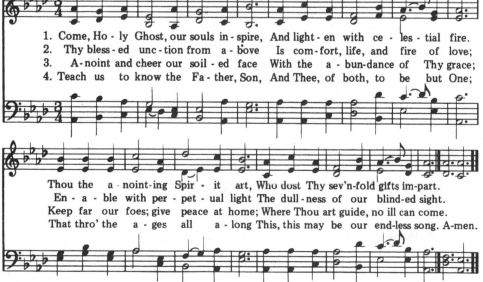

1. Come, Ho - ly Ghost, our souls in - spire, And light - en with ce - les - tial fire.
2. Thy bless - ed unc - tion from a - bove Is com - fort, life, and fire of love;
3. A - noint and cheer our soil - ed face With the a - bun-dance of Thy grace;
4. Teach us to know the Fa - ther, Son, And Thee, of both, to be but One;

Thou the a - noint-ing Spir - it art, Who dost Thy sev'n-fold gifts im-part.
En - a - ble with per - pet - ual light The dull-ness of our blind-ed sight.
Keep far our foes; give peace at home; Where Thou art guide, no ill can come.
That thro' the a - ges all a - long This, this may be our end-less song. A-men.

THE HOLY SPIRIT

189 O Spread the Tidings 'Round

I will pray the Father, and He will give you another Comforter. John 14:16

COMFORTER 12 12 12 6 Ref.

Frank Bottome, 1890

William J. Kirkpatrick, 1890

1. O spread the ti-dings 'round wher-ev-er man is found, Wher-
2. The long, long night is past, the morn-ing breaks at last, And
3. Lo, the great King of kings with heal-ing in His wings, To
4. O bound-less love di-vine! how shall this tongue of mine To

ev-er hu-man hearts and hu-man woes a-bound; Let ev-ery Chris-tian
hushed the dread-ful wail and fu-ry of the blast, As o'er the gold-en
ev-ery cap-tive soul a full de-liv-'rance brings; And through the va-cant
wond-'ring mor-tals tell the match-less grace di-vine—That I, a child of

tongue pro-claim the joy-ful sound: The Com-fort-er has come!
hills the day ad-vanc-es fast! The Com-fort-er has come!
cells the song of tri-umph rings; The Com-fort-er has come!
hell, should in His im-age shine! The Com-fort-er has come!

Refrain

The Com-fort-er has come, the Com-fort-er has come! The

Ho-ly Ghost from Heav'n, the Fa-ther's pro-mise giv'n; O spread the ti-dings

THE HOLY SPIRIT

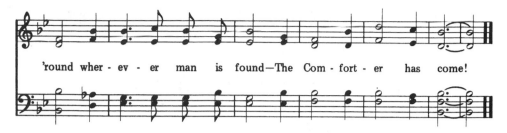

'round wher - ev - er man is found—The Com - fort - er has come!

We Are Gathered for Thy Blessing 190

He shall baptize you with the Holy Ghost and with fire. Matt. 3:11

TABERNACLE 8 7 8 7 Ref.

Paul Rader, 1920

Paul Rader, 1920

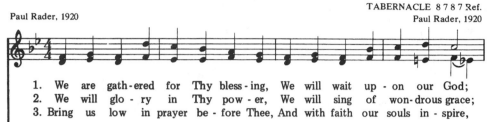

1. We are gath-ered for Thy bless-ing, We will wait up - on our God;
2. We will glo - ry in Thy pow - er, We will sing of won-drous grace;
3. Bring us low in prayer be - fore Thee, And with faith our souls in - spire,

We will trust in Him who loved us, And who bought us with His blood.
In our midst as Thou hast prom-ised, Come, O come and take Thy place.
Till we claim by faith the prom-ise Of the Ho - ly Ghost and fire.

Refrain

Spir - it, now melt and move All of our hearts with love,

Breathe on us from a - bove With old - time pow'r. A - men.

THE HOLY SPIRIT

191 Spirit of God in the Clear Running Water

The wind bloweth where it listeth . . . so is every one that is born of the Spirit. John 3:8

MEDICAL MISSION SISTERS Irreg.

Miriam Therese Winter, 1965

Miriam Therese Winter, 1965

Unison

1. Spir - it of God in the clear run-ning wa - ter, Blow-ing to great-ness the
2. Down in the mead-ow the wil-lows are moan-ing, Sheep in the pas-ture-land
3. I saw the scar of a year that lay dy - ing, Heard the la - ment of a
4. Spir - it of God, ev - ery man's heart is lone - ly, Watch-ing and wait-ing and

trees on the hill— Spir - it of God in the fin - ger of morn-ing,
can - not lie still; Spir - it of God, cre - a - tion is groan-ing—
lone whip-poor-will; Spir - it of God, see that cloud cry - ing—
hun - gry un - til— Spir - it of God, man longs that you on - ly Ful -

Fill the earth, bring it to birth, And blow where You will.
Fill the earth, bring it to birth, And blow where You will.
Fill the earth, bring it to birth, And blow where You will.
fill the earth, bring it to birth, And blow where You will.

Blow, blow, blow till I be But breath of the Spir - it blow-ing in me.

THE HOLY SPIRIT

Joys Are Flowing Like a River 192

He shall give you another Comforter, that He may abide with you forever. John 14:16

BLESSED QUIETNESS 8 7 8 7 Ref.

Manie P. Ferguson, 1900

W. S. Marshall, 19th century
Arr. by James M. Kirk, 1900

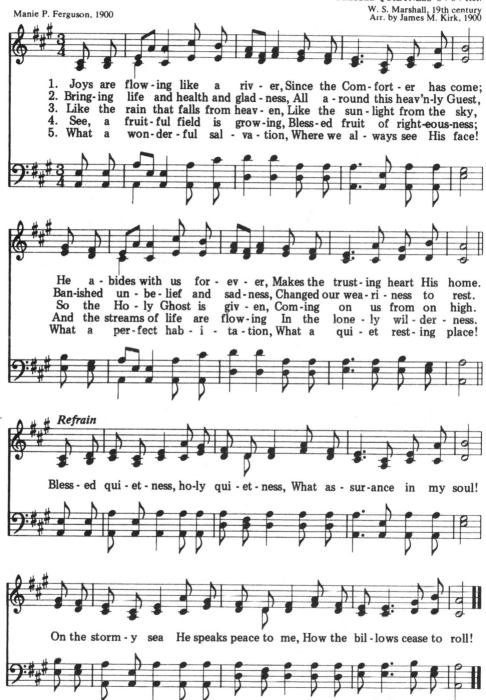

1. Joys are flow-ing like a riv-er, Since the Com-fort-er has come;
2. Bring-ing life and health and glad-ness, All a-round this heav'n-ly Guest,
3. Like the rain that falls from heav-en, Like the sun-light from the sky,
4. See, a fruit-ful field is grow-ing, Bless-ed fruit of right-eous-ness;
5. What a won-der-ful sal-va-tion, Where we al-ways see His face!

He a-bides with us for-ev-er, Makes the trust-ing heart His home.
Ban-ished un-be-lief and sad-ness, Changed our wea-ri-ness to rest.
So the Ho-ly Ghost is giv-en, Com-ing on us from on high.
And the streams of life are flow-ing In the lone-ly wil-der-ness.
What a per-fect hab-i-ta-tion, What a qui-et rest-ing place!

Refrain

Bless-ed qui-et-ness, ho-ly qui-et-ness, What as-sur-ance in my soul!

On the storm-y sea He speaks peace to me, How the bil-lows cease to roll!

THE HOLY SPIRIT

193 Gracious Spirit, Dwell with Me

A new spirit will I put within you. Ezek. 36:26

REDHEAD 777777

Thomas T. Lynch, 1855

Richard Redhead, 1853

1. Gra - cious Spir - it, dwell with me: I my - self would gra - cious be;
2. Truth - ful Spir - it, dwell with me: I my - self would truth - ful be;
3. Might - y Spir - it, dwell with me: I my - self would might - y be;
4. Ho - ly Spir - it, dwell with me: I my - self would ho - ly be;

And with words that help and heal Would Thy life in mine re - veal;
And with wis - dom kind and clear Let Thy life in mine ap - pear;
Might - y so as to pre - vail Where un - aid - ed man must fail;
Sep - a - rate from sin, I would Choose and cher - ish all things good,

And with ac - tions bold and meek Would for Christ my Sav - ior speak.
And with ac - tions broth - er - ly Speak my Lord's sin - cer - i - ty.
Ev - er by a might - y hope Press - ing on and bear - ing up.
And what - ev - er I can be, Give to Him who gave me Thee! A - men.

194 Holy Spirit, Light Divine

He . . . shall also quicken your mortal bodies by His Spirit. Rom. 8:11

MERCY 7777

Andrew Reed, 1817, alt.

Louis M. Gottschalk, 1854
Arr. by Edwin P. Parker, c. 1880

1. Ho - ly Spir - it, Light di - vine, Shine up - on this heart of mine;
2. Ho - ly Spir - it, Power di - vine, Cleanse this guilt - y heart of mine;
3. Ho - ly Spir - it, Joy di - vine, Cheer this sad - dened heart of mine;
4. Ho - ly Spir - it, all di - vine, Dwell with - in this heart of mine;

THE HOLY SPIRIT

Chase the shades of night a - way, Turn my dark - ness in - to day.
Long hath sin with - out con - trol Held do - min - ion o'er my soul.
Bid my man - y woes de - part, Heal my wound-ed, bleed-ing heart.
Cast down ev - ery i - dol throne, Reign su-preme, and reign a - lone. A - men.

Hover o'er Me, Holy Spirit 195

. . . Be filled with the Spirit. Eph. 5:18

FILL ME NOW 8 7 8 7 Ref.

Elwood H. Stokes, 1879

John R. Sweney, 1879

1. Hov - er o'er me, Ho - ly Spir - it, Bathe my trem - bling heart and brow;
2. Thou canst fill me, gra - cious Spir - it, Though I can - not tell Thee how;
3. I am weak - ness, full of weak - ness, At Thy sa - cred feet I bow;
4. Cleanse and com - fort, bless and save me, Bathe, O bathe my heart and brow;

Fill me with Thy hal - lowed pres - ence, Come, O come and fill me now.
But I need Thee, great - ly need Thee, Come, O come and fill me now.
Blest di - vine, e - ter - nal Spir - it, Fill with pow'r and fill me now.
Thou art com - fort - ing and sav - ing, Thou art sweet - ly fill - ing now.

Refrain

Fill me now, fill me now, Je - sus, come and fill me now;

Fill me with Thy hal - lowed pres - ence, Come, O come and fill me now.

THE HOLY SPIRIT

196 O Breath of Life

Wilt Thou not revive us again . . . ? Psa. 85:6

SPIRITUS VITAE 9 8 9 8

Bessie P. Head, c. 1914

Mary J. Hammond, c. 1920

1. O Breath of Life, come sweep-ing through us, Re - vive Thy
2. O Wind of God, come bend us, break us, Till hum - bly
3. O Breath of Love, come breathe with - in us, Re - new - ing
4. Re - vive us, Lord! Is zeal a - bat - ing While har - vest

church with life and pow'r; O Breath of Life, come, cleanse, re -
we con - fess our need; Then in Thy ten - der - ness re -
thought and will and heart; Come, Love of Christ, a - fresh to
fields are vast and white? Re - vive us, Lord, the world is

new us, And fit Thy church to meet this hour.
make us, Re - vive, re - store, for this we plead.
win us, Re - vive Thy church in ev - ery part.
wait - ing, E - quip Thy church to spread the light. A-men.

197 Come, Holy Spirit, Heavenly Dove

The love of God is shed abroad in our hearts by the Holy Ghost . . . Rom. 5:5

ST. AGNES C.M.

Isaac Watts, 1707

John B. Dykes, 1866

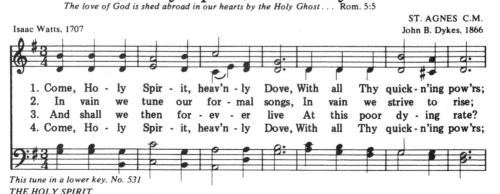

1. Come, Ho - ly Spir - it, heav'n - ly Dove, With all Thy quick-n'ing pow'rs;
2. In vain we tune our for - mal songs, In vain we strive to rise;
3. And shall we then for - ev - er live At this poor dy - ing rate?
4. Come, Ho - ly Spir - it, heav'n - ly Dove, With all Thy quick-n'ing pow'rs;

This tune in a lower key, No. 531
THE HOLY SPIRIT

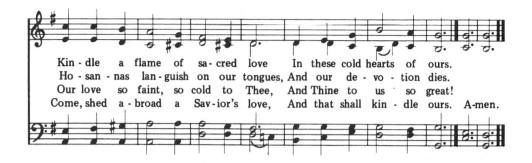

Kin - dle a flame of sa - cred love In these cold hearts of ours.
Ho - san - nas lan - guish on our tongues, And our de - vo - tion dies.
Our love so faint, so cold to Thee, And Thine to us so great!
Come, shed a - broad a Sav - ior's love, And that shall kin - dle ours. A-men.

Spirit of God, Descend upon My Heart 198

If we live in the Spirit, let us also walk in the Spirit. Gal. 5:25

MORECAMBE 10 10 10 10

George Croly, 1867

Frederick C. Atkinson, 1870

1. Spir - it of God, de - scend up - on my heart; Wean it from
2. I ask no dream, no proph - et ec - sta - sies, No sud - den
3. Hast Thou not bid us love Thee, God and King? All, all Thine
4. Teach me to feel that Thou art al - ways nigh; Teach me the
5. Teach me to love Thee as Thine an - gels love, One ho - ly

earth, through all its puls - es move; Stoop to my weak - ness, might - y
rend - ing of the veil of clay, No an - gel vis - it - ant, no
own, soul, heart and strength and mind. I see Thy cross—there teach my
strug - gles of the soul to bear, To check the ris - ing doubt, the
pas - sion fill - ing all my frame; The bap - tism of the heav'n - de-

as Thou art, And make me love Thee as I ought to love.
o - p'ning skies; But take the dim - ness of my soul a - way.
heart to cling: O let me seek Thee, and O let me find.
reb - el sigh; Teach me the pa - tience of un - an - swered prayer.
scend - ed Dove, My heart an al - tar, and Thy love the flame. A-men.

THE HOLY SPIRIT

199 Brethren, We Have Met to Worship

Behold, I will rain bread from heaven for you. Exo. 16:4

HOLY MANNA 8 7 8 7 D.
Columbian Harmony, 1825
Attr. to William Moore

Attr. to George Atkins, 19th century

1. Breth-ren, we have met to wor-ship And a-dore the Lord our God;
2. Breth-ren, see poor sin-ners round you Slum-b'ring on the brink of woe;
3. Sis-ters, will you join and help us? Mo-ses' sis-ter aid-ed him;
4. Let us love our God su-preme-ly, Let us love each oth-er too;

Will you pray with all your pow-er, While we try to preach the Word?
Death is com-ing, hell is mov-ing— Can you bear to let them go?
Will you help the trem-bling mour-ners Who are strug-gling hard with sin?
Let us love and pray for sin-ners Till our God makes all things new.

All is vain un-less the Spir-it Of the Ho-ly One comes down;
See our fa-thers and our moth-ers And our chil-dren sink-ing down;
Tell them all a-bout the Sav-ior—Tell them that He will be found;
Then He'll call us home to heav-en, At His ta-ble we'll sit down;

Breth-ren, pray, and ho-ly man-na Will be show-ered all a-round.
Breth-ren, pray, and ho-ly man-na Will be show-ered all a-round.
Sis-ters, pray, and ho-ly man-na Will be show-ered all a-round.
Christ will gird Him-self and serve us With sweet man-na all a-round.

THE CHURCH

The Church's One Foundation 200

Other foundation can no man lay than that is laid . . . Jesus Christ. I Cor. 3:11

AURELIA 7 6 7 6 D.

Samuel J. Stone, 1868

Samuel S. Wesley, 1864

1. The Church's one foun-da-tion Is Je-sus Christ her Lord;
2. E-lect from ev-ery na-tion, Yet one o'er all the earth,
3. Though with a scorn-ful won-der Men see her sore op-pressed,
4. 'Mid toil and trib-u-la-tion, And tu-mult of her war,
5. Yet she on earth hath un-ion With God, the Three in One,

She is His new cre-a-tion, By wa-ter and the word:
Her char-ter of sal-va-tion, One Lord, one faith, one birth;
By schisms rent a-sun-der, By her-e-sies dis-tressed:
She waits the con-sum-ma-tion Of peace for-ev-er-more;
And mys-tic sweet com-mun-ion With those whose rest is won:

From heav'n He came and sought her To be His ho-ly bride;
One ho-ly name she bless-es, Par-takes one ho-ly food,
Yet saints their watch are keep-ing, Their cry goes up, "How long?"
Till with the vi-sion glo-rious Her long-ing eyes are blest,
O hap-py ones and ho-ly! Lord, give us grace that we,

With His own blood He bought her, And for her life He died.
And to one hope she press-es, With ev-ery grace en-dued.
And soon the night of weep-ing Shall be the morn of song.
And the great Church vic-to-rious Shall be the Church at rest.
Like them, the meek and low-ly, On high may dwell with Thee. A-men.

This tune in a lower key, No. 560

ITS NATURE AND FELLOWSHIP

201 Built on the Rock the Church Doth Stand

And upon this rock I will build My church. Matt. 16:18

Nicolai F. S. Grundtvig, 1837
Trans. by Carl Doving, 1909
Adapt. by Fred C. M. Hansen, c. 1927

KIRKEN DEN ER ET 8 8 8 8 8 8 8
Ludvig M. Lindeman, 1840

1. Built on the Rock the church doth stand, E - ven when stee - ples are fall - ing; Crum-bled have spires in ev - ery land, Bells still are chim - ing and call - ing, Call - ing the young and old to rest, But a - bove all the soul dis-tressed, Long-ing for life ev - er - last - ing.

2. Sure - ly in tem - ples made with hands, God the most high is not dwell - ing; High a - bove earth His tem - ple stands, All earth-ly tem - ples ex - cel - ling. Yet He whom heav'ns can - not con - tain Chose to a - bide on earth with men, Built in our bod - ies His tem - ple.

3. We are God's house of liv - ing stones, Built for His own hab - i - ta - tion; He fills our hearts, his hum - ble thrones, Grant-ing us life and sal - va - tion; Were two or three to seek His face, He in their midst would show His grace, Bless-ings up - on them be - stow - ing.

4. Now we may gath - er with our King E'en in the low - li - est dwell - ing; Prais - es to Him we there may bring, His won-drous mer - cy forth - tell - ing. Je - sus His grace to us ac - cords; Spir - it and life are all His words; His truth doth hal - low the tem - ple. A - men.

THE CHURCH

Jesus, with Thy Church Abide 202

The church of the living God, the pillar and ground of the truth. I Tim. 3:15

LITANY OF THE PASSION 7 7 7 6

Thomas B. Pollock, 1871

John B. Dykes, 1875

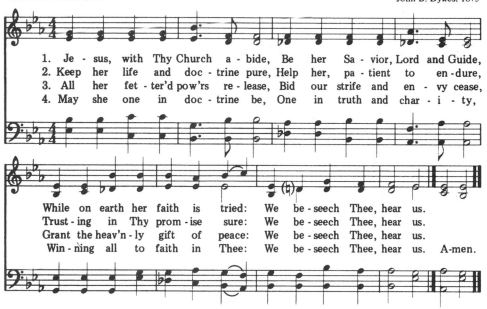

1. Je - sus, with Thy Church a - bide, Be her Sa - vior, Lord and Guide,
2. Keep her life and doc - trine pure, Help her, pa - tient to en - dure,
3. All her fet - ter'd pow'rs re - lease, Bid our strife and en - vy cease,
4. May she one in doc - trine be, One in truth and char - i - ty,

While on earth her faith is tried: We be - seech Thee, hear us.
Trust - ing in Thy prom - ise sure: We be - seech Thee, hear us.
Grant the heav'n - ly gift of peace: We be - seech Thee, hear us.
Win - ning all to faith in Thee: We be - seech Thee, hear us. A - men.

I Love Thy Kingdom, Lord 203

Lord, I have loved the habitation of Thy house. Psa. 26:8

ST. THOMAS S.M.

Timothy Dwight, 1800

Aaron Williams, 1763

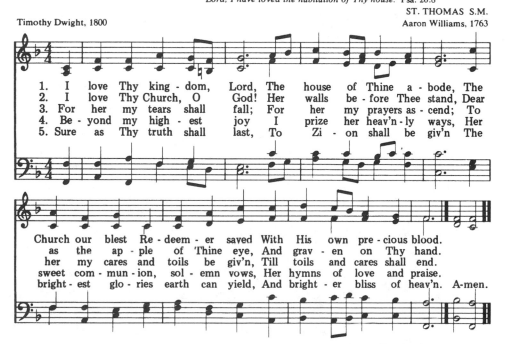

1. I love Thy king - dom, Lord, The house of Thine a - bode, The
2. I love Thy Church, O God! Her walls be - fore Thee stand, Dear
3. For her my tears shall fall; For her my prayers as - cend; To
4. Be - yond my high - est joy I prize her heav'n - ly ways, Her
5. Sure as Thy truth shall last, To Zi - on shall be giv'n The

Church our blest Re - deem - er saved With His own pre - cious blood.
as the ap - ple of Thine eye, And grav - en on Thy hand.
her my cares and toils be giv'n, Till toils and cares shall end.
sweet com - mun - ion, sol - emn vows, Her hymns of love and praise.
bright - est glo - ries earth can yield, And bright - er bliss of heav'n. A - men.

ITS NATURE AND FELLOWSHIP

204 There's a Quiet Understanding

Where two or three are gathered in My name, there am I . . . Matt. 18:20

QUIET UNDERSTANDING Irreg.

Tedd Smith, 1973

Tedd Smith, 1973

1. There's a qui - et un - der-stand - ing when we're gath - ered
2. And we know when we're to - geth - er, shar - ing love and

in the Spir - it, It's a prom - ise that He gives us,
un - der-stand - ing, That our broth - ers and our sis - ters

when we gath-er in His name. There's a love we feel in Je - sus,
feel the one-ness that He brings. Thank You, thank You, thank You, Je - sus,

there's a man - na that He feeds us, It's a prom - ise
for the way You love and feed us, For the man - y

that He gives us
ways You lead us, When we gath-er in His name. Thank You, thank You, Lord.

THE CHURCH

Renew Thy Church, Her Ministries 205

O Lord, revive Thy work in the midst of the years. Hab. 3:2

ALL IS WELL 10 6 10 6 8 8 8 6

Kenneth L. Cober, 1960

Traditional English melody
The Sacred Harp, 1844

1. Re - new Thy church, her min - is - tries re - store: Both to serve and a - dore.
2. Teach us Thy Word, re - veal its truth di - vine, On our path let it shine;
3. Teach us to pray, for Thou art ev - er near, Thy still voice let us hear.
4. Teach us to love, with strength of heart and mind, Ev - ery - one, all man - kind,

Make her a - gain as salt through-out the land, And as light from a stand.
Tell of Thy works, Thy might - y acts of grace, From each page show Thy face.
Our souls are rest - less till they rest in Thee, This our glad des - ti - ny.
Break down old walls of prej - u - dice and hate, Leave us not to our fate.

'Mid som - ber shad - ows of the night, Where greed and ha - treds spread their blight,
As Thou hast loved us, sent Thy Son, And our sal - va - tion now is won,
Be - fore Thy pres - ence keep us still That we may find for us Thy will,
As Thou hast loved and giv'n Thy life To end hos - til - i - ty and strife,

O send us forth with pow'r en - dued, Help us, Lord, be re - newed.
O let our hearts with love be stirred, Help us, Lord, know thy Word.
And seek Thy guid - ance ev - ery day, Teach us, Lord, how to pray.
O share Thy grace from heav'n a - bove, Teach us, Lord, how to love. A - men.

Words copyright 1966 by K. L. Cober;

206 Faith of Our Fathers

Earnestly contend for the faith which was once delivered unto the saints. Jude 3

ST. CATHERINE 8 8 8 8 8 8
Henri F. Hemy, 1864
Arr. by James G. Walton, 1874

Frederick W. Faber, 1849

1. Faith of our fa - thers! liv - ing still   In spite of dun - geon, fire and sword:
2. Our fa-thers, chained in pris - ons dark, Were still in heart and con-science free:
3. Faith of our fa - thers! we will strive To win all na - tions un - to thee,
4. Faith of our fa - thers! we will love Both friend and foe in all our strife:

O   how our hearts beat high with joy When-e'er we hear that glo - rious word!
How sweet would be their chil-dren's fate, If they like them could die   for thee!
And thro' the truth that comes from God, Man-kind shall then be   tru - ly free.
And preach thee too   as   love knows how, By kind - ly words and   vir - tuous life:

Faith of   our fa - thers, ho - ly faith! We will   be true to thee till death!
Faith of   our fa - thers, ho - ly faith! We will   be true to thee till death!
Faith of   our fa - thers, ho - ly faith! We will   be true to thee till death!
Faith of   our fa - thers, ho - ly faith! We will   be true to thee till death! A - men.

207 Blest Be the Tie That Binds

For ye are all one in Christ Jesus. Gal. 3:28

DENNIS S.M.
Johann G. Nageli, 1773-1836
Arr. by Lowell Mason, 1845

John Fawcett, 1782

1. Blest   be   the   tie   that   binds   Our   hearts   in   Chris - tian   love;
2. Be - fore   our   Fa - ther's throne   We   pour   our   ar - dent   prayers;
3. We   share   our   mu - tual   woes,   Our   mu - tual   bur - dens   bear;
4. When   we   a - sun - der part,   It   gives   us   in - ward   pain;

THE CHURCH

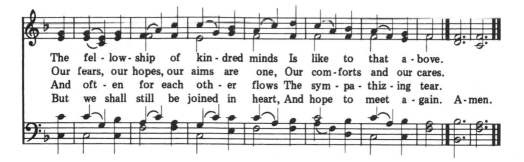

The fel-low-ship of kin-dred minds Is like to that a-bove.
Our fears, our hopes, our aims are one, Our com-forts and our cares.
And oft-en for each oth-er flows The sym-pa-thiz-ing tear.
But we shall still be joined in heart, And hope to meet a-gain. A-men.

There's a Church within Us, O Lord 208

For, behold, the kingdom of God is within you. Luke 17:21

Kent Schneider, 1967

THE CHURCH WITHIN US Irreg.
Kent Schneider, 1967

Unison

1. There's a church with-in us, O Lord; There's a church with-
2. There's po-ten-tial with-in us, O Lord; Some-thing stir-ring with-
3. There's a fire with-in us, O Lord; A new life a-
4. There's some building to be done, O Lord; There's some building to be
5. There's the church with-in us, O Lord; There's the church with-

in us, O Lord; Not a build-ing, but a soul, Not a por-tion,
in us, O Lord; Some-thing strain-ing to have birth, To be vis-i-
burn-ing, O Lord; A new fire for a life, Com-bat-ting
done, O Lord; Not with steel, not with stone, But with lives which
in us, O Lord; Not a build-ing but one soul, Not a por-tion,

but a whole; There's a church with-in us, O Lord.
ble on earth, There's po-ten-tial with-in us, O Lord.
pres-ent strife, There's a fire with-in us, O Lord.
are Your own, There's the church to be built, O Lord.
but a whole, We are Your church in the world.

ITS NATURE AND FELLOWSHIP

209 Glorious Things of Thee Are Spoken

Glorious things are spoken of thee, O city of God. Psa. 87:3

AUSTRIAN HYMN 8 7 8 7 D.

John Newton, 1779

Franz Joseph Haydn, 1797

1. Glo-rious things of thee are spo-ken, Zi-on, cit-y of our God;
2. See the streams of liv-ing wa-ters, Spring-ing from e-ter-nal love,
3. Round each hab-i-ta-tion hov-ering, See the cloud and fire ap-pear
4. Sav-ior, if of Zi-on's cit-y, I through grace a mem-ber am,

He whose word can-not be bro-ken Formed thee for His own a-bode;
Well sup-ply thy sons and daugh-ters, And all fear of want re-move:
For a glo-ry and a cov-ering, Show-ing that the Lord is near!
Let the world de-ride or pit-y, I will glo-ry in Thy name;

On the Rock of A-ges found-ed, What can shake thy sure re-pose?
Who can faint, while such a riv-er Ev-er will their thirst as-suage?
Thus de-riv-ing from their ban-ner Light by night and shade by day;
Fad-ing is the world's best pleas-ure, All its boast-ed pomp and show;

With sal-va-tion's walls sur-round-ed, Thou mayst smile at all thy foes.
Grace which, like the Lord, the Giv-er, Nev-er fails from age to age.
Safe they feed up-on the man-na Which He gives them when they pray.
Sol-id joys and last-ing treas-ure None but Zi-on's chil-dren know. A-men.

This tune in a lower key. No. 464

THE CHURCH: ITS NATURE AND FELLOWSHIP

Here, O My Lord, I See Thee 210

The things which are not seen are eternal. II Cor. 4:18

LANGRAN 10 10 10 10

Horatius Bonar, 1855

James Langran, 1861

1. Here, O my Lord, I see Thee face to face;
2. Here would I feed up - on the bread of God;
3. I have no help but Thine; nor do I need
4. Mine is the sin, but Thine the right - eous - ness;

Here would I touch and han - dle things un - seen,
Here drink with Thee the roy - al wine of heav'n;
An - oth - er arm save Thine to lean up - on;
Mine is the guilt, but Thine the cleans - ing blood.

Here grasp with firm - er hand th'e - ter - nal grace,
Here would I lay a - side each earth - ly load,
It is e - nough, my Lord, e - nough in - deed;
Here is my robe, my ref - uge, and my peace;

And all my wea - ri - ness up - on Thee lean.
Here taste a - fresh the calm of sin for - giv'n.
My strength is in Thy might, Thy might a - lone.
Thy blood, Thy right - eous - ness, O Lord, my God. A - men.

THE LORD'S SUPPER

211 Bread of the World in Mercy Broken

Take, eat: this is My body which is broken for you. I Cor. 11:24

Reginald Heber, 1827

EUCHARISTIC HYMN 9 8 9 8

John S. B. Hodges, 1868

1. Bread of the world in mer - cy bro - ken, Wine of the
2. Look on the heart by sor - row bro - ken, Look on the

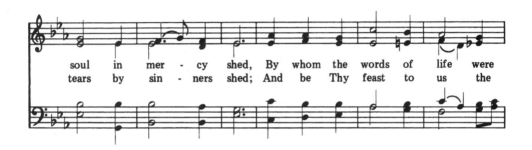

soul in mer - cy shed, By whom the words of life were
tears by sin - ners shed; And be Thy feast to us the

spo - ken, And in whose death our sins are dead:
to - ken That by Thy grace our souls are fed! A - men.

212 According to Thy Gracious Word

This do in remembrance of Me. Luke 22:19

MARTYRDOM C.M.

James Montgomery, 1825

Hugh Wilson, c. 1800

1. Ac - cord - ing to Thy gra - cious word, In meek hu - mil - i - ty, This
2. Thy bod - y, bro - ken for my sake, My bread from heav'n shall be; Thy
3. Re - mem - ber Thee and all Thy pains, And all Thy love to me: Yea,
4. And when these fail - ing lips grow dumb, And mind and mem - ory flee, When

THE CHURCH

will I do, my dy-ing Lord, I will re-mem-ber Thee.
cup of bless-ing I will take, And thus re-mem-ber Thee.
while a breath, a pulse re-mains, Will I re-mem-ber Thee.
Thou shalt in Thy king-dom come, Je-sus, re-mem-ber me. A-men.

Let Us Break Bread Together 213

He took bread, and blessed it, and brake, and gave to them. Luke 24:30

LET US BREAK BREAD Irreg.

Traditional Spiritual

Traditional Spiritual
Arr. by Carlton R. Young

Unison

1. Let us break bread to-geth-er on our knees; Let us break bread to-
2. Let us drink the cup to-geth-er on our knees; Let us drink the cup to-
3. Let us praise God to-geth-er on our knees; Let us praise God to-

Refrain

geth-er on our knees.
geth-er on our knees.
geth-er on our knees. When I fall on my knees, With my

face to the ris-ing sun, O Lord, have mer-cy on me.

THE LORD'S SUPPER

214 We Bless the Name of Christ the Lord

For thus it becometh us to fulfill all righteousness. Matt. 3:15

RETREAT L.M.

Samuel F. Coffman, 1872-1954

Thomas Hastings, 1842

1. We bless the name of Christ the Lord, We bless Him for His ho - ly Word,
2. We fol - low Him with pure de - light To sanc - ti - fy His sa - cred rite;
3. Bap - tized in God—the Fa - ther, Son, And Ho - ly Spir - it—Three in One,
4. By grace we "Ab - ba, Fa - ther" cry; By grace the Com - fort - er comes nigh;

Who loved to do His Fa-ther's will, And all His right-eous-ness ful - fill.
And thus our faith with wa-ter seal, To prove o - be-dience that we feel.
With con-science free, we rest in God, In love and peace thro' Je - sus' blood.
And for Thy grace our love shall be For - ev - er, on - ly, Lord, for Thee. A-men.

215 Come, Holy Spirit, Dove Divine

We are buried with Him by baptism . . . Rom. 6:4

MARYTON L.M.

Adoniram Judson, 1832

H. Percy Smith, 1874

1. Come, Ho - ly Spir - it, Dove di - vine, On these bap - tis - mal wa - ters shine,
2. We love Thy name, we love Thy laws, And joy - ful - ly em - brace Thy cause;
3. We sink be - neath the wa - ter's face; And thank Thee for Thy sav - ing grace;
4. And as we rise with Thee to live, O let the Ho - ly Spir - it give

And teach our hearts, in high-est strain, To praise the Lamb for sin-ners slain.
We love Thy cross, the shame, the pain, O Lamb of God, for sin - ners slain.
We die to sin, and seek a grave With Thee, be-neath the yield-ing wave.
The seal - ing unc - tion from a - bove, The joy of life, the fire of love. A - men.

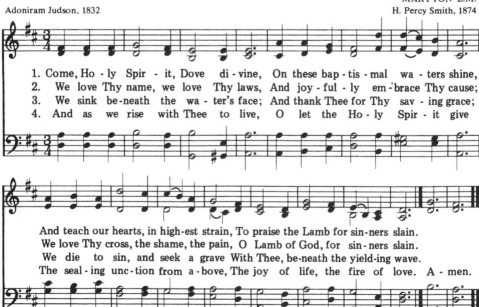

See Israel's Gentle Shepherd Stand 216

And He took them up in His arms . . . and blessed them. Mark 10:16

SERENITY C.M.

Philip Doddridge, 1755

William V. Wallace, 1856

1. See Is - rael's gen - tle Shep - herd stand With all en - gag - ing charms;
2. "Per - mit them to ap - proach," He cries, "Nor scorn their hum - ble name;
3. We bring them, Lord, in thank - ful hands, And yield them up to Thee;

Hark, how He calls the ten - der lambs, And folds them in His arms!
For 'twas to bless such souls as these The Lord of an - gels came."
Joy - ful that we our - selves are Thine, Thine let our off - spring be. A - men.

This tune in a lower key, No. 73

Savior, Who Thy Flock Art Feeding 217

Suffer the little children to come unto Me . . . Mark 10:14

BROCKLESBURY 8 7 8 7

William A. Mühlenberg, 1826

Charlotte A. Barnard, 1868

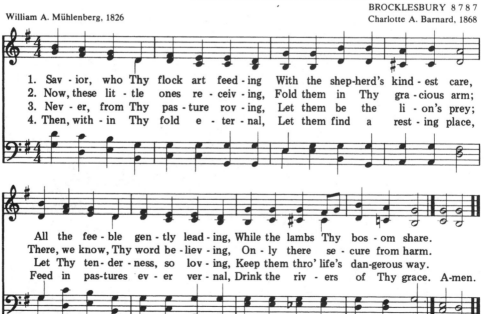

1. Sav - ior, who Thy flock art feed - ing With the shep - herd's kind - est care,
2. Now, these lit - tle ones re - ceiv - ing, Fold them in Thy gra - cious arm;
3. Nev - er, from Thy pas - ture rov - ing, Let them be the li - on's prey;
4. Then, with - in Thy fold e - ter - nal, Let them find a rest - ing place,

All the fee - ble gen - tly lead - ing, While the lambs Thy bos - om share.
There, we know, Thy word be - liev - ing, On - ly there se - cure from harm.
Let Thy ten - der - ness, so lov - ing, Keep them thro' life's dan - gerous way.
Feed in pas - tures ev - er ver - nal, Drink the riv - ers of Thy grace. A - men.

DEDICATION OF CHILDREN

218 The Bible Stands Like a Rock Undaunted

. . . The word of God, which liveth and abideth forever. I Pet. 1:23

RIDGE LINE Irreg. Ref.

Haldor Lillenas, 1917

Donald P. Hustad, 1973

Unison

1. The Bi - ble stands like a rock un - daunt - ed 'Mid the rag - ing storms of
2. The Bi - ble stands like a moun - tain tow - 'ring Far a - bove the works of
3. The Bi - ble stands and it will for - ev - er, When the world has passed a-
4. The Bi - ble stands ev - ery test we give it, For its Au - thor is di-

time; Its pag - es burn with the truth e - ter - nal, And they
man; Its truth by none ev - er was re - fut - ed, And de-
way; By in - spi - ra - tion it has been giv - en, All its
vine; By grace a - lone I ex - pect to live it, And to

glow with a light sub - lime.
stroy it they nev - er can.
pre - cepts I will o - bey.
prove it and make it mine.

Refrain

The Bi - ble stands tho' the hills may tum - ble,

It will firm - ly stand when the earth shall crum - ble; I will plant my feet on its

firm foun - da - tion, For the Bi - ble stands, The Bi - ble stands.

THE SCRIPTURES

O Word of God Incarnate 219

The entrance of Thy words giveth light . . . Psa. 119:130

MUNICH 7 6 7 6 D.
Neuvermehrtes Gesangbuch, Meiningen, 1693
Arr. by Felix Mendelssohn, 1847

William W. How, 1867

1. O Word of God in - car - nate, O Wis - dom from on high,
2. The Church from her dear Mas - ter Re - ceived the gift di - vine,
3. It float - eth like a ban - ner Be - fore God's host un - furled;
4. O make Thy Church, dear Sav - ior, A lamp of pur - est gold,

O Truth un - changed, un - chang - ing, O Light of our dark sky;
And still that light she lift - eth O'er all the earth to shine.
It shin - eth like a bea - con A - bove the dark - ling world.
To bear be - fore the na - tions Thy true light as of old.

We praise Thee for the ra - diance That from the hal - lowed page,
It is the gold - en cas - ket Where gems of truth are stored;
It is the chart and com - pass That o'er life's surg - ing sea,
O teach Thy wan - d'ring pil - grims By this their path to trace,

A lan - tern to our foot - steps, Shines on from age to age.
It is the heav'n - drawn pic - ture Of Christ, the liv - ing Word.
'Mid mists and rocks and quick - sands, Still guides, O Christ, to Thee.
Till, clouds and dark - ness end - ed, They see Thee face to face. A - men.

THE SCRIPTURES

220 Break Thou the Bread of Life

He looked up to heaven, and blessed, and brake the loaves . . . Mark 6:41

BREAD OF LIFE 6 4 6 4 D.

Mary A. Lathbury, 1877

William F. Sherwin, 1877

1. Break Thou the bread of life, Dear Lord, to me, As Thou didst break the loaves Be-side the sea; Be-yond the sa-cred page I seek Thee, Lord, My spir-it pants for Thee, O liv-ing Word.
2. Bless Thou the truth, dear Lord, To me, to me, As Thou didst bless the bread By Gal-i-lee; Then shall all bond-age cease, All fet-ters fall; And I shall find my peace, My All in all.
3. Thou art the bread of life, O Lord, to me, Thy ho-ly Word the truth That sav-eth me; Give me to eat and live With Thee a-bove; Teach me to love Thy truth, For Thou art love.
4. O send Thy Spir-it, Lord, Now un-to me, That He may touch my eyes And make me see: Show me the truth con-cealed With-in Thy Word, And in Thy Book re-vealed I see the Lord. A-men.

221 The Heavens Declare Thy Glory, Lord

The law of the Lord is perfect, converting the soul. Psa. 19:7

WINCHESTER NEW L.M.

Isaac Watts, 1719
Based on Psalm 19

Georg Rebenlein's *Musicalisch Handbuch*, Hamburg, 1690
Arr. by William H. Havergal, 1847

1. The heav'ns de-clare Thy glo-ry, Lord, In ev-ery star Thy wis-dom shines;
2. The roll-ing sun, the chang-ing light, And nights and days Thy pow'r con-fess;
3. Great Sun of Right-eous-ness, a-rise, Bless the dark world with heav'nly light;
4. Thy no-blest won-ders here we view In souls re-newed, and sins for-giv'n;

THE SCRIPTURES

But when our eyes be-hold Thy Word, We read Thy name in fair-er lines.
But the blest vol-ume Thou hast writ, Re-veals Thy jus-tice and Thy grace.
Thy gos-pel makes the sim-ple wise, Thy laws are pure, Thy judg-ments right.
Lord, cleanse my sins, my soul re-new, And make Thy Word my guide to heav'n. A-men.

Sing Them Over Again to Me 222

Lord, to whom shall we go? Thou hast the words of eternal life. John 6:68

WORDS OF LIFE 8 6 8 6 6 6 Ref.

Philip P. Bliss, 1874

Philip P. Bliss, 1874

1. Sing them o-ver a-gain to me, Won-der-ful words of Life;
2. Christ, the bless-ed One, gives to all Won-der-ful words of Life;
3. Sweet-ly ech-o the gos-pel call, Won-der-ful words of Life;

Let me more of their beau-ty see, Won-der-ful words of Life.
Sin-ner, list to the lov-ing call, Won-der-ful words of Life.
Of-fer par-don and peace to all, Won-der-ful words of Life.

Words of life and beau-ty, Teach me faith and du-ty:
All so free-ly giv-en, Woo-ing us to Heav-en:
Je-sus, on-ly Sav-ior, Sanc-ti-fy for-ev-er:

Refrain

1 2

Beau-ti-ful words, won-der-ful words, Won-der-ful words of Life. Life.

THE SCRIPTURES

223 God Hath Spoken by His Prophets

God . . . spake in time past unto the fathers by the prophets . . . Heb. 1:1

HYMN TO JOY 8 7 8 7 D.

George W. Briggs, 1952

Ludwig van Beethoven, 1824

1. God hath spo - ken by His proph-ets, Spo - ken His un-chang - ing Word;
2. God hath spo - ken by Christ Je - sus, Christ, the ev - er - last - ing Son,
3. God yet speak - eth by His Spir - it—Speak-ing to the hearts of men,

Each from age to age pro-claim - ing God the One, the right-eous Lord!
Bright-ness of the Fa - ther's glo - ry, With the Fa - ther ev - er one;
In the age - long word de - clar - ing God's own mes - sage, now as then.

'Mid the world's de - spair and tur - moil One firm an - chor hold - ing fast,
Spo - ken by the Word In - car - nate, God of God ere time be - gan,
Through the rise and fall of na - tions One sure faith yet stand - eth fast:

God is on His throne e - ter - nal, He a - lone the First and Last.
Light of Light, to earth de-scend-ing, Man, re - veal - ing God to man.
God a - bides, His Word un-chang-ing, God a - lone the First and Last. A-men.

Words from "Ten New Bible Hymns," copyright 1953 by the Hymn Society of America; used by permission.

THE SCRIPTURES

How Firm a Foundation 224

Heaven and earth shall pass away: but My words shall not . . . Luke 21:33

FOUNDATION 11 11 11 11
Traditional American melody
Caldwell's *Union Harmony*, 1837

Rippon's *Selection of Hymns*, 1787

1. How firm a foun - da - tion, ye saints of the Lord,
2. "Fear not, I am with thee; O be not dis - mayed,
3. "When through the deep wa - ters I call thee to go,
4. "When through fier - y tri - als thy path - way shall lie,
5. "The soul that on Je - sus hath leaned for re - pose,

Is laid for your faith in His ex - cel - lent Word!
For I am thy God, and will still give thee aid;
The riv - ers of sor - row shall not o - ver - flow;
My grace, all suf - fi - cient, shall be thy sup - ply:
I will not, I will not de - sert to his foes;

What more can He say than to you He hath said,
I'll strength - en thee, help thee, and cause thee to stand,
For I will be with thee, thy trou - bles to bless,
The flame shall not hurt thee; I on - ly de - sign
That soul, though all hell should en - deav - or to shake,

To you who for ref - uge to Je - sus have fled?
Up - held by my right - eous, om - nip - o - tent hand.
And sanc - ti - fy to thee thy deep - est dis - tress.
Thy dross to con - sume, and thy gold to re - fine.
I'll nev - er, no, nev - er, no, nev - er for - sake!" A - men.

Alternate tune, ADESTE FIDELES, No. 103   THE SCRIPTURES

225 Standing on the Promises

Whereby are given unto us exceeding great and precious promises . . . II Pet. 1:4

PROMISES 11 11 11 9 Ref.

R. Kelso Carter, 1886

R. Kelso Carter, 1886

1. Stand-ing on the prom-is-es of Christ my King, Thro' e-ter-nal a-ges let His prais-es ring; Glo-ry in the high-est, I will shout and sing, Stand-ing on the prom-is-es of God.
2. Stand-ing on the prom-is-es that can-not fail, When the howl-ing storms of doubt and fear as-sail, By the liv-ing Word of God I shall pre-vail,
3. Stand-ing on the prom-is-es of Christ the Lord, Bound to Him e-ter-nal-ly by love's strong cord, O-ver-com-ing dai-ly with the Spir-it's sword,
4. Stand-ing on the prom-is-es I can-not fall, Lis-t'ning ev-ery mo-ment to the Spir-it's call, Rest-ing in my Sav-ior as my all in all,

Refrain

Stand-ing, stand-ing, stand-ing on the prom-is-es, Stand-ing on the prom-is-es of God my Sav-ior; Stand-ing, stand-ing, stand-ing on the prom-is-es, I'm stand-ing on the prom-is-es of God.

Holy Bible, Book Divine 226

O how love I Thy law! it is my meditation all the day! Psa. 119:97

ALETTA 7 7 7 7

John Burton, 1803

William B. Bradbury, 1858

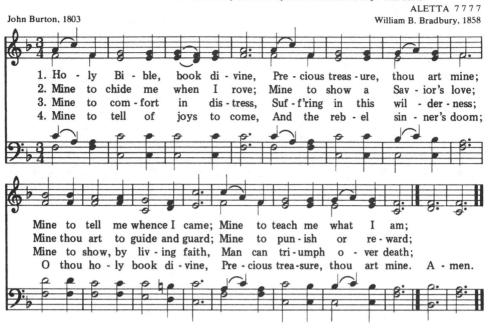

1. Ho - ly Bi - ble, book di - vine, Pre - cious treas - ure, thou art mine;
2. Mine to chide me when I rove; Mine to show a Sav - ior's love;
3. Mine to com - fort in dis - tress, Suf - f'ring in this wil - der - ness;
4. Mine to tell of joys to come, And the reb - el sin - ner's doom;

Mine to tell me whence I came; Mine to teach me what I am;
Mine thou art to guide and guard; Mine to pun - ish or re - ward;
Mine to show, by liv - ing faith, Man can tri - umph o - ver death;
O thou ho - ly book di - vine, Pre - cious trea - sure, thou art mine. A - men.

Lord, Thy Word Abideth 227

Forever, O Lord, Thy word is settled in heaven. Psa. 119:89

RAVENSHAW 6 6 6 6

Michael Weisse's *Ein Neu Gesengbüchlen,* Behmen, 1531
Arr. by William H. Monk, 1861

Henry W. Baker, 1861

1. Lord, Thy Word a - bid - eth, And our foot - steps guid - eth;
2. When our foes are near us, Then Thy Word doth cheer us,
3. When dark clouds are o'er us, And the storms be - fore us,
4. Who can tell the pleas - ure, Who re - count the treas - ure,
5. O that we, dis - cern - ing Its most ho - ly learn - ing,

Who its truth be - liev - eth Light and joy re - ceiv - eth.
Word of con - so - la - tion, Mes - sage of sal - va - tion.
Then its light di - rect - eth, And our way pro - tect - eth.
By Thy Word im - part - ed To the sim - ple - heart - ed?
Lord, may love and fear Thee, Ev - er - more be near Thee! A - men.

THE SCRIPTURES

228 I Saw the Cross of Jesus

Having made peace through the blood of His cross . . . Col. 1:20

WHITFIELD 7 6 7 6 D.
Source unknown

Frederick Whitfield, 1861

1. I saw the cross of Je - sus When bur - dened with my sin;
2. I love the cross of Je - sus, It tells me what I am—
3. I trust the cross of Je - sus In ev - ery try - ing hour,
4. Safe in the cross of Je - sus! There let my wea - ry heart

I sought the cross of Je - sus To give me peace with - in;
A vile and guilt - y crea - ture Saved on - ly through the Lamb;
My sure and cer - tain ref - uge, My nev - er - fail - ing tow'r,
Still rest in peace un - shak - en Till with Him, ne'er to part;

I brought my soul to Je - sus, He cleansed it in His blood;
No right - eous - ness nor mer - it, No beau - ty can I plead;
In ev - ery fear and con - flict I more than con - queror am;
And then in strains of glo - ry I'll sing His won - drous pow'r,

And in the cross of Je - sus I found my peace with God.
Yet in the cross I glo - ry, My ti - tle there I read.
Liv - ing I'm safe, or dy - ing, Thro' Christ, the ris - en Lamb.
Where sin can nev - er en - ter, And death is known no more.

THE GOSPEL

O the Deep, Deep Love of Jesus 229

Having loved His own . . . He loved them unto the end. John 13:1

S. Trevor Francis, 1834-1925

TON-Y-BOTEL 8 7 8 7 D.

Thomas J. Williams, 1890

1. O the deep, deep love of Je - sus, Vast, un - meas-ured, bound-less, free!
2. O the deep, deep love of Je - sus, Spread His praise from shore to shore!
3. O the deep, deep love of Je - sus, Love of ev - ery love the best;

Roll - ing as a might - y o - cean In its full - ness o - ver me,
How He lov - eth, ev - er lov - eth, Chang-eth nev - er, nev - er - more;
'Tis an o - cean vast of bless-ing, 'Tis a ha - ven sweet of rest,

Un - der-neath me, all a - round me, Is the cur - rent of Thy love;
How He watch - es o'er His loved ones, Died to call them all His own;
O the deep, deep love of Je - sus, 'Tis a Heav'n of Heav'ns to me;

Lead - ing on-ward, lead-ing home-ward To my glo - rious rest a-bove.
How for them He in - ter - ced - eth, Watch-eth o'er them from the throne.
And it lifts me up to glo - ry, For it lifts me up to Thee. A - men.

This tune in a higher key, No. 463

THE WORK OF CHRIST

230 There Is a Fountain Filled with Blood

In that day there shall be a fountain opened . . . for sin and for uncleanness. Zech. 13:1

CLEANSING FOUNTAIN C.M.D.

Traditional American melody
Arr. by Lowell Mason, 1830

William Cowper, 1771

1. There is a foun-tain filled with blood Drawn from Im-man-uel's veins;
2. The dy-ing thief re-joiced to see That foun-tain in his day;
3. Dear dy-ing Lamb, Thy pre-cious blood Shall nev-er lose its pow'r,
4. E'er since by faith I saw the stream Thy flow-ing wounds sup-ply,
5. When this poor lisp-ing, stamm'ring tongue Lies si-lent in the grave,

And sin-ners, plunged be-neath that flood, Lose all their guilt-y stains:
And there may I, though vile as he, Wash all my sins a-way:
Till all the ran-somed Church of God Be saved, to sin no more:
Re-deem-ing love has been my theme, And shall be till I die:
Then in a no-bler, sweet-er song, I'll sing Thy pow'r to save:

Lose all their guilt-y stains, Lose all their guilt-y stains; And
Wash all my sins a-way, Wash all my sins a-way; And
Be saved, to sin no more, Be saved, to sin no more; Till
And shall be till I die, And shall be till I die; Re-
I'll sing Thy pow'r to save, I'll sing Thy pow'r to save; Then

sin-ners, plunged be-neath that flood, Lose all their guilt-y stains.
there may I, though vile as he, Wash all my sins a-way.
all the ran-somed Church of God Be saved, to sin no more.
deem-ing love has been my theme, And shall be till I die.
in a no-bler, sweet-er song I'll sing Thy pow'r to save. A-men.

THE GOSPEL

Free from the Law, O Happy Condition 231

Christ hath redeemed us from the curse of the law. Gal. 3:13

ONCE FOR ALL 10 10 9 8 Ref.

Philip P. Bliss, 1873

Philip P. Bliss, 1873

1. Free from the law, O hap-py con-di-tion, Je-sus hath
2. Now are we free—there's no con-dem-na-tion, Je-sus pro-
3. Chil-dren of God, O glo-ri-ous call-ing, Sure-ly His

bled, and there is re-mis-sion; Cursed by the law and bruised by the
vides a per-fect sal-va-tion; "Come un-to Me," O hear His sweet
grace will keep us from fall-ing; Pass-ing from death to life at His

Refrain

fall, Grace hath re-deemed us once for all.
call, Come, and He saves us once for all. Once for all— O sin-ner, re-
call, Bless-ed sal-va-tion once for all.

ceive it; Once for all— O broth-er, be-lieve it; Cling to the

cross, the bur-den will fall, Christ hath re-deemed us once for all.

THE WORK OF CHRIST

232 I Hear the Savior Say

Though your sins be as scarlet, they shall be as white as snow. Isa. 1:18

Elvina M. Hall, 1865

ALL TO CHRIST 6 6 7 7 Ref.
John T. Grape, 1868

1. I hear the Sav - ior say, "Thy strength in - deed is small, Child of
2. Lord, now in - deed I find Thy pow'r and Thine a - lone Can
3. For noth - ing good have I Where - by Thy grace to claim— I'll
4. And when be - fore the throne I stand in Him com - plete, "Je - sus

Refrain

weak-ness, watch and pray, Find in Me thine all in all."
change the lep - er's spots And melt the heart of stone.
wash my gar-ments white In the blood of Cal-v'ry's Lamb.
died my soul to save," My lips shall still re - peat.

Je - sus paid it all,

All to Him I owe; Sin had left a crim - son stain, He washed it white as snow.

233 There's a Wideness in God's Mercy

Thou, O Lord, art a God . . . plenteous in mercy and truth. Psa. 86:15

Frederick W. Faber, 1862

WELLESLEY 8 7 8 7
Lizzie S. Tourjée, 1878

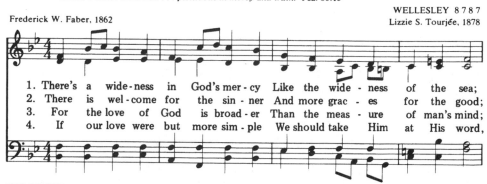

1. There's a wide - ness in God's mer - cy Like the wide - ness of the sea;
2. There is wel - come for the sin - ner And more grac - es for the good;
3. For the love of God is broad - er Than the meas - ure of man's mind;
4. If our love were but more sim - ple We should take Him at His word,

THE GOSPEL

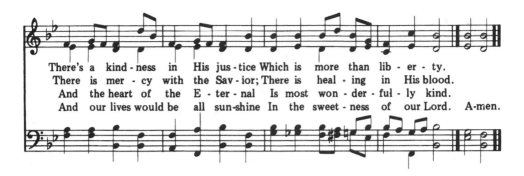

There's a kind-ness in His jus-tice Which is more than lib-er-ty.
There is mer-cy with the Sav-ior; There is heal-ing in His blood.
And the heart of the E-ter-nal Is most won-der-ful-ly kind.
And our lives would be all sun-shine In the sweet-ness of our Lord. A-men.

These Are the Facts 234

I delivered unto you . . . that which I also received . . . I Cor. 15:3

YVONNE 10 10 10 10

Michael Saward, 1971

Norman L. Warren, 1972

Unison

1. These are the facts as we have re-ceived them, These are the truths that the
2. These are the facts as we have re-ceived them, Christ has ful-filled what the
3. These are the facts as we have re-ceived them, We with our Sav-ior have
4. These are the facts as we have re-ceived them, We shall be changed in the

Chris-tian be-lieves, This is the ba-sis of all of our preach-ing,
scrip-tures fore-told, Ad-am's whole fam-'ly in death had been sleep-ing,
died on the cross, Now hav-ing ris-en, our Je-sus lives in us,
blink of an eye, Trum-pets shall sound as we face life im-mor-tal,

Christ died for sin-ners and rose from the tomb.
Christ through His ris-ing re-stores us to life.
Gives us His Spir-it and makes us His home.
This is the vic-t'ry through Je-sus, our Lord. A-men.

THE WORK OF CHRIST

235 "What Must I Do?"

Believe on the Lord Jesus Christ, and thou shalt be saved . . . Acts 16:31

BELIEVE 10 7 10 7 Ref.

Avis B. Christiansen, 1920

Harry D. Clarke, 1920

1. "What must I do?" the trem-bling jail-or cried, When dazed by fear and won-der; "Be-lieve on Christ!" was all that Paul re-plied, "And you shall be saved from sin."
2. What must I do! O wea-ry, trem-bling soul, Just turn to-day to Je-sus; He will re-ceive, for-give and make you whole— Christ a-lone can set you free.
3. His blood is all your plea for sav-ing grace, The pre-cious fount of cleans-ing! O come, ac-cept His love, be-hold His face, And be saved for-ev-er-more.

Refrain

Be-lieve on the Lord Je-sus Christ, Be-lieve on the Lord Je-sus Christ, Be-lieve on the Lord Je-sus Christ, And you shall be saved!

THE GOSPEL

On a Hill Far Away 236

Who for the joy that was set before Him endured the cross, despising the shame . . . Heb. 12:2

OLD RUGGED CROSS Irreg. Ref.

George Bennard, 1913

George Bennard, 1913

1. On a hill far a-way stood an old rug-ged cross, The em-blem of suf-fering and shame; And I love that old cross where the dear-est and best For a world of lost sin-ners was slain.

2. O that old rug-ged cross, so de-spised by the world, Has a won-drous at-trac-tion for me; For the dear Lamb of God left His glo-ry a-bove To bear it to dark Cal-va-ry.

3. In the old rug-ged cross, stained with blood so di-vine, A won - drous beau-ty I see; For 'twas on that old cross Je - sus suf-fered and died To par-don and sanc-ti-fy me.

4. To the old rug-ged cross I will ev-er be true, Its shame and re-proach glad-ly bear; Then He'll call me some day to my home far a-way, Where His glo-ry for-ev-er I'll share.

Refrain

So I'll cher-ish the old rug-ged cross, the old rug-ged cross, Till my tro-phies at last I lay down; I will cling to the old rug-ged cross, the old rug-ged cross, And ex-change it some day for a crown.

THE WORK OF CHRIST

237 What Can Wash Away My Sin?

The blood of Jesus Christ His Son cleanseth us from all sin. I John 1:7

PLAINFIELD 7 8 7 8 Ref.

Robert Lowry, 1876

Robert Lowry, 1876

1. What can wash a-way my sin? Noth-ing but the blood of Je-sus;
2. For my par-don this I see—Noth-ing but the blood of Je-sus;
3. Noth-ing can for sin a-tone—Noth-ing but the blood of Je-sus;
4. This is all my hope and peace—Noth-ing but the blood of Je-sus;

What can make me whole a-gain? Noth-ing but the blood of Je-sus.
For my cleans-ing, this my plea—Noth-ing but the blood of Je-sus.
Naught of good that I have done—Noth-ing but the blood of Je-sus.
This is all my right-eous-ness—Noth-ing but the blood of Je-sus.

Refrain

O! pre-cious is the flow That makes me white as snow;

No oth-er fount I know, Noth-ing but the blood of Je-sus.

238 Depth of Mercy! Can There Be

Thy mercy is great above the heavens . . . Psa. 108:4

SEYMOUR 7 7 7 7

Charles Wesley, 1740

Carl Maria von Weber, 1826

1. Depth of mer-cy! can there be Mer-cy still re-served for me?
2. I have long with-stood His grace, Long pro-voked Him to His face,
3. Lord, in-cline me to re-pent; Let me now my sins la-ment;
4. Still for me the Sav-ior stands, Hold-ing forth His wound-ed hands;

This tune in a lower key, No. 431

THE GOSPEL

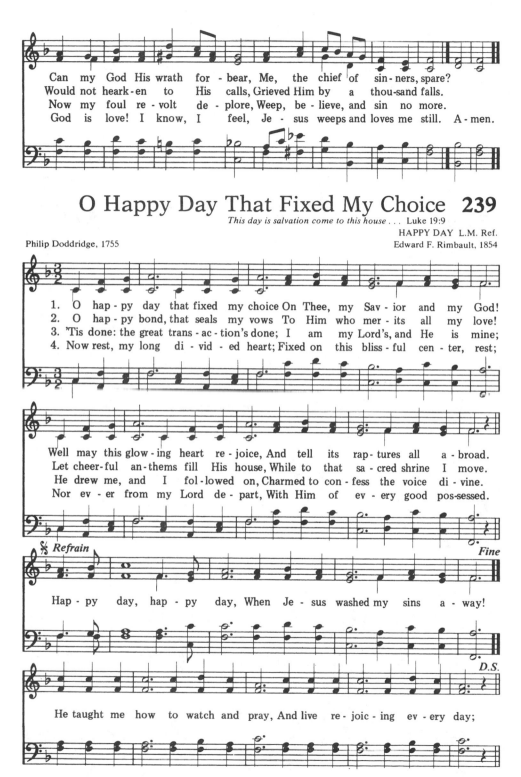

Can my God His wrath for - bear, Me, the chief of sin - ners, spare?
Would not heark - en to His calls, Grieved Him by a thou-sand falls.
Now my foul re - volt de - plore, Weep, be - lieve, and sin no more.
God is love! I know, I feel, Je - sus weeps and loves me still. A - men.

O Happy Day That Fixed My Choice 239

This day is salvation come to this house . . . Luke 19:9

HAPPY DAY L.M. Ref.

Philip Doddridge, 1755

Edward F. Rimbault, 1854

1. O hap - py day that fixed my choice On Thee, my Sav - ior and my God!
2. O hap - py bond, that seals my vows To Him who mer - its all my love!
3. 'Tis done: the great trans - ac - tion's done; I am my Lord's, and He is mine;
4. Now rest, my long di - vid - ed heart; Fixed on this bliss - ful cen - ter, rest;

Well may this glow - ing heart re - joice, And tell its rap - tures all a - broad.
Let cheer-ful an - thems fill His house, While to that sa - cred shrine I move.
He drew me, and I fol - lowed on, Charmed to con - fess the voice di - vine.
Nor ev - er from my Lord de - part, With Him of ev - ery good pos-sessed.

Refrain

Fine

Hap - py day, hap - py day, When Je - sus washed my sins a - way!

D.S.

He taught me how to watch and pray, And live re - joic - ing ev - ery day;

THE WORK OF CHRIST

240 Marvelous Grace of Our Loving Lord

Where sin abounded, grace did much more abound. Rom. 5:20

Julia H. Johnston, 1911

MOODY 9 9 9 9 Ref.
Daniel B. Towner, 1911

1. Mar-vel-ous grace of our lov-ing Lord, Grace that ex-ceeds our
2. Sin and de-spair like the sea waves cold, Threat-en the soul with
3. Dark is the stain that we can-not hide, What can a-vail to
4. Mar-vel-ous, in-fi-nite, match-less grace, Free-ly be-stowed on

sin and our guilt, Yon-der on Cal-va-ry's mount out-poured,
in-fi-nite loss; Grace that is great-er, yes, grace un-told,
wash it a-way? Look! there is flow-ing a crim-son tide;
all who be-lieve; All who are long-ing to see His face,

Refrain

There where the blood of the Lamb was spilt.
Points to the ref-uge, the might-y cross. Grace, grace,
Whit-er than snow you may be to-day. Mar-vel-ous grace,
Will you this mo-ment His grace re-ceive?

God's grace, Grace that will par-don and cleanse with-in; Grace,
in-fi-nite grace, Mar-vel-ous

grace, God's grace, Grace that is great-er than all our sin.
grace, in-fi-nite grace,

THE GOSPEL

Jesus, Thy Blood and Righteousness 241

He hath clothed me with the garments of salvation . . . Isa. 61:10

Nikolaus L. von Zinzendorf, 1739
Trans. by John Wesley, 1740

GERMANY L.M.
William Gardiner's *Sacred Melodies*, 1815

1. Je - sus, Thy blood and right-eous-ness My beau - ty are, my glo - rious dress;
2. Bold shall I stand in Thy great day, For who aught to my charge shall lay?
3. Lord, I be - lieve Thy pre - cious blood, Which, at the mer - cy seat of God
4. Lord, I be - lieve were sin - ners more Than sands up - on the o - cean shore,

'Midst flam-ing worlds, in these ar-rayed, With joy shall I lift up my head.
Ful - ly ab-solved through these I am, From sin and fear, from guilt and shame.
For - ev - er doth for sin-ners plead, For me, e'en for my soul, was shed.
Thou hast for all a ran-som paid, For all a full a - tone-ment made. A-men.

Not What These Hands Have Done 242

Not by works of righteousness which we have done . . . Titus 3:5

Horatius Bonar, 1861

ST. ANDREW S.M.
Joseph Barnby, 1866

1. Not what these hands have done Can save this guilt - y soul; Not
2. Not what I feel or do Can give me peace with God; Not
3. Thy work a - lone, O Christ, Can ease this weight of sin; Thy
4. Thy grace a - lone, O God, To me can par - don speak; Thy
5. I bless the Christ of God; I rest on love di - vine; And,

what this toil - ing flesh has borne Can make my spir - it whole.
all my prayers and sighs and tears Can bear my aw - ful load.
blood a - lone, O Lamb of God, Can give me peace with - in.
power a - lone, O Son of God, Can this sore bon - dage break.
with un - fal - t'ring lip and heart, I call this Sav - ior mine. A-men.

THE WORK OF CHRIST

243 He Took My Feet from the Miry Clay

He brought me up also . . . out of the miry clay, and set my feet upon a rock. Psa. 40:2

Traditional Spiritual

YES, HE DID Irreg.
Traditional Spiritual

1. He took my feet from the mir - y clay, Yes, He did!
2. O my Lord did just what He said, Yes, He did!
3. O Je - sus washed my sins a - way, Yes, He did!
4. He died on the cross to save my soul, Yes, He did!

Yes, He did! And placed them on the rock to stay,
Yes, He did! He healed the sick and He raised the dead,
Yes, He did! And made me hap - py all the day,
Yes, He did! He ran - somed me and made me whole,

Refrain

Yes, He did, Yes, He did! I can tell the world a - bout this,

I can tell the na - tions I'm blest, Tell them that Je - sus

made me whole, And He brought joy, joy to my soul!

THE GOSPEL

Jesus, I Will Trust Thee 244

Lord, if Thou wilt, Thou canst make me clean. Luke 5:12

ST. ALBAN 6 5 6 5 D. Ref.

Mary J. Walker, 1864

Franz Joseph Haydn, 1732-1809

1. Je - sus, I will trust Thee, Trust Thee with my soul, Guilt - y, lost and
2. Je - sus, I must trust Thee, Pon - der - ing Thy ways, Full of love and
3. Je - sus, I do trust Thee, Trust with - out a doubt, Who - so - ev - er

help - less, Thou canst make me whole: There is none in heav - en
mer - cy All Thine earth - ly days: Sin - ners gath - ered round Thee,
com - eth, Thou wilt not cast out: Faith - ful is Thy prom - ise,

Or on earth like Thee: Thou hast died for sin - ners, There-fore, Lord, for me.
Lep - ers sought Thy face: None too vile or loath-some For a Sav - ior's grace.
Pre - cious is Thy blood: These my soul's sal - va - tion, Thou my Sav - ior God!

Refrain

Je - sus, I will trust Thee, Trust Thee with my soul,

Guilt - y, lost and help - less, Thou canst make me whole. A - men.

THE WORK OF CHRIST

245 Wonderful Grace of Jesus

For ye know the grace of our Lord Jesus Christ . . . II Cor. 8:9

WONDERFUL GRACE Irreg. Ref.

Haldor Lillenas, 1918

Haldor Lillenas, 1918

1. Won - der - ful grace of Je - sus, Great - er than all my sin;
2. Won - der - ful grace of Je - sus, Reach - ing to all the lost,
3. Won - der - ful grace of Je - sus, Reach - ing the most de - filed,

How shall my tongue de - scribe it, Where shall its praise be - gin?
By it I have been par - doned, Saved to the ut - ter - most;
By its trans-form - ing pow - er Mak - ing him God's dear child,

Tak - ing a - way my bur - den, Set - ting my spir - it free,
Chains have been torn a - sun - der, Giv - ing me lib - er - ty,
Pur - chas - ing peace and heav - en For all e - ter - ni - ty—

For the won - der - ful grace of Je - sus reach - es me.
For the won - der - ful grace of Je - sus reach - es me.
And the won - der - ful grace of Je - sus reach - es me.

Refrain

the match-less grace of Je - sus,

Won - der - ful the match-less grace of Je - sus, Deep - er than the

THE GOSPEL

might-y roll-ing sea; the roll-ing sea; Won - der-ful
High-er than the moun-tain,

grace, all suf-fi - cient for
spark-ling like a foun-tain, All suf-fi-cient grace for e - ven

me, for e - ven me, Broad - er than the scope of my trans-
me; trans-

gres - sions, Great - er far than all my sin and shame;
gres-sions, sing it! my sin and shame;

O mag - ni - fy the pre-cious name of Je - sus, Praise His name!

THE WORK OF CHRIST

246 Jesus, Lover of My Soul

Thou hast been . . . a refuge from the storm . . . Isa. 25:4

ABERYSTWYTH 7 7 7 7 D.

Charles Wesley, 1740

Joseph Parry, 1879

1. Je - sus, Lov - er of my soul, Let me to Thy bos - om fly,
2. Oth - er ref - uge have I none; Hangs my help - less soul on Thee;
3. Thou, O Christ, art all I want; More than all in Thee I find;
4. Plen - teous grace with Thee is found, Grace to cov - er all my sin;

While the near - er wa - ters roll, While the tem - pest still is high:
Leave, ah! leave me not a - lone, Still sup - port and com - fort me.
Raise the fall - en, cheer the faint, Heal the sick, and lead the blind.
Let the heal - ing streams a - bound; Make and keep me pure with - in.

Hide me, O my Sav - ior, hide, Till the storm of life is past;
All my trust on Thee is stayed, All my help from Thee I bring;
Just and ho - ly is Thy name, I am all un - right - eous - ness;
Thou of life the foun - tain art, Free - ly let me take of Thee;

Safe in - to the ha - ven guide; O re - ceive my soul at last!
Cov - er my de - fense-less head With the shad - ow of Thy wing.
False and full of sin I am, Thou art full of truth and grace.
Spring Thou up with - in my heart, Rise to all e - ter - ni - ty. A - men.

THE GOSPEL

I Lay My Sins on Jesus 247

Who . . . bare our sins in His own body on the tree . . . I Pet. 2:24

AURELIA 7 6 7 6 D.

Horatius Bonar, 1843

Samuel S. Wesley, 1864

1. I lay my sins on Je - sus, The spot - less Lamb of God;
2. I lay my wants on Je - sus; All ful - ness dwells in Him;
3. I rest my soul on Je - sus, This wea - ry soul of mine;
4. I long to be like Je - sus, Meek, lov - ing, low - ly, mild;

He bears them all, and frees us From the ac - curs - ed load:
He heals all my dis - eas - es, He doth my soul re - deem:
His right hand me em - brac - es, I on His breast re - cline:
I long to be like Je - sus, The Fa - ther's ho - ly Child:

I bring my guilt to Je - sus, To wash my crim - son stains
I lay my griefs on Je - sus, My bur - dens and my cares;
I love the name of Je - sus, Im - man - uel, Christ the Lord;
I long to be with Je - sus, A - mid the heav'n - ly throng,

White in His blood most pre - cious, Till not a stain re - mains.
He from them all re - leas - es, He all my sor - rows shares.
Like fra - grance on the breez - es, His name a - broad is poured.
To sing with saints His prais - es, To learn the an - gels' song. A - men.

This tune in a lower key, No. 560

THE WORK OF CHRIST

248 And Can It Be That I Should Gain

While we were yet sinners, Christ died for us. Rom. 5:8

Charles Wesley, 1738

SAGINA L.M.D.
Thomas Campbell, 1825

1. And can it be that I should gain An in - t'rest in the
2. 'Tis mys - tery all! Th' Im - mor - tal dies! Who can ex - plore His
3. He left His Fa - ther's throne a - bove, So free, so in - fi -
4. Long my im - pris - oned spir - it lay Fast bound in sin and
5. No con - dem - na - tion now I dread; Je - sus, and all in

Sav - ior's blood? Died He for me, who caused His pain? For me, who
strange de - sign? In vain the first - born ser - aph tries To sound the
nite His grace; Emp - tied Him - self of all but love, And bled for
na - ture's night; Thine eye dif - fused a quick -'ning ray, I woke, the
Him, is mine! A - live in Him, my liv - ing Head, And clothed in

Him to death pur - sued? A - maz - ing love! how can it be That
depths of love di - vine! 'Tis mer - cy all! let earth a - dore, Let
Ad - am's help - less race; 'Tis mer - cy all, im - mense and free; For,
dun - geon flamed with light; My chains fell off, my heart was free; I
right - eous - ness di - vine, Bold I ap - proach th'e - ter - nal throne, And

Refrain

Thou, my God, shouldst die for me?
an - gel minds in - quire no more.
O my God, it found out me. A - maz - ing love! how
rose, went forth and fol - lowed Thee.
claim the crown, through Christ my own. A - maz-ing love!

THE GOSPEL

can it be That Thou, my God, shouldst die for me. A - men.
How can it be   That Thou, my God,

There Shall Be Showers of Blessing 249

There shall be showers of blessing . . . Ezek. 34:26

SHOWERS OF BLESSING 8 7 8 7 Ref.

Daniel W. Whittle, 1883

James McGranahan, 1883

1. There shall be show-ers of bless - ing: This is the prom-ise of love;
2. There shall be show-ers of bless - ing — Pre-cious re - viv - ing a - gain;
3. There shall be show-ers of bless - ing: Send them up - on us, O Lord;
4. There shall be show-ers of bless - ing: O, that to - day they might fall,

There shall be sea - sons re - fresh - ing, Sent from the Sav - ior a - bove.
O - ver the hills and the val - leys, Sound of a - bun-dance of rain.
Grant to us now a re - fresh - ing, Come, and now hon - or Thy Word.
Now as to God we're con - fess - ing, Now, as on Je - sus we call!

Refrain

Show ers of bless - ing, Show - ers of bless - ing we need:
Show - ers, show - ers of bless - ing,

Mer - cy - drops 'round us are fall - ing, But for the show - ers we plead.

THE WORK OF CHRIST

250 Arise, My Soul, Arise!

He ever liveth to make intercession for them. Heb. 7:25

TOWNER 6 6 6 6 8 8

Charles Wesley. 1742

Traditional American melody
Arr. by Daniel B. Towner, 1909

1. A - rise, my soul, a - rise! Shake off thy guilt - y fears;
2. He ev - er lives a - bove, For me to in - ter - cede;
3. Five bleed - ing wounds He bears, Re - ceived on Cal - va - ry;
4. The Fa - ther hears Him pray, His dear a - noint - ed One;
5. My God is rec - on - ciled, His par - d'ning voice I hear;

The bleed - ing Sac - ri - fice In my be - half ap - pears.
His all - re - deem - ing love, His pre - cious blood to plead;
They pour ef - fec - tual prayers, They strong - ly plead for me;
He can - not turn a - way The pres - ence of His Son:
He owns me for His child, I can no long - er fear;

Be - fore the throne my Sure - ty stands; My name is writ - ten
His blood a - toned for all our race, And sprin - kles now the
"For - give him, O for - give," they cry, "Nor let that ran - somed
His Spir - it an - swers to the blood, And tells me I am
With con - fi - dence I now draw nigh, And "Fa - ther, Ab - ba,

on His hands, My name is writ - ten on His hands.
throne of grace, And sprin - kles now the throne of grace.
sin - ner die! Nor let that ran - somed sin - ner die!"
born of God, And tells me I am born of God.
Fa - ther" cry, And "Fa - ther, Ab - ba, Fa - ther" cry.

THE GOSPEL

My Song Shall Be of Jesus 251

My servants shall sing for joy of heart. Isa. 65:14

Fanny J. Crosby, 1875
Adapt. by E. Margaret Clarkson, 1973

ALSTYNE 7 6 7 6 D.
William H. Doane, 1875

1. My song shall be of Je - sus, His mer - cy crowns my days,
2. My song shall be of Je - sus, When sit - ting at His feet,
3. My song shall be of Je - sus, While press - ing on my way

He fills my cup with bless - ings, And tunes my heart to praise;
I call to mind His good - ness And know my joy's com - plete;
To where my home shines glo - rious In pure and per - fect day.

My song shall be of Je - sus, The pre - cious Lamb of God,
My song shall be of Je - sus, What - ev - er ills be - fall,
And when my soul shall en - ter The man - y man - sions fair,

Who gave Him - self my ran - som, And bought me with His blood.
I'll sing the grace that saves me, And tri - umphs o - ver all.
A song of praise to Je - sus I'll sing for - ev - er there.

THE WORK OF CHRIST

252 O Soul, Are You Weary and Troubled?

Look unto Me, and be ye saved, all the ends of the earth. Isa. 45:22

Helen H. Lemmel, 1922

LEMMEL 9 8 9 8 Ref.
Helen H. Lemmel, 1922

1. O soul, are you wea-ry and troub-led? No light in the
2. Through death in-to life ev-er-last-ing He passed, and we
3. His word shall not fail you— He prom-ised; Be-lieve Him and

dark-ness you see? There's light for a look at the Sav-ior,
fol-low Him there; O-ver us sin no more hath do-min-ion—
all will be well: Then go to a world that is dy-ing,

Refrain

And life more a-bun-dant and free!
For more than con-qu'rors we are! Turn your eyes up-on Je-
His per-fect sal-va-tion to tell!

sus, Look full in His won-der-ful face; And the things of

earth will grow strange-ly dim In the light of His glo-ry and grace.

THE GOSPEL

A Ruler Once Came to Jesus by Night 253

Except a man be born again, he cannot see the kingdom of God. John 3:3

BORN AGAIN Irreg. Ref.

William T. Sleeper, 1877

George C. Stebbins, 1877

1. A rul-er once came to Je-sus by night To ask Him the
2. Ye chil-dren of men, at-tend to the word So sol-emn-ly
3. O ye who would en-ter that glo-ri-ous rest, And sing with the

way of sal-va-tion and light; The Mas-ter made an-swer in words true and plain,
ut-tered by Je-sus the Lord; And let not this mes-sage to you be in vain,
ran-somed the song of the blest; The life ev-er-last-ing if ye would ob-tain,

Refrain

"Ye must be born a-gain." "Ye must be born a-
a-gain."

gain, Ye must be born a-gain; I ver-i-ly,
a-gain, a-gain;

ver-i-ly say un-to thee, Ye must be born a-gain."
a-gain."

THE CALL OF CHRIST

254 "Whosoever Heareth," Shout, Shout

Whosoever will, let him take the water of life freely. Rev. 22:17

Philip P. Bliss, 1870

WHOSOEVER Irreg. Ref.
Philip P. Bliss, 1870

1. "Who - so - ev - er hear-eth," shout, shout the sound! Spread the bless-ed ti - dings
2. Who - so - ev - er com-eth need not de - lay, Now the door is o - pen,
3. "Who - so - ev - er will," the prom-ise is se - cure; "Who-so - ev - er will," for-

all the world a - round; Tell the joy - ful news wher-ev - er man is found,
en - ter while you may; Je - sus is the true, the on - ly Liv - ing Way:
ev - er must en - dure; "Who - so - ev - er will," 'tis life for - ev - er-more;

Refrain

"Who - so - ev - er will may come." Who - so - ev - er will, who - so - ev - er will!

Send the proc - la - ma - tion o - ver vale and hill; 'Tis a lov - ing

Fa - ther calls the wan - d'rer home: "Who - so - ev - er will may come."

THE GOSPEL

Would You Be Free from the Burden 255

In whom we have redemption through His blood . . . Col. 1:14

POWER IN THE BLOOD 10 9 10 8 Ref.

Lewis E. Jones, 1899

Lewis E. Jones, 1899

1. Would you be free from the bur-den of sin? There's pow'r in the blood,
2. Would you be free from your pas-sion and pride? There's pow'r in the blood,
3. Would you be whit-er, much whit-er than snow? There's pow'r in the blood,
4. Would you do serv-ice for Je-sus your King? There's pow'r in the blood,

pow'r in the blood; Would you o'er e-vil a vic-to-ry win? There's
pow'r in the blood; Come for a cleans-ing to Cal-va-ry's tide? There's
pow'r in the blood; Sin-stains are lost in its life-giv-ing flow; There's
pow'r in the blood; Would you live dai-ly His prais-es to sing? There's

Refrain

won-der-ful pow'r in the blood. There is pow'r,   pow'r, won-der-work-ing pow'r
                                        there is

In the blood   of the Lamb;   There is pow'r,   pow'r,
    In the blood   of the Lamb;   there is

won-der-work-ing pow'r In the pre-cious blood of the Lamb.

THE CALL OF CHRIST

256 Come to the Savior Now

The Master is come, and calleth for thee. John 11:28

John M. Wigner, 1871

INVITATION 6 6 6 6 D.
Frederick C. Maker, 1881

1. Come to the Sav-ior now, He gen-tly calls to you;
2. Come to the Sav-ior now, You who have wan-dered far;
3. Bring to the Sav-ior Ev-ery bur-den there may be;

In true re-pent-ance bow, In full com-mit-ment, too;
Re-new your sol-emn vow, For His by right you are;
Hear now His lov-ing call, "Cast all your care on Me."

His word has prom-ised us Sal-va-tion, peace, and love,
Come, like poor wan-dering sheep Re-turn-ing to the fold;
Come, and for ev-ery grief In Je-sus you will find

True joy on earth be-low, A home in heav'n a-bove.
His arm will safe-ly keep, His love will not grow cold.
Help, com-fort and re-lief, A lov-ing friend and kind.

The Savior Is Waiting 257

Today if ye will hear His voice, harden not your hearts . . . Heb. 3:7,8

CARMICHAEL 11 7 11 7 Ref.

Ralph Carmichael, 1958

Ralph Carmichael, 1958

1. The Sav - ior is wait - ing to en - ter your heart, Why don't you
2. If you'll take one step t'ward the Sav - ior, my friend, You'll find His

let Him come in? There's noth-ing in this world to keep you a - part,
arms o - pen wide; Re-ceive Him, and all of your dark-ness will end,

Refrain

What is your an - swer to Him?
With - in your heart He'll a - bide. Time af - ter time He has

wait - ed be - fore, And now He is wait - ing a - gain To

see if you're will-ing to o - pen the door, O, how He wants to come in.

THE CALL OF CHRIST

258 Come, Every Soul by Sin Oppressed

He is able also to save them to the uttermost . . . Heb. 7:25

John H. Stockton, 1874

MINERVA C.M. Ref.
John H. Stockton, 1874

1. Come, ev - ery soul by sin op - pressed, There's mer - cy with the Lord;
2. For Je - sus shed His pre - cious blood, Rich bless - ings to be - stow;
3. Yes, Je - sus is the Truth, the Way, That leads you in - to rest:
4. Come, then, and join this ho - ly band, And on to glo - ry go,

And He will sure - ly give you rest By trust - ing in His word.
Plunge now in - to the crim - son flood That wash - es white as snow.
Be - lieve in Him with - out de - lay, And you are ful - ly blest.
To dwell in that ce - les - tial land, Where joys im - mor - tal flow.

Refrain

On - ly trust Him, on - ly trust Him, On - ly trust Him now.
He will save you, He will save you, He will save you now.

259 Are You Weary, Heavy Laden?

Come unto Me, all ye that labor and are heavy laden . . . Matt. 11:28

John M. Neale, 1862
Based on an early Greek hymn

STEPHANOS 8 5 8 3
Henry W. Baker, 1868

1. Are you wea - ry, heav - y lad - en, Are you sore dis - tressed?
2. Has He marks to lead me to Him, If He be my Guide?
3. Is there di - a - dem, as Mon - arch, That His brow a - dorns?
4. If I still hold close - ly to Him, What has He at last?
5. If I ask Him to re - ceive me, Will He tell me nay?

THE GOSPEL

"Come to Me," says One, "and, com - ing, Be at rest."
"In His feet and hands are wound - prints, And His side."
"Yes, a crown, in ver - y sure - ty, But of thorns."
"Sor - row van - quished, la - bor end - ed, Jor - dan passed."
"Not till earth and not till heav - en Pass a - way." A - men.

Just As I Am, without One Plea 260

Him that cometh to Me I will in no wise cast out. John 6:37

WOODWORTH L.M. Coda

Charlotte Elliott, 1834

William B. Bradbury, 1849

1. Just as I am, with - out one plea But that Thy blood was
2. Just as I am, and wait - ing not To rid my soul of
3. Just as I am, though tossed a - bout With man - y a con - flict,
4. Just as I am, poor, wretch - ed, blind; Sight, rich - es, heal - ing
5. Just as I am, Thou wilt re - ceive, Wilt wel - come, par - don,

shed for me, And that Thou bidd'st me come to Thee, O
one dark blot, To Thee whose blood can cleanse each spot, O
man - y a doubt, Fight - ings and fears with - in, with - out, O
of the mind, Yea, all I need, in Thee I find, O
cleanse, re - lieve; Be - cause Thy prom - ise I be - lieve, O

Coda (after last stanza)

Lamb of God, I come! I come!
Lamb of God, I come! I come!
Lamb of God, I come! I come!
Lamb of God, I come! I come!
Lamb of God, I come! I come! O Lamb of God, I come. A - men.

THE CALL OF CHRIST

261 The Whole World Was Lost

I am the light of the world . . . John 8:12

LIGHT OF THE WORLD 11 8 11 8 Ref.

Philip P. Bliss, 1875

Philip P. Bliss, 1875

1. The whole world was lost in the dark-ness of sin; The Light of the
2. No dark-ness have we who in Je-sus a-bide, The Light of the
3. Ye dwell-ers in dark-ness with sin-blind-ed eyes, The Light of the
4. No need of the sun-light in heav-en, we're told, The Light of the

world is Je-sus; Like sun-shine at noon-day His glo-ry shone in,
world is Je-sus; We walk in the Light when we fol-low our Guide,
world is Je-sus; Go wash at His bid-ding and light will a-rise,
world is Je-sus; The Lamb is the Light in the Cit-y of Gold,

Refrain

The Light of the world is Je-sus. Come to the Light, 'tis

shin-ing for thee; Sweet-ly the Light has dawned up-on me;

Once I was blind, but now I can see; The Light of the world is Je-sus.

THE GOSPEL

O Jesus, Thou Art Standing 262

If any man . . . open the door, I will come in to him. Rev. 3:20

ST. HILDA 7 6 7 6 D.

Justin H. Knecht, 1799, and
Edward Husband, 1871

William W. How, 1867

1. O Je - sus, Thou art stand - ing Out - side the fast - closed door,
2. O Je - sus, Thou art knock - ing; And lo! that hand is scarred,
3. O Je - sus, Thou art plead - ing In ac - cents meek and low,

In low - ly pa - tience wait - ing To pass the thresh - old o'er:
And thorns Thy brow en - cir - cle, And tears Thy face have marred:
"I died for you, My chil - dren, And will ye treat Me so?"

Shame on us, Chris - tian bro - thers, His Name and sign who bear,
O love that pass - eth knowl - edge, So pa - tient - ly to wait!
O Lord, with shame and sor - row We o - pen now the door;

O shame, thrice shame up - on us, To keep Him stand - ing there!
O sin that hath no e - qual, So fast to bar the gate!
Dear Sav - ior, en - ter, en - ter, And leave us nev - er - more! A-men.

THE CALL OF CHRIST

263 Somebody's Knocking at Your Door

Behold, I stand at the door and knock . . . Rev. 3:20

Traditional Spiritual

SOMEBODY'S KNOCKING Irreg.
Traditional Spiritual

Unison

(Ref.) Some-bod-y's knock-ing at your door, Some-bod-y's knock-ing at your door,

O sin-ner, why don't you an-swer? Some-bod-y's knock-ing at your door.

Verses (with refrain)

1. Knocks like Je-sus,
2. Can't you hear Him? Some-bod-y's knock-ing at your door.
3. An-swer Je-sus,

Knocks like Je-sus,
Can't you hear Him? Some-bod-y's knock-ing at your door,
An-swer Je-sus,

D.S.

O sin-ner, why don't you an-swer? Some-bod-y's knock-ing at your door.

THE GOSPEL

Have You Any Room for Jesus? 264

Today if ye will hear His voice, harden not your hearts . . . Heb. 3:15

Source unknown
Adapt. by Daniel W. Whittle, 1878

ANY ROOM 8 7 8 7 Ref.
C. C. Williams, 1878

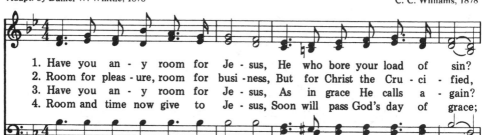

1. Have you an - y room for Je - sus, He who bore your load of sin?
2. Room for pleas - ure, room for busi - ness, But for Christ the Cru - ci - fied,
3. Have you an - y room for Je - sus, As in grace He calls a - gain?
4. Room and time now give to Je - sus, Soon will pass God's day of grace;

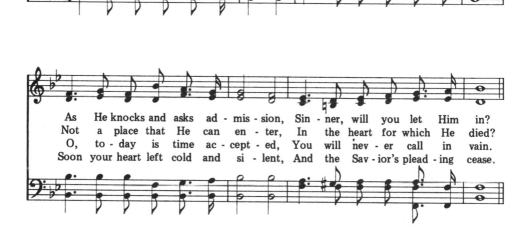

As He knocks and asks ad - mis - sion, Sin - ner, will you let Him in?
Not a place that He can en - ter, In the heart for which He died?
O, to - day is time ac - cept - ed, You will nev - er call in vain.
Soon your heart left cold and si - lent, And the Sav - ior's plead - ing cease.

Refrain

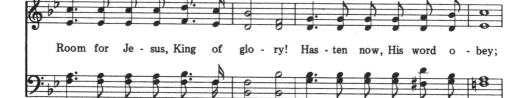

Room for Je - sus, King of glo - ry! Has - ten now, His word o - bey;

Swing the heart's door wide - ly o - pen, Bid Him en - ter while you may.

THE CALL OF CHRIST

265 I've a Message from the Lord

When he looketh upon it, he shall live. Num. 21:8

William A. Ogden, 1887

LOOK AND LIVE Irreg. Ref.
William A. Ogden, 1887

1. I've a mes-sage from the Lord, Hal-le-lu-jah! The mes-sage un-to you I'll
give; 'Tis re-cord-ed in His word, Hal-le-lu-jah! It is
on-ly that you "look and live."

2. I've a mes-sage full of love, Hal-le-lu-jah! A mes-sage, O my friend, for
you; 'Tis a mes-sage from a-bove, Hal-le-lu-jah! Je-sus
said it and I know 'tis true. Look and live, O sin-ner,

3. Life is of-fered un-to you, Hal-le-lu-jah! E-ter-nal life your soul shall
have, If you'll on-ly look to Him, Hal-le-lu-jah! Look to
Je-sus, who a-lone can save. Look and live, O sin-ner,

Refrain

live, Look to Je-sus now and live; 'Tis re-
live, Look and live,

cord-ed in His word, Hal-le-lu-jah! It is on-ly that you look and live.

THE GOSPEL

Softly and Tenderly Jesus Is Calling 266

Come unto Me, all ye that labor and are heavy laden . . . Matt. 11:28

Will L. Thompson, 1880

THOMPSON 11 7 11 7 Ref.
Will L. Thompson, 1880

1. Soft - ly and ten - der - ly Je - sus is call - ing, Call - ing for
2. Why should we tar - ry when Je - sus is plead - ing, Plead - ing for
3. Time is now fleet - ing, the mo - ments are pass - ing, Pass - ing from
4. O for the won - der - ful love He has prom - ised, Prom - ised for

you and for me; See, on the por - tals He's wait - ing and watch - ing,
you and for me? Why should we lin - ger and heed not His mer - cies,
you and from me; Shad - ows are gath - er - ing, death's night is com - ing,
you and for me! Though we have sinned, He has mer - cy and par - don,

Refrain

Watch - ing for you and for me.
Mer - cies for you and for me?
Com - ing for you and for me.
Par - don for you and for me.

Come home, come home,
Come home, come home,

Ye who are wea - ry, come home; Ear - nest - ly, ten - der - ly,

Je - sus is call - ing, Call - ing, O sin - ner, come home!

THE CALL OF CHRIST

267 Out of My Bondage, Sorrow and Night

He hath sent Me . . . to proclaim liberty to the captives . . . Isa. 61:1

William T. Sleeper, 1887

JESUS, I COME Irreg.
George C. Stebbins, 1887

1. Out of my bond-age, sor-row and night, Je-sus, I come, Je-sus, I come;
2. Out of my shame-ful fail-ure and loss, Je-sus, I come, Je-sus, I come;
3. Out of un-rest and ar-ro-gant pride, Je-sus, I come, Je-sus, I come;
4. Out of the fear and dread of the tomb, Je-sus, I come, Je-sus, I come;

In-to Thy free-dom, glad-ness and light, Je-sus, I come to Thee.
In-to the glo-rious gain of Thy cross, Je-sus, I come to Thee.
In-to Thy bless-ed will to a-bide, Je-sus, I come to Thee.
In-to the joy and light of Thy home, Je-sus, I come to Thee.

Out of my sick-ness in-to Thy health, Out of my want and in-to Thy wealth,
Out of earth's sor-rows in-to Thy balm, Out of life's storms and in-to Thy calm,
Out of my-self to dwell in Thy love, Out of de-spair in-to rap-tures a-bove,
Out of the depths of ru-in un-told, In-to the peace of Thy shel-ter-ing fold,

Out of my sin and in-to Thy-self, Je-sus, I come to Thee.
Out of dis-tress to ju-bi-lant psalm, Je-sus, I come to Thee.
Up-ward for aye on wings like a dove, Je-sus, I come to Thee.
Ev-er Thy glo-rious face to be-hold, Je-sus, I come to Thee.

THE GOSPEL

If You Are Tired of the Load of Your Sin 268

Behold, now is the accepted time . . . now is the day of salvation. II Cor. 6:2

McCONNELSVILLE 10 8 10 8 Ref.

Lelia N. Morris, 1898

Lelia N. Morris, 1898

1. If you are tired of the load of your sin, Let Je-sus come
2. If 'tis for pu-ri-ty now that you sigh, Let Je-sus come
3. If there's a tem-pest your voice can-not still, Let Je-sus come
4. If you would join the glad songs of the blest, Let Je-sus come

in-to your heart; If you de-sire a new life to be-gin,
in-to your heart; Foun-tains for cleans-ing are flow-ing near by,
in-to your heart; If there's a void this world nev-er can fill,
in-to your heart; If you would en-ter the man-sions of rest,

Refrain

Let Je-sus come in-to your heart. Just now your

doubt-ings give o'er; Just now re-ject Him no more; Just now throw

o-pen the door; Let Je-sus come in-to your heart.

THE CALL OF CHRIST

269 Come, Ye Sinners, Poor and Needy

Him that cometh to Me I will in no wise cast out. John 6:37

Joseph Hart, 1759
Refrain, source unknown

ARISE 8 7 8 7 Ref.
Traditional American melody

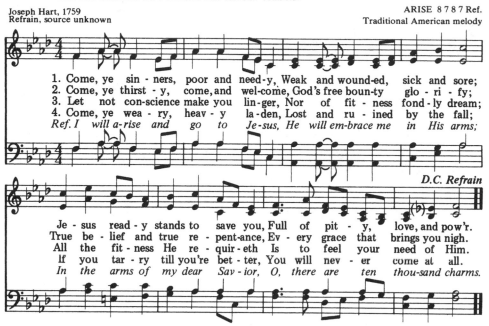

1. Come, ye sin-ners, poor and need-y, Weak and wound-ed, sick and sore;
2. Come, ye thirst-y, come, and wel-come, God's free boun-ty glo-ri-fy;
3. Let not con-science make you lin-ger, Nor of fit-ness fond-ly dream;
4. Come, ye wea-ry, heav-y la-den, Lost and ru-ined by the fall;
Ref. I will a-rise and go to Je-sus, He will em-brace me in His arms;

D.C. Refrain

Je-sus read-y stands to save you, Full of pit-y, love, and pow'r.
True be-lief and true re-pent-ance, Ev-ery grace that brings you nigh.
All the fit-ness He re-quir-eth Is to feel your need of Him.
If you tar-ry till you're bet-ter, You will nev-er come at all.
In the arms of my dear Sav-ior, O, there are ten thou-sand charms.

270 I Am Coming to the Cross

If we confess our sins, He is faithful and just to forgive . . . I John 1:9

William McDonald, 1870

TRUSTING 7 7 7 7 Ref.
William G. Fischer, 1870

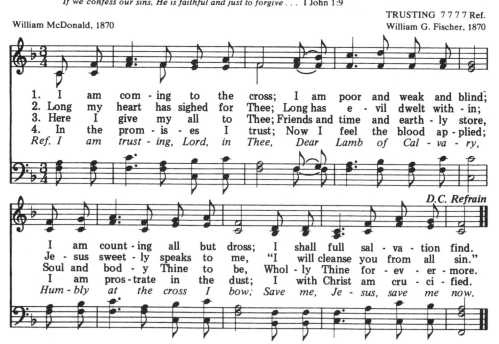

1. I am com-ing to the cross; I am poor and weak and blind;
2. Long my heart has sighed for Thee; Long has e-vil dwelt with-in;
3. Here I give my all to Thee; Friends and time and earth-ly store,
4. In the prom-is-es I trust; Now I feel the blood ap-plied;
Ref. I am trust-ing, Lord, in Thee, Dear Lamb of Cal-va-ry,

D.C. Refrain

I am count-ing all but dross; I shall full sal-va-tion find.
Je-sus sweet-ly speaks to me, "I will cleanse you from all sin."
Soul and bod-y Thine to be, Whol-ly Thine for-ev-er-more.
I am pros-trate in the dust; I with Christ am cru-ci-fied.
Hum-bly at the cross I bow; Save me, Je-sus, save me now.

THE GOSPEL

Sinners Jesus Will Receive 271

This man receiveth sinners ... Luke 15:2

Erdmann Neumeister, 1718
Trans. by Emma F. Bevan, 1858

NEUMEISTER 7 7 7 7 Ref.
James McGranahan, 1883

1. Sin - ners Je - sus will re - ceive; Sound this word of grace to all
2. Come, and He will give you rest; Trust Him, for His word is plain;
3. Now my heart con-demns me not, Pure be - fore the law I stand;
4. Christ re - ceiv - eth sin - ful men, E - ven me with all my sin;

Who the heav'n - ly path - way leave, All who lin - ger, all who fall.
He will take the sin - ful - est; Christ re - ceiv - eth sin - ful men.
He who cleansed me from all spot, Sat - is - fied its last de - mand.
Purged from ev - ery spot and stain, Heav'n with Him I en - ter in.

Refrain

Sing it o'er and o'er a - gain, Christ re -
Sing it o'er and o'er a - gain,

ceiv - eth sin - ful men; Make the mes - sage
Christ re - ceiv - eth sin - ful men; Make the mes -

clear and plain, Christ re - ceiv - eth sin - ful men.
sage clear and plain,

THE CALL OF CHRIST

272 Jesus Is Tenderly Calling You Home

Today if ye will hear His voice, harden not your hearts . . . Heb. 3:15

Fanny J. Crosby, 1883

CALLING TODAY Irreg. Ref.
George C. Stebbins, 1883

1. Je - sus is ten - der - ly call - ing you home, Call - ing to - day,
2. Je - sus is call - ing the wea - ry to rest, Call - ing to - day,
3. Je - sus is wait - ing, O come to Him now, Wait - ing to - day,
4. Je - sus is plead - ing, O list to His voice: Hear Him to - day,

call - ing to - day, Why from the sun - shine of love will you roam
call - ing to - day, Bring Him your bur - den and you shall be blest;
wait - ing to - day, Come with your sins, at His feet low - ly bow;
hear Him to - day, They who be - lieve on His name shall re - joice;

Refrain

Far - ther and far - ther a - way? Call - ing to - day,
He will not turn you a - way.
Come, and no long - er de - lay.
Quick - ly a - rise and a - way. Call - ing, call - ing to - day, to - day,

Call - ing to - day, Je - sus is
Call - ing, call - ing to - day, to - day, Je - sus is ten - der - ly

call - ing, Is ten - der - ly call - ing to - day.
call - ing to - day,

THE GOSPEL

"Give Me Thy Heart," Says the Father 273

My son, give Me thine heart . . . Prov. 23:26

ZERUIAH 10 10 10 10 Ref.

Eliza E. Hewitt, 1898

William J. Kirkpatrick, 1898

1. "Give Me thy heart," says the Fa-ther a-bove, No gift so pre-cious to
2. "Give Me thy heart," says the Sav-ior of men, Call-ing in mer-cy a-
3. "Give Me thy heart," says the Spir-it di-vine, "All that thou hast, to My

Him as our love; Soft-ly He whis-pers, wher-ev-er thou art,
gain and a-gain; "Turn now from sin, and from e-vil de-part,
keep-ing re-sign; Grace more a-bound-ing is Mine to im-part,

Refrain

"Grate-ful-ly trust Me, and give Me thy heart."
Have I not died for thee? give Me thy heart." "Give Me thy heart,
Make full sur-ren-der and give Me thy heart."

give Me thy heart," Hear the soft whis-per, wher-ev-er thou art: From this dark

world He would draw thee a-part; Speak-ing so ten-der-ly, "Give Me thy heart."

THE CALL OF CHRIST

274 I've Heard the King

I will come in to him, and will sup with him, and he with Me. Rev. 3:20

Grant C. Tullar, 1953

HIGHLANDS 9 12 9 12 Ref.

Donald P. Hustad, 1953

1. I've heard the King! The King of heav-en! Nor can I e'er for-get the
2. I've heard the King! The King of glo-ry; For whom my heart's door o-pened
3. I've heard the King! O, had I missed Him, My life for-ev-er-more could
4. I've heard the King! and now I'm tell-ing To all the world the gos-pel

mu-sic of His voice. I've heard the King! His call I've an-swered. I've made the
wide and He came in. I've heard the King! O, bless-ed hear-ing, His voice spoke
not re-gain the loss. From heav'n He came, the world to ran-som, And this He
of un-dy-ing love, That oth-ers too may catch the mu-sic His voice can

Refrain

King of heav'n my ev-er-last-ing choice.
peace and par-don for my guilt and sin. He came to me, and with Him came a
did one day on Cal-v'ry's cru-el cross.
bring, and find their way to heav'n a-bove.

bless-ing. He spoke to me, and glo-ry filled my soul; His voice I heard, so

charm-ing and so won-drous. I've heard the King, and hear-ing am made whole.

THE GOSPEL

Come, We That Love the Lord 275

Let the children of Zion be joyful in their King. Psa. 149:2

Isaac Watts, 1707
Refrain, Robert Lowry, 1867

MARCHING TO ZION 6 6 8 8 6 6 Ref.

Robert Lowry, 1867

1. Come, we that love the Lord, And let our joys be known,
2. Let those re - fuse to sing Who nev - er knew our God,
3. The hill of Zi - on yields A thou - sand sa - cred sweets
4. Then let our songs a - bound, And ev - ery tear be dry;

Join in a song with sweet ac - cord, Join in a song with sweet ac - cord
But chil - dren of the heav'n - ly King, But chil - dren of the heav'n - ly King
Be - fore we reach the heav'n - ly fields, Be - fore we reach the heav'n - ly fields
We're march - ing thro' Im-manuel's ground, We're march - ing thro' Im-manuel's ground

And thus sur - round the throne, And thus sur - round the throne.
May speak their joys a - broad, May speak their joys a - broad.
Or walk the gold - en streets, Or walk the gold - en streets.
To fair - er worlds on high, To fair - er worlds on high.

Refrain

We're march - ing to Zi - on, Beau - ti - ful, beau - ti - ful Zi - on;
We're march - ing on to Zi - on,

We're march - ing up - ward to Zi - on, The beau - ti - ful cit - y of God.

Alternate tune without refrain. ST. THOMAS, No. 23

SONGS OF WITNESS

276 In the Stars His Handiwork I See

When I consider Thy heavens . . . what is man, that Thou art mindful of him? Psa. 8:3,4

HE'S EVERYTHING TO ME Irreg.

Ralph Carmichael, 1964

Ralph Carmichael, 1964

Unison

1. In the stars His hand-i-work I see, On the wind He speaks in maj-es-ty,
2. I will cel - e - brate na-tiv - i - ty For it has a place in his-to-ry,

Though He ruleth o - ver land and sea, What is that to me?
Sure, He came to set His people free, What is that to

me? Till by faith I met Him face to face, And I felt the won-der of His grace,

Then I knew that He was more than just a God who did-n't care, who lived a-way out

there, And now He walks be-side me day by day, Ev - er watch-ing o'er me lest I stray,

THE GOSPEL

Helping me to find that nar-row way, He's ev-ery-thing to me.

Jesus My Lord Will Love Me Forever 277

Whether we live, therefore, or die, we are the Lord's. Rom. 14:8

ELLSWORTH 10 10 9 6 Ref.

Norman J. Clayton, 1943

Norman J. Clayton, 1943

1. Je-sus my Lord will love me for-ev-er, From Him no pow'r of e-vil can sev-er, He gave His life to ran-som my soul, Now I be-long to Him;
2. Once I was lost in sin's deg-ra-da-tion, Je-sus came down to bring me sal-va-tion, Lift-ed me up from sor-row and shame, Now I be-long to Him;
3. Joy floods my soul for Je-sus has saved me, Freed me from sin that long had en-slaved me, His pre-cious blood He gave to re-deem, Now I be-long to Him;

Refrain

Now I be-long to Je-sus, Je-sus be-longs to me,

Not for the years of time a-lone, But for e-ter-ni-ty.

SONGS OF WITNESS

278 Jesus Is All the World to Me

I have called you friends. John 15:15

ELIZABETH Irreg.
Will L. Thompson, 1904

Will L. Thompson, 1904

1. Je - sus is all the world to me, My life, my joy, my all;
2. Je - sus is all the world to me, My Friend in tri - als sore;
3. Je - sus is all the world to me, And true to Him I'll be;
4. Je - sus is all the world to me, I want no bet - ter friend;

He is my strength from day to day, With - out Him I would fall.
I go to Him for bless - ings, and He gives them o'er and o'er.
O, how could I this Friend de - ny, When He's so true to me?
I trust Him now, I'll trust Him when Life's fleet - ing days shall end.

When I am sad to Him I go, No oth - er one can cheer me so;
He sends the sun-shine and the rain, He sends the har-vest's gold - en grain;
Fol - low - ing Him I know I'm right, He watch - es o'er me day and night;
Beau - ti - ful life with such a Friend; Beau - ti - ful life that has no end;

When I am sad He makes me glad, He's my Friend.
Sun - shine and rain, har - vest of grain, He's my Friend.
Fol - low - ing Him by day and night, He's my Friend.
E - ter - nal life, e - ter - nal joy, He's my Friend.

THE GOSPEL

Alas! and Did My Savior Bleed? 279

Surely He hath borne our griefs, and carried our sorrows. Isa. 53:4

Isaac Watts, 1707
Refrain, Ralph E. Hudson, 1885

HUDSON C.M. Ref.
Ralph E. Hudson, 1885

1. A - las! and did my Sav - ior bleed? And did my Sov -'reign die?
2. Was it for crimes that I have done He groaned up - on the tree?
3. Well might the sun in dark - ness hide, And shut his glo - ries in,
4. But drops of grief can ne'er re - pay The debt of love I owe:

Would He de - vote that sa - cred head For sin - ners such as I?
A - maz - ing pit - y! grace un - known! And love be - yond de - gree!
When Christ, the might - y Mak - er, died For man the crea - ture's sin.
Here, Lord, I give my - self a - way, 'Tis all that I can do!

Refrain

At the cross, at the cross where I first saw the light, And the

bur - den of my heart rolled a - way, (rolled a - way,) It was there by faith

I re - ceived my sight, And now I am hap - py all the day!

Alternate tune without refrain, MARTYRDOM, No. 156

SONGS OF WITNESS

280 I Have a Song I Love to Sing

Let the redeemed of the Lord say so . . . Psa. 107:2

Edwin O. Excell, 1884

OTHELLO C.M. Ref.
Edwin O. Excell, 1884

1. I have a song I love to sing, Since I have been re-deemed,
2. I have a Christ who sat-is-fies, Since I have been re-deemed;
3. I have a wit-ness bright and clear, Since I have been re-deemed,
4. I have a home pre-pared for me, Since I have been re-deemed,

Of my Re-deem-er, Sav-ior, King, Since I have been re-deemed.
To do His will my high-est prize, Since I have been re-deemed.
Dis-pel-ling ev-ery doubt and fear, Since I have been re-deemed.
Where I shall dwell e-ter-nal-ly, Since I have been re-deemed.

Refrain

Since I have been re-deemed, Since I have been re-
Since I have been re-deemed, Since I have been re-deemed,

deemed, I will glo-ry in His name; Since I have been re-
Since I have been re-deemed, Since

deemed, I will glo-ry in my Sav-ior's name.
I have been re-deemed,

THE GOSPEL

What a Wonderful Change in My Life 281

If any man be in Christ, he is a new creature . . . II Cor. 5:17

Rufus H. McDaniel, 1914

McDANIEL 12 8 12 8 Ref.
Charles H. Gabriel, 1914

1. What a won-der-ful change in my life has been wrought Since Je-sus came
2. I have ceased from my wand-'ring and go-ing a-stray, Since Je-sus came
3. There's a light in the val-ley of death now for me, Since Je-sus came
4. I shall go there to dwell in that Cit-y, I know, Since Je-sus came

in-to my heart! I have light in my soul for which long I have sought,
in-to my heart! And my sins, which were man-y, are all washed a-way,
in-to my heart! And the gates of the Cit-y be-yond I can see,
in-to my heart! And I'm hap-py, so hap-py, as on-ward I go,

Refrain

Since Je-sus came in-to my heart! Since Je-sus came in-to my
Since Je-sus came in, came

heart, Since Je-sus came in-to my heart, Floods of joy o'er my
in-to my heart, Since Je-sus came in, came in-to my heart,

soul like the sea bil-lows roll, Since Je-sus came in-to my heart.

SONGS OF WITNESS

282 Nor Silver nor Gold Hath Obtained

Redeemed . . . with the precious blood of Christ. I Pet. 1:18, 19

James M. Gray, 1900

PRICELESS 12 11 12 11 Ref.

Daniel B. Towner, 1900

1. Nor sil-ver nor gold hath ob-tained my re-demp-tion, Nor rich-es of
2. Nor sil-ver nor gold hath ob-tained my re-demp-tion, The guilt on my
3. Nor sil-ver nor gold hath ob-tained my re-demp-tion, The ho-ly com-
4. Nor sil-ver nor gold hath ob-tained my re-demp-tion, The way in-to

earth could have saved my poor soul; The blood of the cross is my
con-science too heav-y had grown; The blood of the cross is my
mand-ment for-bade me draw near; The blood of the cross is my
heav-en could not thus be bought; The blood of the cross is my

on-ly foun-da-tion, The death of my Sav-ior now mak-eth me whole.
on-ly foun-da-tion, The death of my Sav-ior could on-ly a-tone.
on-ly foun-da-tion, The death of my Sav-ior re-mov-eth my fear.
on-ly foun-da-tion, The death of my Sav-ior re-demp-tion hath wrought.

Refrain

I am re-deemed, but not with sil-ver; I am
I am re-deemed,

bought, but not with gold; Bought with a price —
I am bought, Bought with a price —

THE GOSPEL

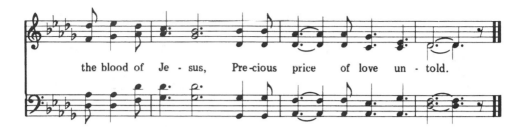

the blood of Je - sus, Pre-cious price of love un - told.

All My Life Long I Had Panted 283

He satisfieth the longing soul, and filleth the hungry soul with goodness. Psa. 107:9

SATISFIED 8 7 8 7 Ref.

Clara T. Williams, 1881

Ralph E. Hudson, 1881

1. All my life long I had pant-ed For a drink from some cool spring
2. Feed-ing on the husks a-round me Till my strength was al-most gone,
3. Poor I was, and sought for rich-es, Some-thing that would sat-is-fy;
4. Well of wa-ter, ev-er spring-ing, Bread of life, so rich and free,

That I hoped would quench the burn-ing Of the thirst I felt with-in.
Longed my soul for some-thing bet-ter, On-ly still to hun-ger on.
But the dust I gath-ered round me On-ly mocked my soul's sad cry.
Un-told wealth that nev-er fail-eth, My Re-deem-er is to me.

Refrain

Hal - le - lu - jah! I have found Him—Whom my soul so long has craved!

Je - sus sat - is - fies my long-ings; Thro' His blood I now, am saved.

284 Yesterday He Died for Me

Christ died for our sins according to the scriptures . . . I Cor. 15:3

Jack Wyrtzen, 1966

YESTERDAY, TODAY AND TOMORROW Irreg.

Don Wyrtzen, 1966

THE GOSPEL

285 Redeemed, How I Love to Proclaim It

In whom we have redemption through His blood . . . Eph. 1:7

Fanny J. Crosby, 1882

ADA 9 8 9 8 Ref.
A. L. Butler, 1966

Unison

1. Re - deemed, how I love to pro - claim it! Re - deemed by the blood of the Lamb; Re - deemed thro' His in - fi - nite mer - cy, His child, and for - ev - er, I am.
2. Re - deemed and so hap - py in Je - sus, No lan - guage my rap - ture can tell; I know that the light of His pres - ence With me doth con - tin - ual - ly dwell.
3. I think of my bless - ed Re - deem - er, I think of Him all the day long; I sing, for I can - not be si - lent; His love is the theme of my song.

Refrain

Re - deemed, re - deemed, Re - deemed by the blood of the Lamb; Re - deemed thro' His in - fi - nite mer - cy, His child, and for - ev - er, I am.

THE GOSPEL

Years I Spent in Vanity and Pride 286

And when they were come to . . . Calvary, there they crucified Him. Luke 23:33

CALVARY 9 9 9 4 Ref.

William R. Newell, 1895

Daniel B. Towner, 1895

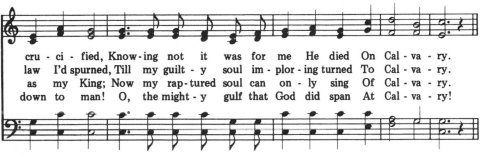

1. Years I spent in van - i - ty and pride, Car - ing not my Lord was
2. By God's Word at last my sin I learned, Then I trem - bled at the
3. Now I've giv'n to Je - sus ev - ery - thing; Now I glad - ly own Him
4. O, the love that drew sal - va - tion's plan! O, the grace that brought it

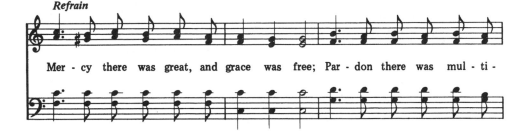

cru - ci - fied, Know - ing not it was for me He died On Cal - va - ry.
law I'd spurned, Till my guilt - y soul im - plor - ing turned To Cal - va - ry.
as my King; Now my rap - tured soul can on - ly sing Of Cal - va - ry.
down to man! O, the might - y gulf that God did span At Cal - va - ry!

Refrain

Mer - cy there was great, and grace was free; Par - don there was mul - ti -

plied to me; There my bur - dened soul found lib - er - ty, At Cal - va - ry.

SONGS OF WITNESS

287 My Faith Has Found a Resting Place

While we were yet sinners, Christ died for us. Rom. 5:8

LANDAS C.M. Ref.
Norse melody
Arr. by William J. Kirkpatrick, 1891

Lidie H. Edmunds, 1891

1. My faith has found a rest-ing place, Not in de-vice nor creed;
2. E-nough for me that Je-sus saves, This ends my fear and doubt;
3. My heart is lean-ing on the Word, The writ-ten Word of God,
4. My great Phy-si-cian heals the sick, The lost He came to save;

I trust the Ev-er-liv-ing One, His wounds for me shall plead.
A sin-ful soul I come to Him, He'll nev-er cast me out.
Sal-va-tion by my Sav-ior's name, Sal-va-tion through His blood.
For me His pre-cious blood He shed, For me His life He gave.

Refrain

I need no oth-er ar-gu-ment, I need no oth-er plea,

It is e-nough that Je-sus died, And that He died for me.

288 Amazing Grace! How Sweet the Sound

God is able to make all grace abound toward you . . . II Cor. 9:8

AMAZING GRACE C.M.
Traditional American melody
Arr. by Edwin O. Excell, 1900

John Newton, 1779
St. 4, source unknown

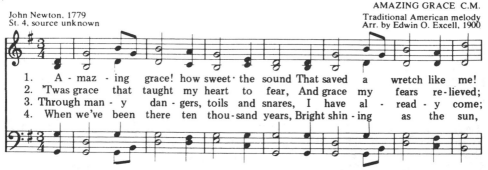

1. A-maz-ing grace! how sweet the sound That saved a wretch like me!
2. 'Twas grace that taught my heart to fear, And grace my fears re-lieved;
3. Through man-y dan-gers, toils and snares, I have al-read-y come;
4. When we've been there ten thou-sand years, Bright shin-ing as the sun,

THE GOSPEL

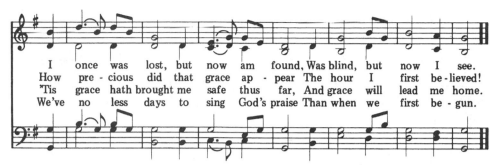

I once was lost, but now am found, Was blind, but now I see.
How pre-cious did that grace ap-pear The hour I first be-lieved!
'Tis grace hath brought me safe thus far, And grace will lead me home.
We've no less days to sing God's praise Than when we first be-gun.

Down at the Cross Where My Savior Died 289

. . . Having made peace by the blood of His cross. Col. 1:20

GLORY TO HIS NAME 9 9 9 5 Ref.

Elisha A. Hoffman, 1878

John H. Stockton, 1878

1. Down at the cross where my Sav-ior died, Down where for cleans-ing from
2. I am so won-drous-ly saved from sin, Je-sus so sweet-ly a-
3. O pre-cious foun-tain that saves from sin, I am so glad I have
4. Come to this foun-tain so rich and sweet; Cast your poor soul at the

sin I cried, There to my heart was the blood ap-plied; Glo-ry to His name!
bides with-in, There at the cross where He took me in; Glo-ry to His name!
en-tered in; There Je-sus saves me and keeps me clean; Glo-ry to His name!
Sav-ior's feet; Plunge in to-day and be made com-plete; Glo-ry to His name!

Refrain

Glo-ry to His name, Glo-ry to His name;

There to my heart was the blood ap-plied; Glo-ry to His name!

SONGS OF WITNESS

290 I Belong to the King

... We are the children of God. Rom. 8:16

Ida R. Smith, 1896

CLIFTON Irreg. Ref.
J. Lincoln Hall, 1896

1. I be-long to the King, I'm a child of His love, I shall dwell in His
2. I be-long to the King, and He loves me, I know, For His mer-cy and
3. I be-long to the King, and His prom-ise is sure, That we all shall be

pal-ace so fair; For He tells of its bliss in yon heav-en a-bove, And His
kind-ness, so free, Are un-ceas-ing-ly mine where-so-ev-er I go, And my
gath-ered at last In His king-dom a-bove, by life's wa-ters so pure, When this

Refrain

chil-dren its splen-dors shall share.
ref-uge un-fail-ing is He.   I be-long to the King, I'm a
life with its tri-als is past.

child of His love, And He nev-er for-sak-eth His own; He will call me some

day to His pal-ace a-bove, I shall dwell by His glo-ri-fied throne.

THE GOSPEL

All My Sins Have Been Forgiven   291

Who forgiveth all thine iniquities; who healeth all thy diseases. Psa. 103:3

Phillip F. Hiller, 1767
Trans. by Esther Bergen, 1959

GREENVILLE 8 7 8 7 D.
Jean J. Rousseau, 1823

1. All my sins have been for-giv - en; God is mer - ci - ful to me;
2. My ac - count is closed for - ev - er; Je - sus Christ has paid it all;
3. How my count-less sins de-pressed me, Gave me sor - row, shame and tears,
4. Now my soul shall live for - ev - er; No more can the Foe con-demn;

Faith has claimed the Sav - ior's prom - ise, Grace and par - don, full and free;
Shed His blood my sin to cov - er, Paid the price to save my soul;
How His wrath and an - ger crushed me, Filled my heart with doubts' and fears;
Noth - ing from God's love can sev - er, Peace and joy are found in Him.

O my soul, be ev - er prais - ing For the great Re - deem - er's love;
There is now no con - dem - na - tion, I am ful - ly rec - on - ciled;
But my soul cried out in an - guish, Called for mer - cy and for grace,
Thus I jour - ney on to heav - en, Cross death's por - tals joy - ful - ly;

Joy - ous songs to Him be rais - ing, Un - to God in heav'n a - bove.
What a won - der - ful sal - va - tion, For a sin - ner so de - filed!
Je - sus heard my sup - pli - ca - tion, Grant-ed par - don and re - lease.
All my sins have been for - giv - en, God is mer - ci - ful to me.

SONGS OF WITNESS

292 Out of the Depths to the Glory Above

I will extol Thee, O Lord; for Thou hast lifted me up. Psa. 30:1

LILLENAS 10 10 10 7 Ref.

Avis B. Christiansen, 1918

Haldor Lillenas, 1918

1. Out of the depths to the glo - ry a - bove, I have been lift - ed in won - der - ful love; From ev - ery fet - ter my spir - it is free— For Je - sus has lift - ed me!

2. Out of the world in - to heav - en - ly rest, In - to the land of the ran - somed and blest; There in the glo - ry with Him I shall be— For Je - sus has lift - ed me!

3. Out of my - self in - to Him I a - dore, There to a - bide in His love ev - er - more; Thro' end - less a - ges His glo - ry to see— My Je - sus has lift - ed me!

Refrain

Je - sus has lift - ed me! lift - ed me! Je - sus has lift - ed me! lift - ed me! Out of the night in - to glo - ri - ous light, Yes, Je - sus has lift - ed me! lift - ed me!

THE GOSPEL

Naught Have I Gotten 293

For by grace are ye saved through faith . . . Eph. 2:8

ONLY A SINNER 10 10 9 9 Ref.

James M. Gray, 1905

Daniel B. Towner, 1905

1. Naught have I got-ten but what I re-ceived; Grace hath be-stowed it since
2. Once I was fool-ish, and sin ruled my heart, Caus-ing my foot-steps from
3. Tears un-a-vail-ing, no mer-it had I; Mer-cy had saved me, or
4. Suf-fer a sin-ner whose heart o-ver-flows, Lov-ing his Sav-ior to

I have be-lieved; Boast-ing ex-clud-ed, pride I a-base; I'm
God to de-part; Je-sus hath found me, hap-py my case; I
else I must die; Sin had a-larmed me, fear-ing God's face; But
tell what he knows; Once more to tell it would I em-brace—I'm

Refrain

on-ly a sin-ner saved by grace!
now am a sin-ner saved by grace!
now I'm a sin-ner saved by grace! On-ly a sin-ner saved by grace!
on-ly a sin-ner saved by grace!

On-ly a sin-ner saved by grace! This is my sto-ry, to

God be the glo-ry—I'm on-ly a sin-ner saved by grace!

SONGS OF WITNESS

294 I Stand Amazed in the Presence

God, who is rich in mercy, for His great love wherewith He loved us . . . Eph. 2:4

MY SAVIOR'S LOVE 8 7 8 7 Ref.

Charles H. Gabriel, 1905

Charles H. Gabriel, 1905

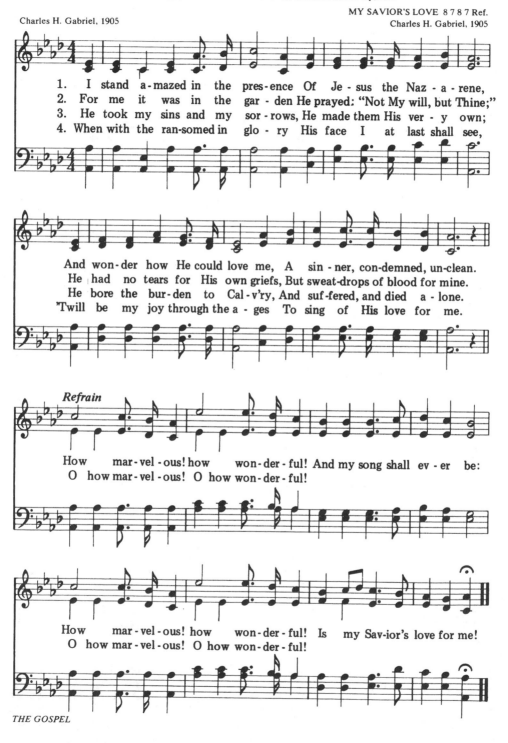

1. I stand a-mazed in the pres-ence Of Je - sus the Naz - a - rene,
2. For me it was in the gar - den He prayed: "Not My will, but Thine;"
3. He took my sins and my sor - rows, He made them His ver - y own;
4. When with the ran-somed in glo - ry His face I at last shall see,

And won-der how He could love me, A sin - ner, con-demned, un-clean.
He had no tears for His own griefs, But sweat-drops of blood for mine.
He bore the bur-den to Cal - v'ry, And suf-fered, and died a - lone.
'Twill be my joy through the a - ges To sing of His love for me.

Refrain

How mar-vel-ous! how won-der-ful! And my song shall ev - er be:
O how mar-vel-ous! O how won-der-ful!

How mar-vel-ous! how won-der-ful! Is my Sav-ior's love for me!
O how mar-vel-ous! O how won-der-ful!

THE GOSPEL

I Know Not Why God's Wondrous Grace 295

For I know whom I have believed . . . II Tim. 1:12

EL NATHAN C.M. Ref.

Daniel W. Whittle, 1883

James McGranahan, 1883

1. I know not why God's won-drous grace To me He hath made known,
2. I know not how this sav - ing faith To me He did im - part,
3. I know not how the Spir - it moves, Con-vinc - ing men of sin,
4. I know not when my Lord may come, At night or noon-day fair,

Nor why, un - wor - thy, Christ in love Re-deemed me for His own.
Nor how be - liev - ing in His Word Wrought peace with-in my heart.
Re - veal - ing Je - sus through the Word, Cre - at - ing faith in Him.
Nor if I'll walk the vale with Him, Or "meet Him in the air."

Refrain

But "I know whom I have be - liev - ed, And am per-suad-ed that He is

a - ble To keep that which I've com-mit - ted Un-to Him a-gainst that day."

SONGS OF WITNESS

296 I Will Sing the Wondrous Story

And they sing the song . . . of the Lamb, saying, Great and marvelous are Thy works. Rev. 15:3

WONDROUS STORY 8 7 8 7 Ref.

Francis H. Rowley, 1886

Peter P. Bilhorn, 1886

1. I will sing the won-drous sto - ry Of the Christ who died for me,
2. I was lost but Je - sus found me, Found the sheep that went a - stray,
3. I was bruised but Je - sus healed me; Faint was I from man - y a fall;
4. Days of dark - ness still come o'er me, Sor-row's paths I oft - en tread,

How He left His home in glo - ry For the cross of Cal - va - ry.
Threw His lov - ing arms a - round me, Drew me back in - to His way.
Sight was gone, and fears pos-sessed me, But He freed me from them all.
But the Sav - ior still is with me; By His hand I'm safe - ly led.

Refrain

Yes, I'll sing the won-drous sto - ry Of the
Yes, I'll sing the won-drous sto - ry

Christ who died for me, Sing it with the saints in
Of the Christ who died for me, Sing it with

glo - ry Gath-ered by the crys-tal sea.
the saints in glo - ry, Gath-ered by the crys-tal sea.

THE GOSPEL

O, What a Savior, That He Died for Me 297

Whosoever believeth in Him should . . . have everlasting life. John 3:16

VERILY 10 10 10 6 Ref.

James McGranahan, 1878

James McGranahan, 1878

1. O, what a Sav - ior, that He died for me! From con - dem -
2. All my in - iq - ui - ties on Him were laid, All my in -
3. Though poor and need - y I can trust my Lord, Though weak and
4. Though all un - wor - thy, yet I will not doubt, For him that

na - tion He hath made me free; "He that be - liev - eth on the
debt - ed - ness by Him was paid; All who be - lieve on Him, the
sin - ful I be - lieve His Word; O, glad mes - sage! ev - ery
com - eth, He will not cast out; "He that be - liev - eth," O the

Refrain

Son," saith He, "Hath ev - er - last - ing life."
Lord hath said, "Hath ev - er - last - ing life." "Ver - i - ly, ver - i - ly,
child of God "Hath ev - er - last - ing life."
good news shout, "Hath ev - er - last - ing life!"

I say un - to you, Ver - i - ly, ver - i - ly," mes - sage ev - er new;

"He that be - liev - eth on the Son," 'tis true, "Hath ev - er - last - ing life."

SONGS OF WITNESS

298 Saved! Saved! Saved!

For there is none other name under heaven . . . whereby we must be saved. Acts 4:12

HICKMAN 9 9 9 9 Ref.

Oswald J. Smith, 1918

Roger M. Hickman, 1918

Unison

1. Saved! saved! saved! my sins are all for - giv'n; Christ is
2. Saved! saved! saved! by grace and grace a - lone; O, what
3. Saved! saved! saved! O, joy be - yond com - pare! Christ my

mine! I'm on my way to heav'n; Once a guilt - y
won - drous love to me was shown, In my stead Christ
life and I His con - stant care; Yield - ing all and

sin - ner, lost, un - done, Now a child of God, saved thro' His Son.
Je - sus bled and died, Bore my sins, for me was cru - ci - fied.
trust - ing Him a - lone, Liv - ing now each mo - ment as His own.

Refrain - parts

Saved! I'm saved thro' Christ, my all in all; Saved! I'm saved, what-
my all in all;

ev - er may be - fall; He died up - on the cross for me, He bore the aw - ful

THE GOSPEL

pen - al - ty; And now I'm saved e - ter - nal - ly—I'm saved! saved! saved!

In Loving Kindness Jesus Came 299

He brought me up also out of an horrible pit . . . Psa. 40:2

HE LIFTED ME 8 8 8 6 Ref.

Charles H. Gabriel, 1905

Charles H. Gabriel, 1905

1. In lov - ing kind - ness Je - sus came My soul in mer - cy to re - claim,
2. He called me long be - fore I heard, Be - fore my sin - ful heart was stirred,
3. His brow was pierced with man - y a thorn, His hands by cru - el nails were torn,
4. Now on a high - er plane I dwell, And with my soul I know 'tis well;

And from the depths of sin and shame Thro' grace He lift - ed me.
But when I took Him at His word, For-giv'n He lift - ed me.
When from my guilt and grief, for - lorn, In love He lift - ed me.
Yet how or why, I can - not tell, He should have lift - ed me.

(He lift-ed me.)

Refrain

From sink - ing sand He lift - ed me, With ten - der hand He lift - ed me,

From shades of night to plains of light, O praise His name, He lift - ed me!

300 In Tenderness He Sought Me

Rejoice with me; for I have found my sheep which was lost. Luke 15:6

CLARENDON 7 6 7 6 8 8 Ref.

W. Spencer Walton, 1894

Adoniram J. Gordon, 1894

1. In ten - der - ness He sought me, Wea - ry and sick with sin,
2. He washed the bleed - ing sin - wounds And poured in oil and wine;
3. He point - ed to the nail - prints, For me His blood was shed,
4. I'm sit - ting in His pres - ence, The sun - shine of His face,
5. So while the hours are pass - ing All now is per - fect rest;

And on His shoul - ders brought me Back to His fold a - gain. While
He whis - pered to as - sure me, "I've found thee, thou art Mine;" I
A mock - ing crown so thorn - y Was placed up - on His head: I
While with a - dor - ing won - der His bless - ings I re - trace: It
I'm wait - ing for the morn - ing, The bright - est and the best, When

an - gels in His pres - ence sang Un - til the courts of heav - en rang.
nev - er heard a sweet - er voice; It made my ach - ing heart re - joice!
won - dered what He saw in me To suf - fer such deep ag - o - ny.
seems as if e - ter - nal days Are far too short to sound His praise.
He will call us to His side, To be with Him, His spot - less bride.

Refrain

O the love that sought me! O the blood that bought me! O the grace that

brought me to the fold, Won - drous grace that brought me to the fold!

THE GOSPEL

Saved by the Blood of the Crucified One 301

Unto Him that . . . washed us from our sins in His own blood. Rev. 1:5

GLORY, I'M SAVED 10 11 11 10 Ref.

S. J. Henderson, 1903

Daniel B. Towner, 1903

1. Saved by the blood of the Cru - ci - fied One! Now ran - somed from
2. Saved by the blood of the Cru - ci - fied One! The an - gels re -
3. Saved by the blood of the Cru - ci - fied One! The Fa - ther— He
4. Saved by the blood of the Cru - ci - fied One! All hail to the

sin and a new work be - gun, Sing praise to the Fa - ther and
joic - ing be - cause it is done; A child of the Fa - ther, joint
spake, and His will— it was done; Great price of my par - don, His
Fa - ther, all hail to the Son, All hail to the Spir - it, the

praise to the Son, Saved by the blood of the Cru - ci - fied One!
heir with the Son, Saved by the blood of the Cru - ci - fied One!
own pre - cious Son; Saved by the blood of the Cru - ci - fied One!
great Three in One! Saved by the blood of the Cru - ci - fied One!

Refrain

Saved! Saved! My sins are all par-doned, my guilt is all gone!
Saved, I'm saved! glo - ry, I'm saved!

Saved! saved! I am saved by the blood of the Cru - ci - fied One!
Saved, I'm saved! glo - ry, I'm saved!

SONGS OF WITNESS

302 I Love to Tell the Story

And they sang a new song saying, Thou art worthy . . . Rev. 5:9

HANKEY 7 6 7 6 D. Ref.

A. Catherine Hankey, 1866.

William G. Fischer, 1869

1. I love to tell the sto - ry Of un - seen things a -
2. I love to tell the sto - ry, More won - der - ful it
3. I love to tell the sto - ry, 'Tis pleas - ant to re -
4. I love to tell the sto - ry, For those who know it

bove, Of Je - sus and His glo - ry, Of Je - sus and His
seems Than all the gold - en fan - cies Of all our gold - en
peat What seems, each time I tell it, More won - der - ful - ly
best Seem hun - ger - ing and thirst - ing To hear it like the

love. I love to tell the sto - ry Be - cause I know 'tis
dreams. I love to tell the sto - ry, It did so much for
sweet. I love to tell the sto - ry, For some have nev - er
rest. And when, in scenes of glo - ry, I sing the new, new

true; It sat - is - fies my long - ings As noth - ing else can do.
me; And that is just the rea - son I tell it now to thee.
heard The mes - sage of sal - va - tion From God's own Ho - ly Word.
song, 'Twill be the old, old sto - ry That I have loved so long.

Refrain

I love to tell the sto - ry, 'Twill be my theme in glo - ry,

To tell the old, old sto - ry Of Je - sus and His love.

Talk About a Soul 303

I will declare what He hath done for my soul. Psa. 66:16

HERE'S ONE Irreg.

Traditional Spiritual
Adapt. by John F. Wilson

Traditional Spiritual
Arr. by John F. Wilson

Unison

1. Talk a - bout a soul that's been con - vert - ed, Here's one, here's one,
2. Talk a - bout a soul that loves his Je - sus, Here's one, here's one,

Talk a - bout a soul that's been con - vert - ed, Here's one, here's one,
Talk a - bout a soul that loves his Je - sus, Here's one, here's one,

Ev - er since I heard the Gos - pel sto - ry, I've been walk - ing up the
In old Sa - tan's snares I once was fall - ing Till I heard the voice of

path to glo - ry, Talk a - bout a soul that's been con-vert-ed, Here's one.
my Lord call - ing, Talk a - bout a soul that's been con-vert-ed, Here's one.

SONGS OF WITNESS

304 There Is a Name I Love to Hear

We love Him, because He first loved us. I John 4:19

O, HOW I LOVE JESUS C.M. Ref.

Frederick Whitfield, 1855

Traditional American melody

1. There is a name I love to hear, I love to sing its
2. It tells me of a Sav - ior's love, Who died to set me
3. It tells me what my Fa - ther hath In store for ev - ery
4. It tells of One whose lov - ing heart Can feel my deep - est

worth; It sounds like mu - sic in my ear, The sweet-est name on earth.
free; It tells me of His pre - cious blood, The sin - ner's per - fect plea.
day, And though I tread a dark-some path, Yields sun-shine all the way.
woe, Who in each sor - row bears a part, That none can bear be - low.

Refrain

O, how I love Je - sus, O, how I love Je - sus,

O, how I love Je - sus, Be - cause He first loved me!

305 I Am Not Skilled to Understand

Him hath God exalted with His right hand to be a . . . Savior. Acts 5:31

GREENWELL 8 8 8 7

Dora Greenwell, 1873

William J. Kirkpatrick, 1885

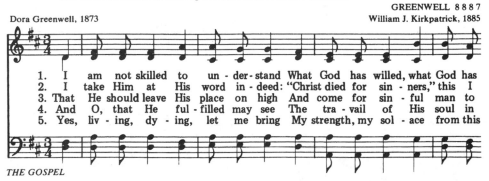

1. I am not skilled to un - der-stand What God has willed, what God has
2. I take Him at His word in - deed: "Christ died for sin - ners," this I
3. That He should leave His place on high And come for sin - ful man to
4. And O, that He ful - filled may see The tra - vail of His soul in
5. Yes, liv - ing, dy - ing, let me bring My strength, my sol - ace from this

THE GOSPEL

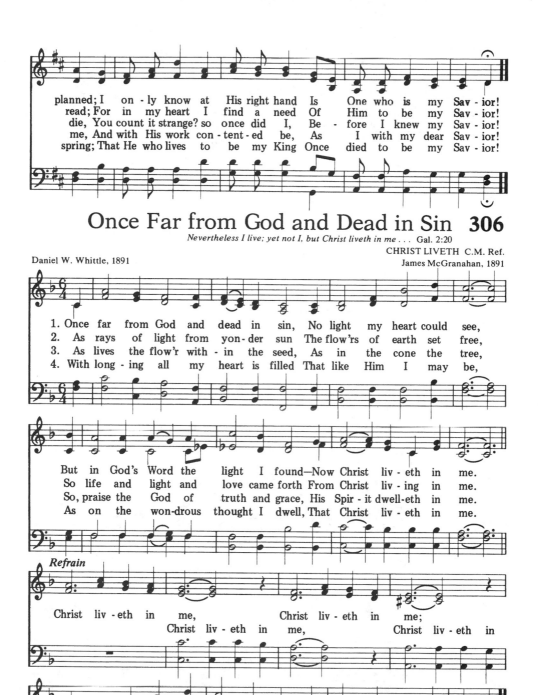

planned; I on-ly know at His right hand Is One who is my Sav-ior!
read; For in my heart I find a need Of Him to be my Sav-ior!
die, You count it strange? so once did I, Be-fore I knew my Sav-ior!
me, And with His work con-tent-ed be, As I with my dear Sav-ior!
spring; That He who lives to be my King Once died to be my Sav-ior!

Once Far from God and Dead in Sin 306

Nevertheless I live; yet not I, but Christ liveth in me . . . Gal. 2:20

CHRIST LIVETH C.M. Ref.

Daniel W. Whittle, 1891

James McGranahan, 1891

1. Once far from God and dead in sin, No light my heart could see,
2. As rays of light from yon-der sun The flow'rs of earth set free,
3. As lives the flow'r with-in the seed, As in the cone the tree,
4. With long-ing all my heart is filled That like Him I may be,

But in God's Word the light I found—Now Christ liv-eth in me.
So life and light and love came forth From Christ liv-ing in me.
So, praise the God of truth and grace, His Spir-it dwell-eth in me.
As on the won-drous thought I dwell, That Christ liv-eth in me.

Refrain

Christ liv-eth in me, Christ liv-eth in me;
Christ liv-eth in me, Christ liv-eth in

O what a sal-va-tion this—That Christ liv-eth in me.
me; O

307 There's Not a Friend

There is a friend that sticketh closer than a brother. Prov. 18:24

NO, NOT ONE 10 6 10 6 Ref.

Johnson Oatman, Jr., c. 1890

George C. Hugg, c. 1890

1. There's not a friend like the low-ly Je-sus, No, not one! no, not one!
2. No friend like Him is so high and ho-ly, No, not one! no, not one!
3. There's not an hour that He is not near us, No, not one! no, not one!
4. Did ev-er saint find this friend for-sake him? No, not one! no, not one!
5. Was e'er a gift like the Sav-ior giv-en? No, not one! no, not one!

None else could heal all our soul's dis-eas-es, No, not one! no, not one!
And yet no friend is so meek and low-ly, No, not one! no, not one!
No night so dark but His love can cheer us, No, not one! no, not one!
Or sin-ner find that He would not take him? No, not one! no, not one!
Will He re-fuse us a home in heav-en? No, not one! no, not one!

Refrain

Je-sus knows all a-bout our strug-gles, He will guide till the day is done;

There's not a friend like the low-ly Je-sus, No, not one! no, not one!

THE GOSPEL

My Hope Is in the Lord 308

Christ in you, the hope of glory. Col. 1:27

Norman J. Clayton, 1945

WAKEFIELD 6 6 6 6 Ref.
Norman J. Clayton, 1945

1. My hope is in the Lord Who gave Him-self for me,
2. No mer-it of my own His an-ger to sup-press,
3. And now for me He stands Be-fore the Fa-ther's throne,
4. His grace has planned it all, 'Tis mine but to be-lieve,

And paid the price of all my sin at Cal-va-ry.
My on-ly hope is found in Je-sus' right-eous-ness.
He shows His wound-ed hands, and names me as His own.
And rec-og-nize His work of love and Christ re-ceive.

Refrain

For me He died, For me He lives,
For me He died, For me He lives,

And ev-er-last-ing life and light He free-ly gives.

Copyright 1945 by Norman J. Clayton, in "Word of Life Melodies No. 2." Assigned to Norman Clayton Publishing Co.
© Renewal 1973 by Norman Clayton Publishing Co. Used by permission.

SONGS OF WITNESS

309 I Heard the Voice of Jesus Say

Come unto Me, all ye that labor . . . and I will give you rest. Matt. 11:28

VOX DILECTI C.M.D.

Horatius Bonar, 1846

John B. Dykes, 1868

1. I heard the voice of Je - sus say, "Come un - to Me and rest;
2. I heard the voice of Je - sus say, "Be - hold, I free - ly give
3. I heard the voice of Je - sus say, "I am this dark world's Light;

Lay down, thou wea - ry one, lay down Thy head up - on My breast."
The liv - ing wa - ter; thirst - y one, Stoop down, and drink, and live."
Look un - to Me, thy morn shall rise, And all thy day be bright."

I came to Je - sus as I was, Wea - ry, and worn, and sad;
I came to Je - sus, and I drank Of that life - giv - ing stream;
I looked to Je - sus, and I found In Him my Star, my Sun;

I found in Him a rest - ing place, And He has made me glad.
My thirst was quenched, my soul re - vived, And now I live in Him.
And in that Light of life I'll walk, Till trav - 'ling days are done.

THE GOSPEL: SONGS OF WITNESS

Under His Wings I Am Safely Abiding 310

Under His wings shalt thou trust. Psa. 91:4

HINGHAM 11 10 11 10 Ref.

William O. Cushing, c. 1896

Ira D. Sankey, 1896

1. Un - der His wings I am safe - ly a - bid - ing; Though the night
2. Un - der His wings, what a ref - uge in sor - row! How the heart
3. Un - der His wings, O what pre - cious en - joy - ment! There will I

deep - ens and tem - pests are wild, Still I can trust Him— I
yearn - ing - ly turns to His rest! Oft - en when earth has no
hide till life's tri - als are o'er; Shel - tered, pro - tect - ed, no

know He will keep me; He has re - deemed me and I am His child.
balm for my heal - ing, There I find com - fort and there I am blest.
e - vil can harm me; Rest - ing in Je - sus I'm safe ev - er - more.

Refrain

Un - der His wings, un - der His wings, Who from His love can sev - er?

Un - der His wings my soul shall a - bide, Safe - ly a - bide for - ev - er.

LIFE IN CHRIST: FAITH AND ASSURANCE

311 Though the Angry Surges Roll

Which hope we have as an anchor of the soul . . . Heb. 6:19

MY ANCHOR HOLDS Irreg. Ref.

W. C. Martin, 1902

Daniel B. Towner, 1902

1. Though the an - gry surg - es roll On my tem - pest - driv - en soul,
2. Might - y tides a - bout me sweep, Per - ils lurk with - in the deep,
3. I can feel the an - chor fast As I meet each sud - den blast,
4. Trou - bles al - most 'whelm the soul; Griefs like bil - lows o'er me roll;

I am peace - ful, for I know, Wild - ly though the winds may blow,
An - gry clouds o'er - shade the sky, And the tem - pest ris - es high;
And the ca - ble, though un - seen, Bears the heav - y strain be - tween;
Tempt - ers seek to lure a - stray; Storms ob - scure the light of day:

I've an an - chor safe and sure That can ev - er - more en - dure.
Still I stand the tem - pest's shock, For my an - chor grips the Rock.
Thro' the storm I safe - ly ride, Till the turn - ing of the tide.
But in Christ I can be bold, I've an an - chor that shall hold.

Refrain

And it holds, my an - chor holds; Blow your wild - est, then, O
And it holds, my an - chor holds; Blow your wild - est,

gale, On my bark so small and frail; By His grace I shall not
then, O gale,

LIFE IN CHRIST

fail, For my an - chor holds, my an-chor holds.
For my an - chor holds, it firm - ly holds,

'Tis So Sweet to Trust in Jesus 312

That we should be to the praise of His glory, who first trusted in Christ. Eph. 1:12

TRUST IN JESUS 8 7 8 7 Ref.

Louisa M. R. Stead, 1882

William J. Kirkpatrick, 1882

1. 'Tis so sweet to trust in Je - sus, Just to take Him at His word;
2. O how sweet to trust in Je - sus, Just to trust His cleans - ing blood;
3. Yes, 'tis sweet to trust in Je - sus, Just from sin and self to cease;
4. I'm so glad I learned to trust Thee, Pre - cious Je - sus, Sav - ior, Friend;

Just to rest up - on His prom-ise; Just to know, "Thus saith the Lord."
Just in sim - ple faith to plunge me 'Neath the heal - ing, cleans - ing flood!
Just from Je - sus sim - ply tak - ing Life and rest, and joy and peace.
And I know that Thou art with me, Wilt be with me to the end.

Refrain

Je - sus, Je - sus, how I trust Him! How I've proved Him o'er and o'er!

Je - sus, Je - sus, pre - cious Je - sus! O for grace to trust Him more!

FAITH AND ASSURANCE

313 My Hope Is Built on Nothing Less

Other foundation can no man lay than that is laid, which is Jesus Christ. I Cor. 3:11

SOLID ROCK L.M. Ref.

Edward Mote, 1834

William B. Bradbury, 1863

1. My hope is built on noth-ing less Than Je - sus' blood and right-eous-ness;
2. When dark-ness veils His love - ly face, I rest on His un-chang-ing grace;
3. His oath, His cov - e - nant, His blood Sup-port me in the whelm-ing flood;
4. When He shall come with trum-pet sound, O may I then in Him be found;

I dare not trust the sweet-est frame, But whol-ly lean on Je - sus' name.
In ev - er-y high and storm - y gale, My an - chor holds with - in the veil.
When all a - round my soul gives way He then is all my hope and stay.
Dressed in His right - eous - ness a - lone, Fault - less to stand be - fore the throne.

Refrain

On Christ the sol - id Rock I stand; All oth - er ground

is sink - ing sand, All oth - er ground is sink - ing sand.

LIFE IN CHRIST

Dying with Jesus, by Death Reckoned 314

Who are kept by the power of God through faith unto salvation. I Pet. 1:5

WHITTLE 10 10 10 10 Ref.

Daniel W. Whittle, 1893

May W. Moody, 1893

1. Dy - ing with Je - sus, by death reck-oned mine; Liv - ing with Je - sus a
2. Nev - er a tri - al that He is not there, Nev - er a bur - den that
3. Nev - er a heart-ache and nev - er a groan, Nev - er a tear-drop and
4. Nev - er a weak-ness that He doth not feel, Nev - er a sick - ness that

new life di - vine; Look-ing to Je - sus till glo - ry doth shine, Mo-ment by
He doth not bear, Nev - er a sor - row that He doth not share, Mo-ment by
nev - er a moan; Nev - er a dan - ger, but there on the throne, Mo-ment by
He can - not heal; Mo-ment by mo-ment, in woe or in weal, Je - sus my

Refrain

mo-ment, O Lord, I am Thine.
mo-ment, I'm un - der His care.
mo-ment, He thinks of His own. Mo-ment by mo-ment I'm kept in His love;
Sav - ior a - bides with me still.

Mo-ment by mo-ment I've life from a - bove; Look-ing to Je - sus till

glo - ry doth shine; Mo - ment by mo - ment, O Lord, I am Thine.

315 O Holy Savior, Friend Unseen

It is better to trust in the Lord than to put confidence in man. Psa. 118:8

FLEMMING 8 8 8 6

Charlotte Elliott, 1834

Friedrich F. Flemming, 1811

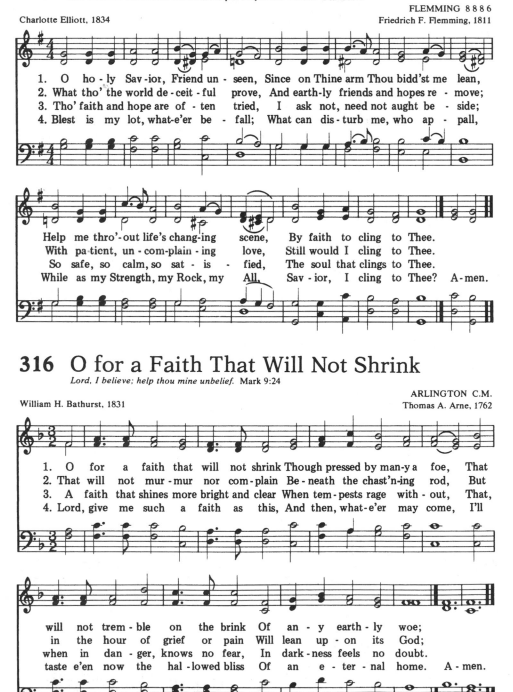

1. O ho-ly Sav-ior, Friend un-seen, Since on Thine arm Thou bidd'st me lean,
2. What tho' the world de-ceit-ful prove, And earth-ly friends and hopes re-move;
3. Tho' faith and hope are of-ten tried, I ask not, need not aught be-side;
4. Blest is my lot, what-e'er be-fall; What can dis-turb me, who ap-pall,

Help me thro'-out life's chang-ing scene, By faith to cling to Thee.
With pa-tient, un-com-plain-ing love, Still would I cling to Thee.
So safe, so calm, so sat-is-fied, The soul that clings to Thee.
While as my Strength, my Rock, my All, Sav-ior, I cling to Thee? A-men.

316 O for a Faith That Will Not Shrink

Lord, I believe; help thou mine unbelief. Mark 9:24

ARLINGTON C.M.

William H. Bathurst, 1831

Thomas A. Arne, 1762

1. O for a faith that will not shrink Though pressed by man-y a foe, That
2. That will not mur-mur nor com-plain Be-neath the chast'n-ing rod, But
3. A faith that shines more bright and clear When tem-pests rage with-out, That,
4. Lord, give me such a faith as this, And then, what-e'er may come, I'll

will not trem-ble on the brink Of an-y earth-ly woe;
in the hour of grief or pain Will lean up-on its God;
when in dan-ger, knows no fear, In dark-ness feels no doubt.
taste e'en now the hal-lowed bliss Of an e-ter-nal home. A-men.

LIFE IN CHRIST

Blessed Assurance, Jesus Is Mine 317

I will sing praises unto my God while I have any being. Psa. 146:2

ASSURANCE 9 10 9 9 Ref.

Fanny J. Crosby, 1873

Phoebe P. Knapp, 1873

1. Bless - ed as - sur - ance, Je - sus is mine! O, what a fore-taste of
2. Per - fect sub - mis - sion, per - fect de - light, Vi - sions of rap - ture now
3. Per - fect sub - mis - sion, all is at rest, I in my Sav - ior am

glo - ry di - vine! Heir of sal - va - tion, pur - chase of God,
burst on my sight; An - gels de - scend - ing, bring from a - bove
hap - py and blest; Watch - ing and wait - ing, look - ing a - bove,

Refrain

Born of His Spir - it, washed in His blood.
Ech - oes of mer - cy, whis - pers of love. This is my sto - ry, this is my
Filled with His good-ness, lost in His love.

song, Prais - ing my Sav - ior all the day long; This is my sto - ry,

this is my song, Prais - ing my Sav - ior all the day long.

FAITH AND ASSURANCE

318 When We Walk with the Lord

If ye continue in My word, then are ye My disciples indeed. John 8:31

John H. Sammis, 1887

TRUST AND OBEY 6 6 9 D. Ref.

Daniel B. Towner, 1887

1. When we walk with the Lord in the light of His Word,
2. Not a shad - ow can rise, not a cloud in the skies,
3. Not a bur - den we bear, not a sor - row we share,
4. But we nev - er can prove the de - lights of His love
5. Then in fel - low - ship sweet we will sit at His feet,

What a glo - ry He sheds on our way! While we do His good
But His smile quick - ly drives it a - way; Not a doubt nor a
But our toil He doth rich - ly re - pay; Not a grief nor a
Un - til all on the al - tar we lay; For the fa - vor He
Or we'll walk by His side in the way; What He says we will

will He a - bides with us still, And with all who will
fear, not a sigh nor a tear, Can a - bide while we
loss, not a frown nor a cross, But is blest if we
shows and the joy He be - stows Are for them who will
do, where He sends we will go— Nev - er fear, on - ly

Refrain

trust and o - bey. Trust and o - bey, for there's no oth - er

way To be hap - py in Je - sus, But to trust and o - bey.

LIFE IN CHRIST

Trust in the Lord with All Your Heart 319

Trust in the Lord with all thine heart . . . Prov. 3:5

LOVELESS 8 7 8 7 Ref.

Thomas O. Chisholm, 1937

Wendell P. Loveless, 1937

1. Trust in the Lord with all your heart, This is God's gra-cious com-mand;
2. Trust in the Lord who rul-eth all, See-eth all things as they are,
3. Trust in the Lord—His eye will guide All thro' your path-way a-head,

In all your ways ac-knowl-edge Him, So shall you dwell in the land.
Be it a bird-ling in its nest, Or yon-der ut-ter-most star.
He hath re-deemed and He will keep, Trust Him and be not a-fraid.

Refrain

Trust in the Lord, O trou-bled soul, Rest in the arms of His care; What-
care, of His care;

ev-er your lot, it mat-ter-eth not, For noth-ing can trou-ble you there;

Trust in the Lord, O trou-bled soul, Noth-ing can trou-ble you there.

FAITH AND ASSURANCE

320 Simply Trusting Every Day

Commit thy way unto the Lord; trust also in Him ... Psa. 37:5

Edgar P. Stites, 1876

TRUSTING JESUS 7 7 7 7 Ref.
Ira D. Sankey, 1876

1. Sim - ply trust - ing ev - ery day, Trust - ing through a storm - y way;
2. Bright - ly doth His Spir - it shine In - to this poor heart of mine;
3. Sing - ing if my way is clear, Pray - ing if the path be drear;
4. Trust - ing Him while life shall last, Trust - ing Him till earth be past;

E - ven when my faith is small, Trust - ing Je - sus—that is all.
While He leads I can - not fall, Trust - ing Je - sus—that is all.
If in dan - ger, for Him call, Trust - ing Je - sus—that is all.
Till with - in the jas - per wall, Trust - ing Je - sus—that is all.

Refrain

Trust - ing as the mo - ments fly, Trust - ing as the days go by;

Trust - ing Him what - e'er be - fall, Trust - ing Je - sus—that is all.

LIFE IN CHRIST

Savior, Like a Shepherd Lead Us **321**

When He putteth forth His own sheep, He goeth before them. John 10:4

Hymns for the Young, 1836
Attr. to Dorothy A. Thrupp

BRADBURY 8 7 8 7 D.
William B. Bradbury, 1859

1. Sav - ior, like a shep-herd lead us, Much we need Thy ten-der care;
2. We are Thine, do Thou be-friend us, Be the guard-ian of our way;
3. Thou hast prom-ised to re-ceive us, Poor and sin-ful though we be;
4. Ear - ly let us seek Thy fa - vor, Ear - ly let us do Thy will;

In Thy pleas-ant pas-tures feed us, For our use Thy folds pre-pare:
Keep Thy flock, from sin de-fend us, Seek us when we go a-stray:
Thou hast mer - cy to re-lieve us, Grace to cleanse, and pow'r to free:
Bless - ed Lord and on - ly Sav - ior, With Thy love our bos-oms fill:

Bless - ed Je - sus, bless - ed Je - sus, Thou hast bought us, Thine we are;
Bless - ed Je - sus, bless - ed Je - sus, Hear, O hear us when we pray;
Bless - ed Je - sus, bless - ed Je - sus, Ear - ly let us turn to Thee;
Bless - ed Je - sus, bless - ed Je - sus, Thou hast loved us, love us still;

Bless - ed Je - sus, bless - ed Je - sus, Thou hast bought us, Thine we are.
Bless - ed Je - sus, bless - ed Je - sus, Hear, O hear us when we pray.
Bless - ed Je - sus, bless - ed Je - sus, Ear - ly let us turn to Thee.
Bless - ed Je - sus, bless - ed Je - sus, Thou hast loved us, love us still.

FAITH AND ASSURANCE

322 The Lord's Our Rock, in Him We Hide

A man shall be . . . like the shadow of a great rock in a weary land. Isa. 32:2

Vernon J. Charlesworth, c. 1880
Adapt. by Ira D. Sankey, 1885

SHELTER L.M. Ref.
Ira D. Sankey, 1885

1. The Lord's our rock, in Him we hide, A shel-ter in the time of storm;
2. A shade by day, de-fense by night, A shel-ter in the time of storm;
3. The rag-ing storms may round us beat, A shel-ter in the time of storm;
4. O Rock di-vine, O Ref-uge dear, A shel-ter in the time of storm;

Se-cure what-ev-er ill be-tide, A shel-ter in the time of storm.
No fears a-larm, no foes af-fright, A shel-ter in the time of storm.
We'll nev-er leave our safe re-treat, A shel-ter in the time of storm.
Be Thou our help-er ev-er near, A shel-ter in the time of storm.

Refrain

O, Je-sus is a rock in a wea-ry land, A wea-ry land, a wea-ry land;

O, Je-sus is a rock in a wea-ry land, A shel-ter in the time of storm.

LIFE IN CHRIST

My Father Is Rich in Houses and Lands 323

We are the children of God; and if children, then heirs. Rom. 8:16,17

BINGHAMTON 10 11 11 11 Ref.

Harriett E. Buell, 1877

John B. Sumner, 1877

1. My Fa - ther is rich in hous - es and lands, He hold - eth the
2. My Fa - ther's own Son, the Sav - ior of men, Once wan - dered on
3. I once was an out - cast stran - ger on earth, A sin - ner by
4. A tent or a cot - tage, why should I care? They're build - ing a

wealth of the world in His hands! Of ru - bies and dia - monds, of
earth as the poor - est of them; But now He is reign - ing for -
choice, and an al - ien by birth; But I've been a - dopt - ed, my
pal - ace for me o - ver there; Though ex - iled from home, yet

sil - ver and gold, His cof - fers are full, He has rich - es un - told.
ev - er on high, And will give me a home in heav'n by and by.
name's writ - ten down, An heir to a man - sion, a robe, and a crown.
still I may sing: All glo - ry to God, I'm a child of the King.

Refrain

I'm a child of the King, A child of the King:

With Je - sus my Sav - ior, I'm a child of the King.

FAITH AND ASSURANCE

324 Be Still, My Soul

Be still, and know that I am God. Psa. 46:10

Katharina A. von Schlegel, 1752
Trans. by Jane L. Borthwick, 1855

FINLANDIA 10 10 10 10 10 10
Jean Sibelius, 1899
Arr. for *The Hymnal*, 1933

1. Be still, my soul! the Lord is on thy side; Bear pa-tient-ly the cross of grief or pain; Leave to thy God to or-der and pro-vide; In ev-ery change He faith-ful will re-main. Be still, my soul! thy best, thy heav'n-ly Friend Thro' thorn-y ways leads to a joy-ful end.

2. Be still, my soul! thy God doth un-der-take To guide the fu-ture as He has the past. Thy hope, thy con-fi-dence let noth-ing shake; All now mys-te-rious shall be bright at last. Be still, my soul! the waves and winds still know His voice who ruled them while He dwelt be-low.

3. Be still, my soul! the hour is has-t'ning on When we shall be for-ev-er with the Lord, When dis-ap-point-ment, grief, and fear are gone, Sor-row for-got, love's pur-est joys re-stored. Be still, my soul! when change and tears are past, All safe and bless-ed we shall meet at last.

LIFE IN CHRIST

My Shepherd Will Supply My Need   325

He will feed His flock like a shepherd . . . Isa. 40:11

RESIGNATION C.M.D.

Psalm 23, paraphrased
Isaac Watts, 1719

Traditional American melody
Southern Harmony, 1855

1. My Shep-herd will sup-ply my need; Je - ho - vah is His name:
2. When I walk through the shades of death Thy pres-ence is my stay;
3. The sure pro - vi - sions of my God At - tend me all my days;

In pas - tures fresh He makes me feed, Be - side the liv - ing stream.
One word of Thy sup-port - ing breath Drives all my fears a - way.
O may Thy house be my a - bode, And all my work be praise.

He brings my wand-'ring spir - it back, When I for - sake His ways;
Thy hand, in sight of all my foes, Doth still my ta - ble spread;
There would I find a set - tled rest, While oth - ers go and come;

And leads me, for His mer - cy's sake, In paths of truth and grace.
My cup with bless-ings o - ver-flows, Thine oil a-noints my head.
No more a stran-ger, nor a guest, But like a child at home. A-men.

FAITH AND ASSURANCE

326 God of Our Life, through All the Circling

Thou art the same, and Thy years shall have no end. Psa. 102:27

SANDON 10 4 10 4 10 10

Hugh T. Kerr, 1916; alt., 1928

Charles H. Purday, 1860

1. God of our life, through all the cir-cling years, We trust in Thee;
2. God of the past, our times are in Thy hand; With us a-bide.
3. God of the com-ing years, through paths un-known We fol-low Thee;

In all the past, through all our hopes and fears, Thy hand we see.
Lead us by faith to hope's true prom-ised land; Be Thou our guide.
When we are strong, Lord, leave us not a-lone; Our ref-uge be.

With each new day, when morn-ing lifts the veil,
With Thee to bless, the dark-ness shines as light,
Be Thou for us in life our dai-ly bread,

We own Thy mer-cies, Lord, which nev-er fail.
And faith's fair vi-sion chang-es in-to sight.
Our heart's true home when all our years have sped. A-men.

LIFE IN CHRIST

In Heavenly Love Abiding 327

If ye keep My commandments, ye shall abide in My love. John 15:10

NYLAND 7 6 7 6 D.

Anna L. Waring, 1850

Traditional Finnish melody
Arr. by David Evans, 1927

1. In heav'n - ly love a - bid - ing, No change my heart shall fear;
2. Wher - ev - er He may guide me No want shall turn me back;
3. Green pas - tures are be - fore me Which yet I have not seen;

And safe is such con - fid - ing, For noth - ing chang - es here.
My Shep - herd is be - side me And noth - ing can I lack.
Bright skies will soon be o'er me Where dark - est clouds have been.

The storm may roar with - out me, My heart may low be laid;
His wis - dom ev - er wak - eth, His sight is nev - er dim;
My hope I can - not meas - ure, My path to life is free;

But God is round a - bout me, And can I be dis - mayed?
He knows the way He tak - eth, And I will walk with Him.
My Sav - ior has my treas - ure, And He will walk with me. A - men.

Music from "The Revised Church Hymnary" by permission of Oxford University Press.

FAITH AND ASSURANCE

328 Anywhere with Jesus I Can Safely Go

Lo, I am with you always . . . Matt. 28:20

Jessie B. Pounds, 1887, and
Helen C. Dixon, c. 1915

SECURITY 11 11 11 11 Ref.
Daniel B. Towner, 1887

1. An-y-where with Je-sus I can safe-ly go; An-y-where He leads me in this world be-low; An-y-where with-out Him dear-est joys would fade; An-y-where with Je-sus I am not a-fraid.

2. An-y-where with Je-sus I am not a-lone, Oth-er friends may fail me, He is still my own; Though His hand may lead me o-ver drear-y ways, An-y-where with Je-sus is a house of praise.

3. An-y-where with Je-sus o-ver land and sea, Tell-ing souls in dark-ness of sal-va-tion free; Read-y as He sum-mons me to go or stay, An-y-where with Je-sus when He points the way.

Refrain

An-y-where! an-y-where! Fear I can-not know;

An-y-where with Je-sus I can safe-ly go.

LIFE IN CHRIST

Walk in the Light! 329

If we walk in the light, as He is in the light . . . I John 1:7

MANOAH C.M.

Bernard Barton, 1826

Henry W. Greatorex's *Collection*, 1851

1. Walk in the light! and you shall know That fel-low-ship of love
2. Walk in the light! and you shall find Your heart made tru-ly His,
3. Walk in the light! and you shall see Your dark-ness pass a-way,
4. Walk in the light! and you shall share Your path, though thorn-y, bright;

His Spir-it on-ly can be-stow Who reigns in light a-bove.
Who dwells in cloud-less light en-shrined, In whom no dark-ness is.
Be-cause the light has come to be, In which is per-fect day.
For God in grace walks with you there, And God Him-self is light. A-men.

I Am Trusting Thee, Lord Jesus 330

Trust ye in the Lord for ever . . . Isa. 26:4

BULLINGER 8 5 8 3

Frances R. Havergal, 1874

Ethelbert W. Bullinger, 1874

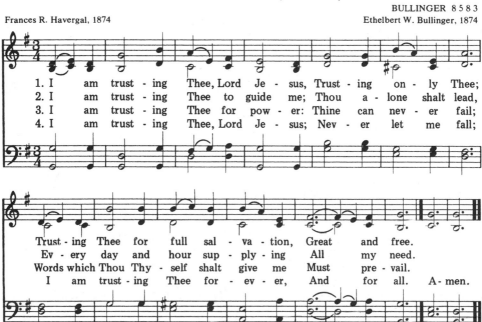

1. I am trust-ing Thee, Lord Je-sus, Trust-ing on-ly Thee;
2. I am trust-ing Thee to guide me; Thou a-lone shalt lead,
3. I am trust-ing Thee for pow-er: Thine can nev-er fail;
4. I am trust-ing Thee, Lord Je-sus; Nev-er let me fall;

Trust-ing Thee for full sal-va-tion, Great and free.
Ev-ery day and hour sup-ply-ing All my need.
Words which Thou Thy-self shalt give me Must pre-vail.
I am trust-ing Thee for-ev-er, And for all. A-men.

FAITH AND ASSURANCE

331 He's Got the Whole World in His Hands

In whose hand is the soul of every living thing . . . Job 12:10

Traditional Spiritual

WHOLE WORLD Irreg.
Traditional Spiritual

Unison

1. He's got the whole wide world in His hands, He's got the whole wide world in His hands, He's got the whole wide world in His hands, He's got the whole world in His hands.
2. He's got the wind and the rain in His hands, He's got the wind and the rain in His hands, He's got the wind and the rain in His hands, He's got the whole world in His hands.
3. He's got the ti - ny lit - tle ba - by in His hands, He's got the ti - ny lit - tle ba - by in His hands, He's got the ti - ny lit - tle ba - by in His hands, He's got the whole world in His hands.
4. He's got you and me, broth-er, in His hands, He's got you and me, sis - ter, in His hands, He's got you and me, broth-er, in His hands, He's got the whole world in His hands. He's got the whole world in His hands.

Coda (after last stanza)

332 To Talk with God

Rest in the Lord and wait patiently for Him. Psa. 37:7

Traditional Hindi hymn

HINDI Irreg.
Martin West, 1969

Solo   Group

1. To talk with God, no breath is lost, Talk on, talk on, talk on!
2. To walk with God, no strength is lost, Walk on, walk on, walk on!
3. To wait on God, no time is lost, Wait on, wait on, wait on!

LIFE IN CHRIST: FAITH AND ASSURANCE

O to Be Like Thee! Blessed Redeemer **333**

... To be conformed to the image of His Son. Rom. 8:29

RONDINELLA 10 9 10 9 Ref.

Thomas O. Chisholm, 1897

William J. Kirkpatrick, 1897

1. O to be like Thee! bless - ed Re - deem - er, This is my con - stant
2. O to be like Thee! full of com - pas - sion, Lov - ing, for - giv - ing,
3. O to be like Thee! low - ly in spir - it, Ho - ly and harm - less,
4. O to be like Thee! while I am plead - ing, Pour out Thy Spir - it,

long - ing and prayer. Glad - ly I'll for - feit all of earth's treas - ures,
ten - der and kind, Help - ing the help - less, cheer - ing the faint - ing,
pa - tient and brave; Meek - ly en - dur - ing cru - el re - proach - es,
fill with Thy love; Make me a tem - ple meet for Thy dwell - ing,

Refrain

Je - sus, Thy per - fect like - ness to wear.
Seek - ing the wan - d'ring sin - ner to find.
Will - ing to suf - fer oth - ers to save.   O to be like Thee!
Fit me for life and heav - en a - bove.

O to be like Thee, Bless - ed Re - deem - er, pure as Thou art! Come in Thy

sweet - ness, come in Thy full - ness; Stamp Thine own im - age deep on my heart.

HOPE AND ASPIRATION

334 More Like Jesus Would I Be

Abide in Me, and I in you. As the branch cannot bear fruit of itself . . . John 15:4

MORE LIKE JESUS 7 7 7 7 D.

Fanny J. Crosby, 1867

William H. Doane, 1867

1. More like Je - sus would I be, Let my Sav - ior dwell in me;
2. If He hears the rav - en's cry, If His ev - er watch - ful eye
3. More like Je - sus when I pray, More like Je - sus day by day;

Fill my soul with peace and love, Make me gen - tle as a dove;
Marks the spar - rows when they fall, Sure - ly He will hear my call:
May I rest me by His side, Where the tran - quil wa - ters glide:

More like Je - sus while I go, Pil - grim in this world be - low;
He will teach me how to live, All my sin - ful thoughts for - give;
Born of Him, through grace re - newed, By His love my will sub - dued,

Poor in spir - it would I be; Let my Sav - ior dwell in me.
Pure in heart I still would be; Let my Sav - ior dwell in me.
Rich in faith I still would be; Let my Sav - ior dwell in me.

LIFE IN CHRIST

Jesus, My Lord, My God, My All   335

Lord . . . Thou knewest that I love Thee. John 21:17

HOLY FAITH 8 8 8 8 8 8

Henry Collins, 1854

George C. Martin, 1889

1. Je - sus, my Lord, my God, my All, Hear me, blest Sav - ior,
2. Je - sus, too late I Thee have sought, How can I love Thee
3. Je - sus, what didst Thou find in me, That Thou hast dealt so
4. Je - sus, of Thee shall be my song, To Thee my heart and

when I call; Hear me, and from Thy dwel - ling place
as I ought? And how ex - tol Thy match - less fame,
lov - ing - ly? How great the joy that Thou hast brought,
soul be - long, All that I have or am is Thine,

Unison

Pour down the rich - es of Thy grace. Je - sus, my Lord, I
The glo - rious beau - ty of Thy name? Je - sus, my Lord, I
So far ex - ceed - ing hope or thought! Je - sus, my Lord, I
And Thou, blest Sav - ior, Thou art mine. Je - sus, my Lord, I

Parts

Thee a - dore, O make me love Thee more and more. A - men.

HOPE AND ASPIRATION

336 I Want a Principle Within

I exercise myself, to have always a conscience void of offense . . . Acts 24:16

Charles Wesley, 1749

LLANGLOFFAN C.M.D.
Traditional Welsh melody

1. I want a prin-ci-ple with-in Of watch-ful, god-ly fear,
2. From Thee that I no more may stray, No more Thy good-ness grieve,
3. Al-might-y God of truth and love, To me Thy pow'r im-part;

A sen-si-bil-i-ty of sin, A pain to feel it near.
Grant me the fil-ial awe, I pray, The ten-der con-science give.
The bur-den from my soul re-move, The hard-ness from my heart.

Help me the first ap-proach to feel Of pride or wrong de-sire;
Quick as the ap-ple of an eye, O God, my con-science make!
O may the least o-mis-sion pain My re-a-wak-ened soul,

To catch the wan-dering of my will, And quench the kind-ling fire.
A-wake my soul when sin is nigh, And keep it still a-wake.
And drive me to that grace a-gain, Which makes the wound-ed whole. A-men.

LIFE IN CHRIST

I Would Be True 337

Be thou an example of the believers . . . I Tim. 4:12

PEEK 11 10 11 10 10

Howard A. Walter, 1907

Joseph Y. Peek, 1909

1. I would be true, for there are those who trust me; I would be
2. I would be friend of all— the foe, the friend-less; I would be
3. I would be learn-ing day by day the les-sons My heav'n-ly
4. I would be prayer-ful through each bus-y mo-ment; I would be

pure, for there are those who care: I would be strong, for there is
giv-ing, and for-get the gift; I would be hum-ble, for I
Fa-ther gives me in His Word; I would be quick to hear His
con-stant-ly in touch with God; I would be tuned to hear His

much to suf-fer; I would be brave, for there is much to
know my weak-ness; I would look up, and laugh, and love, and
light-est whis-per, And prompt and glad to do the things I've
slight-est whis-per, I would have faith to keep the path Christ

dare; I would be brave, for there is much to dare.
lift; I would look up, and laugh, and love, and lift.
heard; And prompt and glad to do the things I've heard.
trod; I would have faith to keep the path Christ trod. A-men.

HOPE AND ASPIRATION

338 Lord, I Want to Be a Christian

Desire the sincere milk of the Word, that ye may grow thereby. I Pet. 2:2

Traditional Spiritual

I WANT TO BE A CHRISTIAN Irreg.
Traditional Spiritual

1. Lord, I want to be a Chris-tian In-a my heart, in-a my heart, Lord, I want to be a Chris-tian In-a my heart.
2. Lord, I want to be more lov-ing In-a my heart, in-a my heart, Lord, I want to be more lov-ing In-a my heart.
3. Lord, I want to be more ho-ly In-a my heart, in-a my heart, Lord, I want to be more ho-ly In-a my heart.
4. Lord, I want to be like Je-sus In-a my heart, in-a my heart, Lord, I want to be like Je-sus In-a my heart.

Refrain

In-a my heart, In-a my heart, In-a my heart, In-a my heart,

Lord, I want to be a Chris-tian In-a my heart.
Lord, I want to be more lov-ing In-a my heart.
Lord, I want to be more ho-ly In-a my heart.
Lord, I want to be like Je-sus In-a my heart.

LIFE IN CHRIST

More About Jesus Would I Know 339

But grow in grace, and in the knowledge of our Lord and Savior Jesus Christ. II Pet. 3:18

SWENEY L.M. Ref.

Eliza E. Hewitt, 1887

John R. Sweney, 1887

1. More a - bout Je - sus would I know, More of His grace to oth - ers show;
2. More a - bout Je - sus let me learn, More of His ho - ly will dis - cern;
3. More a - bout Je - sus; in His Word, Hold-ing com-mun-ion with my Lord;
4. More a - bout Je - sus on His throne, Rich-es in glo - ry all His own;

More of His sav - ing ful - ness see, More of His love who died for me.
Spir - it of God, my teach - er be, Show-ing the things of Christ to me.
Hear - ing His voice in ev - ery line, Mak-ing each faith - ful say - ing mine.
More of His king-dom's sure in-crease; More of His com - ing, Prince of Peace.

Refrain

More, more a - bout Je - sus, More, more a - bout Je - sus;

More of His sav - ing ful - ness see, More of His love who died for me.

HOPE AND ASPIRATION

340 I Need Thee Every Hour

Bow down Thine ear, O Lord, and hear me: for I am poor and needy. Psa. 86:1

Annie S. Hawks, 1872

NEED 6 4 6 4 Ref.
Robert Lowry, 1872

1. I need Thee ev-ery hour, Most gra-cious Lord; No ten-der voice like
2. I need Thee ev-ery hour, Stay Thou near by; Temp-ta-tions lose their
3. I need Thee ev-ery hour In joy or pain; Come quick-ly and a-
4. I need Thee ev-ery hour, Most Ho-ly One; O make me Thine in-

Refrain

Thine Can peace af - ford.
pow'r When Thou art nigh.   I need Thee, O I need Thee; Ev - ery hour I
bide Or life is vain.
deed, Thou bless - ed Son!

need Thee; O bless me now, my Sav - ior, I come to Thee!

341 Lord Jesus, Think on Me

According to Thy mercy remember Thou me . . . Psa. 25:7

Synesius of Cyrene, c. 410
Trans. by Allen W. Chatfield, 1876

DAMON S.M.
William Damon's *Psalms,* 1579

1. Lord Je - sus, think on me And purge a - way my sin;
2. Lord Je - sus, think on me, With care and woe op - pressed;
3. Lord Je - sus, think on me Nor let me go a - stray;
4. Lord Je - sus, think on me, That when the flood is past,

LIFE IN CHRIST

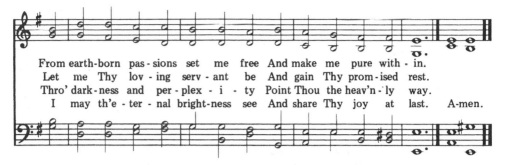

From earth-born pas-sions set me free And make me pure with-in.
Let me Thy lov-ing serv-ant be And gain Thy prom-ised rest.
Thro' dark-ness and per-plex-i-ty Point Thou the heav'n-ly way.
I may th'e-ter-nal bright-ness see And share Thy joy at last. A-men.

There Is a Place of Quiet Rest 342

Draw nigh to God, and He will draw nigh to you. James 4:8

McAFEE C.M. Ref.

Cleland B. McAfee, 1901

Cleland B. McAfee, 1901

1. There is a place of qui-et rest Near to the heart of God,
2. There is a place of com-fort sweet Near to the heart of God,
3. There is a place of full re-lease Near to the heart of God,

A place where sin can-not mo-lest, Near to the heart of God.
A place where we our Sav-ior meet, Near to the heart of God.
A place where all is joy and peace, Near to the heart of God.

Refrain

O Je-sus, blest Re-deem-er Sent from the heart of God,

Hold us who wait be-fore Thee Near to the heart of God.

HOPE AND ASPIRATION

343 Earthly Pleasures Vainly Call Me

We . . . are changed into the same image from glory to glory. II Cor. 3:18

James Rowe, 1912

SPRING HILL C.M. Ref.
Bentley D. Ackley, 1912

1. Earth-ly pleas-ures vain-ly call me, I would be like Je - sus;
2. He has bro-ken ev-ery fet - ter, I would be like Je - sus;
3. All the way from earth to glo - ry, I would be like Je - sus;
4. That in heav-en He may meet me, I would be like Je - sus;
   would be like Je - sus;

Noth-ing world-ly shall en-thrall me, I would be like Je - sus.
That my soul may serve Him bet - ter, I would be like Je - sus.
Tell-ing o'er and o'er the sto - ry, I would be like Je - sus.
That His words "Well done" may greet me, I would be like Je - sus.
    would be like Je - sus.

Refrain

Be like Je - sus, this my song, In the home and in the throng;

Be like Je - sus, all day long! I would be like Je - sus.

LIFE IN CHRIST

Be Thou My Vision 344

What things were gain to me, those I counted loss for Christ. Phil. 3:7

Irish hymn, c. 8th century
Trans. by Mary E. Byrne, 1905
Versified by Eleanor H. Hull, 1912

SLANE 10 10 10 10
Traditional Irish melody
Arr. by Donald P. Hustad, 1973

Unison

1. Be Thou my Vi - sion, O Lord of my heart;
2. Be Thou my Wis - dom, and Thou my true Word;
3. Rich - es I heed not, nor man's emp - ty praise,
4. High King of heav - en, my vic - to - ry won,

Naught be all else to me, save that Thou art—
I ev - er with Thee and Thou with me, Lord;
Thou mine in - her - i - tance, now and al - ways;
May I reach heav - en's joys, O bright heav'n's Sun!

Thou my best thought, by day or by night,
Thou my great Fa - ther, I Thy true son;
Thou and Thou on - ly, first in my heart,
Heart of my own heart, what - ev - er be - fall,

Wak - ing or sleep - ing, Thy pres - ence my light.
Thou in me dwell - ing, and I with Thee one.
High King of heav - en, my Treas - ure Thou art.
Still be my Vi - sion, O Rul - er of all. A - men.

Words used by permission of Chatto and Windus Ltd.

HOPE AND ASPIRATION

345 Savior, Thy Dying Love

... Faith which worketh by love. Gal. 5:6

Sylvanus D. Phelps, 1862

SOMETHING FOR THEE 64646664

Robert Lowry, 1871

1. Sav - ior, Thy dy - ing love Thou gav - est me, Nor should I
2. At the blest mer - cy - seat Plead-ing for me, My fee - ble
3. Give me a faith - ful heart, Like-ness to Thee, That each de -
4. All that I am and have— Thy gifts so free— In joy, in

aught with-hold, Dear Lord, from Thee: In love my soul would bow, My heart ful-
faith looks up, Je - sus, to Thee: Help me the cross to bear, Thy won-drous
part - ing day Henceforth may see Some work of love be - gun, Some deed of
grief, thro' life, Dear Lord, for Thee! And when Thy face I see, My ran-somed

fill its vow, Some of - fering bring Thee now, Some-thing for Thee.
love de-clare, Some song to raise, or prayer, Some-thing for Thee.
kind - ness done, Some wan - d'rer sought and won, Some-thing for Thee.
soul shall be Through all e - ter - ni - ty, Some-thing for Thee. A - men.

346 O for a Heart to Praise My God

I will praise Thee, O Lord, with my whole heart. Psa. 9:1

Charles Wesley, 1742

AZMON C.M.
Carl G. Gläser, 1784-1829
Arr. by Lowell Mason, 1839

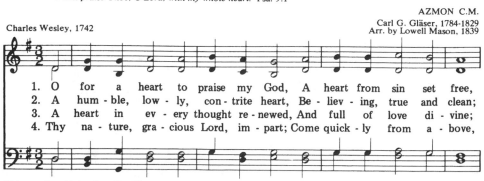

1. O for a heart to praise my God, A heart from sin set free,
2. A hum - ble, low - ly, con - trite heart, Be - liev - ing, true and clean;
3. A heart in ev - ery thought re - newed, And full of love di - vine;
4. Thy na - ture, gra - cious Lord, im - part; Come quick - ly from a - bove,

This tune in a higher key, No. 90

LIFE IN CHRIST

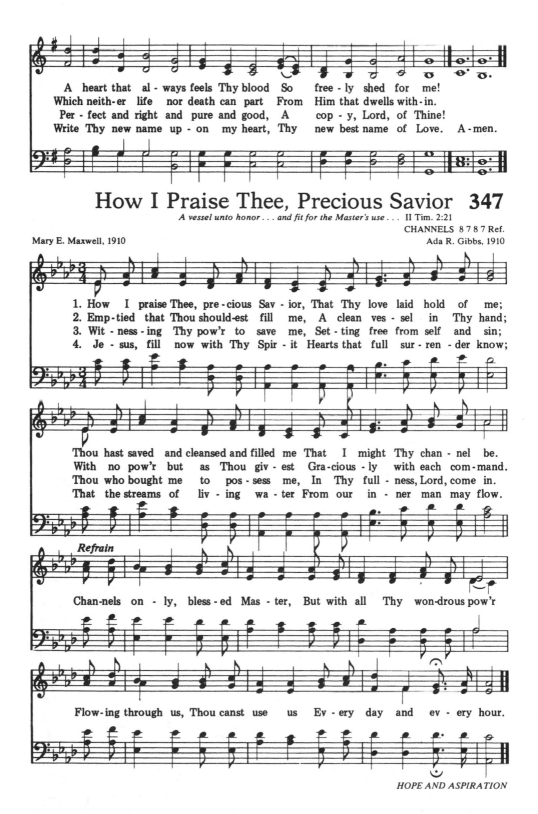

A heart that al-ways feels Thy blood So free-ly shed for me!
Which neith-er life nor death can part From Him that dwells with-in.
Per-fect and right and pure and good, A cop-y, Lord, of Thine!
Write Thy new name up-on my heart, Thy new best name of Love. A-men.

How I Praise Thee, Precious Savior 347

A vessel unto honor . . . and fit for the Master's use . . . II Tim. 2:21

CHANNELS 8 7 8 7 Ref.

Mary E. Maxwell, 1910

Ada R. Gibbs, 1910

1. How I praise Thee, pre-cious Sav-ior, That Thy love laid hold of me;
2. Emp-tied that Thou should-est fill me, A clean ves-sel in Thy hand;
3. Wit-ness-ing Thy pow'r to save me, Set-ting free from self and sin;
4. Je-sus, fill now with Thy Spir-it Hearts that full sur-ren-der know;

Thou hast saved and cleansed and filled me That I might Thy chan-nel be.
With no pow'r but as Thou giv-est Gra-cious-ly with each com-mand.
Thou who bought me to pos-sess me, In Thy full-ness, Lord, come in.
That the streams of liv-ing wa-ter From our in-ner man may flow.

Refrain

Chan-nels on-ly, bless-ed Mas-ter, But with all Thy won-drous pow'r

Flow-ing through us, Thou canst use us Ev-ery day and ev-ery hour.

HOPE AND ASPIRATION

348 Nearer, My God, to Thee

It is good for me to draw near to God . . . Psa. 73:28

Sarah F. Adams, 1841
Based on Gen. 28:10-22

BETHANY 6 4 6 4 6 6 6 4
Lowell Mason, 1856

1. Near - er, my God, to Thee, Near - er to Thee! E'en though it
2. Though like the wan - der - er, The sun gone down, Dark - ness be
3. There let the way ap - pear Steps un - to heav'n; All that Thou
4. Then, with my wak - ing thoughts Bright with Thy praise, Out of my
5. Or if on joy - ful wing, Cleav - ing the sky, Sun, moon, and

be a cross That rais - eth me; Still all my song shall be, Near - er, my
o - ver me, My rest a stone; Yet in my dreams I'd be Near - er, my
send - est me In mer - cy giv'n; An - gels to beck - on me Near - er, my
ston - y griefs, Beth - el I'll raise; So by my woes to be Near - er, my
stars for - got, Up - ward I fly, Still all my song shall be Near - er, my

God, to Thee, Near - er, my God, to Thee, Near - er to Thee. A - men.

349 May the Mind of Christ My Savior

Let this mind be in you which was also in Christ Jesus . . . Phil. 2:5

Kate B. Wilkinson, 1925

ST. LEONARDS 8 7 8 5
A. Cyril Barham-Gould, 1925

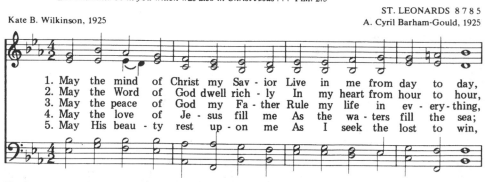

1. May the mind of Christ my Sav - ior Live in me from day to day,
2. May the Word of God dwell rich - ly In my heart from hour to hour,
3. May the peace of God my Fa - ther Rule my life in ev - ery - thing,
4. May the love of Je - sus fill me As the wa - ters fill the sea;
5. May His beau - ty rest up - on me As I seek the lost to win,

Words copyright used by permission of Gordon Hitchcock, Surrey.

LIFE IN CHRIST

By His love and pow'r con-trol-ling All I do and say.
So that all may see I tri-umph On-ly through His pow'r.
That I may be calm to com-fort Sick and sor-row-ing.
Him ex-alt-ing, self a-bas-ing, This is vic-to-ry.
And may they for-get the chan-nel, See-ing on-ly Him. A-men.

Open My Eyes, That I May See 350

Open Thou mine eyes, that I may behold wondrous things out of Thy law. Psa. 119:18

SCOTT Irreg.

Clara H. Scott, 1895

Clara H. Scott, 1895

1. O-pen my eyes, that I may see Glimps-es of truth Thou hast for me;
2. O-pen my ears, that I may hear Voic-es of truth Thou send-est clear;
3. O-pen my mouth, and let me bear Glad-ly the warm truth ev-ery-where;

Place in my hands the won-der-ful key That shall un-clasp and set me free.
And while the wave-notes fall on my ear, Ev-ery-thing false will dis-ap-pear.
O-pen my heart, and let me pre-pare Love with Thy chil-dren thus to share.

Refrain

Si-lent-ly now I wait for Thee, Read-y, my God, Thy will to see;

O-pen my eyes, il-lu-mine me, Spir-it di-vine!
O-pen my ears, il-lu-mine me, Spir-it di-vine!
O-pen my heart, il-lu-mine me, Spir-it di-vine! A-men.

HOPE AND ASPIRATION

351 O Love That Will Not Let Me Go

The Lord hath appeared . . . saying, Yea, I have loved thee with an everlasting love. Jer. 31:3

George Matheson, 1882

ST. MARGARET 8 8 8 8 6
Albert L. Peace, 1884

1. O Love that will not let me go, I rest my wea - ry
2. O Light that fol - l'west all my way, I yield my flick - 'ring
3. O Joy that seek - est me through pain, I can - not close my
4. O Cross that lift - est up my head, I dare not ask to

soul in Thee; I give Thee back the life I owe, That
torch to Thee; My heart re - stores its bor - rowed ray, That
heart to Thee; I trace the rain - bow through the rain, And
fly from Thee; I lay in dust life's glo - ry dead, And

in Thine o - cean depths its flow May rich - er, full - er be.
in Thy sun - shine's blaze its day May bright - er, fair - er be.
feel the prom - ise is not vain That morn shall tear - less be.
from the ground there blos - soms red Life that shall end - less be. A - men.

352 O for a Closer Walk with God

What doth the Lord require of thee . . . to walk humbly with thy God. Micah 6:8

William Cowper, 1772

BEATITUDO C.M.
John B. Dykes, 1875

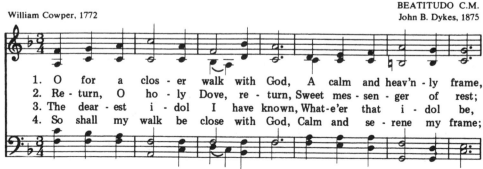

1. O for a clos - er walk with God, A calm and heav'n - ly frame,
2. Re - turn, O ho - ly Dove, re - turn, Sweet mes - sen - ger of rest;
3. The dear - est i - dol I have known, What - e'er that i - dol be,
4. So shall my walk be close with God, Calm and se - rene my frame;

LIFE IN CHRIST

A light to shine up - on the road That leads me to the Lamb.
I hate the sins that made Thee mourn, And drove Thee from my breast.
Help me to tear it from Thy throne, And wor - ship on - ly Thee.
So pur - er light shall mark the road That leads me to the Lamb. A - men.

Nearer, Still Nearer 353

For to me to live is Christ, and to die is gain. Phil. 1:21

MORRIS 9 10 9 10

Lelia N. Morris, 1898

Lelia N. Morris, 1898

1. Near - er, still near - er, close to Thy heart, Draw me, my Sav - ior, so pre - cious Thou
2. Near - er, still near - er, noth - ing I bring, Naught as an of - f'ring to Je - sus my
3. Near - er, still near - er, Lord, to be Thine, Sin with its fol - lies I glad - ly re -
4. Near - er, still near - er, while life shall last, Till safe in glo - ry my an - chor is

art; Fold me, O fold me close to Thy breast, Shel - ter me safe in that
King; On - ly my sin - ful, now con-trite heart, Grant me the cleans-ing Thy
sign; All of its pleas-ures, pomp and its pride, Give me but Je - sus, my
cast; Thro' end-less a - ges, ev - er to be Near - er, my Sav - ior, still

"Ha - ven of Rest," Shel - ter me safe in that "Ha - ven of Rest."
blood doth im - part, Grant me the cleans-ing Thy blood doth im-part.
Lord cru - ci - fied, Give me but Je - sus, my Lord cru - ci - fied.
near - er to Thee, Near - er, my Sav - ior, still near - er to Thee. A - men.

HOPE AND ASPIRATION

354 I Am Thine, O Lord

Let us draw near with a true heart . . . Heb. 10:22

Fanny J. Crosby, 1875

I AM THINE 10 7 10 7 Ref.
William H. Doane, 1875

1. I am Thine, O Lord, I have heard Thy voice, And it
2. Con - se - crate me now to Thy serv - ice, Lord, By the
3. O, the pure de - light of a sin - gle hour That be -
4. There are depths of love that I can - not know Till I

told Thy love to me; But I long to rise in the arms of faith,
pow'r of grace di - vine; Let my soul look up with a stead-fast hope,
fore Thy throne I spend, When I kneel in prayer, and with Thee, my God,
cross the nar - row sea; There are heights of joy that I may not reach

Refrain

And be clos - er drawn to Thee.
And my will be lost in Thine.
I com - mune as friend with friend! Draw me near - er,
Till I rest in peace with Thee.

near - er, bless - ed Lord, To the cross where Thou hast died; Draw me

near - er, near - er, near - er, bless-ed Lord, To Thy pre - cious, bleed - ing side.

LIFE IN CHRIST

I'm Pressing on the Upward Way 355

I press toward the mark for the prize . . . Phil. 3:14

Johnson Oatman, Jr., 1898

HIGHER GROUND L.M. Ref.
Charles H. Gabriel, 1898

1. I'm press-ing on the up-ward way, New heights I'm gain-ing ev-ery
2. My heart has no de-sire to stay Where doubts a-rise and fears dis-
3. I want to live a-bove the world, Though Sa-tan's darts at me are
4. I want to scale the ut-most height, And catch a gleam of glo-ry

day; Still pray-ing as I'm on-ward bound, "Lord, plant my
may; Though some may dwell where these a-bound, My prayer, my
hurled; For faith has caught the joy-ful sound, The song of
bright; But still I'll pray till heav'n I've found, "Lord, lead me

Refrain

feet on high-er ground."
aim is high-er ground. Lord, lift me up and let me stand
saints on high-er ground.
on to high-er ground."

By faith on heav-en's ta-ble-land, A high-er plane

than I have found; Lord, plant my feet on high-er ground.

HOPE AND ASPIRATION

356 Draw Thou My Soul, O Christ

Master, I will follow Thee whithersoever Thou goest. Matt. 8:19

Lucy Larcom, 1892

ST. EDMUND 6 4 6 4 6 6 6 4
Arthur S. Sullivan, 1872

1. Draw Thou my soul, O Christ, Clos - er to Thine; Breathe in - to
2. Lead forth my soul, O Christ, One with Thine own, Joy - ful to
3. Not for my - self a - lone May my prayer be; Lift Thou Thy

ev - ery wish Thy will di - vine; Raise my low self a - bove, Won by Thy
fol - low Thee Thro' paths un - known; In Thee my strength re - new; Give me Thy
world, O Christ, Clos - er to Thee; Cleanse it from guilt and wrong; Teach it sal-

death - less love; Ev - er, O Christ, thro' mine Let Thy life shine.
work to do; Thro' me Thy truth be shown, Thy love made known.
va - tion's song, Till earth, as heav'n, ful - fill God's ho - ly will. A - men.

357 "Take Up Your Cross," the Savior Said

If any man will come after Me, let him . . . take up his cross, and follow Me. Matt. 16:24

Charles W. Everest, 1833

QUEBEC L.M.
Henry Baker, 1854

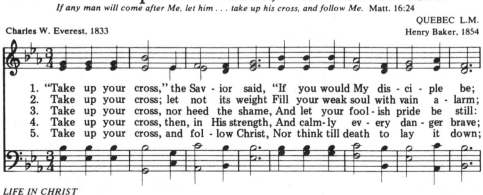

1. "Take up your cross," the Sav - ior said, "If you would My dis - ci - ple be;
2. Take up your cross; let not its weight Fill your weak soul with vain a - larm;
3. Take up your cross, nor heed the shame, And let your fool - ish pride be still:
4. Take up your cross, then, in His strength, And calm - ly ev - ery dan - ger brave;
5. Take up your cross, and fol - low Christ, Nor think till death to lay it down;

LIFE IN CHRIST

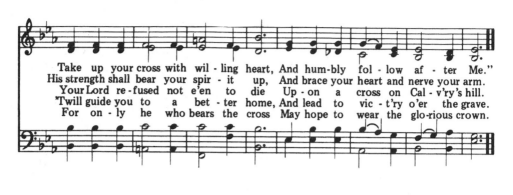

Take up your cross with wil - ling heart, And hum-bly fol - low af - ter Me."
His strength shall bear your spir - it up, And brace your heart and nerve your arm.
Your Lord re - fused not e'en to die Up - on a cross on Cal - v'ry's hill.
'Twill guide you to a bet - ter home, And lead to vic - t'ry o'er the grave.
For on - ly he who bears the cross May hope to wear the glo - ri-ous crown.

We Praise Thee, O God 358

Wilt Thou not revive us again: that Thy people may rejoice in Thee? Psa. 85:6

William P. Mackay, 1863

REVIVE US AGAIN 11 11 Ref.
John J. Husband, c. 1880

1. We praise Thee, O God, for the Son of Thy love, For Je - sus who
2. We praise Thee, O God, for Thy Spir - it of light, Who has shown us our
3. All glo - ry and praise to the Lamb that was slain, Who has borne all our
4. Re - vive us a - gain, fill each heart with Thy love; May each soul be re -

Refrain

died and is now gone a - bove.
Sav - ior and scat - tered our night.
sins, and has cleansed ev - ery stain. Hal - le - lu - jah! Thine the glo - ry, Hal - le -
kin-dled with fire from a - bove.

lu - jah! A - men; Hal - le - lu - jah! Thine the glo - ry; Re - vive us a - gain.

HOPE AND ASPIRATION

359 More Love to Thee, O Christ

This I pray, that your love may abound yet more and more. Phil. 1:9

MORE LOVE TO THEE 6 4 6 4 6 6 4 4

Elizabeth P. Prentiss, 1856·

William H. Doane, 1870

1. More love to Thee, O Christ, More love to Thee! Hear Thou the
2. Once earth-ly joy I craved, Sought peace and rest; Now Thee a-
3. Let sor-row do its work, Send grief and pain; Sweet are Thy
4. Then shall my lat-est breath Whis-per Thy praise; This be the

prayer I make On bend-ed knee; This is my ear-nest plea:
lone I seek, Give what is best; This all my prayer shall be:
mes-sen-gers, Sweet their re-frain, When they can sing with me:
part-ing cry My heart shall raise; This still its prayer shall be:

More love, O Christ, to Thee, More love to Thee, More love to Thee! A-men.

360 Speak, Lord, in the Stillness

Speak, Lord: for Thy servant heareth. I Sam. 3:9

QUIETUDE 6 5 6 5

E. May Grimes, 1920

Harold Green, c. 1925

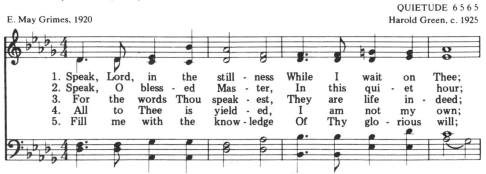

1. Speak, Lord, in the still-ness While I wait on Thee;
2. Speak, O bless-ed Mas-ter, In this qui-et hour;
3. For the words Thou speak-est, They are life in-deed;
4. All to Thee is yield-ed, I am not my own;
5. Fill me with the know-ledge Of Thy glo-rious will;

Copyright used by permission of the Africa Evangelical Fellowship/SAGM, London.

LIFE IN CHRIST

Hushed my heart to lis-ten In ex-pect-an-cy.
Let me see Thy face, Lord, Feel Thy touch of power.
Liv-ing bread from heav-en, Now my spir-it feed!
Bliss-ful, glad sur-ren-der, I am Thine a-lone.
All Thine own good pleas-ure In Thy child ful-fill. A-men.

Jesus, Keep Me Near the Cross 361

God forbid that I should glory, save in the cross . . . Gal. 6:14

NEAR THE CROSS 7 6 7 6 Ref.

Fanny J. Crosby, 1869

William H. Doane, 1869

1. Je-sus, keep me near the cross, There a pre-cious foun-tain
2. Near the cross, a trem-bling soul, Love and mer-cy found me;
3. Near the cross! O Lamb of God, Bring its scenes be-fore me;
4. Near the cross I'll watch and wait, Hop-ing, trust-ing ev-er,

Free to all, a heal-ing stream, Flows from Cal-v'ry's moun-tain.
There the Bright and Morn-ing Star Sheds its beams a-round me.
Help me walk from day to day With its shad-ows o'er me.
Till I reach the gold-en strand Just be-yond the riv-er.

Refrain

In the cross, in the cross Be my glo-ry ev-er;

Till my rap-tured soul shall find Rest be-yond the riv-er.

HOPE AND ASPIRATION

362 More Like the Master

That . . . ye might be partakers of the divine nature . . . II Pet. 1:4

Charles H. Gabriel, 1906

HANFORD 10 10 11 11 Ref.
Charles H. Gabriel, 1906

1. More like the Mas-ter I would ev - er be, More of His meek-ness, more hu-mil - i - ty; More zeal to la - bor, more cour-age to be true, More con - se - cra-tion for work He bids me do.

2. More like the Mas-ter is my dai - ly prayer, More strength to car - ry cross - es I must bear; More ear-nest ef - fort to bring His king-dom in, More of His Spir - it, the wan-der - er to win.

3. More like the Mas-ter I would live and grow, More of His love to oth - ers I would show; More self - de - ni - al like His in Gal - i - lee, More like the Mas - ter I long to ev - er be.

Refrain

Take Thou my heart, I would be Thine a - lone; Take Thou my heart and make it all Thine own. Purge me from sin, O Lord, I now im-

Take my heart, O take my heart, I would be Thine a - lone; Take my heart, O take my heart and make it all Thine own. Purge Thou me from ev-ery sin, O Lord, I

LIFE IN CHRIST

plore, Wash me and keep me Thine for - ev - er - more.
now im - plore, Wash and keep, O wash and keep me Thine for - ev - er - more.

Lord, I Hear of Showers of Blessing 363

. . . The times of refreshing shall come from the presence of the Lord. Acts 3:19

EVEN ME 8 7 8 7 6 7

Elizabeth Codner, 1860

William B. Bradbury, 1862

1. Lord, I hear of show'rs of bless - ing Thou art scat - t'ring full and free;
2. Pass me not, O gra - cious Fa - ther, Sin - ful though my heart may be;
3. Pass me not, O ten - der Sav - ior, Let me love and cling to Thee;
4. Love of God, so pure and change - less, Blood of Christ, so rich, so free,

Show'rs the thirst - y land re - fresh - ing; Let some drops now fall on me;
Thou mightst leave me, but the rath - er Let Thy mer - cy light on me;
I am long - ing for Thy fa - vor; While Thou'rt call - ing, O call me,
Grace of God, so strong and bound - less, Mag - ni - fy them all in me,

E - ven me, E - ven me, Let some drops now fall on me.
E - ven me, E - ven me, Let Thy mer - cy light on me.
E - ven me, E - ven me, While Thou'rt call - ing, O call me.
E - ven me, E - ven me, Mag - ni - fy them all in me. A - men.

HOPE AND ASPIRATION

364 Jesus, Thy Boundless Love to Me

... And to know the love of Christ, which passeth knowledge. Eph. 3:19

Paul Gerhardt, 1653
Trans. by John Wesley, 1739

ST. CATHERINE 8 8 8 8 8 8
Henri F. Hemy, 1864
Arr. by James G. Walton, 1874

1. Je - sus, Thy bound-less love to me No thought can reach, no tongue de-clare;
2. O Love, how cheer-ing is Thy ray! All fear be - fore Thy pres-ence flies;
3. In suf-fering be Thy love my peace; In weak - ness be Thy love my pow'r;

O knit my thank-ful heart to Thee, And reign with - out a ri - val there!
Care, an - guish, sor - row, melt a - way, Wher-e'er Thy heal - ing beams a - rise:
And when the storms of life shall cease, O Je - sus, in that sol - emn hour,

Thine whol-ly, Thine a - lone, I'd live, My-self to Thee en - tire - ly give.
O Je - sus, noth-ing may I see, Noth-ing de - sire, or seek, but Thee!
In death as life be Thou my guide, And save me, who for me hast died. A-men.

365 I Am Weak, but Thou Art Strong

Let the weak say, I am strong. Joel 3:10

Source unknown

CLOSER WALK Irreg.
Source unknown

Unison

1. I am weak, but Thou art strong; Je - sus, keep me from all wrong;
2. Thro' this world of toil and snares, If I fal - ter, Lord, who cares?
3. When my fee - ble life is o'er, Time for me will be no more;
Ref. Just a clos - er walk with Thee, Grant it, Je - sus, is my plea,

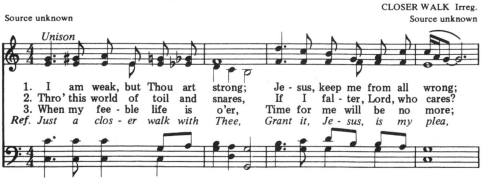

LIFE IN CHRIST

D.C. Refrain

I'll be sat - is - fied as long / As I walk, let me walk close to Thee.
Who with me my bur - den shares? / None but Thee, dear Lord, none but Thee.
Guide me gent - ly, safe - ly o'er / To Thy king - dom shore, to Thy shore.
Dai - ly walk-ing close to Thee, / *Let it be, dear Lord, let it be.*

My Faith Looks Up to Thee 366

Looking unto Jesus the author and finisher of our faith. Heb. 12:2

Ray Palmer, 1830

OLIVET 6 6 4 6 6 6 4
Lowell Mason, 1832

1. My faith looks up to Thee, Thou Lamb of Cal - va - ry,
2. May Thy rich grace im - part Strength to my faint - ing heart,
3. While life's dark maze I tread, And griefs a - round me spread,
4. When ends life's tran - sient dream, When death's cold, sul - len stream

Sav - ior di - vine! Now hear me while I pray, Take all my
My zeal in - spire; As Thou hast died for me, O may my
Be Thou my guide; Bid dark - ness turn to day, Wipe sor - row's
Shall o'er me roll; Blest Sav - ior, then, in love, Fear and dis -

guilt a - way, O let me from this day Be whol - ly Thine!
love to Thee Pure, warm, and change - less be, A liv - ing fire!
tears a - way, Nor let me ev - er stray From Thee a - side.
trust re - move; O bear me safe a - bove, A ran - somed soul! A-men.

HOPE AND ASPIRATION

367 Fill All My Vision, Savior, I Pray

They saw no man, save Jesus only. Matt. 17:8

Avis B. Christiansen, 1940

HAMMONTREE 9 9 9 9 Ref.
Homer Hammontree, 1940

1. Fill all my vi - sion, Sav - ior, I pray, Let me see on - ly
2. Fill all my vi - sion, ev - ery de - sire Keep for Thy glo - ry;
3. Fill all my vi - sion, let naught of sin Shad - ow the bright - ness

Je - sus to - day; Though thro' the val - ley Thou lead - est me,
my soul in - spire With Thy per - fec - tion, Thy ho - ly love
shin - ing with - in. Let me see on - ly Thy bless - ed face,

Refrain

Give me Thy glo - ry and beau - ty to see.
Flood - ing my path - way with light from a - bove. Fill all my vi - sion,
Feast - ing my soul on Thy in - fi - nite grace.

Sav - ior di - vine, Till with Thy glo - ry my spir - it shall shine. Fill all my

vi - sion, that all may see Thy ho - ly im - age re - flect - ed in me.

LIFE IN CHRIST: HOPE AND ASPIRATION

My Life, My Love I Give to Thee 368

That they might live . . . unto Him which died for them. II Cor. 5:15

DUNBAR 8 8 8 6 Ref.

Ralph E. Hudson, 1882

C. R. Dunbar, 1882

1. My life, my love I give to Thee, Thou Lamb of God who died for me;
2. I now be-lieve Thou dost re-ceive, For Thou hast died that I might live;
3. O Thou who died on Cal-va-ry, To save my soul and make me free,
Ref. — I'll live for Him who died for me, How hap-py then my life shall be!

O may I ev-er faith-ful be, My Sav-ior and my God!
And now hence-forth I'll trust in Thee, My Sav-ior and my God!
I'll con-se-crate my life to Thee, My Sav-ior and my God!
I'll live for Him who died for me, My Sav-ior and my God!

D.C. Refrain

I Can Hear My Savior Calling 369

Master, I will follow Thee whithersoever Thou goest. Matt. 8:19

NORRIS 8 8 8 9 Ref.

E. W. Blandy, 1890

John S. Norris, 1890

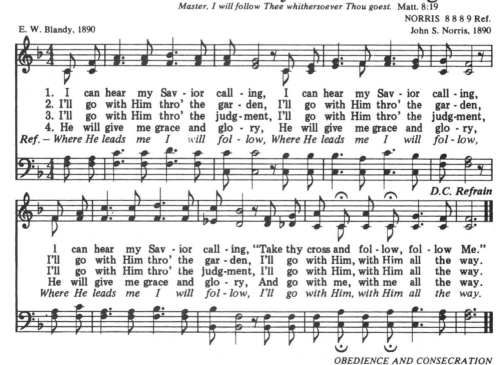

1. I can hear my Sav-ior call-ing, I can hear my Sav-ior call-ing,
2. I'll go with Him thro' the gar-den, I'll go with Him thro' the gar-den,
3. I'll go with Him thro' the judg-ment, I'll go with Him thro' the judg-ment,
4. He will give me grace and glo-ry, He will give me grace and glo-ry,
Ref. — Where He leads me I will fol-low, Where He leads me I will fol-low,

I can hear my Sav-ior call-ing, "Take thy cross and fol-low, fol-low Me."
I'll go with Him thro' the gar-den, I'll go with Him, with Him all the way.
I'll go with Him thro' the judg-ment, I'll go with Him, with Him all the way.
He will give me grace and glo-ry, And go with me, with me all the way.
Where He leads me I will fol-low, I'll go with Him, with Him all the way.

D.C. Refrain

OBEDIENCE AND CONSECRATION

370 Teach Me Thy Will, O Lord

Teach me to do Thy will; for Thou art my God. Psa. 143:10

TEACH ME 64646664

Katherine A. Grimes, 1935

William M. Runyan, 1935

1. Teach me Thy will, O Lord, teach me Thy way; Teach me to
2. Teach me Thy won-drous grace, bound-less and free; Lord, let Thy
3. Teach me by pain Thy power, teach me by love; Teach me to
4. Teach Thou my lips to sing, my heart to praise; Be Thou my

know Thy Word, teach me to pray. What-e'er seems best to Thee, that be my
bless-ed face shine up-on me. Heal Thou sin's ev-ery smart, dwell Thou with-
know each hour Thou art a-bove. Teach me as seem-eth best in Thee to
Lord and King thro' all my days. Teach Thou my soul to cry, "Be Thou, dear

ear-nest plea, So that Thou draw-est me clos-er each day.
in my heart; Grant that I nev-er part, Sav-ior, from Thee.
find sweet rest; Lean-ing up-on Thy breast, all doubt re-move.
Sav-ior, nigh, Teach me to live, to die, saved by Thy grace." A-men.

371 Just As I Am, Thine Own to Be

Wherewithal shall a young man cleanse his way? Psa. 119:9

JUST AS I AM 8886

Marianne Hearn, 1887

Joseph Barnby, 1892

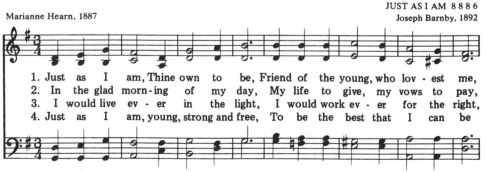

1. Just as I am, Thine own to be, Friend of the young, who lov-est me,
2. In the glad morn-ing of my day, My life to give, my vows to pay,
3. I would live ev-er in the light, I would work ev-er for the right,
4. Just as I am, young, strong and free, To be the best that I can be

LIFE IN CHRIST

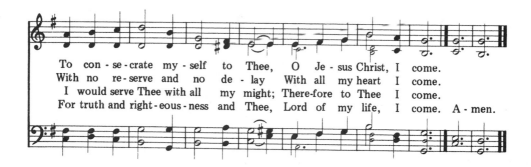

To con - se - crate my - self to Thee, O Je - sus Christ, I come.
With no re - serve and no de - lay With all my heart I come.
I would serve Thee with all my might; There-fore to Thee I come.
For truth and right - eous - ness and Thee, Lord of my life, I come. A - men.

Have Thine Own Way, Lord 372

We are the clay, and Thou our potter . . . Isa. 64:8

ADELAIDE 5 4 5 4 D.

Adelaide A. Pollard, 1902

George C. Stebbins, 1907

1. Have Thine own way, Lord! Have Thine own way! Thou art the
2. Have Thine own way, Lord! Have Thine own way! Search me and
3. Have Thine own way, Lord! Have Thine own way! Wound - ed and
4. Have Thine own way, Lord! Have Thine own 'way! Hold o'er my

Pot - ter, I am the clay. Mold me and make me aft - er Thy
try me, Mas - ter, to - day! Whit - er than snow, Lord, wash me just
wea - ry, help me, I pray! Pow - er— all pow - er— sure - ly is
be - ing ab - so - lute sway! Fill with Thy Spir - it till all shall

will, While I am wait - ing yield - ed and still.
now, As in Thy pres - ence hum - bly I bow.
Thine! Touch me and heal me, Sav - ior di - vine!
see Christ on - ly, al - ways, liv - ing in me! A - men.

OBEDIENCE AND CONSECRATION

373 All to Jesus I Surrender

Lo, we have left all, and have followed Thee. Mark 10:28

SURRENDER 8 7 8 7 Ref.

Judson W. VanDeVenter, 1896

Winfield S. Weeden, 1896

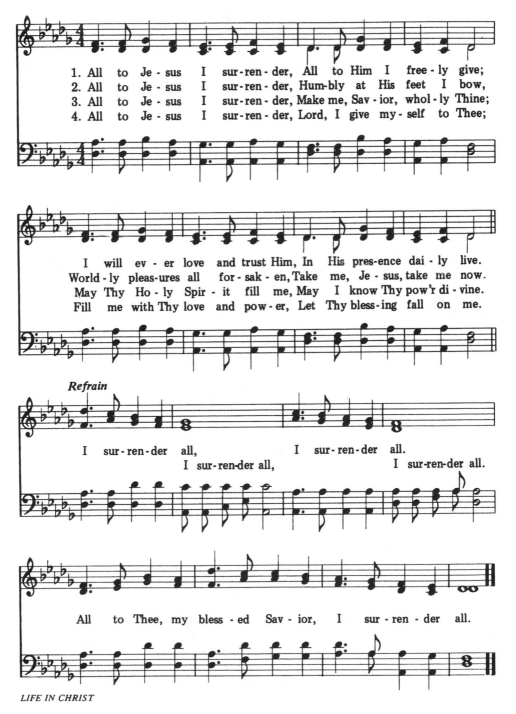

1. All to Je-sus I sur-ren-der, All to Him I free-ly give;
2. All to Je-sus I sur-ren-der, Hum-bly at His feet I bow,
3. All to Je-sus I sur-ren-der, Make me, Sav-ior, whol-ly Thine;
4. All to Je-sus I sur-ren-der, Lord, I give my-self to Thee;

I will ev-er love and trust Him, In His pres-ence dai-ly live.
World-ly pleas-ures all for-sak-en, Take me, Je-sus, take me now.
May Thy Ho-ly Spir-it fill me, May I know Thy pow'r di-vine.
Fill me with Thy love and pow-er, Let Thy bless-ing fall on me.

Refrain

I sur-ren-der all, I sur-ren-der all.
I sur-ren-der all, I sur-ren-der all.

All to Thee, my bless-ed Sav-ior, I sur-ren-der all.

LIFE IN CHRIST

Take Thou Our Minds, Dear Lord 374

Thou shalt love the Lord thy God . . . with all thy mind. Matt. 22:37

HALL 10 10 10 10

William H. Foulkes, 1918

Calvin W. Laufer, 1918

1. Take Thou our minds, dear Lord, we hum - bly pray;
2. Take Thou our hearts, O Christ, they are Thine own;
3. Take Thou our wills, Most High! hold Thou full sway;
4. Take Thou our - selves, O Lord, heart, mind and will;

Give us the mind of Christ each pass - ing day;
Come Thou with - in our souls and claim Thy throne;
Have in our in - most souls Thy per - fect way;
Through our sur - ren - dered souls Thy plans ful - fill.

Teach us to know the truth that sets us free;
Help us to shed a - broad Thy death - less love;
Guard Thou each sa - cred hour from self - ish ease;
We yield our - selves to Thee— time, tal - ents, all!

Grant us in all our thoughts to hon - or Thee.
Use us to make the earth like heav'n a - bove.
Guide Thou our or - dered lives as Thou dost please.
We hear, and hence - forth heed Thy sov - ereign call. A-men.

OBEDIENCE AND CONSECRATION

375 God Himself Is with Us

The Lord is in His holy temple: let all the earth keep silence before Him. Hab. 2:20

Gerhard Tersteegen, 1729
Trans., *Hymnal 1940*

WUNDERBARER KÖNIG 6 6 8 D. 3 3 6 6
Joachim Neander's *Bundes-lieder,* 1680

1. God Him-self is with us; Let us all a - dore Him, And with awe ap-
2. Come, a - bide with - in me; Let my soul, like Ma - ry, Be Thine earth-ly
3. Glad - ly we sur - ren - der Earth's de-ceit - ful treas-ures, Pride of life and

pear be - fore Him. God is here with - in us; Soul, in si - lence
sanc - tu - ar - y. Come, in - dwell-ing Spir - it, With trans - fig - ured
sin - ful pleas - ures; Glad - ly, Lord, we of - fer Thine to be for-

fear Him, Hum-bly, fer-vent - ly draw near Him. Now His own who have known
splen-dor; Love and hon-or will I ren - der. Where I go here be - low
ev - er, Soul and life and each en - deav - or. Thou a - lone shalt be known

God, in wor - ship low - ly, Yield their spir - its whol - ly.
Let me bow be - fore Thee, Know Thee and a - dore Thee.
Lord of all our be - ing, Life's true way de - cree - ing. A - men.

LIFE IN CHRIST

Make Me a Captive, Lord 376

He that loseth his life for My sake shall find it. Matt. 10:39

George Matheson, 1890

DIADEMATA S.M.D.
George J. Elvey, 1868

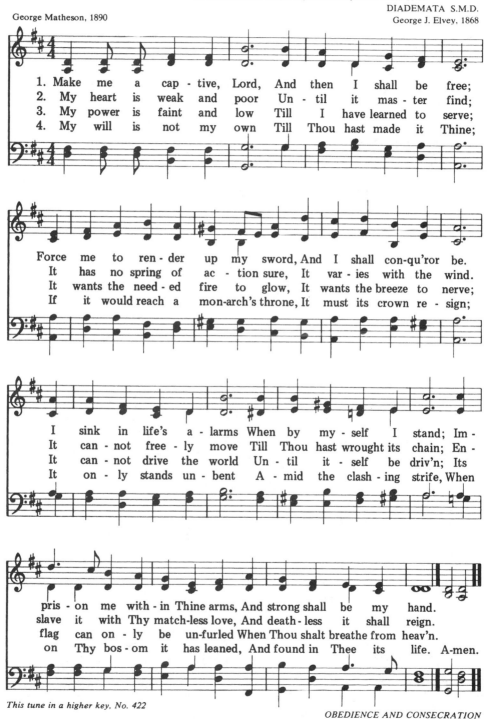

1. Make me a cap - tive, Lord, And then I shall be free;
2. My heart is weak and poor Un - til it mas - ter find;
3. My power is faint and low Till I have learned to serve;
4. My will is not my own Till Thou hast made it Thine;

Force me to ren - der up my sword, And I shall con-qu'ror be.
It has no spring of ac - tion sure, It var - ies with the wind.
It wants the need - ed fire to glow, It wants the breeze to nerve;
If it would reach a mon-arch's throne, It must its crown re - sign;

I sink in life's a - larms When by my - self I stand; Im -
It can - not free - ly move Till Thou hast wrought its chain; En -
It can - not drive the world Un - til it - self be driv'n; Its
It on - ly stands un - bent A - mid the clash - ing strife, When

pris - on me with - in Thine arms, And strong shall be my hand.
slave it with Thy match-less love, And death - less it shall reign.
flag can on - ly be un-furled When Thou shalt breathe from heav'n.
on Thy bos - om it has leaned, And found in Thee its life. A-men.

This tune in a higher key, No. 422

OBEDIENCE AND CONSECRATION

377 Jesus, Savior, All I Have Is Thine

. . . A vessel unto honor, . . . meet for the Master's use. II Tim. 2:21

VOSS Irreg.

Herman Voss, 1940

Herman Voss, 1940

1. Je - sus, Sav - ior, all I have is Thine, Bod - y, soul and
2. Je - sus, Sav - ior, I would die to sin, Come, O come and
3. Je - sus, Sav - ior, in this qui - et hour, May I feel Thy

will I now re - sign. Make me, keep me faith - ful un - to
live in me a - gain. Mold me, fill me till the world shall
Spir - it's strength and pow'r; Take me, use me as Thou wilt each

Thee, Je - sus, Sav - ior, through e - ter - ni - ty.
see Je - sus, Sav - ior, liv - ing now in me.
day, Je - sus, Sav - ior, this I hum - bly pray. A - men.

378 Lord, Speak to Me, That I May Speak

The things that thou hast heard of me . . . commit thou to faithful men. II Tim. 2:2

CANONBURY L.M.

Frances R. Havergal, 1872

Robert A. Schumann, 1839

1. Lord, speak to me, that I may speak In liv - ing ech - oes of Thy tone;
2. O teach me, Lord, that I may teach The pre - cious things Thou dost im - part;
3. O fill me with Thy full - ness, Lord, Un - til my ver - y heart o'er - flow
4. O use me, Lord, use e - ven me, Just as Thou wilt and when and where;

LIFE IN CHRIST

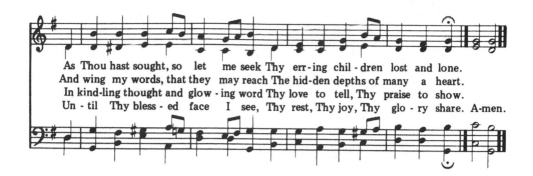

As Thou hast sought, so let me seek Thy err-ing chil-dren lost and lone.
And wing my words, that they may reach The hid-den depths of many a heart.
In kind-ling thought and glow-ing word Thy love to tell, Thy praise to show.
Un-til Thy bless-ed face I see, Thy rest, Thy joy, Thy glo-ry share. A-men.

Teach Me Thy Way, O Lord 379

Teach me Thy way, O Lord, and lead me in a plain path. Psa. 27:11

CAMACHA 6 4 6 4 6 6 6 4

B. Mansell Ramsey, 1919

B. Mansell Ramsey, 1919

1. Teach me Thy way, O Lord, Teach me Thy way! Thy guid-ing grace af-ford—
2. When I am sad at heart, Teach me Thy way! When earth-ly joys de-part,
3. When doubts and fears a-rise, Teach me Thy way! When storms o'er-spread the skies,
4. Long as my life shall last, Teach me Thy way! Wher-e'er my lot be cast,

Teach me Thy way! Help me to walk a-right, More by faith,
Teach me Thy way! In hours of lone-li-ness, In times of
Teach me Thy way! Shine thro' the cloud and rain, Thro' sor-row,
Teach me Thy way! Un-til the race is run, Un-til the

less by sight; Lead me with heav'n-ly light, Teach me Thy way!
dire dis-tress, In fail-ure or suc-cess, Teach me Thy way!
toil and pain; Make Thou my path-way plain, Teach me Thy way!
jour-ney's done, Un-til the crown is won, Teach me Thy way! A-men.

OBEDIENCE AND CONSECRATION

380 Living for Jesus a Life That Is True

That ye might walk worthy of the Lord . . . Col. 1:10

LIVING 10 10 10 10 Ref.

Thomas O. Chisholm, 1917

C. Harold Lowden, 1915

1. Liv-ing for Je-sus a life that is true, Striv-ing to please Him in all that I do; Yield-ing al-le-giance, glad-heart-ed and free, This is the path-way of bless-ing for me.
2. Liv-ing for Je-sus who died in my place, Bear-ing on Cal-v'ry my sin and dis-grace; Such love con-strains me to an-swer His call, Fol-low His lead-ing and give Him my all.
3. Liv-ing for Je-sus wher-ev-er I am, Do-ing each du-ty in His ho-ly name; Will-ing to suf-fer af-flic-tion and loss, Deem-ing each tri-al a part of my cross.
4. Liv-ing for Je-sus through earth's lit-tle while, My dear-est treas-ure, the light of His smile; Seek-ing the lost ones He died to re-deem, Bring-ing the wea-ry to find rest in Him.

Refrain

O Je-sus, Lord and Sav-ior, I give my-self to Thee, For Thou, in Thy a-tone-ment, Didst give Thy-self for me; I own no oth-er Mas-ter, My heart shall be Thy

LIFE IN CHRIST

throne; My life I give, hence-forth to live, O Christ, for Thee a - lone.

Not I, but Christ 381

Nevertheless I live; yet not I, but Christ liveth in me. Gal. 2:20

EXALTATION 11 10 11 10

Ada A. Whiddington, c. 1880

C. H. Forrest, 1925

1. Not I, but Christ, be hon - ored, loved, ex - alt - ed; Not I, but Christ,
2. Not I, but Christ, to gen - tly soothe in sor - row; Not I, but Christ,
3. Not I, but Christ, in low - ly, si - lent la - bor; Not I, but Christ,
4. Christ, on - ly Christ, ere long will fill my vi - sion; Glo - ry ex - cel -

be seen, be known, be heard; Not I, but Christ, in ev - ery look and
to wipe the fall - ing tear; Not I, but Christ, to lift the wea - ry
in hum - ble, ear - nest toil; Christ, on - ly Christ! no show, no os - ten -
ling, soon, full soon, I'll see—Christ, on - ly Christ, my ev - ery wish ful -

ac - tion; Not I, but Christ, in ev - ery thought and word.
bur - den! Not I, but Christ, to hush a - way all fear.
ta - tion! Christ, none but Christ, the gath - 'rer of the spoil.
fil - ing—Christ, on - ly Christ, my All in all to be. A - men.

382 Only One Life to Offer

But this I say, brethren, the time is short . . . I Cor. 7:29

Avis B. Christiansen, 1937

ONLY ONE LIFE Irreg.
Merrill Dunlop, 1937

1. On - ly one life to of - fer— Je - sus, my Lord and King;
2. On - ly this hour is mine, Lord—May it be used for Thee;
3. On - ly one life to of - fer— Take it, dear Lord, I pray;

On - ly one tongue to praise Thee And of Thy mer - cy sing (for-ev-er);
May ev - ery pass - ing mo-ment Count for e - ter - ni - ty (my Sav-ior);
Noth-ing from Thee with-hold-ing, Thy will I now o - bey (my Je-sus);

On - ly one heart's de - vo - tion—Sav-ior, O may it be Con - se -
Souls all a - bout are dy - ing, Dy - ing in sin and shame; Help me
Thou who hast free - ly giv - en Thine all in all for me, Claim this

crat - ed a - lone to Thy match - less glo - ry, Yield-ed ful - ly to Thee.
bring them the mes - sage of Cal - v'ry's re-demp-tion In Thy glo - ri - ous name.
life for Thine own, to be used, my Sav - ior, Ev - ery mo-ment for Thee.

LIFE IN CHRIST

"Are Ye Able," Said the Master 383

Jesus said . . . Can ye drink of the cup that I drink of? Mark 10:38

BEACON HILL 8 7 8 7 Ref.

Earl Marlatt, 1925

Harry S. Mason, 1924

1. "Are ye a - ble," said the Mas - ter, "To be cru - ci - fied with me?"
2. "Are ye a - ble," to re - mem - ber, When a thief lifts up his eyes,
3. "Are ye a - ble," when the shad-ows Close a - round you with the sod,
4. "Are ye a - ble?" still the Mas - ter Whis-pers down e - ter - ni - ty,

"Yea," the stur - dy dream-ers an-swered, "To the death we fol - low Thee."
That his par-doned soul is wor - thy Of a place in par - a - dise?
To be - lieve that spir - it tri - umphs, To com-mend your soul to God?
And he - ro - ic spir - its an - swer Now, as then in Gal - i - lee.

Refrain

"Lord, we are a - ble," our spir - its are Thine. Re - mold them,

make us like Thee, di - vine: Thy guid - ing ra - diance a - bove us shall

be A bea - con to God, To love and loy - al - ty. A - men.

Words used by permission of Earl B. Marlatt.

OBEDIENCE AND CONSECRATION

384 All for Jesus! All for Jesus!

Present your bodies a living sacrifice . . . Rom. 12:1

WYCLIFF 8 7 8 7

Mary D. James, 1889

John Stainer, 1887

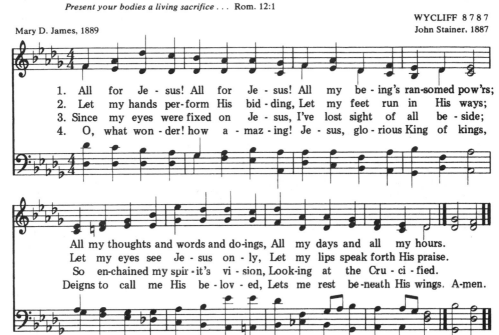

1. All for Je - sus! All for Je - sus! All my be - ing's ran-somed pow'rs;
2. Let my hands per-form His bid - ding, Let my feet run in His ways;
3. Since my eyes were fixed on Je - sus, I've lost sight of all be - side;
4. O, what won - der! how a - maz - ing! Je - sus, glo - rious King of kings,

All my thoughts and words and do-ings, All my days and all my hours.
Let my eyes see Je - sus on - ly, Let my lips speak forth His praise.
So en-chained my spir - it's vi - sion, Look-ing at the Cru - ci - fied.
Deigns to call me His be - lov - ed, Lets me rest be -neath His wings. A-men.

385 Take My Life and Let It Be

Ye are bought with a price; therefore glorify God in your body . . . I Cor. 6:20

HENDON 7 7 7 7 7

Frances R. Havergal, 1874

Henri A. César Malan, 1827

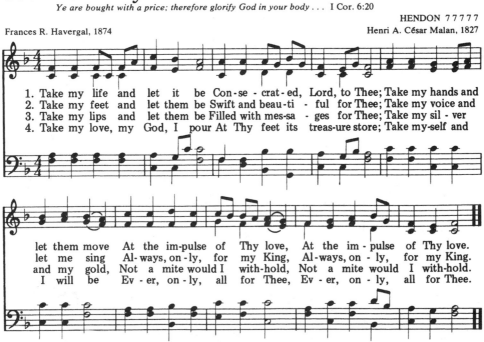

1. Take my life and let it be Con - se - crat - ed, Lord, to Thee; Take my hands and
2. Take my feet and let them be Swift and beau-ti - ful for Thee; Take my voice and
3. Take my lips and let them be Filled with mes-sa - ges for Thee; Take my sil - ver
4. Take my love, my God, I pour At Thy feet its treas-ure store; Take my-self and

let them move At the im-pulse of Thy love, At the im - pulse of Thy love.
let me sing Al- ways, on - ly, for my King, Al - ways, on - ly, for my King.
and my gold, Not a mite would I with-hold, Not a mite would I with-hold.
I will be Ev - er, on - ly, all for Thee, Ev - er, on - ly, all for Thee.

Lord Jesus, I Long to Be Perfectly Whole 386

Wash me, and I shall be whiter than snow. Psa. 51:7

FISCHER 11 11 11 11 Ref.

James L. Nicholson, 1872

William G. Fischer, 1872

1. Lord Je-sus, I long to be per-fect-ly whole; I want You for-ev - er to
2. Lord Je-sus, look down from Your throne in the skies, And help me to make a com-
3. Lord Je-sus, for this I most hum-bly en-treat, I wait, bless-ed Lord, at Your
4. Lord Je-sus, You see that I pa-tient-ly wait, Come now, and with-in me a

live in my soul, Break down ev - ery i - dol, cast out ev - ery foe;
plete sac - ri - fice; I give up my - self, and what - ev - er I know,
cru - ci - fied feet; By faith, for my cleans-ing I see Your blood flow,
new heart cre - ate; To those who have sought You, You nev - er said "No,"

Refrain

Now wash me and I shall be whit - er than snow. Whit - er than snow, yes,

whit - er than snow; Now wash me, and I shall be whit - er than snow.

PURITY AND HOLINESS

387 Search Me, O God

Search me, O God, and know my heart . . . Psa. 139:23

J. Edwin Orr, 1936

MAORI 10 10 10 10
Traditional Maori melody

1. Search me, O God, and know my heart to-day; Try me, O Sav-ior, know my thoughts, I pray. See if there be some wick-ed way in me; Cleanse me from ev-ery sin and set me free.

2. I praise Thee, Lord, for cleans-ing me from sin; Ful-fill Thy Word and make me pure with-in. Fill me with fire where once I burned with shame; Grant my de-sire to mag-ni-fy Thy name.

3. Lord, take my life and make it whol-ly Thine; Fill my poor heart with Thy great love di-vine. Take all my will, my pas-sion, self and pride; I now sur-ren-der, Lord— in me a-bide.

4. O Ho-ly Spir-it, re-viv-al comes from Thee; Send a re-viv-al— start the work in me. Thy Word de-clares Thou wilt sup-ply our need; For bless-ings now, O Lord, I hum-bly plead.

388 God Who Touches Earth with Beauty

He hath made every thing beautiful in His time. Eccl. 3:11

Mary S. Edgar, 1925

GENEVA 8 5 8 5
C. Harold Lowden, 1925

1. God who touch-es earth with beau-ty, Make my heart a-new;

2. Like Your springs and run-ning wa-ters Make me crys-tal pure,

3. Like Your danc-ing waves in sun-light Make me glad and free,

4. Like the arch-ing of the heav-ens Lift my thoughts a-bove,

5. God who touch-es earth with beau-ty, Make my heart a-new;

LIFE IN CHRIST

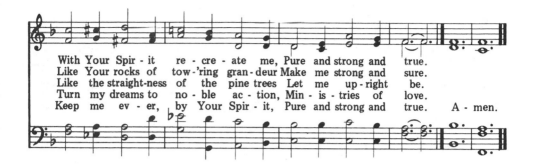

With Your Spir - it re - cre - ate me, Pure and strong and true.
Like Your rocks of tow-'ring gran-deur Make me strong and sure.
Like the straight-ness of the pine trees Let me up - right be.
Turn my dreams to no - ble ac - tion, Min - is - tries of love.
Keep me ev - er, by Your Spir - it, Pure and strong and true. A - men.

Purer in Heart, O God 389

Every man that hath this hope in Him purifieth himself . . . I John 3:3

PURER IN HEART 6 4 6 4 6 6 4 4

Fannie E. Davison, 1877

James H. Fillmore, 1877

1. Pur - er in heart, O God, Help me to be; May I de -
2. Pur - er in heart, O God, Help me to be; Teach me to
3. Pur - er in heart, O God, Help me to be; Un - til Thy

vote my life Whol - ly to Thee: Watch Thou my way - ward feet,
do Thy will Most lov - ing - ly: Be Thou my friend and guide,
ho - ly face One day I see: Keep me from se - cret sin,

Guide me with coun - sel sweet; Pur - er in heart Help me to be.
Let me with Thee a - bide; Pur - er in heart Help me to be.
Reign Thou my soul with - in; Pur - er in heart Help me to be.

PURITY AND HOLINESS

390 More Holiness Give Me

Till we all come . . . unto the measure of the stature of the fulness of Christ. Eph. 4:13

Philip P. Bliss, 1873

MY PRAYER 6 5 6 5 D.
Philip P. Bliss, 1873

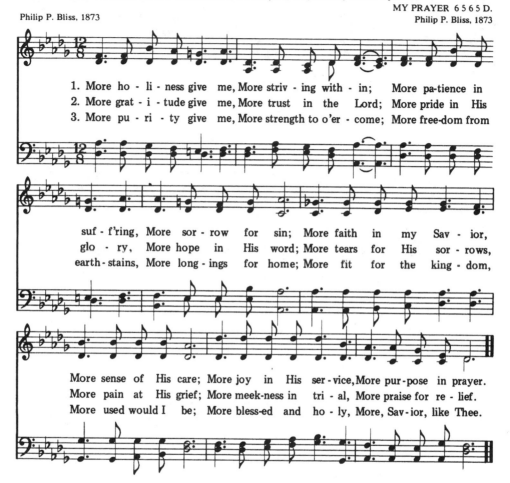

1. More ho - li - ness give me, More striv - ing with - in; More pa - tience in
2. More grat - i - tude give me, More trust in the Lord; More pride in His
3. More pu - ri - ty give me, More strength to o'er - come; More free-dom from

suf - f'ring, More sor - row for sin; More faith in my Sav - ior,
glo - ry, More hope in His word; More tears for His sor - rows,
earth - stains, More long - ings for home; More fit for the king - dom,

More sense of His care; More joy in His ser - vice, More pur - pose in prayer.
More pain at His grief; More meek-ness in tri - al, More praise for re - lief.
More used would I be; More bless-ed and ho - ly, More, Sav - ior, like Thee.

391 We Are Climbing Jacob's Ladder

Behold a ladder . . . and the top of it reached to heaven. Gen. 28:12

Traditional Spiritual

JACOB'S LADDER 8 8 8 5
Traditional Spiritual

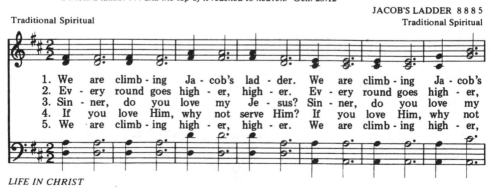

1. We are climb - ing Ja - cob's lad - der. We are climb - ing Ja - cob's
2. Ev - ery round goes high - er, high - er. Ev - ery round goes high - er,
3. Sin - ner, do you love my Je - sus? Sin - ner, do you love my
4. If you love Him, why not serve Him? If you love Him, why not
5. We are climb - ing high - er, high - er. We are climb - ing high - er,

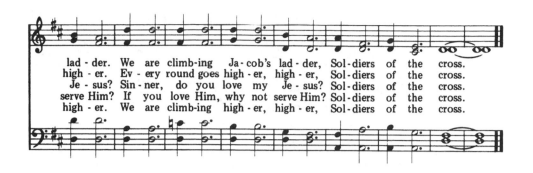

lad - der. We are climb-ing Ja-cob's lad - der, Sol-diers of the cross.
high - er. Ev - ery round goes high - er, high - er, Sol-diers of the cross.
Je - sus? Sin - ner, do you love my Je - sus? Sol-diers of the cross.
serve Him? If you love Him, why not serve Him? Sol-diers of the cross.
high - er. We are climb-ing high - er, high - er, Sol-diers of the cross.

Take Time to Be Holy 392

Follow peace with all men, and holiness . . . Heb. 12:14

HOLINESS 6 5 6 5 D.

William D. Longstaff, 1882

George C. Stebbins, 1890

1. Take time to be ho - ly, Speak oft with thy Lord; A - bide in Him
2. Take time to be ho - ly, The world rush - es on; Spend much time in
3. Take time to be ho - ly, Let Him be thy guide, And run not be -
4. Take time to be ho - ly, Be calm in thy soul; Each thought and each

al - ways, And feed on His Word. Make friends of God's chil - dren; Help
se - cret With Je - sus a - lone; By look - ing to Je - sus, Like
fore Him What - ev - er be - 'tide; In joy or in sor - row Still
mo - tive Be - neath His con - trol; Thus led by His Spir - it To

those who are weak; For - get - ting in noth - ing His bless - ing to seek.
Him thou shalt be; Thy friends in thy con - duct His like - ness shall see.
fol - low thy Lord, And, look - ing to Je - sus, Still trust in His Word.
foun - tains of love, Thou soon shalt be fit - ted For ser - vice a - bove.

393 There's within My Heart a Melody

We know that we have passed from death to life . . . I John 3:14

SWEETEST NAME 9 7 9 7 Ref.

Luther B. Bridgers, 1909

Luther B. Bridgers, 1909

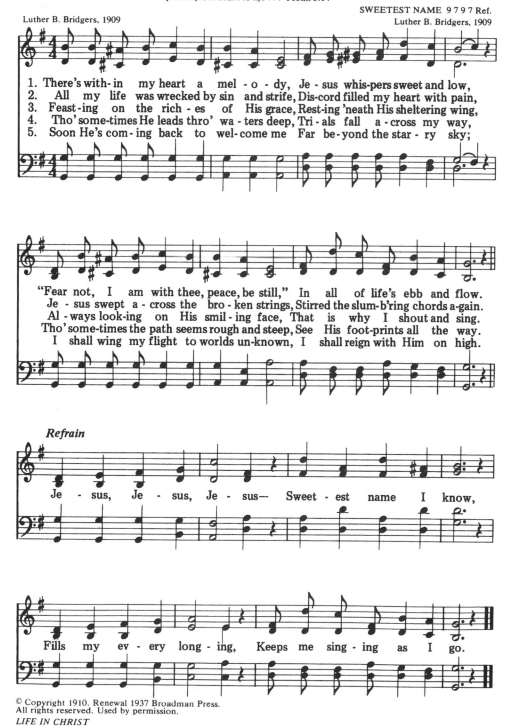

1. There's with-in my heart a mel-o-dy, Je-sus whis-pers sweet and low,
2. All my life was wrecked by sin and strife, Dis-cord filled my heart with pain,
3. Feast-ing on the rich-es of His grace, Rest-ing 'neath His sheltering wing,
4. Tho' some-times He leads thro' wa-ters deep, Tri-als fall a-cross my way,
5. Soon He's com-ing back to wel-come me Far be-yond the star-ry sky;

"Fear not, I am with thee, peace, be still," In all of life's ebb and flow.
Je-sus swept a-cross the bro-ken strings, Stirred the slum-b'ring chords a-gain.
Al-ways look-ing on His smil-ing face, That is why I shout and sing.
Tho' some-times the path seems rough and steep, See His foot-prints all the way.
I shall wing my flight to worlds un-known, I shall reign with Him on high.

Refrain

Je-sus, Je-sus, Je-sus— Sweet-est name I know,

Fills my ev-ery long-ing, Keeps me sing-ing as I go.

LIFE IN CHRIST

Jesus, I Am Resting, Resting 394

Looking unto Jesus the author and finisher of our faith. Heb. 12:2

TRANQUILLITY 8 7 8 5 D. Ref.

Jean S. Pigott, 1876

James Mountain, 1876

1. Je - sus, I am rest - ing, rest - ing In the joy of what Thou art;
2. O, how great Thy lov - ing kind - ness, Vast - er, broad - er than the sea!
3. Sim - ply trust - ing Thee, Lord Je - sus, I be - hold Thee as Thou art,
4. Ev - er lift Thy face up - on me As I work and wait for Thee;
(Ref.) Je - sus, I am rest - ing, rest - ing In the joy of what Thou art;

I am find - ing out the great - ness Of Thy lov - ing heart.
O, how mar - vel - ous Thy good - ness, Lav - ished all on me!
And Thy love, so pure, so change - less, Sat - is - fies my heart;
Rest - ing 'neath Thy smile, Lord Je - sus, Earth's dark shad - ows flee.
I am find - ing out the great - ness Of Thy lov - ing heart.

Fine

Thou hast bid me gaze up - on Thee, And Thy beau - ty fills my soul,
Yes, I rest in Thee, Be - lov - ed, Know what wealth of grace is Thine,
Sat - is - fies its deep - est long - ings, Meets, sup - plies its ev - ery need,
Bright - ness of my Fa - ther's glo - ry, Sun - shine of my Fa - ther's face,

D.C. Refrain

For by Thy trans - form - ing pow - er, Thou hast made me whole.
Know Thy cer - tain - ty of prom - ise, And have made it mine.
Com - pass - eth me round with bless - ings: Thine is love in - deed!
Keep me ev - er trust - ing, rest - ing, Fill me with Thy grace.

PEACE AND JOY

395 Lord of Our Life, and God of Our Salvation

Help us, O God of our salvation, for the glory of Thy name. Psa. 79:9

Philip Pusey, 1834
Based on Matthaus A. von Löwenstern, 1644

FLEMMING 11 11 11 5
Friedrich F. Flemming, 1811

1. Lord of our life, and God of our sal - va - tion, Star of our
2. Lord, Thou canst help when earth - ly ar - mor fail - eth; Lord, Thou canst
3. Peace in our hearts, our e - vil thoughts as - suag - ing; Peace in Thy
4. Grant us Thy help till back - ward they are driv - en; Grant them Thy

night, and hope of ev - ery na - tion, Hear and re - ceive Thy
save when dead - ly sin as - sail - eth; Lord, o'er Thy Church nor
Church, where broth - ers are en - gag - ing; Peace, when the world its
truth, that they may be for - giv - en; Grant peace on earth, or,

Church's sup - pli - ca - tion, Lord God Al - might - y.
death nor hell pre - vail - eth: Grant us Thy peace, Lord:
bus - y war is wag - ing: Calm Thy foes' rag - ing.
af - ter we have striv - en, Peace in Thy heav - en. A - men.

396 Peace, Perfect Peace

Thou wilt keep Him in perfect peace, whose mind is stayed on Thee. Isa. 26:3

PAX TECUM Irreg.
George T. Caldbeck, 1877
Arr. by Charles J. Vincent, 1877

Edward H. Bickersteth, 1875

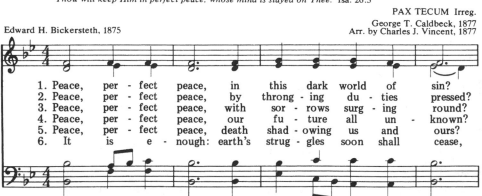

1. Peace, per - fect peace, in this dark world of sin?
2. Peace, per - fect peace, by throng - ing du - ties pressed?
3. Peace, per - fect peace, with sor - rows surg - ing round?
4. Peace, per - fect peace, our fu - ture all un - known?
5. Peace, per - fect peace, death shad - owing us and ours?
6. It is e - nough: earth's strug - gles soon shall cease,

LIFE IN CHRIST

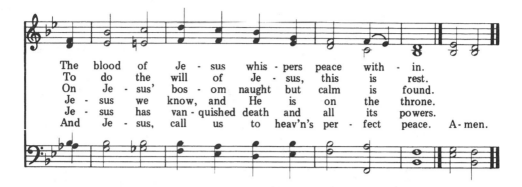

The blood of Je - sus whis - pers peace with - in.
To do the will of Je - sus, this is rest.
On Je - sus' bos - om naught but calm is found.
Je - sus we know, and He is on the throne.
Je - sus has van - quished death and all its po wers.
And Je - sus, call us to heav'n's per - fect peace. A - men.

Like a River Glorious 397

Then had Thy peace been as a river . . . Isa. 48:18

WYE VALLEY 6 5 6 5 D. Ref.

Frances R. Havergal, 1878

James Mountain, 1876

1. Like a riv - er glo - rious Is God's per - fect peace, O - ver all vic - to - rious
2. Hid - den in the hol - low Of His bless - ed hand, Nev - er foe can fol - low,
3. Ev - ery joy or tri - al Fall - eth from a - bove, Traced up - on our di - al

In its bright in - crease; Per - fect, yet it flow - eth Full - er ev - ery day,
Nev - er trai - tor stand; Not a surge of wor - ry, Not a shade of care,
By the Sun of Love. We may trust Him ful - ly All for us to do;

Refrain

Per - fect, yet it grow - eth Deep - er all the way.
Not a blast of hur - ry Touch the spir - it there. Stayed up - on Je - ho - vah,
They who trust Him whol - ly Find Him whol - ly true.

Hearts are ful - ly blest; Find - ing, as He prom - ised, Per - fect peace and rest.

PEACE AND JOY

398 I Come to the Garden Alone

Mary Magdalene came and told the disciples that she had seen the Lord. John 20:18

GARDEN Irreg. Ref.

C. Austin Miles, 1912

C. Austin Miles, 1912

1. I come to the gar-den a - lone, While the dew is still on the ros - es; And the voice I hear, fall - ing on my ear, The Son of God dis - clos - es.

2. He speaks, and the sound of His voice Is so sweet the birds hush their sing - ing, And the mel - o - dy that He gave to me With-in my heart is ring - ing.

3. I'd stay in the gar - den with Him Though the night a - round me be fall - ing, But He bids me go; through the voice of woe, His voice to me is call - ing.

Refrain

And He walks with me, and He talks with me, And He tells me I am His own, And the joy we share as we tar - ry there, None oth - er has ev - er known.

LIFE IN CHRIST

There Is Sunshine in My Soul Today 399

For God, who commanded the light to shine out of darkness, hath shined in our hearts . . . II Cor. 4:6

SUNSHINE 9 6 8 6 Ref.

Eliza E. Hewitt, 1887

John R. Sweney, 1887

1. There is sun - shine in my soul to - day, More glo - ri - ous and bright
2. There is mu - sic in my soul to - day, A car - ol to my King,
3. There is spring - time in my soul to - day, For when the Lord is near
4. There is glad - ness in my soul to - day, And hope and praise and love,

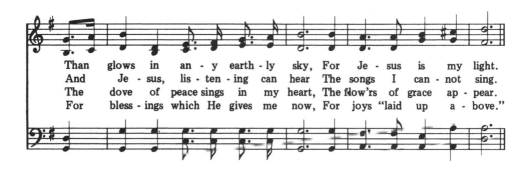

Than glows in an - y earth - ly sky, For Je - sus is my light.
And Je - sus, lis - ten - ing can hear The songs I can - not sing.
The dove of peace sings in my heart, The flow'rs of grace ap - pear.
For bless - ings which He gives me now, For joys "laid up a - bove."

Refrain

O there's sun - shine, bless - ed sun - shine, When the peace - ful, hap - py mo - ments

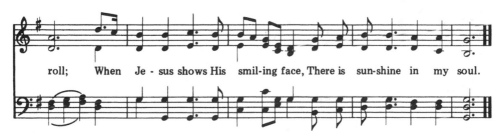

roll; When Je - sus shows His smil - ing face, There is sun - shine in my soul.

PEACE AND JOY

400 O Safe to the Rock That Is Higher than I

Lead me to the rock that is higher than I. Psa. 61:2

William O. Cushing, 1876

HIDING IN THEE 11 11 11 11 Ref.
Ira D. Sankey, 1877

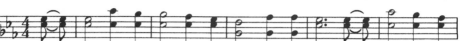

1. O safe to the Rock that is high - er than I, My soul in its
2. In the calm of the noon-tide, in sor-row's lone hour, In times when temp-
3. How oft in the con-flict, when pressed by the foe, I have fled to my

con - flicts and sor - rows would fly; So sin - ful, so wea - ry, Thine,
ta - tion casts o'er me its pow'r; In the tem - pests of life, on its
Ref - uge and breathed out my woe; How oft - en, when tri - als like

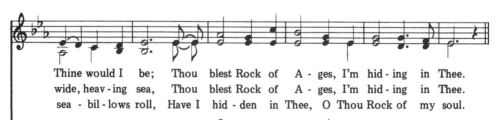

Thine would I be; Thou blest Rock of A - ges, I'm hid - ing in Thee.
wide, heav - ing sea, Thou blest Rock of A - ges, I'm hid - ing in Thee.
sea - bil - lows roll, Have I hid - den in Thee, O Thou Rock of my soul.

Refrain

Hid - ing in Thee, Hid - ing in Thee, Thou blest Rock of A-ges, I'm hid - ing in Thee.

LIFE IN CHRIST

When Peace Like a River Attendeth 401

Bless the Lord, O my soul, and forget not all His benefits . . . Psa. 103:2

Horatio G. Spafford, 1873

VILLE DU HAVRE 11 8 11 9 Ref.

Philip P. Bliss, 1876

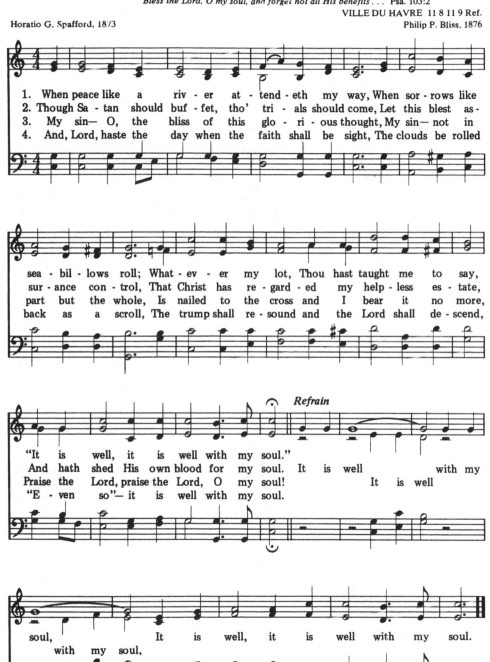

1. When peace like a riv-er at-tend-eth my way, When sor-rows like
2. Though Sa-tan should buf-fet, tho' tri-als should come, Let this blest as-
3. My sin— O, the bliss of this glo-ri-ous thought, My sin— not in
4. And, Lord, haste the day when the faith shall be sight, The clouds be rolled

sea-bil-lows roll; What-ev-er my lot, Thou hast taught me to say,
sur-ance con-trol, That Christ has re-gard-ed my help-less es-tate,
part but the whole, Is nailed to the cross and I bear it no more,
back as a scroll, The trump shall re-sound and the Lord shall de-scend,

Refrain

"It is well, it is well with my soul." It is well with my
And hath shed His own blood for my soul. It is well
Praise the Lord, praise the Lord, O my soul! It is well
"E-ven so"— it is well with my soul.

soul, It is well, it is well with my soul.
with my soul,

PEACE AND JOY

402 A Wonderful Savior Is Jesus My Lord

I will put thee in a clift of the rock, and will cover thee with My hand. Exo. 33:22

KIRKPATRICK 11 8 11 8 Ref.

Fanny J. Crosby, 1890

William J. Kirkpatrick, 1890

1. A won-der-ful Sav-ior is Je-sus my Lord, A won-der-ful
2. A won-der-ful Sav-ior is Je-sus my Lord, He tak-eth my
3. With num-ber-less bless-ings each mo-ment He crowns, And, filled with His
4. When clothed in His bright-ness, trans-port-ed I rise To meet Him in

Sav-ior to me; He hid-eth my soul in the cleft of the rock, Where
bur-den a-way; He hold-eth me up, and I shall not be moved, He
full-ness di-vine, I sing in my rap-ture, O glo-ry to God For
clouds of the sky, His per-fect sal-va-tion, His won-der-ful love, I'll

Refrain

riv-ers of pleas-ure I see.
giv-eth me strength as my day.
such a Re-deem-er as mine!
shout with the mil-lions on high.

He hid-eth my soul in the cleft of the rock

That shad-ows a dry, thirst-y land; He hid-eth my life in the depths of His love,

And cov-ers me there with His hand, And cov-ers me there with His hand.

LIFE IN CHRIST

Walking in Sunlight All of My Journey 403

He that followeth Me shall not walk in darkness . . . John 8:12

HEAVENLY SUNLIGHT 10 9 10 9 Ref.

Henry J. Zelley, 1899

George H. Cook, 1899

1. Walk-ing in sun-light all of my jour-ney, O-ver the moun-tains,
2. Shad-ows a-round me, shad-ows a-bove me Nev-er con-ceal my
3. In the bright sun-light, ev-er re-joic-ing, Press-ing my way to

through the deep vale; Je-sus has said, "I'll nev-er for-sake thee,"
Sav-ior and Guide; He is the Light, in Him is no dark-ness;
man-sions a-bove; Sing-ing His prais-es glad-ly I'm walk-ing,

Refrain

Prom-ise di-vine that nev-er can fail.
Ev-er I'm walk-ing close to His side. Heav-en-ly sun-light,
Walk-ing in sun-light, sun-light of love.

heav-en-ly sun-light, Flood-ing my soul with glo-ry di-vine; Hal-le-

lu-jah! I am re-joic-ing, Sing-ing His prais-es, Je-sus is mine.

PEACE AND JOY

404 I Have a Song That Jesus Gave Me

Singing and making melody in your heart to the Lord. Eph. 5:19

Elton M. Roth, 1924

HEART MELODY Irreg. Ref.
Elton M. Roth, 1924

1. I have a song that Je-sus gave me, It was sent from heav'n a-bove; There nev-er was a sweet-er mel-o-dy, 'Tis a mel-o-dy of love.

2. I love the Christ who died on Cal-v'ry, For He washed my sins a-way; He put with-in my heart a mel-o-dy, And I know it's there to stay.

3. 'Twill be my end-less theme in glo-ry, With the an-gels I will sing; 'Twill be a song with glo-rious har-mo-ny, When the courts of heav-en ring.

Refrain

In my heart there rings a mel-o-dy, There rings a mel-o-dy with heav-en's har-mo-ny; In my heart there rings a mel-o-dy; There rings a mel-o-dy of love.

LIFE IN CHRIST

Come, Come, Ye Saints 405

All things work together for good to them that love God. . . Rom. 8:28

ALL IS WELL 10 6 10 6 8 8 8 6

Avis B. Christiansen, 1966
Based on William Clayton, 1846

Traditional English melody
The Sacred Harp, 1844

1. Come, come, ye saints, no toil nor la - bor fear, But with joy wend your way;
2. What though the path you tread be rough and steep? Have no fear, He is near!
3. God hath pre-pared a glo-rious Home a - bove Round His throne, for His own,
4. With long - ing hearts we wait the prom-ised day When the trump we shall hear,

Though hard to you life's jour - ney may ap - pear, Grace shall be as your day.
His might - y arm un - to the end will keep; Soon His call you shall hear.
Where they may rest for - ev - er in His love, Toil and tears all un-known.
That sum-mons us from earth-ly cares a - way, At His side to ap-pear!

God's hand of love shall be your guide, And all your need He will pro-vide;
Then fol - low on, fresh cour-age take, For God His own will ne'er for-sake,
There they shall sing e - ter - nal praise To Him who saved them by His grace.
But un - til then we'll la - bor on In pa-tience till our course is run,

His pow'r shall ev - ery foe dis - pel, All is well, All is well!
Till in His pres - ence they shall dwell! All is well, All is well!
Through heaven's courts the song shall swell, All is well, All is well!
Al - though the hour we may not tell, All is well, All is well!

PEACE AND JOY

406 There's a Peace in My Heart

I will never leave thee, nor forsake thee. Heb. 13:5

CONSTANTLY ABIDING 12 8 12 9 Ref.

Anne S. Murphy, 1908

Anne S. Murphy, 1908

1. There's a peace in my heart that the world nev-er gave, A peace it can
2. All the world seemed to sing of a Sav-ior and King, When peace sweetly
3 This treas-ure I have in a tem-ple of clay, While here on His

not take a-way; Tho' the tri-als of life may sur-round like a cloud,
came to my heart; Troub-les all fled a-way and my night turned to day,
foot-stool I roam: But He's com-ing to take me some glo-ri-ous day,

Refrain

I've a peace that has come there to stay! Con - stant-ly a-
Bless-ed Je-sus, how glorious Thou art! Con-stant-ly a-bid - ing,
O - ver there to my heav-en-ly home!

bid - ing, Je - sus is mine;
con-stant-ly a - bid-ing, Je-sus is mine, yes, Je-sus is mine;

Con - stant-ly a-bid - ing, rap - ture di-
Con-stant-ly a-bid - ing, con-stant-ly a-bid-ing, rap-ture di-vine, O

LIFE IN CHRIST

vine; He nev-er leaves me lone - ly, whis-pers,
rap-ture di-vine; He nev-er leaves me, nev-er leaves me lone-ly, whis-pers,

O so kind: "I will nev-er leave thee," Je - sus is mine.
whis-pers, O so kind: nev-er leave thee, Je-sus, Je-sus is mine.

Dear Lord and Father of Mankind 407

. . . Sitting at the feet of Jesus, clothed, and in His right mind. Luke 8:35

REST 8 6 8 8 6

John G. Whittier, 1872

Frederick C. Maker, 1887

1. Dear Lord and Fa - ther of man - kind, For - give our fool - ish
2. In sim - ple trust like theirs who heard, Be - side the Syr - ian
3. Drop Thy still dews of qui - et - ness, Till all our striv - ings
4. Breathe through the heats of our de - sire Thy cool - ness and Thy

ways! Re - clothe us in our right - ful mind; In pur - er
Sea, The gra - cious call - ing of the Lord, Let us, like
cease; Take from our souls the strain and stress, And let our
balm; Let sense be dumb, let flesh re - tire; Speak through the

lives Thy serv - ice find, In deep - er rev - 'rence, praise.
them, with - out a word, Rise up and fol - low Thee.
or - dered lives con - fess The beau - ty of Thy peace.
earth - quake, wind, and fire, O still small voice of calm! A-men.

PEACE AND JOY

408 I Will Sing of My Redeemer

Jesus Christ; who gave Himself for us, that He might redeem us . . . Titus 2:13, 14

HYFRYDOL 8 7 8 7 Ref.

Philip P. Bliss, c. 1876

Rowland H. Prichard, c. 1830

1. I will sing of my Re-deem-er And His won-drous love to me;
2. I will tell the won-drous sto-ry, How my lost es-tate to save,
3. I will praise my dear Re-deem-er, His tri-umph-ant power I'll tell,
4. I will sing of my Re-deem-er And His heav'n-ly love for me;

On the cru-el cross He suf-fered, From the curse to set me free.
In His bound-less love and mer-cy, He the ran-som free-ly gave.
How the vic-to-ry He giv-eth O-ver sin and death and hell.
He from death to life hath brought me, Son of God, with Him to be.

Refrain

Sing, O sing of my Re-deem-er, With His blood He pur-chased me,

On the cross He sealed my par-don, Paid the debt, and made me free.

LIFE IN CHRIST

Loved with Everlasting Love 409

I am persuaded that (nothing) shall be able to separate us from the love of God . . . Rom. 8:38, 39

EVERLASTING LOVE 7 7 7 7 D.

George W. Robinson, 1890

James Mountain, c. 1890

1. Loved with ev - er - last - ing love, Led by grace that love to know;
2. Heav'n a - bove is soft - er blue, Earth a - round is sweet - er green!
3. Things that once were wild a - larms Can - not now dis - turb my rest;
4. His for - ev - er, on - ly His; Who the Lord and me shall part?

Gra - cious Spir - it from a - bove, Thou hast taught me it is so!
Some - thing lives in ev - ery hue Christ - less eyes have nev - er seen:
Closed in ev - er - last - ing arms, Pil - lowed on the lov - ing breast.
Ah, with what a rest of bliss Christ can fill the lov - ing heart!

O, this full and per - fect peace! O, this trans - port all di - vine!
Birds with glad - der songs o'er - flow, Flow'rs with deep - er beau - ties shine,
O, to lie for - ev - er here, Doubt and care and self re - sign,
Heav'n and earth may fade and flee, First - born light in gloom de - cline;

1.

In a love which can - not cease, I am His, and He is mine. mine.
Since I know, as now I know, I am His, and He is mine. mine.
While He whis - pers in my ear, I am His, and He is mine. mine.
But while God and I shall be, I am His, and He is mine. mine.

2.

PEACE AND JOY

410 O What a Wonderful, Wonderful Day

If any man be in Christ, he is a new creature. II Cor. 5:17

HEAVEN CAME DOWN Irreg. Ref.

John W. Peterson, 1961

John W. Peterson, 1961

1. O what a won - der - ful, won - der - ful day— Day I will
2. Born of the Spir - it with life from a - bove In - to God's
3. Now I've a hope that will sure - ly en - dure Aft - er the

nev - er for - get; Aft - er I'd wan - dered in dark - ness a - way,
fam - ily di - vine, Jus - ti - fied ful - ly thro' Cal - va - ry's love,
pass - ing of time; I have a fu - ture in heav - en for sure,

Je - sus my Sav - ior I met. O what a ten - der, com - pas - sion - ate friend—
O what a stand - ing is mine! And the trans - ac - tion so quick - ly was made
There in those man - sions sub - lime. And it's be - cause of that won - der - ful day

He met the need of my heart; Shad - ows dis - pel - ling, With
When as a sin - ner I came, Took of the of - fer Of
When at the cross I be - lieved; Rich - es e - ter - nal And

LIFE IN CHRIST

joy I am tell - ing, He made all the dark - ness de - part!
grace He did prof - fer— He saved me, O praise His dear name!
bless - ings su - per - nal From His pre - cious hand I re - ceived.

Refrain

Heav - en came down and glo - ry filled my soul, (filled my soul,)

When at the cross the Sav - ior made me whole; (made me whole;) My

sins were washed a - way And my night was turned to day—

Heav - en came down and glo - ry filled my soul! (filled my soul!)

PEACE AND JOY

411 Happiness Is to Know the Savior

Blessed is everyone that feareth the Lord . . . happy shalt thou be . . . Psa. 128:1, 2

HAPPINESS IS THE LORD Irreg. Ref.

Ira. F. Stanphill, 1968

Ira F. Stanphill, 1968

Unison

1. Hap-pi-ness is to know the Sav-ior, Liv-ing a life with-in His fa-vor,
2. Hap-pi-ness is a new cre-a-tion—"Je-sus and me" in close re-la-tion,
3. Hap-pi-ness is to be for-giv-en, Liv-ing a life that's worth the liv-in',

[1] (to vs. 2)

Hav-ing a change in my be-hav-ior—Hap-pi-ness is the Lord;
Hav-ing a part in His sal-va-tion—
Tak-ing a trip that leads to heav-en—

[2]

Hap-pi-ness is the Lord. Real joy is mine, no mat-ter if tear-drops start; I've

D.C. (to vs. 3) **[3]**

found the se-cret—it's Je-sus in my heart! Hap-pi-ness is the

Lord, Hap-pi-ness is the Lord, Hap-pi-ness is the Lord!

LIFE IN CHRIST: PEACE AND JOY

Just When I Need Him Jesus Is Near 412

God is our refuge and strength, a very present help in trouble. Psa. 46:1

William C. Poole, 1907

GABRIEL 9 9 9 6 Ref.
Charles H. Gabriel, 1907

1. Just when I need Him Je-sus is near, Just when I fal-ter,
2. Just when I need Him Je-sus is true, Nev-er for-sak-ing
3. Just when I need Him Je-sus is strong, Bear-ing my bur-dens
4. Just when I need Him He is my all, An-swer-ing when up-

just when I fear; Read-y to help me, read-y to cheer,
all the way through; Giv-ing for bur-dens pleas-ures a-new,
all the day long; For all my sor-row giv-ing a song,
on Him I call; Ten-der-ly watch-ing lest I should fall,

Refrain

Just when I need Him most. Just when I need Him most,

Just when I need Him most; Je-sus is near to

com-fort and cheer, Just when I need Him most.

COMFORT AND ENCOURAGEMENT

413 God Is My Strong Salvation

The Lord is my light and my salvation; whom shall I fear? Psa. 27:1

WEDLOCK 7 6 7 6
Traditional American melody
The Sacred Harp. 1844
Arr. by Donald P. Hustad. 1973

James Montgomery, 1822

Unison

1. God is my strong sal-va-tion: What foe have I to fear? In darkness and temp-
2. Place on the Lord re-li-ance; My soul, with cour-age wait; His truth be thine af-

ta-tion, My light, my help is near. Tho' hosts en-camp a-round me, Firm in the
fi-ance, When faint and des-o-late. His might thy heart shall strengthen, His love thy

fight I stand; What ter-ror can con-found me, With God at my right hand?
joy in-crease; Mer-cy thy days shall length-en; The Lord will give thee peace. A-men.

414 Mid All the Traffic of the Ways

It is good for me to draw near to God . . . Psa. 73:28

ST. AGNES C.M.
John B. Dykes, 1866

John Oxenham, 1917

1. Mid all the traf-fic of the ways, Tur-moils with-out, with-in,
2. A lit-tle shrine of qui-et-ness, All sa-cred to Thy-self,
3. A lit-tle shel-ter from life's stress, Where I may lay me prone,
4. A lit-tle place of mys-tic grace, Of self and sin swept bare,

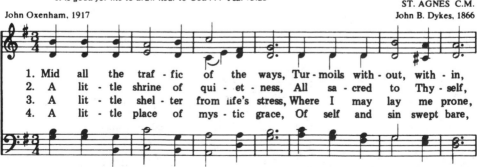

This tune in a lower key, No. 531
Words used by permission of Miss Theo Oxenham, Worthing, Sussex.

LIFE IN CHRIST

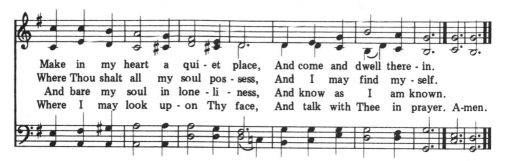

Make in my heart a qui-et place, And come and dwell there-in.
Where Thou shalt all my soul pos-sess, And I may find my-self.
And bare my soul in lone-li-ness, And know as I am known.
Where I may look up-on Thy face, And talk with Thee in prayer. A-men.

There Is a Balm in Gilead 415

Is there no balm in Gilead; is there no physician there? Jer. 8:22

BALM IN GILEAD Irreg.
Traditional Spiritual

Traditional Spiritual

Unison

(Ref.) There is a balm in Gil-e-ad To make the wound-ed whole,

Fine

There is a balm in Gil-e-ad To heal the sin-sick soul.

1. Some-times I feel dis-cour-aged, And think my work's in vain,
2. If you can-not preach like Pe-ter, If you can-not pray like Paul,

D.C. Refrain

But then the Ho-ly Spir-it Re-vives my soul a-gain.
You can tell the love of Je-sus, And say, "He died for all."

COMFORT AND ENCOURAGEMENT

416 Does Jesus Care?

Casting all your care upon Him; for He careth for you. I Pet. 5:7

Frank E. Graeff, 1901

MY SAVIOR CARES Irreg. Ref.
J. Lincoln Hall, 1901

1. Does Je - sus care when my heart is pained Too deep - ly for
2. Does Je - sus care when my way is dark With a name - less
3. Does Je - sus care when I've tried and failed To re - sist some temp-
4. Does Je - sus care when I've said good - by To the dear - est on

mirth and song; As the bur - dens press and the cares dis - tress, And the
dread and fear? As the day - light fades in - to deep night shades, Does He
ta - tion strong; When for my deep grief I find no re - lief, Though my
earth to me, And my sad heart aches till it near - ly breaks—Is it

Refrain

way grows wea - ry and long?
care e - nough to be near?   O yes, He cares; I know He cares, His
tears flow all the night long?
aught to Him? Does He see?

heart is touched with my grief; When the days are wea - ry, the

long nights drear - y, I know my Sav - ior cares. (He cares).

LIFE IN CHRIST

What a Fellowship, What a Joy Divine   **417**

The eternal God is thy refuge, and underneath are the everlasting arms. Deut. 33:27

SHOWALTER 10 9 10 9 Ref.

Elisha A. Hoffman, 1887

Anthony J. Showalter, 1887

1. What a fel-low-ship, what a joy di-vine, Lean-ing on the ev-er-
2. O how sweet to walk in this pil-grim way, Lean-ing on the ev-er-
3. What have I to dread, what have I to fear, Lean-ing on the ev-er-

last-ing arms; What a bless-ed-ness, what a peace is mine,
last-ing arms; O, how bright the path grows from day to day,
last-ing arms? I have bless-ed peace with my Lord so near,

Refrain

Lean-ing on the ev-er-last-ing arms. Lean - ing,
Lean-ing on the ev-er-last-ing arms. Lean-ing on Je-sus,
Lean-ing on the ev-er-last-ing arms.

lean - ing, Safe and se-cure from all a-larms; Lean -
lean-ing on Je-sus,   Lean-ing on

ing, lean - ing, Lean-ing on the ev-er-last-ing arms.
Je - sus, lean-ing on Je-sus,

COMFORT AND ENCOURAGEMENT

418 In the Hour of Trial

God is faithful, who will not suffer you to be tempted above that ye are able . . . I Cor. 10:13

PENITENCE 6 5 6 5 D.

James Montgomery, 1834

Spencer Lane, 1875

1. In the hour of tri - al, Je - sus, plead for me, Lest, by base de -
2. With for - bid - den plea - sures Would this vain world charm, Or its sor - did
3. Should Thy mer - cy send me Sor - row, toil, and woe; Or should pain at -

ni - al, I de - part from Thee; When Thou seest me wa - ver, With a
trea - sures Spread to work me harm; Bring to my re - mem - brance Sad Geth -
tend me On my path be - low; Grant that I may nev - er Fail Thy

look re - call; Nor for fear or fa - vor Suf - fer me to fall.
sem - a - ne, Or, in dark - er sem - blance, Rug - ged Cal - va - ry.
hand to see; Grant that I may ev - er Cast my care on Thee. A - men.

419 Father, Whate'er of Earthly Bliss

I have learned, in whatsoever state I am . . . to be content. Phil. 4:11

NAOMI C.M.

Anne Steele, 1760
Adapt. by Augustus M. Toplady, 1776

Johann G. Nägeli, 1832
Arr. by Lowell Mason, 1836

1. Fa - ther, what - e'er of earth - ly bliss Thy sov - 'reign will de - nies,
2. Give me a calm, a thank - ful heart, From ev - ery mur - mur free;
3. Let the sweet hope that Thou art mine My path of life at - tend;

LIFE IN CHRIST

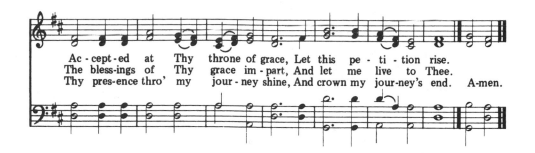

Ac - cept - ed at Thy throne of grace, Let this pe - ti - tion rise.
The bless - ings of Thy grace im - part, And let me live to Thee.
Thy pres - ence thro' my jour - ney shine, And crown my jour - ney's end. A - men.

If Thou but Suffer God to Guide Thee 420

Cast thy burden upon the Lord, and He shall sustain thee . . . Psa. 55:22

Georg Neumark, 1641
Trans. by Catherine Winkworth, 1855
Based on Psalm 55

NEUMARK 989888
Georg Neumark, 1657

1. If thou but suf - fer God to guide thee, And hope in Him through
2. On - ly be still and wait His lei - sure In cheer - ful hope, with
3. Sing, pray, and keep His ways un - swerv - ing; In all thy la - bor

all thy ways, He'll give thee strength, what - e'er be - tide thee,
heart con - tent To take what - e'er thy Fa - ther's plea - sure
faith - ful be, And trust His Word; though un - de - serv - ing,

And bear thee thro' the e - vil days; Who trusts in God's un -
And all - dis - cern - ing love hath sent; Nor doubt our in - most
Thou yet shalt find it true for thee; God nev - er will for -

chang - ing love Builds on the rock that naught can move.
wants are known To Him who chose us for His own.
sake in need The soul that trusts in Him in - deed. A - men.

421 Be Not Dismayed Whate'er Betide

Casting all your care on Him; for He careth for you. I Pet. 5:7

Civilla D. Martin, 1904

GOD CARES C.M. Ref.
W. Stillman Martin, 1904

1. Be - not dis - mayed what-e'er be - tide, God will take care of you;
2. Through days of toil when heart doth fail, God will take care of you;
3. All you may need He will pro-vide, God will take care of you;
4. No mat - ter what may be the test, God will take care of you;

Be - neath His wings of love a - bide, God will take care of you.
When dan - gers fierce your path as - sail, God will take care of you.
Noth - ing you ask will be de - nied, God will take care of you.
Lean, wea - ry one, up - on His breast, God will take care of you.

Refrain

God will take care of you, Through ev - ery day, o'er all the way;

He will take care of you, God will take care of you.

LIFE IN CHRIST

Give to the Winds Your Fears **422**

Commit thy way unto the Lord . . . and He shall bring it to pass. Psa. 37:5

Paul Gerhardt, 1653
Trans. by John Wesley, 1739
Based on Psalm 37

DIADEMATA S.M.D.
George J. Elvey, 1868

1. Give to the winds your fears, Hope, and be un - dis-mayed;
2. Still heav - y is your heart? Still sink your spir - its down?
3. Far, far a - bove your thought His coun - sel shall ap - pear,

God hears your sighs and counts your tears, God shall lift up your head,
Cast off the weight, let fear de - part, And ev - ery care be gone.
When ful - ly He the work has wrought That caused your need-less fear.

Through waves and clouds and storms He gen - tly clears the way;
He ev - ery - where has sway And all things serve His mind;
Leave to His sov - ereign will To choose and to com - mand:

Wait for His time, so shall the night Soon end in joy - ous day.
His ev - ery act pure bless-ing is, His path un - sul - lied light
With won - der filled, you then shall own How wise, how strong His hand. A-men.

This tune in a lower key, No. 519

COMFORT AND ENCOURAGEMENT

423 Come, Ye Disconsolate

Let us then with confidence draw near to the throne of grace . . . Heb. 4:16

St. 1, 2, Thomas Moore, 1824
St. 3, Thomas Hastings, 1831

CONSOLATOR 11 10 11 10
Samuel Webbe, 1792

1. Come, ye dis - con - so - late, wher - e'er ye lan - guish; Come to the
2. Joy of the des - o - late, Light of the stray - ing, Hope of the
3. Here see the Bread of Life; see wa - ters flow - ing Forth from the

mer - cy - seat, fer - vent - ly kneel; Here bring your wound - ed hearts, here tell your
pen - i - tent, fade - less and pure, Here speaks the Com - fort - er, ten - der - ly
throne of God, pure from a - bove; Come to the feast of love; come, ev - er

an - guish; Earth has no sor - row that heav'n can - not heal.
say - ing, "Earth has no sor - row that heav'n can - not cure."
know - ing Earth has no sor - row but heav'n can re - move. A - men.

424 Immortal Love, Forever Full

If I may but touch His garment, I shall be whole. Matt. 9:21

John G. Whittier, 1866

SERENITY C.M.
William V. Wallace, 1856

1. Im - mor - tal Love, for - ev - er full, For - ev - er flow - ing free,
2. We may not climb the heav'n - ly steeps To bring the Lord Christ down;
3. But warm, sweet, ten - der, e - ven yet A pres - ent help is He;
4. The heal - ing of His seam - less dress Is by our beds of pain;
5. O Lord and Mas - ter of us all, What - e'er our name or sign,

This tune in a lower key, No. 73

LIFE IN CHRIST

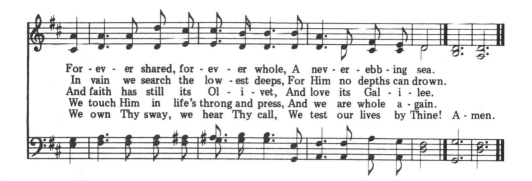

For - ev - er shared, for - ev - er whole, A nev - er - ebb - ing sea.
In vain we search the low - est deeps, For Him no depths can drown.
And faith has still its Ol - i - vet, And love its Gal - i - lee.
We touch Him in life's throng and press, And we are whole a - gain.
We own Thy sway, we hear Thy call, We test our lives by Thine! A - men.

We Would See Jesus; for the Shadows 425

Sir, we would see Jesus. John 12:21

CONSOLATION 11 10 11 10

Anna B. Warner, 1852

Arr. from Felix Mendelssohn, 1834

1. We would see Je - sus; for the shad - ows length - en A - cross this
2. We would see Je - sus; the great rock foun - da - tion Where - on our
3. We would see Je - sus; sense is all too bind - ing, And heav'n ap-
4. We would see Je - sus; this is all we're need - ing; Strength, joy and

lit - tle land - scape of our life; We would see Je - sus, our weak faith to
feet were set by sov'reign grace; Not life nor death, with all their ag - i -
pears too dim, too far a - way. We would see Thee, Thy - self our hearts re -
will - ing - ness come with the sight; We would see Je - sus, dy - ing, ris - en,

strength - en, For the last wea - ri - ness, the fi - nal strife.
ta - tion, Can thence re - move us, if we see His face.
mind - ing What Thou hast suf - fered, our great debt to pay.
plead - ing, Then wel - come day, and fare - well mor - tal night. A - men.

426 Is Your Burden Heavy?

Surely He hath borne our griefs and carried our sorrows . . . Isa. 53:4

REACH OUT TO JESUS Irreg.

Ralph Carmichael, 1968

Ralph Carmichael, 1968

1. Is your bur-den heav-y as you bear it all a-lone? Does the
2. Is the life you're liv-ing filled with sor-row and de-spair? Does the

road you trav-el har-bor dan-ger yet un-known? Are you grow-ing
fu-ture press you with its wor-ry and its care? Are you tired and

wea-ry in the strug-gle of it all? Je-sus will help you when
friend-less, have you al-most lost your way? Je-sus will help you—just

on His name you call.
come to Him to-day.
He is al-ways there hear-ing ev-ery prayer,

Faith-ful and true, Walk-ing by our side, in His love we hide all the day

LIFE IN CHRIST

through. When you get dis-cour-aged, just re-mem - ber what to

do— Reach out to Je - sus, He's reach - ing out to you,

Jesus, My Savior, Look on Me 427

When He saw the multitudes, He was moved with compassion on them . . . Matt. 9:36

Charlotte Elliott, 1869

SULLIVAN 8 8 8 4
Arthur S. Sullivan, 1874

1. Je - sus, my Sav - ior, look on me, For I am wea - ry and op-pressed;
2. Look down on me, for I am weak; I feel the toil-some jour-ney's length:
3. I am be - wil-dered on my way, Dark and tem-pest-uous is the night:
4. When Sa - tan flings his fi - ery darts, I look to Thee, my ter - rors cease;
5. Thou wilt my ev - ery want sup - ply, E'en to the end, what-e'er be - fall;

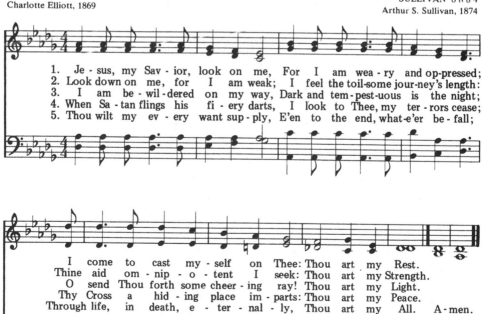

I come to cast my - self on Thee: Thou art my Rest.
Thine aid om - nip - o - tent I seek: Thou art my Strength.
O send Thou forth some cheer - ing ray! Thou art my Light.
Thy Cross a hid - ing place im - parts: Thou art my Peace.
Through life, in death, e - ter - nal - ly, Thou art my All. A - men.

COMFORT AND ENCOURAGEMENT

428 Lord, I Have Shut the Door

And when thou hast shut thy door, pray to thy Father . . . Matt. 6:6

SANCTUARY 6 4 6 4 D.

William M. Runyan, 1923

William M. Runyan, 1923

1. Lord, I have shut the door, Speak now the word Which in the din and throng Could not be heard; Hushed now my in - ner heart, Whis - per Thy will, While I have come a - part, While all is still.
2. Lord, I have shut the door, Here do I bow; Speak, for my soul at - tent Turns to Thee now. Re - buke Thou what is vain, Coun-sel my soul, Thy ho - ly will re - veal, My will con - trol.
3. In this blest qui - et - ness Clam - or - ings cease; Here in Thy pres - ence dwells In - fi - nite peace; Yon - der, the strife and cry, Yon-der, the sin: Lord, I have shut the door, Thou art with - in!
4. Lord, I have shut the door, Strength - en my heart; Yon - der a - waits the task— I share a part. On - ly through grace be-stowed May I be true; Here, while a - lone with Thee, My strength re - new. A-men.

429 Prayer Is the Soul's Sincere Desire

Praying always with all prayer and supplication in the Spirit. Eph. 6:18

CAMPMEETING C.M.

James Montgomery, 1818

Traditional American melody
Arr. by Robert G. McCutchan, 1935

1. Prayer is the soul's sin - cere de - sire, Un - ut - tered or ex-pressed; The
2. Prayer is the sim - plest form of speech That in - fant lips can try; Prayer,
3. Prayer is the con - trite sin - ner's voice, Re - turn - ing from his ways; While
4. Prayer is the Chris - tian's vi - tal breath, The Chris-tian's na - tive air, His
5. O Thou, by whom we come to God, The Life, the Truth, the Way, The

motion of a hidden fire That trembles in the breast.
the sublimest strains that reach The Majesty on high.
angels in their songs rejoice And cry, "Behold, he prays!"
watch-word at the gates of death: He enters heav'n with prayer.
path of prayer Thyself hast trod: Lord, teach us how to pray! A-men.

From Every Stormy Wind That Blows 430

I will commune with thee from above the mercy seat. Exo. 25:22

Hugh Stowell, 1828

RETREAT L.M.
Thomas Hastings, 1842

1. From every storm-y wind that blows, From ev-ery swell-ing
2. There is a place where Je-sus sheds The oil of glad-ness
3. There is a scene where spir-its blend, Where friend holds fel-low-
4. Ah! whith-er could we flee for aid, When tempt-ed, des-o-
5. Ah! there on ea-gle wings we soar, And sin and sense mo-

tide of woes, There is a calm, a sure re-treat:
on our heads; A place than all be-side more sweet:
ship with friend; Though sun-dered far, by faith they meet
late, dis-mayed: Or how the hosts of hell de-feat,
lest no more: And heav'n comes down our souls to greet,

'Tis found be-neath the mer-cy seat.
It is the blood-bought mer-cy seat.
A-round one com-mon mer-cy seat.
Had suf-f'ring saints no mer-cy seat.
While glo-ry crowns the mer-cy seat. A-men.

PRAYER

431 Come, My Soul, Your Plea Prepare

Ask, and it shall be given you . . . Matt. 7:7

SEYMOUR 7 7 7 7

John Newton, 1779

Carl Maria von Weber, 1826

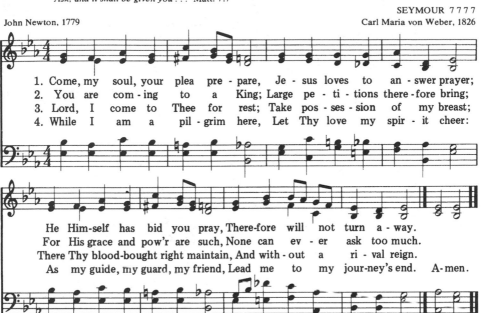

1. Come, my soul, your plea pre - pare, Je - sus loves to an - swer prayer;
2. You are com - ing to a King; Large pe - ti - tions there - fore bring;
3. Lord, I come to Thee for rest; Take pos - ses - sion of my breast;
4. While I am a pil - grim here, Let Thy love my spir - it cheer:

He Him-self has bid you pray, There-fore will not turn a - way.
For His grace and pow'r are such, None can ev - er ask too much.
There Thy blood-bought right maintain, And with - out a ri - val reign.
As my guide, my guard, my friend, Lead me to my jour-ney's end. A-men.

This tune in a higher key, No. 238

432 Talk with Us, Lord

Did not our heart burn within us, while He talked with us . . . Luke 24:32

GRÄFENBERG C.M.

Praxis Pietatis Melica, Berlin, 1647
Johann Crüger, 1647

Charles Wesley, 1740

1. Talk with us, Lord, Thy - self re - veal, While here o'er earth we rove;
2. With Thee con - vers - ing, we for - get All time and toil and care;
3. Thou call - est me to seek Thy face, 'Tis all I wish to seek;
4. Let this my ev - ery hour em - ploy, Till I Thy glo - ry see

Speak to our hearts, and let us feel The kin-dling of Thy love.
La - bor is rest, and pain is sweet, If Thou, my God, art here.
To hear the whis-pers of Thy grace, And hear Thee in me speak.
En - ter in - to my Mas-ter's joy, And find my heav'n in Thee. A - men.

LIFE IN CHRIST

'Tis the Blessed Hour of Prayer 433

He shall call upon me, and I will answer Him . . . Psa. 91:15

Fanny J. Crosby, 1880

BLESSED HOUR Irreg. Ref.
William H. Doane, 1880

1. 'Tis the bless - ed hour of prayer, when our hearts low - ly bend,
2. 'Tis the bless - ed hour of prayer, when the Sav - ior draws near,
3. 'Tis the bless - ed hour of prayer, when the tempt - ed and tried
4. At the bless - ed hour of prayer, trust - ing Him we be - lieve

And we gath - er to Je - sus, our Sav - ior and Friend; If we
With a ten - der com - pas - sion His chil - dren to hear; When He
To the Sav - ior who loves them their sor - row con - fide; With a
That the bless - ings we're need - ing we'll sure - ly re - ceive; In the

come to Him in faith, His pro - tec - tion to share, What a balm for the
tells us we may cast at His feet ev - ery care, What a balm for the
sym - pa - thiz - ing heart He re - moves ev - ery care, What a balm for the
full - ness of this trust we shall lose ev - ery care; What a balm for the

Refrain

wea - ry! O how sweet to be there! Bless - ed hour of prayer, Bless - ed

hour of prayer; What a balm for the wea - ry! O how sweet to be there!

PRAYER

434 Sweet Hour of Prayer

Now Peter and John went up together . . . at the hour of prayer. Acts 3:1

William Walford, 1845

SWEET HOUR L.M.D.
William B. Bradbury, 1861

1. Sweet hour of prayer, sweet hour of prayer, That calls me from a world of care,
2. Sweet hour of prayer, sweet hour of prayer, Thy wings shall my pe - ti - tion bear,
3. Sweet hour of prayer, sweet hour of prayer, May I thy con - so - la - tion share,

And bids me at my Fa-ther's throne Make all my wants and wish - es known;
To Him whose truth and faith-ful - ness En - gage the wait - ing soul to bless;
Till, from Mount Pis-gah's loft - y height, I view my home, and take my flight:

In sea - sons of dis-tress and grief, My soul has oft - en found re - lief,
And since He bids me seek His face, Be - lieve His word and trust His grace,
This robe of flesh I'll drop, and rise To seize the ev - er - last - ing prize;

And oft es-caped the tempt - er's snare, By thy re - turn, sweet hour of prayer.
I'll cast on Him my ev - ery care, And wait for thee, sweet hour of prayer.
And shout, while pass-ing through the air, Fare-well, fare-well, sweet hour of prayer!

LIFE IN CHRIST

What a Friend We Have in Jesus 435

By prayer . . . with thanksgiving let your requests be made known unto God. Phil. 4:6

CONVERSE 8 7 8 7 D.

Joseph M. Scriven, 1855

Charles C. Converse, 1868

1. What a Friend we have in Je - sus, All our sins and griefs to bear!
2. Have we tri - als and temp - ta - tions? Is there trou - ble an - y - where?
3. Are we weak and heav - y - la - den, Cum - bered with a load of care?

What a priv - i - lege to car - ry Ev - ery-thing to God in prayer!
We should nev - er be dis - cour - aged, Take it to the Lord in prayer.
Pre - cious Sav - ior, still our ref - uge— Take it to the Lord in prayer.

O what peace we of - ten for - feit, O what need-less pain we bear,
Can we find a friend so faith - ful Who will all our sor - rows share?
Do thy friends de-spise, for-sake thee? Take it to the Lord in prayer;

All be-cause we do not car - ry Ev - ery-thing to God in prayer!
Je - sus knows our ev - ery weak - ness, Take it to the Lord in prayer.
In His arms He'll take and shield thee, Thou wilt find a sol - ace there.

PRAYER

436 I Have a Savior, He's Pleading in Glory

He ever liveth to make intercession for them. Heb. 7:25

INTERCESSION 11 11 12 11 Ref.

S. O'Malley Clough, 1860

Ira D. Sankey, 1875

1. I have a Sav - ior, He's plead - ing in glo - ry, A dear, lov - ing
2. I have a Fa - ther; to me He has giv - en A hope for e -
3. I have a peace; it is calm as a riv - er, A peace that the
4. When He has found you, tell oth - ers the sto - ry, That my lov - ing

Sav - ior, tho' earth-friends be few; And now He is watch - ing in
ter - ni - ty, bless - ed and true; And soon He will call me to
friends of this world nev - er knew: My Sav - ior a - lone is its
Sav - ior is your Sav - ior, too; Then pray that your Sav - ior may

ten - der - ness o'er me, But O, that my Sav - ior were your Sav - ior too!
meet Him in heav - en, But O, that He'd let me bring you with me too!
au - thor and giv - er, And O, could I know it was giv - en for you.
bring them to glo - ry, And prayer will be an - swered—'twas an - swered for you!

Refrain

For you I am pray - ing, For you I am pray - ing,

For you I am pray - ing, I'm pray - ing for you.

LIFE IN CHRIST

I Must Tell Jesus All of My Trials 437

For in that He Himself hath suffered . . . He is able to succor them . . . Heb. 2:18

ORWIGSBURG 10 9 10 9 Ref.

Elisha A. Hoffman, 1894

Elisha A. Hoffman, 1894

1. I must tell Je - sus all of my tri - als; I can - not bear these
2. I must tell Je - sus all of my trou - bles; He is a kind, com -
3. Tempt-ed and tried, I need a great Sav - ior, One who can help my
4. O how the world to e - vil al - lures me! O how my heart is

bur - dens a - lone; In my dis - tress He kind - ly will help me;
pas - sion - ate Friend; If I but ask Him, He will de - liv - er,
bur - dens to bear; I must tell Je - sus, I must tell Je - sus;
tempt - ed to sin! I must tell Je - sus, and He will help me

Refrain

He ev - er loves and cares for His own.
Make of my trou - bles quick - ly an end.
He all my cares and sor - rows will share.   I must tell Je - sus!
O - ver the world the vic - t'ry to win.

I must tell Je - sus! I can - not bear my bur - dens a - lone; I must tell

Je - sus! I must tell Je - sus! Je - sus can help me, Je - sus a - lone.

438 Teach Me to Pray, Lord

Lord, teach us to pray . . . Luke 11:1

Albert S. Reitz, 1925

REITZ 9 9 9 9 Ref.
Albert S. Reitz, 1925

1. Teach me to pray, Lord, teach me to pray; This is my heart-cry
2. Pow-er in prayer, Lord, pow-er in prayer, Here 'mid earth's sin and
3. My weak-ened will, Lord, Thou canst re-new; My sin-ful na-ture
4. Teach me to pray, Lord, teach me to pray; Thou art my pat-tern,

day un-to day; I long to know Thy will and Thy way; Teach me to
sor-row and care; Men lost and dy-ing, souls in de-spair; O give me
Thou canst sub-due; Fill me just now with pow-er a-new, Pow-er to
day un-to day; Thou art my sure-ty, now and for aye; Teach me to

Refrain

pray, Lord, teach me to pray.
pow-er, pow-er in prayer!
pray and pow-er to do! Liv-ing in Thee, Lord, and Thou in
pray, Lord, teach me to pray.

me; Con-stant a-bid-ing, this is my plea; Grant me Thy

pow-er, bound-less and free: Pow-er with men and pow-er with Thee.

LIFE IN CHRIST: PRAYER

He Leadeth Me, O Blessed Thought 439

I am the Lord thy God . . . which leadeth thee . . . Isa. 48:17

Joseph H. Gilmore, 1862

HE LEADETH ME L.M. Ref.
William B. Bradbury, 1864

1. He lead - eth me, O bless - ed thought! O words with heav'n - ly
2. Some-times 'mid scenes of deep - est gloom, Some-times where E - den's
3. Lord, I would clasp Thy hand in mine, Nor ev - er mur - mur
4. And when my task on earth is done, When by Thy grace the

com - fort fraught! What - e'er I do, wher - e'er I be, Still
bow - ers bloom, By wa - ters still, o'er trou - bled sea, Still
nor re - pine; Con - tent, what - ev - er lot I see, Since
vic - t'ry's won, E'en death's cold wave I will not flee, Since

Refrain

'tis God's hand that lead - eth me.
'tis His hand that lead - eth me.
'tis my God that lead - eth me. He lead - eth me, He
God through Jor - dan lead - eth me.

lead - eth me! By His own hand He lead - eth me! His

faith - ful fol - l'wer I would be, For by His hand He lead-eth me.

PILGRIMAGE AND GUIDANCE

440 All the Way My Savior Leads Me

I will guide thee with Mine eye. Psa. 32:8

ALL THE WAY 8 7 8 7 D.

Fanny J. Crosby, 1875

Robert Lowry, 1875

1. All the way my Sav-ior leads me; What have I to ask be - side?
2. All the way my Sav-ior leads me; Cheers each wind-ing path I tread;
3. All the way my Sav-ior leads me; O the full - ness of His love!

Can I doubt His ten-der mer - cy, Who through life has been my guide?
Gives me grace for ev - ery tri - al, Feeds me with the liv-ing bread;
Per-fect rest to me is prom-ised In my Fa-ther's house a - bove;

Heav'n-ly peace, di - vin - est com-fort, Here by faith in Him to dwell!
Though my wea - ry steps may fal - ter, And my soul a-thirst may be,
When my spir - it, clothed im - mor-tal, Wings its flight to realms of day,

For I know, what - e'er be-fall me, Je - sus do - eth all things well;
Gush-ing from the rock be-fore me, Lo! a spring of joy I see,
This my song through end-less a - ges, Je - sus led me all the way.

LIFE IN CHRIST

For I know, what-e'er be-fall me, Je-sus do-eth all things well.
Gush-ing from the rock be-fore me, Lo! a spring of joy I see.
This my song through end-less a-ges, Je-sus led me all the way.

Lead Us, O Father 441

He goeth before them, and the sheep follow Him . . . John 10:4

LANGRAN 10 10 10 10

William H. Burleigh, 1859

James Langran, 1861

1. Lead us, O Fa-ther, in the paths of peace: With-out Thy guid-ing
2. Lead us, O Fa-ther, in the paths of truth: Un-helped by Thee, in
3. Lead us, O Fa-ther, in the paths of right: Blind-ly we stum-ble
4. Lead us, O Fa-ther, to Thy heav'n-ly rest, How-ev-er rough and

hand we go a-stray, And doubts ap-pall, and sor-rows still in-crease;
er-ror's maze we grope, While pas-sion stains and fol-ly dims our youth,
when we walk a-lone, In-volved in shad-ows of a dark-'ning night;
steep the path may be, Thro' joy or sor-row, as Thou deem-est best,

Lead us through Christ, the true and liv-ing Way.
And age comes on un-cheered by faith or hope.
On-ly with Thee we jour-ney safe-ly on.
Un-til our lives are per-fect-ed in Thee. A-men.

PILGRIMAGE AND GUIDANCE

442 Lead, Kindly Light

Thou wilt show me the path of life: at Thy right hand there are pleasures for evermore. Psa. 16:11

LUX BENIGNA 10 4 10 4 10 10

John H. Newman, 1833

John B. Dykes, 1865

1. Lead, kind-ly Light, a - mid th' en-cir-cling gloom, Lead Thou me on;
2. I was not ev - er thus, nor prayed that Thou Shouldst lead me on;
3. So long Thy pow'r hath blest me, sure it still Will lead me on,

The night is dark, and I am far from home; Lead Thou me on:
I loved to choose and see my path; but now Lead Thou me on.
O'er moor and fen, o'er crag and tor - rent, till The night is gone;

Keep Thou my feet; I do not ask to see
I loved the gar - ish day, and, spite of fears,
And with the morn those an - gel fac - es smile,

The dis - tant scene—one step e - nough for me.
Pride ruled my will: re - mem-ber not past years.
Which I have loved long since, and lost a - while. A - men.

Alternate tune, SANDON, No. 44

LIFE IN CHRIST

Jesus, I My Cross Have Taken 443

Lo, we have left all, and have followed Thee. Mark 10:28

ELLESDIE 8 7 8 7 D.

Leavitt's *The Christian Lyre,* 1831
Attr. to Wolfgang A. Mozart, 1756-1791
Arr. by Hubert P. Main, c. 1868

Henry F. Lyte, 1824

1. Je - sus, I my cross have tak - en, All to leave and fol - low Thee;
2. Let the world de - spise and leave me, They have left my Sav - ior too;
3. Man may trou - ble and dis - tress me, 'Twill but drive me to Thy breast;
4. Has - ten on from grace to glo - ry, Armed by faith and winged by prayer;

Des - ti - tute, de - spised, for - sak - en, Thou from hence my all shalt be:
Hu - man hearts and looks de - ceive me; Thou art not, like man, un - true;
Life with tri - als hard may press me, Heav'n will bring me sweet - er rest.
Heav'n's e - ter - nal day's be - fore me, God's own hand shall guide me there.

Per - ish ev - ery fond am - bi - tion, All I've sought, and hoped, and known;
And, while Thou shalt smile up - on me, God of wis - dom, love, and might,
O 'tis not in grief to harm me, While Thy love is left to me;
Soon shall close my earth - ly mis - sion, Swift shall pass my pil - grim days,

Yet how rich is my con - di - tion, God and heav'n are still my own!
Foes may hate and friends may shun me; Show Thy face, and all is bright.
O 'twere not in joy to charm me, Were that joy un - mixed with Thee.
Hope shall change to glad fru - i - tion, Faith to sight, and prayer to praise. A - men.

PILGRIMAGE AND GUIDANCE

444 Take Thou My Hand, O Father

For He hath prepared for them a city. Heb. 11:16

Julie K. Hausmann, 1862
Trans. by Herman Brückner, 1866-1942

SO NIMM DENN MEINE HÄNDE 7 4 7 4 D.
Friedrich Silcher, 1842

1. Take Thou my hand, O Fa - ther, And lead Thou me, Un - til my jour-ney
2. O cov - er with Thy mer - cy My poor, weak heart! Let ev - ery thought re-
3. Tho' naught of Thy great pow - er May move my soul, With Thee thro' night and

end - eth, E - ter - nal - ly. A - lone I will not wan - der One
bel - lious From me de - part. Per - mit Thy child to lin - ger Here
dark - ness I reach the goal. Take then my hands, O Fa - ther, And

sin - gle day; Be Thou my true com-pan - ion And with me stay.
at Thy feet, And blind - ly trust Thy good-ness With faith com-plete.
lead Thou me, Un - til my jour-ney end - eth E - ter - nal - ly. A-men.

445 Children of the Heavenly King

The ransomed of the Lord shall . . . come to Zion with songs and everlasting joy. Isa. 35:10

John Cennick, 1742

VIENNA 7 7 7 7
Justin H. Knecht, 1799

1. Chil - dren of the heav'n-ly King, As we jour - ney let us sing;
2. We are trav - 'ling home to God In the way our fa - thers trod;
3. Fear not, breth - ren, joy - ful stand On the bor - ders of our land;
4. Lord, o - be - dient - ly we'll go, Glad - ly leav - ing all be - low:

Sing our Sav-ior's wor-thy praise, Glo-rious in His works and ways.
They are hap-py now, and we Soon their hap-pi-ness shall see.
Je-sus Christ, our Fa-ther's Son, Bids us un-dis-mayed go on.
On-ly Thou our Lead-er be, And we still will fol-low Thee. A-men.

Jesus, Savior, Pilot Me 446

He commandeth even the winds and water, and they obey Him. Luke 8:25

ARFON 7 7 7 7 D.

Edward Hopper, 1871

Traditional Welsh hymn melody

1. Je - sus, Sav - ior, pi - lot me O - ver life's tem - pes - tuous sea;
2. As a moth - er stills her child, Thou canst hush the o - cean wild;
3. When at last I near the shore, And the fear - ful break - ers roar

Un - known waves be - fore me roll, Hid - ing rock and treach-'rous shoal;
Bois - terous waves o - bey Thy will When Thou say'st to them, "Be still!"
'Twixt me and the peace - ful rest, Then, while lean - ing on Thy breast,

Chart and com - pass came from Thee: Je - sus, Sav - ior, pi - lot me.
Won-drous Sov - 'reign of the sea, Je - sus, Sav - ior, pi - lot me.
May I hear Thee say to me, "Fear not, I will pi - lot thee." A-men.

PILGRIMAGE AND GUIDANCE

447 Because the Lord Is My Shepherd

The Lord is my shepherd; I shall not want. Psa. 23:1

Ralph Carmichael, 1969
Based on Psalm 23

THE NEW 23RD Irreg.
Ralph Carmichael, 1969

Unison

Be-cause the Lord is my Shep-herd, I have ev-ery-thing that I need. He lets me rest in mead-ows green and leads me be-side the qui-et stream. He keeps on giv-ing life to me, and helps me to do what hon-ors Him the most. E-ven when walk-ing thro' the dark val-ley of death, val-ley of death, I will nev-er

LIFE IN CHRIST

be a-fraid, for He is close be-side me. Guard-ing, guid-ing all the
way, He spreads a feast be-fore me in the pres-ence of my
en-e-mies. He wel-comes me as His spe-cial guest with bless-ing ev-er
flow-ing, His good-ness and un-fail-ing kind-ness shall be with me all of my
life, And af-ter-wards I shall live with Him for-ev-er, for-ev-er
in His home, for-ev-er in His home. For-ev-er in His home.

PILGRIMAGE AND GUIDANCE

448 Guide Me, O Thou Great Jehovah

This God is our God . . . He will be our guide even unto death. Psa. 48:14

William Williams, 1745
Trans. by Peter Williams and
William Williams, 1771 and 1772

CWM RHONDDA 8 7 8 7 8 7 7
John Hughes, 1907

1. Guide me, O Thou great Je - ho - vah, Pil - grim through this bar - ren land;
2. O - pen now the crys - tal foun - tain, Whence the healing stream doth flow;
3. When I tread the verge of Jor - dan, Bid my anx - ious fears sub - side;

I am weak, but Thou art might - y; Hold me with Thy pow'r - ful hand;
Let the fire and cloud - y pil - lar Lead me all my jour - ney through;
Death of death, and hell's de - struc - tion, Land me safe on Ca - naan's side;

Bread of heav - en, Bread of heav - en, Feed me till I want no
Strong De - liv - erer, strong De - liv - erer, Be Thou still my strength and
Songs of prais - es, songs of prais - es I will ev - er give to

more, (want no more,) Feed me till I want no more.
shield, (strength and shield,) Be Thou still my strength and shield.
Thee, (give to Thee,) I will ev - er give to Thee. A - men.

LIFE IN CHRIST

I Feel the Winds of God Today 449

Launch out into the deep. Luke 5:4

KINGSFOLD C.M.D.

Jessie Adams, 1907

Traditional English melody
Arr. by Ellwood Shermer Wolf, 1966

1. I feel the winds of God to-day; To - day my sail I lift,
2. It is the wind of God that dries My vain, re - gret - ful tears,
3. If ev - er I for - get Thy love And how that love was shown,

Though heav - y oft with drench-ing spray, And torn with man-y a rift;
Un - til with brav - er thoughts shall rise The pur - er, bright - er years;
Lift high the blood-red flag a - bove; It bears Thy name a - lone.

If hope but light the wa - ter's crest, And Christ my bark will use,
If cast on shores of self - ish ease Or pleas - ure I should be,
Great Pi - lot of my on - ward way, Thou wilt not let me drift;

I'll seek the seas at His be - hest And brave an - oth - er cruise.
Lord, let me feel Thy freshen-ing breeze, And I'll put back to sea.
I feel the winds of God to-day; To - day my sail I lift. A - men.

PILGRIMAGE AND GUIDANCE

450 Jesus, Still Lead On

Therefore for Thy name's sake lead me, and guide me. Psa. 31:3

Nikolaus L. von Zinzendorf, 1721
Trans. by Jane L. Borthwick, 1846

ROCHELLE 5 5 8 8 5 5
Adam Drese, 1698

1. Je - sus, still lead on, Till our rest be won, And, al - though the
2. If the way be drear, If the foe be near, Let not faith - less
3. When we seek re - lief From a long - felt grief, When op - pressed by
4. Je - sus, still lead on, Till our rest be won; Heav'n - ly lead - er,

way be cheer - less, We will fol - low, calm and fear - less;
fears o'er - take us, Let not faith and hope for - sake us;
new temp - ta - tions, Lord, in - crease and per - fect pa - tience;
still di - rect us, Still sup - port, con - sole, pro - tect us,

Guide us by Thy hand To our fa - ther - land.
For, through man - y a woe, To our home we go.
Show us that bright shore Where we weep no more.
Till we safe - ly stand In our fa - ther - land. A - men.

451 I Have Decided to Follow Jesus

Master, I will follow Thee whithersoever Thou goest. Matt. 8:19

Source unknown

ASSAM Irreg.
Folk melody from India

Unison

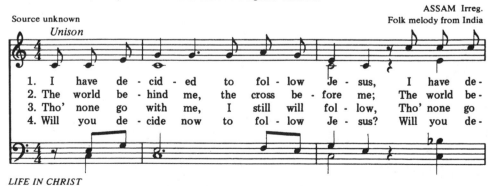

1. I have de - cid - ed to fol - low Je - sus, I have de -
2. The world be - hind me, the cross be - fore me; The world be -
3. Tho' none go with me, I still will fol - low, Tho' none go
4. Will you de - cide now to fol - low Je - sus? Will you de -

LIFE IN CHRIST

cid - ed to fol - low Je - sus, I have de - cid - ed to fol - low
hind me, the cross be - fore me; The world be - hind me, the cross be -
with me, I still will fol - low, Tho' none go with me, I still will
cide now to fol - low Je - sus? Will you de - cide now to fol - low

Je - sus, No turn - ing back, no turn - ing back.
fore me, No turn - ing back, no turn - ing back.
fol - low, No turn - ing back, no turn - ing back.
Je - sus? No turn - ing back, no turn - ing back.

I Want Jesus to Walk with Me 452

I am with thee, and will keep thee . . . whither thou goest. Gen. 28:15

WALK WITH ME Irreg.

Traditional Spiritual

Traditional Spiritual

Unison

1.   I want Je - sus to walk with me;   I want
2. In my tri - als, Lord, walk with me;   In my
3. When I'm in trou - ble, Lord, walk with me;   When I'm in

Je - sus to walk with me;   All a - long my
tri - als, Lord, walk with me;   When my heart is
trou - ble, Lord, walk with me;   When my head is

pil - grim jour - ney, Lord, I want Je - sus to walk with me.
al - most break - ing, Lord, I want Je - sus to walk with me.
bowed in sor - row, Lord, I want Je - sus to walk with me.

453 Encamped Along the Hills of Light

This is the victory that overcometh the world, even our faith. I John 5:4

John H. Yates, 1891

SANKEY C.M.D. Ref.
Ira D. Sankey, 1891

1. En - camped a - long the hills of light, Ye Chris - tian sol - diers, rise,
2. His ban - ner o - ver us is love, Our sword the Word of God;
3. On ev - ery hand the foe we find Drawn up in dread ar - ray;
4. To him that o - ver-comes the foe, White rai - ment shall be giv'n;

And press the bat - tle ere the night Shall veil the glow - ing skies.
We tread the road the saints a - bove With shouts of tri - umph trod.
Let tents of ease be left be - hind, And on - ward to the fray;
Be - fore the an - gels he shall know His name con-fessed in heav'n.

A - gainst the foe in vales be - low Let all our strength be hurled;
By faith they, like a whirl-wind's breath, Swept on o'er ev - ery field;
Sal - va - tion's hel - met on each head, With truth all girt a - bout,
Then on - ward from the hills of light, Our hearts with love a - flame,

Faith is the vic - to - ry, we know, That o - ver-comes the world.
The faith by which they con-quered death Is still our shin - ing shield.
The earth shall trem - ble 'neath our tread, And ech - o with our shout.
We'll van - quish all the hosts of night, In Je - sus' con-quering name.

LIFE IN CHRIST

Awake, My Soul, Stretch Every Nerve 454

Let us run with patience the race that is set before us. Heb. 12:1

CHRISTMAS C.M. Repeats

Philip Doddridge, 1755

Weyman's *Melodia Sacra*, 1815
Arr. from George F. Handel, 1728

1. A - wake, my soul, stretch ev - ery nerve, And press with vig - or on; A heav'n - ly race de - mands thy zeal, And an im - mor - tal crown, And an im - mor - tal crown.
2. A cloud of wit - ness - es a - round Hold thee in full sur - vey: For - get the steps al - read - y trod, And on - ward urge thy way, And on - ward urge thy way.
3. 'Tis God's all - an - i - mat - ing voice, That calls thee from on high; 'Tis His own hand pre - sents the prize To thine as - pir - ing eye, To thine as - pir - ing eye.
4. Blest Sav - ior, in - tro - duced by Thee Have I my race be - gun; And crowned with vic - t'ry, at Thy feet I'll lay my hon - ors down, I'll lay my hon - ors down. A-men.

This tune in a lower key, No. 119

CHALLENGE AND VICTORY

455 Stand Up, Stand Up for Jesus

Watch ye, stand fast in the faith, quit you like men, be strong. I Cor. 16:13

George Duffield, 1858

GEIBEL 7 6 7 6 D. Ref.
Adam Geibel, 1901

Unison

1. Stand up, stand up for Je - sus, Ye sol - diers of the cross;
2. Stand up, stand up for Je - sus, The trum - pet call o - bey;
3. Stand up, stand up for Je - sus, The strife will not be long;

Lift high His roy - al ban - ner, It must not suf - fer loss:
Forth to the might - y con - flict In this His glo - rious day:
This day the noise of bat - tle, The next, the vic - tor's song:

From vic - t'ry un - to vic - t'ry His ar - my shall He lead,
"Ye that are men, now serve Him" A - gainst un - num-bered foes;
To Him that o - ver - com - eth A crown of life shall be;

Till ev - ery foe is van - quished And Christ is Lord in - deed.
Let cour - age rise with dan - ger, And strength to strength op - pose.
He with the King of glo - ry Shall reign e - ter - nal - ly.

LIFE IN CHRIST

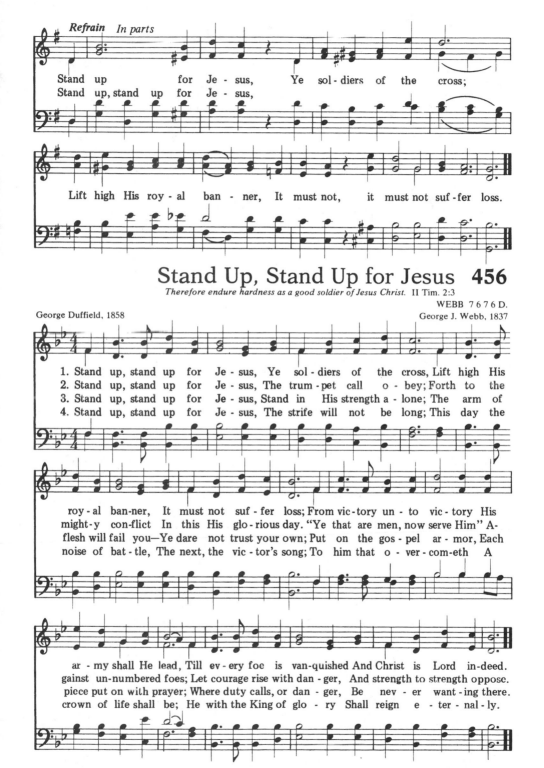

Stand Up, Stand Up for Jesus 456

Therefore endure hardness as a good soldier of Jesus Christ. II Tim. 2:3

WEBB 7 6 7 6 D.

George Duffield, 1858

George J. Webb, 1837

Refrain *In parts*

Stand up for Je - sus, Ye sol - diers of the cross;
Stand up, stand up for Je - sus,

Lift high His roy - al ban - ner, It must not, it must not suf - fer loss.

1. Stand up, stand up for Je - sus, Ye sol - diers of the cross, Lift high His
2. Stand up, stand up for Je - sus, The trum - pet call o - bey; Forth to the
3. Stand up, stand up for Je - sus, Stand in His strength a - lone; The arm of
4. Stand up, stand up for Je - sus, The strife will not be long; This day the

roy - al ban - ner, It must not suf - fer loss; From vic - to - ry un - to vic - to - ry His
might - y con - flict In this His glo - rious day. "Ye that are men, now serve Him" A -
flesh will fail you—Ye dare not trust your own; Put on the gos - pel ar - mor, Each
noise of bat - tle, The next, the vic - tor's song; To him that o - ver - com - eth A

ar - my shall He lead, Till ev - ery foe is van - quished And Christ is Lord in - deed.
gainst un - num - bered foes; Let courage rise with dan - ger, And strength to strength oppose.
piece put on with prayer; Where duty calls, or dan - ger, Be nev - er want - ing there.
crown of life shall be; He with the King of glo - ry Shall reign e - ter - nal - ly.

457 Lead On, O King Eternal

Henceforth there is laid up for me a crown of righteousness . . . II Tim. 4:8

Ernest W. Shurtleff, 1887

LANCASHIRE 7 6 7 6 D.
Henry T. Smart, 1835

1. Lead on, O King E - ter - nal, The day of march has come;
2. Lead on, O King E - ter - nal, Till sin's fierce war shall cease,
3. Lead on, O King E - ter - nal, We fol - low, not with fears;

Hence - forth in fields of con - quest Your tents shall be our home.
And ho - li - ness shall whis - per The sweet A - men of peace;
For glad - ness breaks like morn - ing Wher - e'er Your face ap - pears;

Through days of prep - a - ra - tion Your grace has made us strong,
For not with swords loud clash - ing, Nor roll of stir - ring drums,
Your cross is lift - ed o'er us; We jour - ney in its light:

And now, O King E - ter - nal, We lift our bat - tle song.
With deeds of love and mer - cy The heav'n - ly king - dom comes.
The crown a - waits the con - quest; Lead on, O God of might. A - men.

This tune in a lower key, No. 517
LIFE IN CHRIST

Soldiers of Christ, Arise 458

Be strong in the Lord . . . Put on the whole armor of God. Eph. 6:10, 11

DIADEMATA S.M.D.

Charles Wesley, 1749

George J. Elvey, 1868

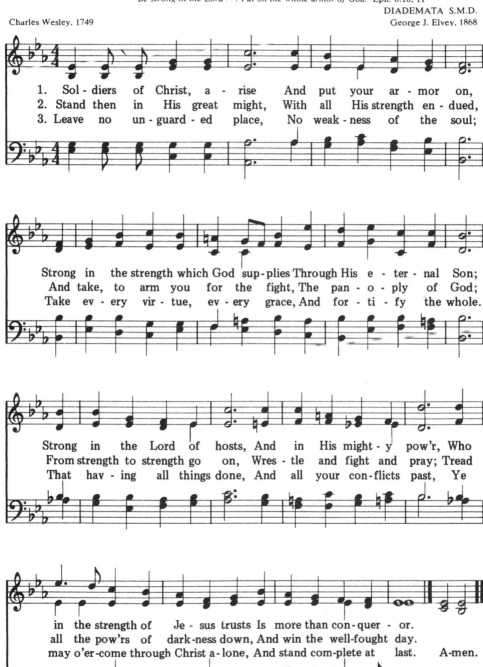

1. Sol - diers of Christ, a - rise And put your ar - mor on,
2. Stand then in His great might, With all His strength en - dued,
3. Leave no un - guard - ed place, No weak - ness of the soul;

Strong in the strength which God sup - plies Through His e - ter - nal Son;
And take, to arm you for the fight, The pan - o - ply of God;
Take ev - ery vir - tue, ev - ery grace, And for - ti - fy the whole.

Strong in the Lord of hosts, And in His might - y pow'r, Who
From strength to strength go on, Wres - tle and fight and pray; Tread
That hav - ing all things done, And all your con - flicts past, Ye

in the strength of Je - sus trusts Is more than con - quer - or.
all the pow'rs of dark - ness down, And win the well-fought day.
may o'er - come through Christ a - lone, And stand com - plete at last. A - men.

This tune in a lower key, No. 376

CHALLENGE AND VICTORY

459 There's a Royal Banner Given for Display

Thou hast given a banner to them . . . that it may be displayed . . . Psa. 60:4

Daniel W. Whittle, 1887

ROYAL BANNER 11 7 11 7 Ref.
James McGranahan, 1887

1. There's a roy - al ban - ner giv - en for dis - play To the sol - diers of the King; As an en - sign fair we lift it up to - day, While as ran - somed ones we sing.

2. Though the foe may rage and gath - er as the flood, Let the stand - ard be dis - played; And be - neath its folds, as sol - diers of the Lord, For the truth be not dis - mayed!

3. O - ver land and sea, wher - ev - er man may dwell, Make the glo - rious ti - dings known; Of the crim - son ban - ner now the sto - ry tell, While the Lord shall claim His own!

4. When the glo - ry dawns—'tis draw - ing ver - y near— It is has - tening day by day; Then be - fore our King the foe shall dis - ap - pear, And the cross the world shall sway!

Refrain

March - ing on, march - ing on, on, on, For Christ count ev - ery - thing but loss! ev - ery - thing, ev - ery - thing but loss! And to crown Him King, we'll toil and sing 'Neath the ban - ner of the cross! Be - neath

LIFE IN CHRIST

Who Is on the Lord's Side? 460

Who is on the Lord's side? Exo. 32:26

ARMAGEDDON 6 5 6 5 D. Ref.
C. Luise Reichardt, 1853
Arr. by John Goss, 1872

Frances R. Havergal, 1877

1. Who is on the Lord's side? Who will serve the King? Who will be His
2. Not for weight of glo - ry, Not for crown and palm, En - ter we the
3. Je - sus, Thou hast bought us, Not with gold or gem, But with Thine own
4. Fierce may be the con - flict, Strong may be the foe, But the King's own

help - ers, Oth - er lives to bring? Who will leave the world's side?
ar - my, Raise the war - rior psalm; But for love that claim - eth
life - blood, For Thy di - a - dem. With Thy bless - ing fill - ing
ar - my None can o - ver - throw. Round His stand - ard rang - ing

Who will face the foe? Who is on the Lord's side? Who for
Lives for whom He died; He whom Je - sus nam - eth Must be
Each who comes to Thee, Thou hast made us will - ing, Thou hast
Vic - t'ry is se - cure; For His truth un - chang - ing Makes the

Him will go? By Thy call of mer - cy, By Thy grace di - vine,
on His side. By Thy love con - strain - ing, By Thy grace di - vine,
made us free. By Thy grand re - demp - tion, By Thy grace di - vine,
tri - umph sure. Joy - ful - ly en - list - ing By Thy grace di - vine,

We are on the Lord's side, Sav - ior, we are Thine. A - men.

CHALLENGE AND VICTORY

461 Rise Up, O Men of God!

Yet a little while, and He ... will come, and will not tarry. Heb. 10:37

William P. Merrill, 1911

FESTAL SONG S.M.
William H. Walter, 1894

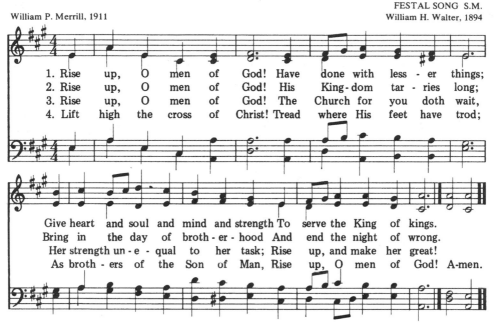

1. Rise up, O men of God! Have done with less-er things;
2. Rise up, O men of God! His King-dom tar-ries long;
3. Rise up, O men of God! The Church for you doth wait,
4. Lift high the cross of Christ! Tread where His feet have trod;

Give heart and soul and mind and strength To serve the King of kings.
Bring in the day of broth-er-hood And end the night of wrong.
Her strength un-e-qual to her task; Rise up, and make her great!
As broth-ers of the Son of Man, Rise up, O men of God! A-men.

Words by permission of "The Presbyterian Outlook," Richmond, Va. (USA).

462 My Soul, Be on Your Guard

Be sober, be vigilant ... 1 Pet. 5:8

George Heath, 1781

LABAN S.M.
Lowell Mason, 1830

1. My soul, be on your guard, Ten thou-sand foes a-rise; The
2. O watch and fight and pray, The bat-tle ne'er give o'er; Re-
3. Ne'er think the vic-t'ry won, Nor lay your ar-mor down; The
4. Fight on, my soul, till death Shall bring you to your God; He'll

hosts of sin are press-ing hard To draw you from the skies.
new it bold-ly ev-ery day, And help di-vine im-plore.
work of faith will not be done Till you ob-tain the crown.
take you at your part-ing breath, To His di-vine a-bode. A-men.

LIFE IN CHRIST

Once to Every Man and Nation **463**

Choose you this day whom ye will serve. Joshua 24:15

James R. Lowell, 1845

TON-Y-BOTEL 8 7 8 7 D.

Thomas J. Williams, 1890

1. Once to ev-ery man and na-tion Comes the mo-ment to de-cide,
2. Then to side with truth is no-ble, When we share her wretch-ed crust,
3. Though the cause of e-vil pros-per, Yet the truth a-lone is strong;

In the strife of truth with false-hood, For the good or e-vil side;
Ere her cause bring fame and prof-it, And 'tis pros-p'rous to be just;
Though her por-tion be the scaf-fold, And up-on the throne be wrong,

Some great cause, some great de-ci-sion, Of-f'ring each the bloom or blight,
Then it is the brave man choos-es While the cow-ard stands a-side,
Yet that scaf-fold sways the fu-ture, And, be-hind the dim un-known,

And the choice goes by for-ev-er 'Twixt that dark-ness and that light.
Till the mul-ti-tude make vir-tue Of the faith they had de-nied.
Stand-eth God with-in the shad-ow Keep-ing watch a-bove His own. A-men.

This tune in a lower key, No. 229
Music copyright used by permission of Gwenlyn Evans, Ltd., Caernarvon.

CHALLENGE AND VICTORY

464 We Are Living, We Are Dwelling

For we know that the whole creation groaneth and travaileth in pain . . . until now. Rom. 8:22

AUSTRIAN HYMN 8 7 8 7 D.

A. Cleveland Coxe, 1840

Franz Joseph Haydn, 1797

1. We are liv-ing, we are dwell-ing In a grand and aw-ful time,
2. Will ye play, then? will ye dal-ly Far be-hind the bat-tle line?
3. Sworn to yield, to wa-ver, nev-er; Con-se-crat-ed, born a-gain;

In an age on a-ges tell-ing; To be liv-ing is sub-lime.
Up! it is Je-ho-vah's ral-ly; God's own arm hath need of thine.
Sworn to be Christ's sol-diers ev-er, On! for Christ at least be men!

Hark! the wak-ing up of na-tions, Hosts ad-vanc-ing to the fray;
Worlds are charg-ing, heav'n be-hold-ing; Thou hast but an hour to fight;
On! let all the soul with-in you For the truth's sake go a-broad!

Hark! what sound-eth is cre-a-tion's Groan-ing for the lat-ter day.
Now, the bla-zoned cross un-fold-ing, On, right on-ward for the right!
Strike! let ev-ery nerve and sin-ew Tell on a-ges, tell for God. A-men.

This tune in a higher key, No. 209

LIFE IN CHRIST

Give of Your Best to the Master 465

Unto whomsoever much is given, of him shall be much required. Luke 12:48

BARNARD 8 7 8 7 D. Ref.

Howard B. Grose, 1851-1939

Charlotte A. Barnard, 1830-1869

1. Give of your best to the Mas-ter, Give of the strength of your youth;
2. Give of your best to the Mas-ter, Give Him first place in your heart;
3. Give of your best to the Mas-ter, Naught else is wor-thy His love;
Ref. Give of your best to the Mas-ter, Give of the strength of your youth;

Fine

Throw your soul's fresh, glow-ing ar - dor In - to the bat-tle for truth.
Give Him first place in your serv-ice, Con - se-crate ev - ery part.
He gave Him-self for your ran - som, Gave up His glo-ry a - bove;
Clad in sal - va-tion's full ar - mor, Join in the bat-tle for truth.

Je - sus has set the ex - am - ple—Daunt-less was He, young and brave;
Give, and to you shall be giv - en— God His be - lov - ed Son gave;
Laid down His life with-out mur - mur, You from sin's ru - in to save;

D.C. Refrain

Give Him your loy - al de - vo - tion, Give Him the best that you have.
Grate-ful - ly seek-ing to serve Him, Give Him the best that you have.
Give Him your heart's ad-o - ra - tion, Give Him the best that you have.

CHALLENGE AND VICTORY

466 God of Grace and God of Glory

Who knoweth whether thou art come to the kingdom for such a time . . . ? Esther 4:14

CWM RHONDDA 8 7 8 7 8 7 7

Harry E. Fosdick, 1930

John Hughes, 1907

1. God of grace and God of glo - ry, On Thy peo - ple
2. Lo! the hosts of e - vil round us Scorn Thy Christ, as-
3. Set our feet on loft - y plac - es; Gird our lives, that

pour Thy pow'r; Crown Thine an-cient church's sto - ry, Bring her bud to
sail His ways! Fears and doubts too long have bound us, Free our hearts to
they may be Ar-mored with all Christ -like grac - es In the fight to

glo - rious flow'r. Grant us wis - dom, Grant us cour - age
faith and praise. Grant us wis - dom, Grant us cour - age
set men free. Grant us wis - dom, Grant us cour - age

For the fac - ing of this hour, For the fac - ing of this hour.
For the liv - ing of these days, For the liv - ing of these days.
That we fail not man nor Thee! That we fail not man nor Thee! A -men.

LIFE IN CHRIST

The Son of God Goes Forth to War **467**

Can ye drink of the cup that I drink of . . . ? Mark 10:38

ALL SAINTS, NEW C.M.D.

Reginald Heber, 1827

Henry S. Cutler, 1872

1. The Son of God goes forth to war, A king-ly crown to gain;
2. The mar-tyr first, whose ea-gle eye Could pierce be-yond the grave,
3. A glo-rious band, the cho-sen few On whom the Spir-it came,
4. A no-ble ar-my, men and boys, The ma-tron and the maid,

His blood-red ban-ner streams a-far: Who fol-lows in His train?
Who saw his Mas-ter in the sky And called on Him to save.
Twelve val-iant saints, their hope they knew And mocked the cross and flame:
A-round the Sav-ior's throne re-joice, In robes of light ar-rayed.

Who best can drink His cup of woe, Tri-um-phant o-ver pain,
Like Him, with par-don on his tongue In midst of mor-tal pain,
They met the ty-rant's bran-dished steel, The li-on's go-ry mane;
They climbed the steep as-cent of heav'n Through per-il, toil, and pain;

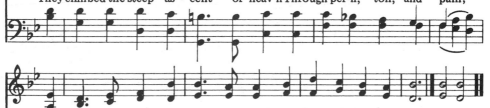

Who pa-tient bears His cross be-low, He fol-lows in His train.
He prayed for them that did the wrong: Who fol-lows in his train?
They bowed their necks the death to feel: Who fol-lows in their train?
O God, to us may grace be giv'n To fol-low in their train! A-men.

CHALLENGE AND VICTORY

468 Soldiers, Who Are Christ's Below

My reward is with me, to give every man according as his work shall be. Rev. 22:12

Latin hymn, *Bourges Breviary*, 1734
Trans. by J. H. Clark, 1865

CRUCIS MILITES 7 7 7 7
Myles B. Foster, 1889

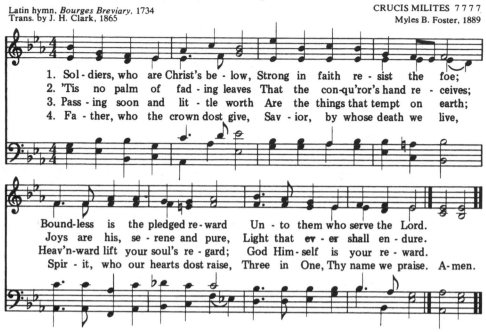

1. Sol - diers, who are Christ's be - low, Strong in faith re - sist the foe;
2. 'Tis no palm of fad - ing leaves That the con-qu'ror's hand re - ceives;
3. Pass - ing soon and lit - tle worth Are the things that tempt on earth;
4. Fa - ther, who the crown dost give, Sav - ior, by whose death we live,

Bound-less is the pledged re - ward Un - to them who serve the Lord.
Joys are his, se - rene and pure, Light that ev - er shall en - dure.
Heav'n-ward lift your soul's re - gard; God Him-self is your re - ward.
Spir - it, who our hearts dost raise, Three in One, Thy name we praise. A - men.

469 Fight the Good Fight with All Thy Might

Fight the good fight of faith. I Tim. 6:12

John S. B. Monsell, 1863

PENTECOST L.M.
William Boyd, 1864

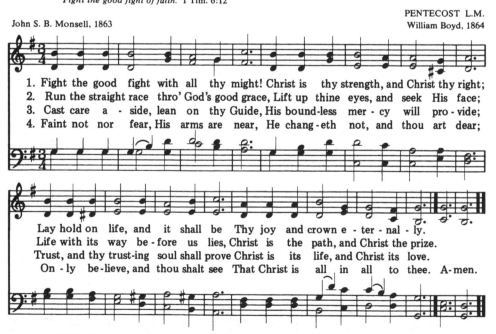

1. Fight the good fight with all thy might! Christ is thy strength, and Christ thy right;
2. Run the straight race thro' God's good grace, Lift up thine eyes, and seek His face;
3. Cast care a - side, lean on thy Guide, His bound-less mer - cy will pro - vide;
4. Faint not nor fear, His arms are near, He chang-eth not, and thou art dear;

Lay hold on life, and it shall be Thy joy and crown e - ter - nal - ly.
Life with its way be - fore us lies, Christ is the path, and Christ the prize.
Trust, and thy trust-ing soul shall prove Christ is its life, and Christ its love.
On - ly be - lieve, and thou shalt see That Christ is all in all to thee. A - men.

LIFE IN CHRIST

Onward, Christian Soldiers 470

Thou therefore endure hardness, as a good soldier of Jesus Christ. II Tim. 2:3

ST. GERTRUDE 6 5 6 5 D. Ref.

Sabine Baring-Gould, 1864

Arthur S. Sullivan, 1871

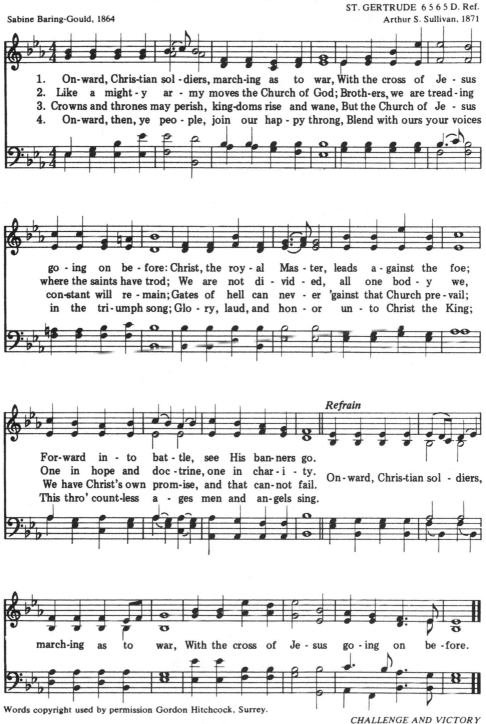

1. On-ward, Chris-tian sol-diers, march-ing as to war, With the cross of Je - sus
2. Like a might-y ar - my moves the Church of God; Broth-ers, we are tread-ing
3. Crowns and thrones may perish, king-doms rise and wane, But the Church of Je - sus
4. On-ward, then, ye peo - ple, join our hap - py throng, Blend with ours your voices

go - ing on be - fore: Christ, the roy - al Mas - ter, leads a - gainst the foe;
where the saints have trod; We are not di - vid - ed, all one bod - y we,
con-stant will re - main; Gates of hell can nev - er 'gainst that Church pre - vail;
in the tri - umph song; Glo - ry, laud, and hon - or un - to Christ the King;

Refrain

For-ward in - to bat - tle, see His ban-ners go.
One in hope and doc - trine, one in char - i - ty.
We have Christ's own prom-ise, and that can-not fail.
This thro' count-less a - ges men and an-gels sing.

On-ward, Chris-tian sol - diers,

march-ing as to war, With the cross of Je - sus go-ing on be - fore.

CHALLENGE AND VICTORY

471 Give Me a Passion for Souls, Dear Lord

My heart's desire and prayer to God . . . is, that they might be saved. Rom. 10:1

Herbert G. Tovey, 1914

BIOLA 9 7 9 7 Ref.
Foss L. Fellers, 1914

1. Give me a pas-sion for souls, dear Lord, A pas-sion to save the lost;
2. Though there are dan-gers un - told and stern Con-front-ing me in the way,
3. How shall this pas-sion for souls be mine? Lord, make Thou the an-swer clear;

O that Thy love were by all a-dored, And wel-comed at an - y cost.
Will - ing - ly still would I go, nor turn, But trust Thee for grace each day.
Help me to throw out the old life -line To those who are strug-gling near.

Refrain

Je - sus, I long, I long to be win - ning Men who are

lost, and con - stant - ly sin - ning; O may this hour be

one of be - gin - ning The sto - ry of par - don to tell.

LIFE IN CHRIST

From Greenland's Icy Mountains 472

Come over . . . and help us. Acts 16:9

MISSIONARY HYMN 7 6 7 6 D.

Reginald Heber, 1819

Lowell Mason, 1824

1. From Green-land's i - cy moun-tains, From In - dia's cor - al strand,
2. What though the spic - y breez - es Blow soft o'er Cey - lon's isle;
3. Shall we, whose souls are light - ed With wis - dom from on high,
4. Waft, waft, ye winds, His sto - ry, And you, ye wa - ters, roll,

Where Af - ric's sun - ny foun - tains Roll down their gold - en sand,
Though ev - ery pros - pect pleas - es, And on - ly man is vile?
Shall we to men be - night - ed The lamp of life de - ny?
Till, like a sea of glo - ry, It spreads from pole to pole:

From man - y an an - cient riv - er, From man - y a palm - y plain,
In vain with lav - ish kind - ness The gifts of God are strown;
Sal - va - tion! O sal - va - tion! The joy - ful sound pro - claim,
Till o'er our ran - somed na - ture The Lamb for sin - ners slain,

They call us to de - liv - er Their land from er - ror's chain.
The hea - then in his blind - ness Bows down to wood and stone.
Till earth's re - mot - est na - tion Has learned Mes - si - ah's name.
Re - deem - er, King, Cre - a - tor, In bliss re - turns to reign. A - men.

EVANGELISM AND MISSIONS

473 Take Up Thy Cross and Follow Me

Whosoever will come after Me, let him . . . take up his cross and follow Me. Mark 8:34

FALLS CREEK 8 6 8 7 Ref.

B. B. McKinney, 1937

B. B. McKinney, 1937

1. "Take up thy cross and fol - low Me," I heard my Mas - ter say;
2. He drew me clos - er to His side, I sought His will to know,
3. It may be through the shad - ows dim, Or o'er the storm - y sea,
4. My heart, my life, my all I bring To Christ who loves me so;

"I gave My life to ran - som thee, Sur - ren - der your all to - day."
And in that will I now a - bide, Wher - ev - er He leads I'll go.
I take my cross and fol - low Him, Wher - ev - er He lead - eth me.
He is my Mas - ter, Lord, and King, Wher - ev - er He leads I'll go.

Refrain

Wher - ev - er He leads I'll go, Wher - ev - er He leads I'll go,

I'll fol - low my Christ who loves me so, Wher - ev - er He leads I'll go.

LIFE IN CHRIST

Remember All the People **474**

Other sheep I have which are not of this fold: them also I must bring. John 10:16

FAR OFF LANDS 7 6 7 6 D.

Hemmets Koralbok, 1921
Traditional Bohemian Brethren melody

Percy Dearmer, 1929

1. Re - mem - ber all the peo - ple Who live in far off lands,
2. Some work in sul - try for - ests Where apes swing to and fro,
3. God bless the men and wo - men Who serve Him o - ver - sea;

In strange and lone - ly cit - ies, Or roam the des - ert sands,
Some fish in might - y riv - ers, Some hunt a - cross the snow.
God raise up more to help them To set the na - tions free,

Or farm the moun - tain pas - tures, Or till the end - less plains
Re - mem - ber all God's chil - dren, Who yet have nev - er heard
Till all the dis - tant peo - ple In ev - ery for - eign place

Where chil - dren wade thro' rice-fields And watch the cam - el trains.
The truth that comes from Je - sus, The glo - ry of His Word.
Shall un - der - stand His king-dom And come in - to His grace. A - men.

EVANGELISM AND MISSIONS

475 The Battle Is the Lord's

For the battle is the Lord's. 1 Sam. 17:47

LEONI 6 6 8 4 D.
Synagogue melody
Arr. by Meyer Lyon, 1770

E. Margaret Clarkson, 1962

1. The bat-tle is the Lord's! The har-vest fields are white:
2. The bat-tle is the Lord's! Not ours is strength or skill,
3. The bat-tle is the Lord's! The Vic-tor cru-ci-fied
4. The bat-tle is the Lord's! Stand still, my soul, and see

How few the reap-ing hands ap-pear, Their strength how slight!
But His a-lone, in sov-ereign grace, To work His will.
Must with the tra-vail of His soul Be sat-is-fied.
The great sal-va-tion God hath wrought Re-vealed for thee.

Yet vic-to-ry is sure— We face a van-quished foe;
Ours, count-ing not the cost, Un-flinch-ing, to o-bey;
The pow'rs of hell shall fail, And all God's will be done,
Then, rest-ing in His might, Lift high His tri-umph song,

Then for-ward with the ris-en Christ To bat-tle go!
And in His time His ho-ly arm Shall win the day.
Till ev-ery soul whom He hath giv'n To Christ be won.
For pow'r, do-min-ion, king-dom, strength To Christ be-long! A-men.

LIFE IN CHRIST

O Christian, Haste, Your Mission High **476**

We declare unto you glad tidings. Acts 13:32

TIDINGS 11 10 11 10 Ref.

Mary A. Thomson, 1868

James Walch, 1875

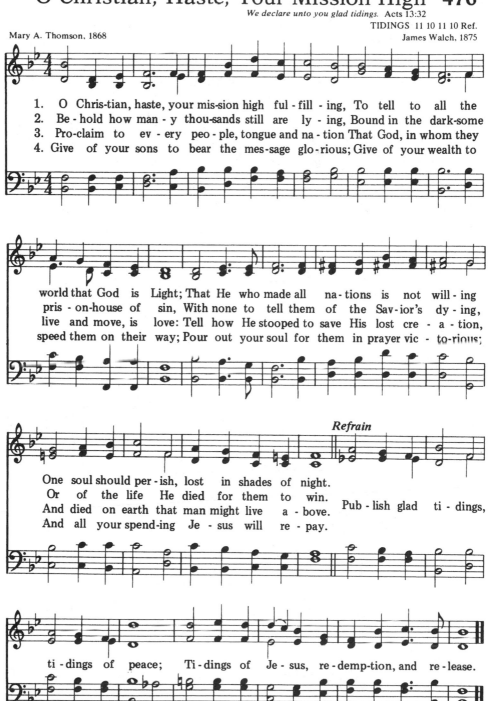

1. O Chris-tian, haste, your mis-sion high ful - fill - ing, To tell to all the
2. Be - hold how man - y thou-sands still are ly - ing, Bound in the dark-some
3. Pro-claim to ev - ery peo - ple, tongue and na - tion That God, in whom they
4. Give of your sons to bear the mes-sage glo-rious; Give of your wealth to

world that God is Light; That He who made all na - tions is not will - ing
pris - on-house of sin, With none to tell them of the Sav-ior's dy - ing,
live and move, is love: Tell how He stooped to save His lost cre - a - tion,
speed them on their way; Pour out your soul for them in prayer vic - to-rious;

Refrain

One soul should per - ish, lost in shades of night.
Or of the life He died for them to win.
And died on earth that man might live a - bove. Pub - lish glad ti - dings,
And all your spend-ing Je - sus will re - pay.

ti - dings of peace; Ti - dings of Je - sus, re - demp-tion, and re - lease.

EVANGELISM AND MISSIONS

477 The Sending, Lord, Springs

Whom shall I send, and who will go for us? Isa. 6:8

SINE NOMINE 10 10 10 Alleluias

William J. Danker, 1966

Ralph Vaughan Williams, 1906

1. The send - ing, Lord, springs from Thy yearn - ing heart.
2. Thy bod - y paid for men of ev - ery race;
3. Where men their broth - ers heart - less - ly op - press,
4. One man in need in bod - y, mind, and soul;
5. One mis - sion takes me o - ver land and sea
6. From ur - ban deeps to or - bits high in space,

God, Thou the send - er, Thou the Sent One art,
To them we wit - ness, Christ, Thy bound - less grace,
Where peo - ple suf - fer, hope - less in dis - tress,
One word in Je - sus' name to make him whole;
And to the Chris - tian broth - er next to me.
Through cross to glo - ry moves one pil - grim race,

And of Thy mis - sion mak - est us a part.
With them, one bod - y, kneel be - fore Thy face.
There we Thy name in deed and word con - fess.
One Lord, one mis - sion leads us to the goal.
Help me to lis - ten, Lord, and speak for Thee.
Prais - ing the Fa - ther - Son - and - Spir - it's grace.

Al - le - lu - ia! Al - le - lu - ia! Al - le - lu - ia! A-men.

A unison setting of this tune, No. 533
Words Copyright 1966 by "Christianity Today". Used by permission.
Music from "The English Hymnal" by permission of Oxford University Press.
LIFE IN CHRIST

Must I Go, and Empty Handed? 478

. . . He that winneth souls is wise. Prov. 11:30

PROVIDENCE 8 7 8 7 Ref.

Charles C. Luther, 1877

George C. Stebbins, 1878

1. "Must I go, and emp-ty hand-ed," Thus my dear Re-deem-er meet?
2. Not at death I shrink nor fal-ter, For my Sav-ior saves me now;
3. O the years in sin-ning wast-ed, Could I but re-call them now,
4. O ye saints, a-rouse, be ear-nest, Up and work while yet 'tis day;

Not one day of serv-ice give Him, Lay no tro-phy at His feet?
But to meet Him emp-ty-hand-ed, Thought of that now clouds my brow.
I would give them to my Sav-ior, To His will I'd glad-ly bow.
Ere the night of death o'er-take you, Strive for souls while still you may.

Refrain

"Must I go, and emp-ty hand-ed?" Must I meet my Sav-ior so?

Not one soul with which to greet Him: Must I emp-ty-hand-ed go?

EVANGELISM AND MISSIONS

479 Christ Was Born in a Distant Land

Behold, I bring you good tidings of great joy . . . Luke 2:10

Gene Bartlett, 1968

RHEA L.M. Ref.
Gene Bartlett, 1968

1. Christ was born in a dis-tant land, Tell the good news, tell the good news,
2. Christ be-came a man on earth, Tell the good news, tell the good news,
3. Christ a-rose and to heav-en went, Tell the good news, tell the good news,
4. Christ still lives in the world to-day, Tell the good news, tell the good news,

Lived on earth for the good of man, Tell the good news, tell the good news.
Gave His life for man's re-birth, Tell the good news, tell the good news.
All may fol-low who re-pent, Tell the good news, tell the good news.
Giv-ing strength to all souls who pray, Tell the good news, tell the good news.

Refrain

Tell the good news, tell the good news, Tell the good news that Christ has come;

Tell the good news, tell the good news, Tell the good news to ev-ery-one.

LIFE IN CHRIST

Rescue the Perishing 480

The Son of man is come to seek and to save that which was lost. Luke 19:10

Fanny J. Crosby, 1869

RESCUE 11 10 11 10 Ref.
William H. Doane, 1870

1. Res - cue the per - ish - ing, care for the dy - ing, Snatch them in pit - y from
2. Though they are slight-ing Him, still He is wait - ing, Wait - ing the pen - i - tent
3. Down in the hu - man heart, crushed by the tempt-er, Feel - ings lie bur - ied that
4. Res - cue the per - ish - ing, du - ty de-mands it; Strength for thy la - bor the

sin and the grave; Weep o'er the err - ing one, lift up the fall - en,
child to re - ceive; Plead with them ear - nest - ly, plead with them gen - tly,
grace can re - store; Touched by a lov - ing heart, wak - ened by kind - ness,
Lord will pro - vide; Back to the nar - row way pa - tient - ly win them;

Refrain

Tell them of Je - sus the might - y to save.
He will for - give if they on - ly be - lieve.
Cords that are bro - ken will vi - brate once more.   Res - cue the per - ish - ing,
Tell the poor wan-d'rer a Sav - ior has died.

care for the dy - ing; Je - sus is mer - ci - ful, Je - sus will save.

EVANGELISM AND MISSIONS

481 So Send I You

As My Father hath sent Me, even so send I you. John 20:21

E. Margaret Clarkson, 1937

TORONTO 11 10 11 10 Ref.
John W. Peterson, 1954

1. So send I you to la - bor un - re - ward - ed, To serve un-
2. So send I you to bind the bruised and bro - ken, O'er wand-'ring
3. So send I you to lone - li - ness and long - ing, With heart a-
4. So send I you to leave your life's am - bi - tion, To die to
5. So send I you to hearts made hard by ha - tred, To eyes made

paid, un - loved, un - sought, un - known, To bear re - buke, to suf - fer
souls to work, to weep, to wake, To bear the bur - dens of a
hung -'ring for the loved and known, For - sak - ing home and kin - dred,
dear de - sire, self - will re - sign, To la - bor long, and love where
blind be - cause they will not see, To spend, though it be blood, to

scorn and scoff - ing— So send I you to toil for Me a - lone.
world a - wea - ry, So send I you to suf - fer for My sake.
friend and dear one— So send I you to know My love a - lone.
men re - vile you— So send I you to lose your life in Mine.
spend and spare not— So send I you to taste of Cal - va - ry.

Refrain (following the final stanza)

"As the Fa - ther hath sent me, So send I you."

LIFE IN CHRIST

Lonely Voices Crying in the City 482

I . . . am as a sparrow alone upon the housetop. Psa. 102:7

LONELY VOICES Irreg.

Billie Hanks, Jr., 1967

Billie Hanks, Jr., 1967

Unison

1. Lone - ly voic - es cry - ing in the cit - y, Lone - ly voic - es
2. Lone - ly fac - es look - ing for the sun - rise, Just to find an -
3. Lone - ly eyes, I see them in the sub - way, Bur - dened by the
4. A - bund - ant life He came to tru - ly give man, But so few His

sound - ing like a child. Lone - ly voic - es come from bus - y peo - ple,
oth - er bus - y day. Lone - ly fac - es all a - round the cit - y,
wor - ries of the day: Men at lei - sure, but they're so un - hap - py,
gift of grace re - ceive. Lone - ly peo - ple live in ev - ery cit - y,

Too dis - turbed to stop a lit - tle while. Lone - ly voic - es
Men a - fraid, but too a - shamed to pray. Lone - ly fac - es
Tired of fool - ish roles they try to play. Lone - ly peo - ple
Men who face a dark and lone - ly grave. Lone - ly fac - es

fill my dreams, Lone - ly voic - es haunt my mem - o - ry.
do I see, Lone - ly fac - es haunt my mem - o - ry.
do I see, Lone - ly peo - ple haunt my mem - o - ry.
do I see, Lone - ly voic - es call - ing out to me.

EVANGELISM AND MISSIONS

483 We've a Story to Tell to the Nations

And this gospel . . . shall be preached in all the world for a witness unto all nations. Matt. 24:14

H. Ernest Nichol, 1896

MESSAGE 10 8 8 7 7 Ref.

H. Ernest Nichol, 1896

1. We've a sto - ry to tell to the na - tions That shall
2. We've a song to be sung to the na - tions That shall
3. We've a mes - sage to give to the na - tions That the
4. We've a Sav - ior to show to the na - tions Who the

turn their hearts to the right, A sto - ry of truth and mer - cy,
lift their hearts to the Lord, A song that shall con - quer e - vil
Lord who reign - eth a - bove Hath sent us His Son to save us,
path of sor - row hath trod, That all of the world's great peo - ples

A sto - ry of peace and light, A sto - ry of peace and light.
And shat - ter the spear and sword, And shat - ter the spear and sword.
And show us that God is love, And show us that God is love.
Might come to the truth of God, Might come to the truth of God.

Refrain

For the dark-ness shall turn to dawn-ing, And the dawn-ing to noon-day bright,

And Christ's great king-dom shall come to earth, The king-dom of love and light.

LIFE IN CHRIST

It Only Takes a Spark 484

If God so loved us, we ought also to love one another. I John 4:11

Kurt Kaiser, 1969

PASS IT ON Irreg.
Kurt Kaiser, 1969

Unison

1. It on - ly takes a spark to get a fire go - ing,
2. What a won - drous time is spring when all the trees are bud - ding,
3. I wish for you, my friend, this hap - pi-ness that I've found,

And soon all those a-round can warm up in its glow-ing.
The birds be-gin to sing, the flow - ers start their bloom-ing,
You can de-pend on Him, it mat - ters not where you're bound.

That's how it is with God's love once you've ex-pe-ri-enced it;
That's how it is with God's love once you've ex-pe-ri-enced it;
I'll shout it from the moun-tain top— I want my world to know;

You spread His love to ev - ery one; You want to pass it on.
You want to sing, it's fresh like spring, You want to pass it on.
The Lord of love has come to me, I want to pass it on.

EVANGELISM AND MISSIONS

485 The Vision of a Dying World

Lift up your eyes, and look on the fields; for they are white. John 4:35

Anne Ortlund, 1966

ALL SAINTS, NEW C.M.D.
Henry S. Cutler, 1872

1. The vi - sion of a dy - ing world Is vast be - fore our eyes;
2. The sav - age hugs his god of stone And fears de - scent of night;
3. To - day, as un - der-stand-ing's bounds Are stretch'd on ev - ery hand,
4. The warn-ing bell of judg-ment tolls, A - bove us looms the cross;

We feel the heart-beat of its need, We hear its fee - ble cries:
The cit - y dwell - er cring - es lone A - mid the gar - ish light:
O clothe Thy Word in bright, new sounds, And speed it o'er the land;
A - round are ev - er - dy - ing souls— How great, how great the loss!

Lord Je - sus Christ, re - vive Thy church In this, her cru - cial hour!
Lord Je - sus Christ, a - rouse Thy church To see their mute dis - tress!
Lord Je - sus Christ, em - pow - er us To preach by ev - ery means!
O Lord, con-strain and move Thy church The glad news to im - part!

Lord Je - sus Christ, a - wake Thy church With Spir - it - giv - en pow'r.
Lord Je - sus Christ, e - quip Thy church With love and ten - der-ness.
Lord Je - sus Christ, em-bold - en us In near and dis-tant scenes.
And Lord, as Thou dost stir Thy church, Be - gin with - in my heart. A-men.

LIFE IN CHRIST

We Have Heard the Joyful Sound 486

Tell of His salvation from day to day. Declare His glory . . . Psa. 96:2, 3

JESUS SAVES 7 6 7 6 7 7 7 6

Priscilla J. Owens, 1868

William J. Kirkpatrick, 1882

1. We have heard the joy - ful sound: Je - sus saves! Je - sus saves!
2. Waft it on the roll - ing tide; Je - sus saves! Je - sus saves!
3. Sing a - bove the bat - tle strife, Je - sus saves! Je - sus saves!
4. Give the winds a might - y voice, Je - sus saves! Je - sus saves!

Spread the ti - dings all a - round: Je - sus saves! Je - sus saves!
Tell to sin - ners far and wide: Je - sus saves! Je - sus saves!
By His death and end - less life, Je - sus saves! Je - sus saves!
Let the na - tions now re - joice— Je - sus saves! Je - sus saves!

Bear the news to ev - ery land, Climb the steeps and cross the waves;
Sing, ye is - lands of the sea; Ech - o back, ye o - cean caves;
Sing it soft - ly through the gloom, When the heart for mer - cy craves;
Shout sal - va - tion full and free, High - est hills and deep - est caves;

On - ward! 'tis our Lord's com - mand; Je - sus saves! Je - sus saves!
Earth shall keep her ju - bi - lee: Je - sus saves! Je - sus saves!
Sing in tri - umph o'er the tomb— Je - sus saves! Je - sus saves!
This our song of vic - to - ry— Je - sus saves! Je - sus saves!

EVANGELISM AND MISSIONS

487 Far, Far Away, in Death and Darkness

Go ye into all the world, and preach the gospel . . . Mark 16:15

James McGranahan, 1886

GO YE 11 10 11 10 Ref.
James McGranahan, 1886

1. Far, far a - way, in death and dark - ness dwell - ing, Mil - lions of souls for-
2. See o'er the world wide o - pen doors in - vit - ing, Sol - diers of Christ, a -
3. "Why will ye die?" the voice of God is call - ing, "Why will ye die?" re-
4. God speed the day, when those of ev - ery na - tion "Glo - ry to God!" tri-

ev - er may be lost; Who, who will go, sal - va - tion's sto - ry tell - ing,
rise and en - ter in! Chris - tians, a - wake! your forc - es all u - nit - ing,
ech - o in His name; Je - sus hath died to save from death ap - pall - ing,
um - phant - ly shall sing; Ran - somed, re - deemed, re - joic - ing in sal - va - tion,

Refrain

Look - ing to Je - sus, mind - ing not the cost?
Send forth the gos - pel, break the chains of sin. "All pow'r is giv - en un - to Me,
Life and sal - va - tion there - fore go pro - claim.
Shout Hal - le - lu - jah, for the Lord is King.

All pow'r is giv - en un - to Me, Go ye in - to all the world and

preach the gos - pel, And lo, I am with you al - way."

LIFE IN CHRIST

Heralds of Christ 488

Make straight in the desert a highway for our God. Isa. 40:3

NATIONAL HYMN 10 10 10 10

Laura S. Copenhaver, 1894

George W. Warren, c. 1892

Trumpets before each stanza.

1. Her - alds of Christ, who bear the King's com-mands,
2. Through des - ert ways, dark fen, and deep mo - rass,
3. Where once the crook-ed trail in dark-ness wound
4. Lord, give us faith and strength the road to build,

Im - mor - tal ti - dings in your mor - tal hands,
Through jun - gles, slug - gish seas, and moun - tain pass,
Let march - ing feet and joy - ous song re - sound,
To see the prom - ise of the day ful - filled,

Pass on and car - ry swift the news ye bring;
Build ye the road, and fal - ter not nor stay;
Where burn the fu - n'ral pyres and cen - sers swing,
When war shall be no more and strife shall cease

Make straight, make straight the high - way of the King.
Pre - pare a - cross the earth the King's high - way.
Make straight, make straight the high - ways of the King.
Up - on the high - way of the Prince of Peace. A-men.

EVANGELISM AND MISSIONS

489 Jesus Shall Reign Where'er the Sun

All kings shall fall down before Him: all nations shall serve Him. Psa. 72:11

Isaac Watts, 1719
Based on Psalm 72

DUKE STREET L.M.
John Hatton, 1793

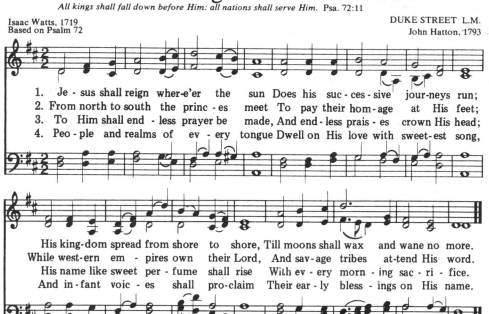

1. Je - sus shall reign wher-e'er the sun Does his suc - ces - sive jour-neys run;
2. From north to south the princ - es meet To pay their hom-age at His feet;
3. To Him shall end - less prayer be made, And end - less prais - es crown His head;
4. Peo - ple and realms of ev - ery tongue Dwell on His love with sweet-est song,

His king-dom spread from shore to shore, Till moons shall wax and wane no more.
While west-ern em - pires own their Lord, And sav - age tribes at-tend His word.
His name like sweet per - fume shall rise With ev - ery morn - ing sac - ri - fice.
And in-fant voic - es shall pro-claim Their ear - ly bless - ings on His name.

490 Fling Out the Banner! Let It Float

Thou hast given a banner to them that fear thee . . . Psa. 60:4

George W. Doane, 1848

WALTHAM L.M.
John B. Calkin, 1872

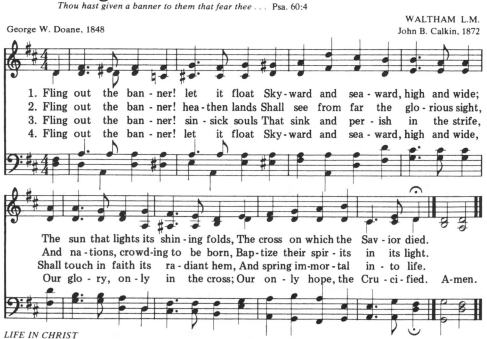

1. Fling out the ban - ner! let it float Sky - ward and sea - ward, high and wide;
2. Fling out the ban - ner! hea - then lands Shall see from far the glo - rious sight,
3. Fling out the ban - ner! sin - sick souls That sink and per - ish in the strife,
4. Fling out the ban - ner! let it float Sky - ward and sea - ward, high and wide,

The sun that lights its shin - ing folds, The cross on which the Sav - ior died.
And na - tions, crowd-ing to be born, Bap - tize their spir - its in its light.
Shall touch in faith its ra - diant hem, And spring im-mor - tal in - to life.
Our glo - ry, on - ly in the cross; Our on - ly hope, the Cru - ci - fied. A-men.

I'll Tell to All That God Is Love 491

Wherever this gospel shall be preached throughout the whole world . . . Mark 14:9

TILL THE WHOLE WORLD KNOWS 8 7 8 7 Ref.

Alfred H. Ackley, 1923

Bentley D. Ackley, 1923

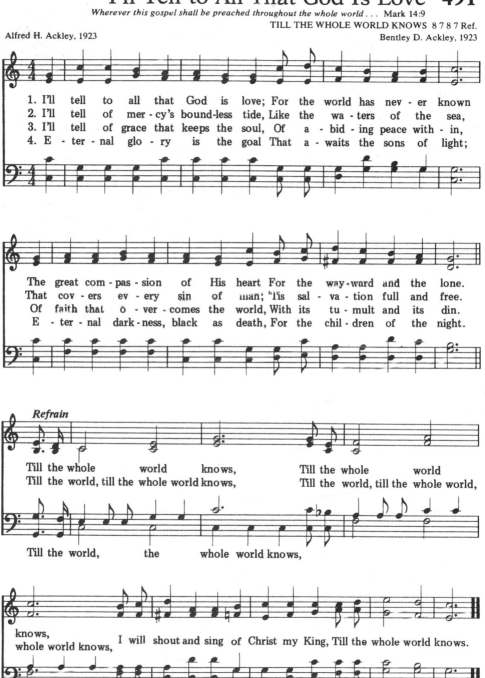

1. I'll tell to all that God is love; For the world has nev - er known
2. I'll tell of mer - cy's bound-less tide, Like the wa - ters of the sea,
3. I'll tell of grace that keeps the soul, Of a - bid - ing peace with - in,
4. E - ter - nal glo - ry is the goal That a - waits the sons of light;

The great com - pas - sion of His heart For the way - ward and the lone.
That cov - ers ev - ery sin of man; 'Tis sal - va - tion full and free.
Of faith that o - ver - comes the world, With its tu - mult and its din.
E - ter - nal dark - ness, black as death, For the chil - dren of the night.

Refrain

Till the whole world knows, Till the whole world
Till the world, till the whole world knows, Till the world, till the whole world,

Till the world, the whole world knows,

knows, I will shout and sing of Christ my King, Till the whole world knows.
whole world knows,

EVANGELISM AND MISSIONS

492 Through All the World

Let the whole earth be filled with His glory. Psa. 72:19

Bryan J. Leech, 1970

CONRAD 14 12 12 14
Paul Liljestrand, 1970

Unison

1. Thro' all the world let ev-ery na-tion sing to God the
2. Thro' all the world let ev-ery man ex-press true right-eous-
3. Thro' all the world let ev-ery man em-brace the gift of
4. If all the world in ev-ery part shall hear, and God re-

King, As Lord may Christ pre-side where now He is de-fied,
ness, May Christ now be the norm to which all men con-form,
grace, May Christ's great light con-sume our dark-est cit-ies' gloom,
vere, We must be moved to care, and in His name to share

And sov-'reign place His throne in lands not yet His own.
His pas-sion cure the sin that fes-ters from with-in.
May Christ's great love ef-face hos-til-i-ties of race.
The lib-er-a-ting word which must be told a-broad.

Thro' all the world let ev-ery na-tion sing to God the King.
Thro' all the world let ev-ery man ex-press true right-eous-ness.
Thro' all the world let ev-ery man em-brace the gift of grace.
Then all the world in ev-ery part shall hear, and God re-vere.

LIFE IN CHRIST

Hark, the Voice of Jesus Calling 493

The harvest truly is great, but the laborers are few . . . Luke 10:2

ELLESDIE 8 7 8 7 D.

Leavitt's *The Christian Lyre*, 1831
Attr. to Wolfgang A. Mozart, 1756-1791
Arr. by Hubert P. Main, c. 1868

Daniel March, 1868

1. Hark, the voice of Je - sus call - ing, "Who will go and work to - day?
2. If you can - not be the watch - man Stand - ing high on Zi - on's wall,
3. Let none hear you i - dly say - ing, "There is noth - ing I can do,"

Fields are white, and har - vests wait - ing, Who will bear the sheaves a - way?"
Point - ing out the path to heav - en, Off - 'ring life and peace to all,
While the souls of men are dy - ing, And the Mas - ter calls for you:

Loud and long the Mas - ter call - eth, Rich re - ward He of - fers free;
If you can - not speak like an - gels, If you can - not preach like Paul,
Take the task He gives you glad - ly; Let His work your pleas - ure be;

Who will an - swer, glad - ly say - ing, "Here am I; send me, send me"?
You can tell the love of Je - sus, You can say, "He died for all."
An - swer quick - ly when He call - eth, "Here am I; send me, send me." A - men.

EVANGELISM AND MISSIONS

494 Eternal God, Whose Power Upholds

Even from everlasting to everlasting, Thou art God. Psa. 90:2

PILGRIM C.M.D.

Henry H. Tweedy, 1929

Traditional American melody
Southern Harmony, 1835

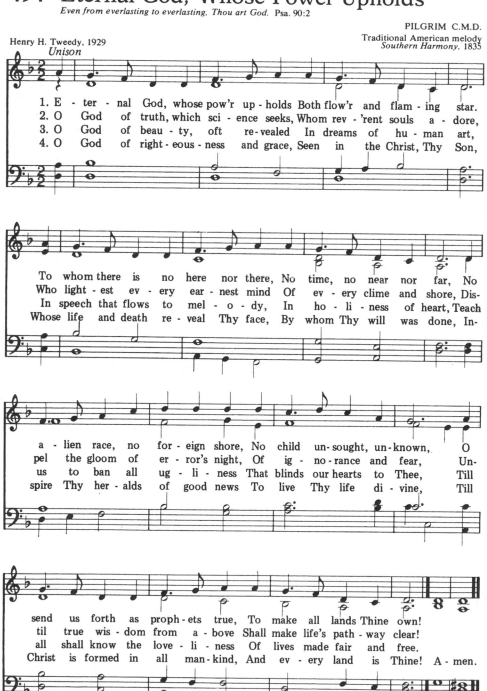

1. E - ter - nal God, whose pow'r up - holds Both flow'r and flam - ing star,
2. O God of truth, which sci - ence seeks, Whom rev - 'rent souls a - dore,
3. O God of beau - ty, oft re - vealed In dreams of hu - man art,
4. O God of right - eous - ness and grace, Seen in the Christ, Thy Son,

To whom there is no here nor there, No time, no near nor far, No
Who light - est ev - ery ear - nest mind Of ev - ery clime and shore, Dis -
In speech that flows to mel - o - dy, In ho - li - ness of heart, Teach
Whose life and death re - veal Thy face, By whom Thy will was done, In -

a - lien race, no for - eign shore, No child un - sought, un - known, O
pel the gloom of er - ror's night, Of ig - no - rance and fear, Un -
us to ban all ug - li - ness That blinds our hearts to Thee, Till
spire Thy her - alds of good news To live Thy life di - vine, Till

send us forth as proph - ets true, To make all lands Thine own!
til true wis - dom from a - bove Shall make life's path - way clear!
all shall know the love - li - ness Of lives made fair and free.
Christ is formed in all man - kind, And ev - ery land is Thine! A - men.

Words used by permission of The Hymn Society of America.

LIFE IN CHRIST: EVANGELISM AND MISSIONS

Must Jesus Bear the Cross Alone? 495

If any man will come after Me, let him . . . take up his cross. Matt. 16:24

Thomas Shepherd, 1693, and others

MAITLAND C.M.
George N. Allen, 1844

1. Must Je - sus bear the cross a - lone, And all the world go free?
2. How hap - py are the saints a - bove, Who once went sor - r'wing here;
3. The con - se - crat - ed cross I'll bear, Till death shall set me free,
4. Up - on the crys - tal pave - ment, down At Je - sus' pierc - ed feet,

No, there's a cross for ev - ery - one, And there's a cross for me.
But now they taste un - min - gled love, And joy with - out a tear.
And then go home my crown to wear, For there's a crown for me.
Joy - ful, I'll cast my gold - en crown, And His dear name re - peat. A - men.

A Charge to Keep I Have 496

Walk worthy of the vocation wherewith ye are called. Eph. 4:1

Charles Wesley, 1762

BOYLSTON S.M.
Lowell Mason, 1832

1. A charge to keep I have, A God to glo - ri - fy, A
2. To serve the pres - ent age, My call - ing to ful - fill; O
3. Arm me with watch - ful care As in Thy sight to live, And
4. Help me to watch and pray, And still on Thee re - ly, O

nev - er - dy - ing soul to save, And fit it for the sky.
may it all my pow'rs en - gage To do my Mas - ter's will!
now Thy serv - ant, Lord, pre - pare A strict ac - count to give!
let me not my trust be - tray, But press to realms on high. A - men.

STEWARDSHIP AND SERVICE

497 There Is Joy in Serving Jesus

Serve the Lord with gladness: come before His presence with singing. Psa. 100:2

Oswald J. Smith, 1931

JOY IN SERVING JESUS Irreg. Ref.
Bentley D. Ackley, 1931

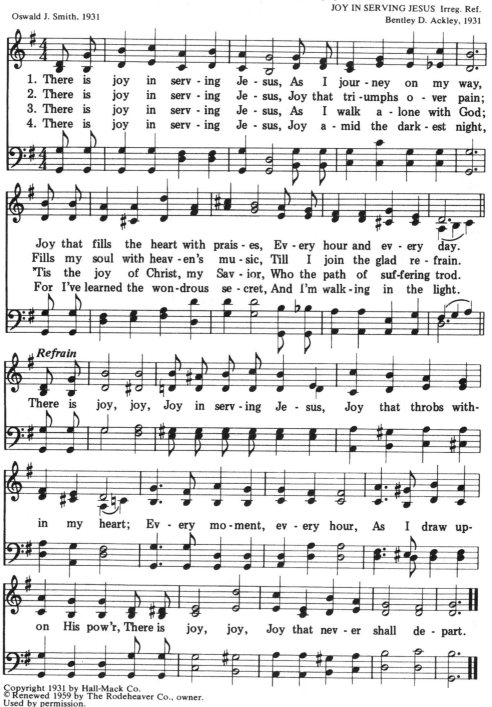

1. There is joy in serv - ing Je - sus, As I jour - ney on my way,
2. There is joy in serv - ing Je - sus, Joy that tri - umphs o - ver pain;
3. There is joy in serv - ing Je - sus, As I walk a - lone with God;
4. There is joy in serv - ing Je - sus, Joy a - mid the dark - est night,

Joy that fills the heart with prais - es, Ev - ery hour and ev - ery day.
Fills my soul with heav - en's mu - sic, Till I join the glad re - frain.
'Tis the joy of Christ, my Sav - ior, Who the path of suf - fering trod.
For I've learned the won - drous se - cret, And I'm walk - ing in the light.

Refrain

There is joy, joy, Joy in serv - ing Je - sus, Joy that throbs with - in my heart; Ev - ery mo - ment, ev - ery hour, As I draw up - on His pow'r, There is joy, joy, Joy that nev - er shall de - part.

LIFE IN CHRIST

Come, All Christians, Be Committed 498

Present your bodies a living sacrifice . . . be ye transformed. Rom. 12:1, 2

BEACH SPRING 8 7 8 7 D.
Traditional American melody
The Sacred Harp, 1844
Arr. by James H. Wood, 1958

Eva B. Lloyd, 1966

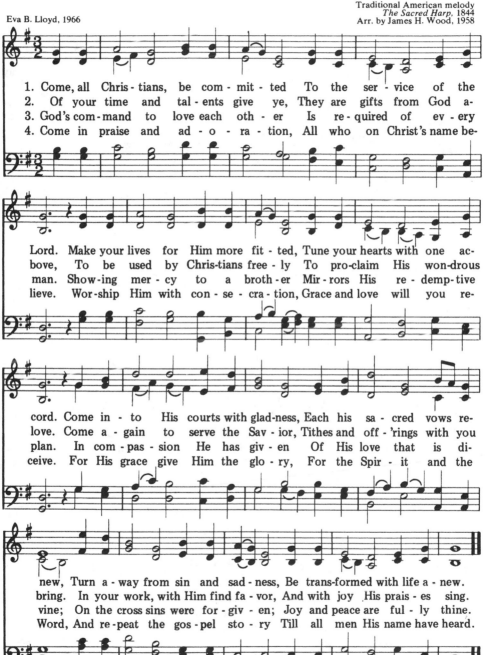

1. Come, all Chris - tians, be com - mit - ted To the ser - vice of the Lord. Make your lives for Him more fit - ted, Tune your hearts with one ac - cord. Come in - to His courts with glad-ness, Each his sa - cred vows re - new, Turn a - way from sin and sad - ness, Be trans-formed with life a - new.

2. Of your time and tal - ents give ye, They are gifts from God a - bove, To be used by Chris-tians free - ly To pro-claim His won-drous love. Come a - gain to serve the Sav - ior, Tithes and off - 'rings with you bring. In your work, with Him find fa - vor, And with joy His prais - es sing.

3. God's com - mand to love each oth - er Is re - quired of ev - ery man. Show-ing mer - cy to a broth - er Mir - rors His re - demp-tive plan. In com - pas - sion He has giv - en Of His love that is di - vine; On the cross sins were for - giv - en; Joy and peace are ful - ly thine.

4. Come in praise and ad - o - ra - tion, All who on Christ's name be - lieve. Wor-ship Him with con - se - cra - tion, Grace and love will you re - ceive. For His grace give Him the glo - ry, For the Spir - it and the Word, And re-peat the gos - pel sto - ry Till all men His name have heard.

STEWARDSHIP AND SERVICE

499 The Master Has Come, and He Calls Us

The Master is come, and calleth for thee. John 11:28

Sarah Doudney, 1871

ASH GROVE 12 11 12 11 D.
Traditional Welsh melody

1. The Mas-ter has come, and He calls us to fol-low The track of the
2. The Mas-ter has called us; the road may be drear-y, And dan-gers and
3. The Mas-ter has called us in life's ear-ly morn-ing, With spir-its as

foot-prints He leaves on our way; Far o-ver the moun-tain and
sor-rows are strewn on the track; But God's Ho-ly Spir-it shall
fresh as the dew on the sod; We turn from the world with its

through the deep hol-low, The path leads us on to the man-sions of day: The
com-fort the wea-ry; We fol-low the Sav-ior and can-not turn back; The
smiles and its scorn-ing, To cast in our lot with the peo-ple of God: The

Mas-ter has called us, the chil-dren who fear Him, Who march 'neath Christ's
Mas-ter has called us: tho' doubt and temp-ta-tion May com-pass our
Mas-ter has called us, His sons and His daugh-ters, We plead for His

LIFE IN CHRIST

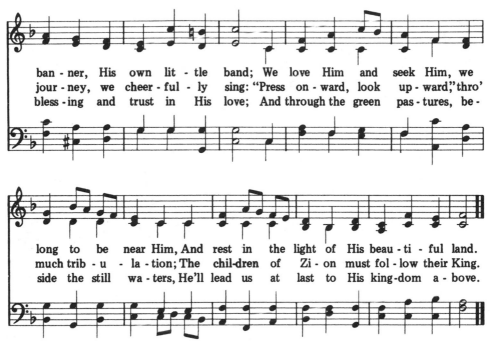

ban - ner, His own lit - tle band; We love Him and seek Him, we
jour - ney, we cheer - ful - ly sing: "Press on - ward, look up - ward,"thro'
bless - ing and trust in His love; And through the green pas - tures, be -

long to be near Him, And rest in the light of His beau - ti - ful land.
much trib - u - la - tion; The chil-dren of Zi - on must fol - low their King.
side the still wa - ters, He'll lead us at last to His king-dom a - bove.

Go, Labor On; Spend, and Be Spent 500

Go out into the highways . . , and compel them to come in. Luke 14:23

TRURO L.M.

Horatius Bonar, 1843

Thomas Williams' *Psalmodia Evangelica,* 1789

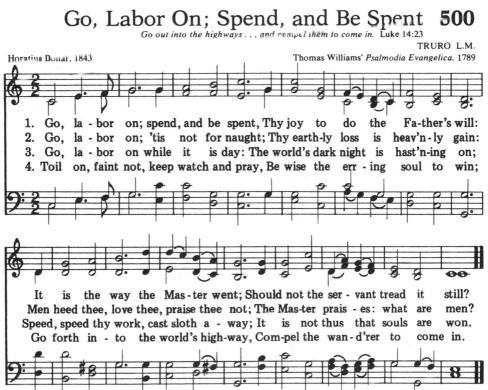

1. Go, la - bor on; spend, and be spent, Thy joy to do the Fa-ther's will:
2. Go, la - bor on; 'tis not for naught; Thy earth-ly loss is heav'n-ly gain:
3. Go, la - bor on while it is day: The world's dark night is hast'n-ing on;
4. Toil on, faint not, keep watch and pray, Be wise the err - ing soul to win;

It is the way the Mas-ter went; Should not the ser - vant tread it still?
Men heed thee, love thee, praise thee not; The Mas-ter prais - es: what are men?
Speed, speed thy work, cast sloth a - way; It is not thus that souls are won.
Go forth in - to the world's high-way, Com-pel the wan - d'rer to come in.

501 Reach Out to Your Neighbor

Thou shalt love thy neighbor as thyself. Matt. 22:39

Roger Copeland, 1971

REACH OUT Irreg. Ref.
Roger Copeland, 1971

Unison

1. Reach out to your neigh-bor, Let him know you real - ly care, Reach
2. Reach out to a stran - ger, To a man who's lost his way; Like a
3. Reach out, like your Sav - ior, When He gave His life for you, Reach

out when he's lone - ly, Let him know some-bod - y's there, Reach
sheep with-out a shep-herd, Who can't find the light of day; Reach
out to all the peo - ple Who don't know what to do; Reach

out in his dark - ness, When the clouds ob - scure his view, Just
out, your broth - er needs you, Needs to know he's not a - lone! So
out and tell of Je - sus, Who has done His great - est part; Just

walk with him, and talk with him, He's wait - ing there for you.
tell him of God's might - y love, And share with him your own.
share the love I'm sing - ing of; Reach out with all your heart!

Refrain

Reach out in a world filled with hope - less - ness and pain; Reach out with a

LIFE IN CHRIST

(heart)
hand full of love! Reach out, the world is wait-ing for some-

one to lead the way! Reach out, reach out to find a brand new day!

Master, No Offering, Costly and Sweet 502

Inasmuch as ye have done it unto one of the least of these . . . Matt. 25:40

LOVE'S OFFERING 6 4 6 4 6 6 4

Edwin P. Parker, 1889

Edwin P. Parker, 1889

1. Mas - ter, no of - fer - ing, Cost - ly and sweet, May we, like
2. Dai - ly our lives would show Weak - ness made strong, Toil - some and
3. Some word of hope for hearts Bur - dened with fears, Some balm of
4. Thus in Thy serv - ice, Lord, Till e - ven - tide Clos - es the

Mag - da - lene, Lay at Thy feet; Yet may love's in - cense rise, Sweet - er than
gloom - y ways Bright-ened with song; Some deeds of kind - ness done, Some souls by
peace for eyes Blind - ed with tears, Some dews of mer - cy shed, Some way-ward
day of life, May we a - bide! And when earth's la - bors cease, Bid us de -

sac - ri - fice, Dear Lord, to Thee, Dear Lord, to Thee.
pa -tience won, Dear Lord, to Thee, Dear Lord, to Thee.
foot-steps led, Dear Lord, to Thee, Dear Lord, to Thee.
part in peace, Dear Lord, to Thee, Dear Lord, to Thee. A-men.

503 Jesus Calls Us; o'er the Tumult

He saith unto them, Follow Me. Matt. 4:19

Cecil F. Alexander, 1852

GALILEE 8 7 8 7
William H. Jude, 1887

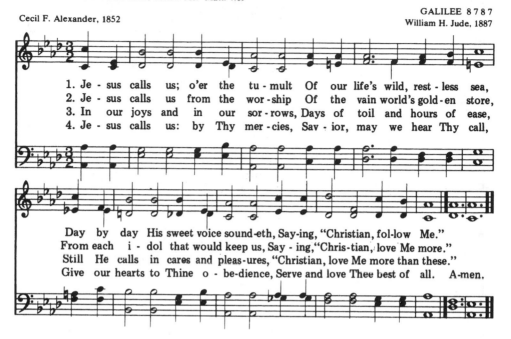

1. Je - sus calls us; o'er the tu - mult Of our life's wild, rest - less sea,
2. Je - sus calls us from the wor - ship Of the vain world's gold - en store,
3. In our joys and in our sor - rows, Days of toil and hours of ease,
4. Je - sus calls us: by Thy mer - cies, Sav - ior, may we hear Thy call,

Day by day His sweet voice sound - eth, Say - ing, "Christian, fol - low Me."
From each i - dol that would keep us, Say - ing, "Chris - tian, love Me more."
Still He calls in cares and pleas - ures, "Christian, love Me more than these."
Give our hearts to Thine o - be - dience, Serve and love Thee best of all. A - men.

504 O Master, Let Me Walk with Thee

He appeared . . . unto two of them, as they walked . . . Mark 16:12

Washington Gladden, 1879

MARYTON L.M.
H. Percy Smith, 1874

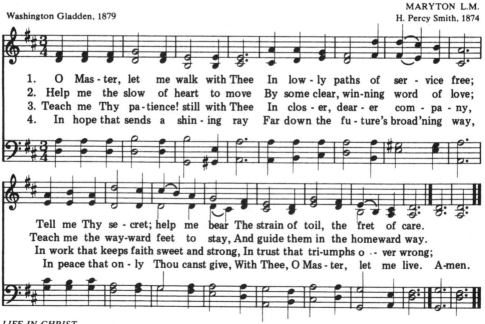

1. O Mas - ter, let me walk with Thee In low - ly paths of ser - vice free;
2. Help me the slow of heart to move By some clear, win - ning word of love;
3. Teach me Thy pa - tience! still with Thee In clos - er, dear - er com - pa - ny,
4. In hope that sends a shin - ing ray Far down the fu - ture's broad'ning way,

Tell me Thy se - cret; help me bear The strain of toil, the fret of care.
Teach me the way - ward feet to stay, And guide them in the homeward way.
In work that keeps faith sweet and strong, In trust that tri - umphs o - ver wrong;
In peace that on - ly Thou canst give, With Thee, O Mas - ter, let me live. A - men.

LIFE IN CHRIST

Out in the Highways and Byways of Life 505

So will I save you and ye shall be a blessing. Zech. 8:13

SCHULER 10 7 10 7 Ref.

Ira B. Wilson, 1909

George S. Schuler, 1924

1. Out in the high-ways and by-ways of life, Man-y are wea-ry and sad;
   are wea-ry and sad;
2. Tell the sweet sto-ry of Christ and His love, Tell of His pow'r to for-give;
   His pow'r to for-give;
3. Give as 'twas giv-en to you in your need, Love as the Mas-ter loved you;
   the Mas-ter loved you;

Car-ry the sun-shine where dark-ness is rife, Mak-ing the sor-row-ing glad.
Oth-ers will trust Him if on-ly you prove True, ev-ery mo-ment you live.
Be to the help-less a help-er in-deed, Un-to your mis-sion be true.

Refrain

Make me a bless-ing, make me a bless-ing, Out of my
life may Je-sus shine; Make me a bless-ing, O Sav-ior,
out of my life

I pray,
I pray Thee, my Sav-ior, Make me a bless-ing to some-one to-day.

STEWARDSHIP AND SERVICE

506 O Jesus, I Have Promised

If any man serve Me, let him follow Me . . . John 12:26

John E. Bode, 1866

ANGEL'S STORY 7 6 7 6 D.
Arthur H. Mann, 1881

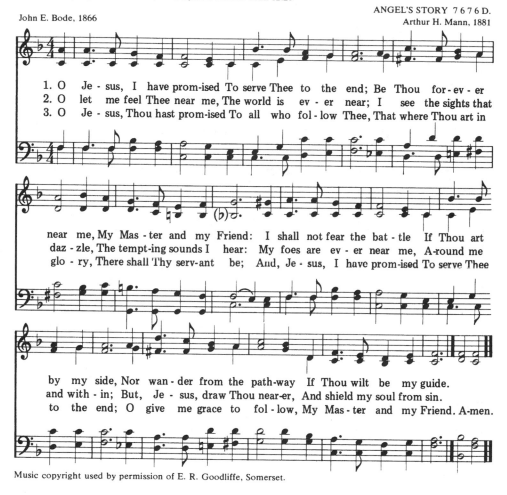

1. O Je - sus, I have prom-ised To serve Thee to the end; Be Thou for - ev - er near me, My Mas - ter and my Friend: I shall not fear the bat - tle If Thou art by my side, Nor wan - der from the path-way If Thou wilt be my guide.

2. O let me feel Thee near me, The world is ev - er near; I see the sights that daz - zle, The tempt-ing sounds I hear: My foes are ev - er near me, A-round me and with - in; But, Je - sus, draw Thou near-er, And shield my soul from sin.

3. O Je - sus, Thou hast prom-ised To all who fol - low Thee, That where Thou art in glo - ry, There shall Thy serv-ant be; And, Je - sus, I have prom-ised To serve Thee to the end; O give me grace to fol - low, My Mas - ter and my Friend. A-men.

Music copyright used by permission of E. R. Goodliffe, Somerset.

507 We Give Thee but Thine Own

Of Thine own have we given Thee. I Chron. 29:14

William W. How, 1858

SCHUMANN S.M.
Mason and Webb's *Cantica Laudis*, 1850

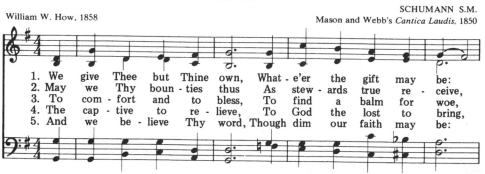

1. We give Thee but Thine own, What - e'er the gift may be:
2. May we Thy boun - ties thus As stew - ards true re - ceive,
3. To com - fort and to bless, To find a balm for woe,
4. The cap - tive to re - lieve, To God the lost to bring,
5. And we be - lieve Thy word, Though dim our faith may be:

LIFE IN CHRIST

All that we have is Thine a - lone, A trust, O Lord, from Thee.
And glad - ly, as Thou bless - est us, To Thee our first-fruits give.
To tend the lone and fa - ther - less, Is an - gels' work be - low.
To teach the way of life and peace— It is a Christ-like thing.
What - e'er for Thine we do, O Lord, We do it un - to Thee. A-men.

I Gave My Life for Thee 508

He died for all, that they . . . should not henceforth live unto themselves . . . II Cor. 5:15

KENOSIS Irreg.

Frances R. Havergal, 1859

Philip P. Bliss, 1873

1. I gave My life for thee, My pre - cious blood I shed,
2. My Fa - ther's house of light, My glo - ry - cir - cled throne
3. I suf - fered much for thee, More than thy tongue can tell,
4. And I have brought to thee, Down from My home a - bove,

That thou might ran - somed be, And quick - ened from the dead;
I left for earth - ly night, For wan - d'rings sad and lone;
Of bit - terest ag - o - ny, To res - cue thee from hell;
Sal - va - tion full and free, My par - don and My love;

I gave, I gave My life for thee, What hast thou given for Me?
I left, I left it all for thee, Hast thou left aught for Me?
I've borne, I've borne it all for thee, What hast thou borne for Me?
I bring, I bring rich gifts to thee, What hast thou brought to Me?

STEWARDSHIP AND SERVICE

509 Is Your Life a Channel of Blessing?

. . . A vessel unto honor, sanctified, and meet for the Master's use. II Tim. 2:21

EUCLID 9 9 10 9 Ref.

Harper G. Smyth, 1903

Harper G. Smyth, 1903

1. Is your life a chan-nel of bless-ing? Is the love of God
2. Is your life a chan-nel of bless-ing? Are you bur-dened for
3. Is your life a chan-nel of bless-ing? Is it dai - ly
4. We can-not be chan-nels of bless-ing If our lives are not

flow - ing through you? Are you tell - ing the lost of the Sav-ior?
those who are lost? Have you urged up-on those who are stray-ing
tell - ing for Him? Have you spo-ken the word of sal - va - tion
free from known sin; We will bar - ri - ers be and a hin-drance

Refrain

Are you read - y His serv-ice to do?
The Sav - ior who died on the cross?
To those who are dy - ing in sin? Make me a chan-nel of
To those we are try - ing to win.

bless-ing to - day, Make me a chan-nel of bless-ing, I pray; My life pos-

sess-ing, my ser-vice bless-ing, Make me a chan-nel of bless-ing to-day.

LIFE IN CHRIST

Am I a Soldier of the Cross? 510

. . . Endure hardness, as a good soldier of Jesus Christ. II Tim. 2:3

Isaac Watts, c. 1724

ARLINGTON C.M.
Thomas A. Arne, 1762

1. Am I a sol - dier of the cross, A fol - l'wer of the Lamb,
2. Must I be car - ried to the skies On flow - ery beds of ease,
3. Are there no foes for me to face? Must I not stem the flood?
4. Sure I must fight if I would reign; In - crease my cour - age, Lord;

And shall I fear to own His cause, Or blush to speak His name?
While oth - ers fought to win the prize, And sailed thro' blood - y seas?
Is this vile world a friend to grace, To help me on to God?
I'll bear the toil, en - dure the pain, Sup - port - ed by Thy word. A - men.

Forth in Thy Name, O Lord, I Go 511

I will go forth in the strength of the Lord. Psa. 71:16

Charles Wesley, 1749

KEBLE L.M.
John B. Dykes, 1875
Arr. by Austin C. Lovelace, 1964

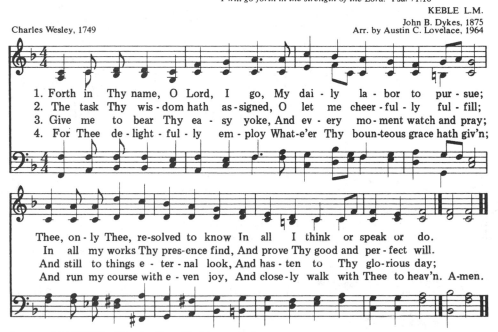

1. Forth in Thy name, O Lord, I go, My dai - ly la - bor to pur - sue;
2. The task Thy wis - dom hath as - signed, O let me cheer - ful - ly ful - fill;
3. Give me to bear Thy ea - sy yoke, And ev - ery mo - ment watch and pray;
4. For Thee de - light - ful - ly em - ploy What-e'er Thy boun-teous grace hath giv'n;

Thee, on - ly Thee, re-solved to know In all I think or speak or do.
In all my works Thy pres-ence find, And prove Thy good and per - fect will.
And still to things e - ter - nal look, And has - ten to Thy glo-rious day;
And run my course with e - ven joy, And close-ly walk with Thee to heav'n. A-men.

STEWARDSHIP AND SERVICE

512 Lord, Whose Love through Humble Service

If any one has the world's goods, and sees his brother in need . . . I John 3:17

HYFRYDOL 8 7 8 7 D.
Rowland H. Prichard, c. 1830

Albert F. Bayly, 1961

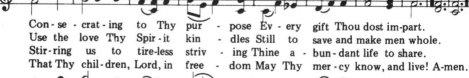

1. Lord, whose love through hum-ble ser - vice Bore the weight of hu - man need,
2. Still Thy chil - dren wan - der home-less; Still the hun-gry cry for bread;
3. As we wor - ship, grant us vi - sion, Till Thy love's re - veal - ing light,
4. Called from wor - ship un - to ser - vice, Forth in Thy dear name we go,

Who did'st on the cross, for - sak - en, Work Thy mer - cy's per - fect deed;
Still the cap - tives long for free - dom; Still in grief men mourn their dead.
In its height and depth and great-ness Dawns up - on our quick-ened sight,
To the child, the youth, the a - ged, Love in liv - ing deeds to show.

We Thy ser - vants bring the wor - ship Not of voice a - lone, but heart;
As, O Lord, Thy deep com - pas - sion Healed the sick and freed the soul,
Mak - ing known the needs and bur - dens Thy com - pas - sion bids us bear,
Hope and health, good-will and com - fort, Coun-sel, aid and peace we give,

Con - se - crat - ing to Thy pur - pose Ev - ery gift Thou dost im-part.
Use the love Thy Spir - it kin - dles Still to save and make men whole.
Stir - ring us to tire-less striv - ing Thine a - bun-dant life to share.
That Thy chil - dren, Lord, in free - dom May Thy mer - cy know, and live! A-men.

LIFE IN CHRIST

In Christ There Is No East or West 513

Ye are all one in Christ Jesus. Gal. 3:28

McKEE C.M.

John Oxenham, 1908

Traditional Spiritual melody
Arr. by Harry T. Burleigh, 1939

Unison

1. In Christ there is no East or West, In Him no South or North,
2. In Him shall true hearts ev-ery-where Their high com-mun-ion find;
3. Join hands, then, broth-ers of the faith, What-e'er your race may be;
4. In Christ now meet both East and West, In Him meet South and North:

But one great fel-low-ship of love Through-out the whole wide earth.
His serv-ice is the gold-en cord Close-bind-ing all man-kind.
Who serves my Fa-ther as a son Is sure-ly kin to me.
All Christ-ly souls are one in Him Through-out the whole wide earth.

Alternate tune, ST. PETER, No. 68
Words used by permission of Miss Theo Oxenham, Worthing, Sussex.

Where Cross the Crowded Ways of Life 514

Whosoever shall give . . . a cup of cold water . . . shall in no wise lose his reward. Matt. 10:42

GERMANY L.M.

Frank M. North, 1903

William Gardiner's *Sacred Melodies*, 1815

1. Where cross the crowd-ed ways of life, Where sound the cries of race and clan,
2. In haunts of wretch-ed - ness and need, On shad-owed thresh-olds dark with fears,
3. The cup of wa - ter giv'n for Thee Still holds the fresh-ness of Thy grace;
4. O Mas - ter, from the moun-tain side, Make haste to heal these hearts of pain,
5. Till sons of men shall learn Thy love And fol - low where Thy feet have trod:

A-bove the noise of self - ish strife, We hear Thy voice, O Son of man!
From paths where hide the lures of greed, We catch the vi - sion of Thy tears.
Yet long these mul - ti-tudes to see The sweet com-pas-sion of Thy face.
A-mong these rest-less throngs a-bide, O tread the cit - y's streets a - gain;
Till glo-rious from Thy heav'n a-bove Shall come the cit - y of our God. A-men.

SOCIAL CONCERN

515 Hope of the World

. . . Lord Jesus Christ, who is our hope. I Tim. 1:1

Georgia E. Harkness, 1954

VICAR 11 10 11 10
V. Earle Copes, 1963

1. Hope of the world, Thou Christ of great com-pas-sion,
2. Hope of the world, God's gift from high-est heav-en,
3. Hope of the world, a-foot on dust-y high-ways,
4. Hope of the world, Who by Thy cross didst save us
5. Hope of the world, O Christ o'er death vic-to-rious,

Speak to our fear-ful hearts by con-flict rent.
Bring-ing to hun-gry souls the bread of life,
Show-ing to wan-dering souls the path of light;
From death and dark de-spair, from sin and guilt;
Who by this sign didst con-quer grief and pain,

Save us, Thy peo-ple, from con-sum-ing pas-sion,
Still let Thy Spir-it un-to us be giv-en,
Walk Thou be-side us lest the tempt-ing by-ways
We ren-der back the love Thy mer-cy gave us;
We would be faith-ful to Thy gos-pel glo-rious:

Who by our own false hopes and aims are spent.
To heal earth's wounds and end her bit-ter strife.
Lure us a-way from Thee to end-less night.
Take Thou our lives, and use them as Thou wilt.
Thou art our Lord! Thou dost for-ev-er reign! A-men.

LIFE IN CHRIST

Father Eternal, Ruler of Creation 516

Thy kingdom come. Thy will be done in earth, as it is in heaven. Matt. 6:10

LANGHAM 11 10 11 10 10

Laurence Housman, 1919

Geoffrey Shaw, 1921

Unison

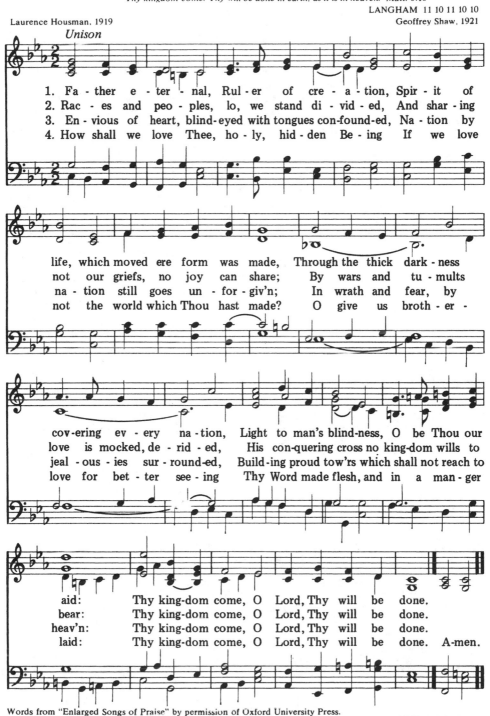

1. Fa - ther e - ter - nal, Rul - er of cre - a - tion, Spir - it of
2. Rac - es and peo - ples, lo, we stand di - vid - ed, And shar - ing
3. En - vious of heart, blind - eyed with tongues con - found - ed, Na - tion by
4. How shall we love Thee, ho - ly, hid - den Be - ing If we love

life, which moved ere form was made, Through the thick dark - ness
not our griefs, no joy can share; By wars and tu - mults
na - tion still goes un - for - giv'n; In wrath and fear, by
not the world which Thou hast made? O give us broth - er -

cov - ering ev - ery na - tion, Light to man's blind - ness, O be Thou our
love is mocked, de - rid - ed, His con - quering cross no king - dom wills to
jeal - ous - ies sur - round - ed, Build - ing proud tow'rs which shall not reach to
love for bet - ter see - ing Thy Word made flesh, and in a man - ger

aid: Thy king - dom come, O Lord, Thy will be done.
bear: Thy king - dom come, O Lord, Thy will be done.
heav'n: Thy king - dom come, O Lord, Thy will be done.
laid: Thy king - dom come, O Lord, Thy will be done. A - men.

SOCIAL CONCERN

517 We Thank Thee That Thy Mandate

They went forth, and preached . . . confirming the words with signs . . . Mark 16:20

Ernest K. Emurian, 1968

LANCASHIRE 7 6 7 6 D.
Henry T. Smart, 1835

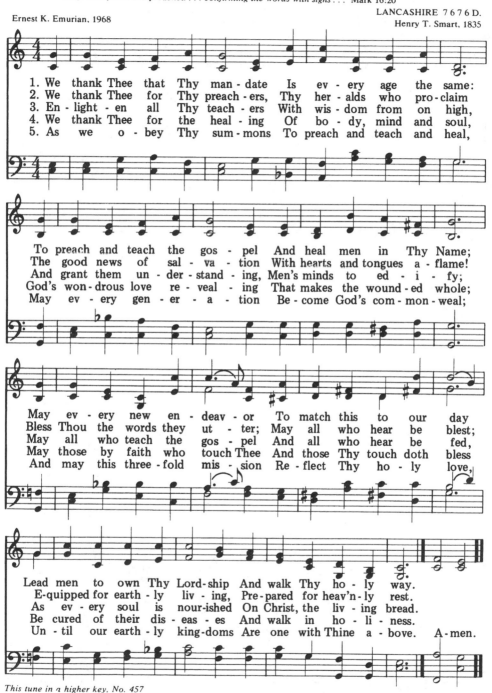

1. We thank Thee that Thy man-date Is ev-ery age the same:
2. We thank Thee for Thy preach-ers, Thy her-alds who pro-claim
3. En-light-en all Thy teach-ers With wis-dom from on high,
4. We thank Thee for the heal-ing Of bo-dy, mind and soul,
5. As we o-bey Thy sum-mons To preach and teach and heal,

To preach and teach the gos-pel And heal men in Thy Name;
The good news of sal-va-tion With hearts and tongues a-flame!
And grant them un-der-stand-ing, Men's minds to ed-i-fy;
God's won-drous love re-veal-ing That makes the wound-ed whole;
May ev-ery gen-er-a-tion Be-come God's com-mon-weal;

May ev-ery new en-deav-or To match this to our day
Bless Thou the words they ut-ter; May all who hear be blest;
May all who teach the gos-pel And all who hear be fed,
May those by faith who touch Thee And those Thy touch doth bless
And may this three-fold mis-sion Re-flect Thy ho-ly love,

Lead men to own Thy Lord-ship And walk Thy ho-ly way.
E-quipped for earth-ly liv-ing, Pre-pared for heav'n-ly rest.
As ev-ery soul is nour-ished On Christ, the liv-ing bread.
Be cured of their dis-eas-es And walk in ho-li-ness.
Un-til our earth-ly king-doms Are one with Thine a-bove. A-men.

This tune in a higher key, No. 457

Words copyright, 1968 by Ernest K. Emurian. Used by permission.

LIFE IN CHRIST

Whatsoever You Do to the Least 518

Come, ye blessed of My Father, inherit the kingdom prepared for you . . . Matt. 25:34

Willard F. Jabusch, 1969

WHATSOEVER YOU DO Irreg. Ref.
Willard F. Jabusch, 1969

(Ref.) What - so - ev - er you do to the least of my broth - ers,

That you do un - to me.

1. { When I was hun - gry, you
     When I was home - less, you
2. { When I was wea - ry, you
     When in a pris - on, you
3. { When I was Ne - gro, or
     You saw me cov - ered with

gave me to eat; When I was thirst - y, you
o - pened your door; When I was na - ked, you
helped me find rest; When I was anx - ious, you
came to my cell; When on a sick - bed, you
Chi - nese, or white; Mocked and in - sult - ed, you
spit - tle and blood; You knew my fea - tures, though

gave me to drink.
gave me your coat.
calmed all my fears. Now en - ter in - to the home of my Fa - ther.
cared for my needs.
car - ried my cross.
grim - y with sweat.

SOCIAL CONCERN

519 Peace in Our Time, O Lord

And the work of righteousness shall be peace. Isa. 32:17

John Oxenham, 1938

DIADEMATA S.M.D.
George J. Elvey, 1868

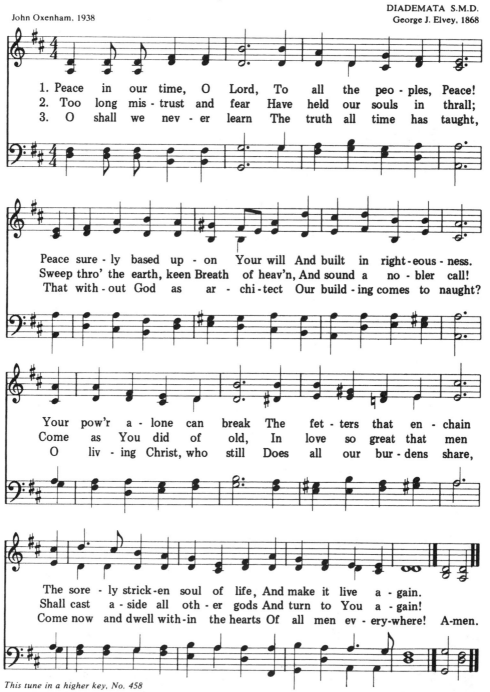

1. Peace in our time, O Lord, To all the peo - ples, Peace!
2. Too long mis-trust and fear Have held our souls in thrall;
3. O shall we nev - er learn The truth all time has taught,

Peace sure - ly based up - on Your will And built in right - eous - ness.
Sweep thro' the earth, keen Breath of heav'n, And sound a no - bler call!
That with - out God as ar - chi - tect Our build - ing comes to naught?

Your pow'r a - lone can break The fet - ters that en - chain
Come as You did of old, In love so great that men
O liv - ing Christ, who still Does all our bur - dens share,

The sore - ly strick - en soul of life, And make it live a - gain.
Shall cast a - side all oth - er gods And turn to You a - gain!
Come now and dwell with - in the hearts Of all men ev - ery-where! A-men.

This tune in a higher key, No. 458

Words used by permission of Miss Theo Oxenham, Worthing, Sussex.

LIFE IN CHRIST

O Beautiful for Spacious Skies 520

Blessed is the nation whose God is the Lord. Psa. 33:12

MATERNA C.M.D.

Katharine L. Bates, 1893

Samuel A. Ward, 1882

1. O beau-ti-ful for spa-cious skies, For am-ber waves of grain,
2. O beau-ti-ful for pil-grim feet, Whose stern im-pas-sioned stress
3. O beau-ti-ful for he-roes proved In lib-er-at-ing strife,
4. O beau-ti-ful for pa-triot dream That sees be-yond the years

For pur-ple moun-tain maj-es-ties A-bove the fruit-ed plain!
A thor-ough-fare for free-dom beat A-cross the wil-der-ness!
Who more than self their coun-try loved, And mer-cy more than life!
Thine al-a-bas-ter cit-ies gleam, Un-dimmed by hu-man tears!

A-mer-i-ca! A-mer-i-ca! God shed His grace on thee,
A-mer-i-ca! A-mer-i-ca! God mend thine ev-ery flaw,
A-mer-i-ca! A-mer-i-ca! May God thy gold re-fine,
A-mer-i-ca! A-mer-i-ca! God shed His grace on thee,

And crown thy good with broth-er-hood From sea to shin-ing sea!
Con-firm thy soul in self-con-trol, Thy lib-er-ty in law!
Till all suc-cess be no-ble-ness, And ev-ery gain di-vine!
And crown thy good with broth-er-hood From sea to shin-ing sea! A-men.

THE CHRISTIAN CITIZEN

521 Not Alone for Mighty Empire

Some trust in chariots . . . but we will remember the name of the Lord. Psa. 20:7

HYFRYDOL 8 7 8 7 D.

William P. Merrill, 1909

Rowland H. Prichard, c. 1830
Arr. by Ralph Vaughan Williams, 1906

1. Not a - lone for might - y em - pire, Stretch-ing far o'er land and sea;
2. Not for bat - tle-ship and for - tress, Not for con-quests of the sword;
3. For the ar - mies of the faith - ful, Souls that passed and left no name;

Not a - lone for boun-teous har - vests, Lift we up our hearts to Thee.
But for con-quests of the spir - it Give we thanks to Thee, O Lord;
For the glo - ry that il - lu-mines Pa - triot lives of death-less fame;

Stand - ing in the liv - ing pres - ent, Mem - o - ry and hope be - tween,
For the her - i - tage of free - dom, For the home, the church, the school;
For our proph-ets and a - pos - tles, Loy - al to the liv - ing Word;

Lord, we would with deep thanks-giv - ing Praise Thee most for things un-seen.
For the o - pen door to man - hood In a land the peo - ple rule.
For all he - roes of the Spir - it, Give we thanks to Thee, O Lord. A - men.

Music from "The English Hymnal;" used by permission of Oxford University Press.

LIFE IN CHRIST

Mine Eyes Have Seen the Glory 522

He is terrible to the kings of the earth. Psa. 76:12

BATTLE HYMN 15 15 15 6 Ref.

Julia W. Howe, 1862

Traditional American melody, c. 1852

1. Mine eyes have seen the glo - ry of the com - ing of the Lord; He is
2. I have seen Him in the watch-fires of a hun - dred cir - cling camps; They have
3. He has sound-ed forth the trum - pet that shall nev - er sound re - treat; He is
4. In the beau - ty of the lil - ies, Christ was born a - cross the sea, With a

tram - pling out the vin - tage where the grapes of wrath are stored; He hath loosed the
build - ed Him an al - tar in the eve - ning dews and damps; I can read His
sift - ing out the hearts of men be - fore His judg-ment seat; O be swift, my
glo - ry in His bos - om that trans - fig - ures you and me; As He died to

fate - ful light-ning of His ter - ri - ble swift sword; His truth is march-ing on.
right-eous sen-tence by the dim and flar - ing lamps; His day is march-ing on.
soul, to an - swer Him! be ju - bi - lant, my feet! Our God is march-ing on.
make men ho - ly, let us live to make men free, While God is march-ing on.

Refrain

Glo - ry! glo - ry, hal - le - lu - jah! Glo - ry! glo - ry, hal - le - lu - jah!

Glo - ry! glo - ry, hal - le - lu - jah! Our God is march - ing on.

THE CHRISTIAN CITIZEN

523 Great God of Nations

O praise the Lord, all ye nations: praise Him, all ye people. Psa. 117:1

Alfred A. Woodhull, 1828

ST. PETERSBURG 8 8 8 8
Arr. from Dimitri S. Bortniansky, 1825

1. Great God of na - tions, now to Thee Our hymn of
2. Thy Name we bless, Al - might - y God, For all the
3. Here free - dom spreads her ban - ner wide And casts her
4. We pray Thee let the gos - pel light Through all our
5. Great God, pre - serve us in Thy fear; In dan - ger

grat - i - tude we raise; With hum - ble heart and bend - ing
kind - ness Thou hast shown To this fair land the Pil - grims
soft and hal - lowed ray; Here Thou our fa - thers' steps didst
land its ra - diance shed; Dis - pel the shades of er - ror's
still our Guard - ian be: O spread Thy truth's bright pre - cepts

knee We of - fer Thee our song of praise.
trod, This land we fond - ly call our own.
guide In safe - ty through their dan - gerous way.
night, And heav'n - ly bless - ings round us spread.
here; Let all the peo - ple wor - ship Thee. A - men.

524 Lord, While for All Mankind We Pray

In righteousness shalt thou be established. Isa. 54:14

John R. Wreford, 1837

HARLECH C.M.
Traditional Welsh melody

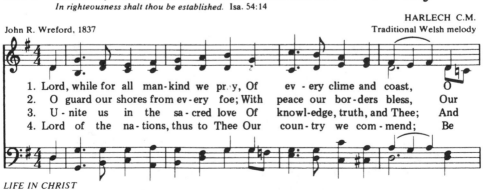

1. Lord, while for all man-kind we pray, Of ev - ery clime and coast, O
2. O guard our shores from ev-ery foe; With peace our bor-ders bless, Our
3. U - nite us in the sa-cred love Of knowl-edge, truth, and Thee; And
4. Lord of the na-tions, thus to Thee Our coun-try we com-mend; Be

LIFE IN CHRIST

hear us for our na-tive land, The land we love the most.
cit - ies with pros-per - i - ty, Our fields with plen-teous-ness.
let our hills and val-leys shout The songs of lib - er - ty.
Thou her ref-uge and her trust, Her ev - er - last-ing friend. A-men.

My Country, 'Tis of Thee 525

Righteousness exalteth a nation: but sin is a reproach to any people. Prov. 14:34

AMERICA 6 6 4 6 6 6 4

Samuel F. Smith, 1832

Thesaurus Musicus, c. 1745

1. My coun - try, 'tis of thee, Sweet land of lib - er - ty,
2. My na - tive coun - try, thee, Land of the no - ble free,
3. Let mu - sic swell the breeze, And ring from all the trees
4. Our fa - thers' God, to Thee, Au - thor of lib - er - ty,

Of thee I sing: Land where my fa - thers died, Land of the
Thy name I love: I love thy rocks and rills, Thy woods and
Sweet free - dom's song: Let mor - tal tongues a - wake, Let all that
To Thee we sing: Long may our land be bright With free - dom's

pil - grims' pride, From ev - ery moun-tain side Let free-dom ring!
tem - pled hills; My heart with rap - ture thrills Like that a - bove.
breathe par - take; Let rocks their si - lence break, The sound pro-long.
ho - ly light; Pro - tect us by Thy might, Great God, our King! A-men.

526 God of Our Fathers

The Lord of hosts is with us; the God of Jacob is our refuge. Psa. 46:7

NATIONAL HYMN 10 10 10 10

Daniel C. Roberts, 1876

George W. Warren, 1892

1. God of our fa-thers, whose al-might-y hand Leads forth in beau-ty all the star-ry band Of shin-ing worlds in splen-dor through the skies, Our grate-ful songs be-fore Thy throne a-rise.

2. Thy love di-vine hath led us in the past; In this free land by Thee our lot is cast; Be Thou our Rul-er, Guard-ian, Guide and Stay, Thy Word our law, Thy paths our cho-sen way.

3. From war's a-larms, from dead-ly pes-ti-lence, Be Thy strong arm our ev-er sure de-fense; Thy true re-lig-ion in our hearts in-crease, Thy boun-teous good-ness nour-ish us in peace.

4. Re-fresh Thy peo-ple on their toil-some way; Lead us from night to nev-er-end-ing day; Fill all our lives with love and grace di-vine; And glo-ry, laud, and praise be ev-er Thine. A-men.

LIFE IN CHRIST

God the Omnipotent! 527

He maketh wars to cease unto the end of the earth . . . Psa. 46:9

Henry F. Chorley, 1842, and
John Ellerton, 1870

RUSSIAN HYMN 11 10 11 9
Alexis F. Lvov, 1833

1. God the Om - nip - o - tent! King, who or - dain - est
2. God the All - mer - ci - ful! Earth hath for - sak - en
3. God the All - right - eous One! Man hath de - fied Thee;
4. So shall Thy peo - ple, with thank - ful de - vo - tion,

Thun - der Thy clar - ion, the light - ning Thy sword;
Meek - ness and mer - cy, and slight - ed Thy Word;
Yet to e - ter - ni - ty stand - eth Thy Word;
Praise Him who saved them from per - il and sword,

Show forth Thy pit - y on high where Thou reign - est;
Let not Thy wrath in its ter - rors a - wak - en;
False - hood and wrong shall not tar - ry be - side Thee;
Sing - ing in cho - rus from o - cean to o - cean,

Give to us peace in our time, O Lord.
Give to us peace in our time, O Lord.
Give to us peace in our time, O Lord.
Peace to the na - tions, and praise to the Lord. A - men.

THE CHRISTIAN CITIZEN

528 Lord of Life and King of Glory

Your children . . . bring them up in the nurture and admonition of the Lord. Eph. 6:4

SICILIAN MARINER'S HYMN 8 7 8 7 8 7

Christian Burke, 1904

Tattersall's *Psalmody*, 1794

1. Lord of life and King of glo - ry, Who didst deign a
2. Grant us then pure hearts and pa - tient, That in all we
3. When our grow - ing sons and daugh-ters Look on life with
4. May we keep our ho - ly call - ing Stain - less in its

child to be, Cra - dled on a moth - er's bo - som,
do or say Lit - tle ones our deeds may cop - y,
ea - ger eyes, Grant us then a deep - er in - sight
fair re - nown, That, when all the work is o - ver

Throned up - on a moth - er's knee: For the chil - dren
And be nev - er led a - stray; Lit - tle feet our
And new pow'rs of sac - ri - fice: Hope to trust them,
And we lay the bur - den down, Then the chil - dren

Thou hast giv - en We must an - swer un - to Thee.
steps may fol - low In a safe and nar - row way.
faith to guide them, Love that noth - ing good de - nies.
Thou hast giv - en Still may be our joy and crown. A - men.

LIFE IN CHRIST

O Perfect Love, All Human Thought 529

. . . And shall be joined unto his wife, and they two shall be one flesh. Eph. 5:31

Dorothy F. Gurney, 1883
St. 4, John Ellerton, 1875

SANDRINGHAM 11 10 11 10
Joseph Barnby, 1889

1. O per-fect Love, all hu-man thought tran-scend-ing,
2. O per-fect Life, be Thou their full as-sur-ance
3. Grant them the joy which bright-ens earth-ly sor-row;
4. Hear us, O Fa-ther, gra-cious and for-giv-ing,

Low-ly we kneel in prayer be-fore Thy throne,
Of ten-der char-i-ty and stead-fast faith,
Grant them the peace which calms all earth-ly strife,
Through Je-sus Christ, Thy co-e-ter-nal Word,

That theirs may be the love which knows no end-ing,
Of pa-tient hope, and qui-et, brave en-dur-ance,
And to life's day the glo-rious, un-known mor-row
Who, with the Ho-ly Ghost, by all things liv-ing

Whom Thou for-ev-er-more dost join in one.
With child-like trust that fears not pain nor death.
That dawns up-on e-ter-nal love and life.
Now and to end-less a-ges art a-dored. A-men.

Words by permission of Oxford University Press, London.

MARRIAGE AND FAMILY

530 Gracious Savior, Who Didst Honor

A woman that feareth the Lord . . . shall be praised. Prov. 31:30

KOMM, O KOMM 8 7 8 7 7 7

Emily L. Shirreff, 1814-1897

Neuvermehrtes Gesangbuch, Meiningen, 1693

1. Gra - cious Sav - ior, who didst hon - or Wom - an - kind as wom - an's son;
2. Je - sus, Son of hu - man moth - er, Bless our moth - er - hood, we pray;
3. Thou who didst with Jo - seph la - bor, Nor didst hum - ble work dis - dain,
4. Thou who didst go forth in sor - row, Toil - ing for the souls of men,

Ver - y man, though God be - got - ten, And with God the Fa - ther one,
Give us grace to lead our chil - dren, Draw them to Thee day by day;
Grant we may Thy foot-steps fol - low Pa - tient - ly through toil or pain;
Thou who shalt draw all men to Thee, Though de - spised, re - ject - ed then;

Grant that wom - an - hood may be Con - se - crat - ed, Lord, to Thee.
May our sons and daugh-ters be Ded - i - cat - ed, Lord, to Thee.
May our qui - et home-life be Lived, O Lord, in Thee, to Thee.
Hum - ble though our in-fluence be, Use it in the world for Thee. A - men.

531 Happy the Home When God Is There

As for me and my house, we will serve the Lord. Josh. 24:15

ST. AGNES C.M.

Henry Ware, Jr., 1846

John B. Dykes, 1866

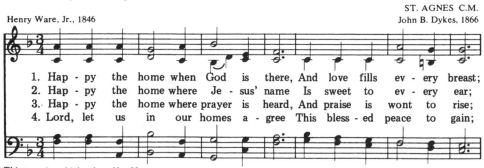

1. Hap - py the home when God is there, And love fills ev - ery breast;
2. Hap - py the home where Je - sus' name Is sweet to ev - ery ear;
3. Hap - py the home where prayer is heard, And praise is wont to rise;
4. Lord, let us in our homes a - gree This bless - ed peace to gain;

This tune in a higher key, No. 83

LIFE IN CHRIST

When one their wish and one their prayer, And one their heav'n-ly rest.
Where chil-dren ear - ly lisp His fame, And par - ents hold Him dear.
Where par-ents love the sa - cred Word, And all its wis - dom prize.
U - nite our hearts in love to Thee, And love to all will reign. A - men.

O Happy Home, Where Thou Art Loved 532

This day is salvation come to this house. Luke 19:9

Carl J. P. Spitta, 1826
Trans. by Sarah B. Findlater, 1858

HENLEY 11 10 11 10
Lowell Mason, 1854

1. O hap - py home, where Thou art loved the dear - est, Thou lov - ing
2. O hap - py home, where each one serves Thee, low - ly, What - ev - er
3. O hap - py home, where Thou art not for - got - ten When joy is
4. Un - til at last, when earth's day's work is end - ed, All meet Thee

Friend and Sav - ior of our race, And where a - mong the guests there nev - er
his ap - point - ed work may be, Till ev - ery com - mon task seems great and
o - ver - flow - ing, full and free; O hap - py home, where ev - ery wound-ed
in the bless - ed home a - bove, From whence Thou camest, where Thou hast as-

com - eth One who can hold such high and hon - ored place.
ho - ly, When it is done, O Lord, as un - to Thee.
spir - it Is brought, Phy - si - cian, Com - fort - er, to Thee.
cend - ed, Thy ev - er - last - ing home of peace and love! A-men.

533 For All the Saints

These all died in faith . . . and confessed that they were . . . pilgrims. Heb. 11:13

SINE NOMINE 10 10 10 Alleluias

William W. How, 1864

Ralph Vaughan Williams, 1906

Unison, stanzas 1, 2 and 6.

1. For all the saints who from their la - bors rest, Who Thee by faith be - fore the world con-fessed, Thy name, O Je - sus, be for - ev - er blest.
2. Thou wast their rock, their fort-ress and their might; Thou, Lord, their cap - tain in the well-fought fight; Thou in the dark - ness drear, their one true light.
6. From earth's wide bounds and o-cean's far-thest coast, Thro' gates of pearl stream in the count-less host, Sing - ing to Fa - ther, Son, and Ho - ly Ghost.

(after stanza 6)

Al - le - lu - ia! Al - le - lu - ia! A - men.

Harmony, stanzas 3, 4, 5.

3. O blest com-mun - ion, fel - low - ship di - vine! We fee - bly strug - gle; they in glo - ry shine. Yet all are one in Thee, for all are Thine.
4. And when the strife is fierce, the war - fare long, Steals on the ear the dis - tant tri-umph song, And hearts are brave a - gain and arms are strong.
5. The gold - en eve - ning bright-ens in the west; Soon, soon to faith - ful war-riors com-eth rest; And sweet the calm of Par - a - dise, the blest.

THE LIFE ETERNAL

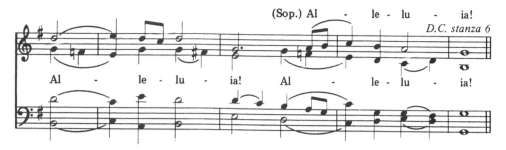

Face to Face with Christ My Savior 534

Now we see through a glass, darkly; but then face to face . . . I Cor. 13:12

Carrie E. Breck, 1898

FACE TO FACE 8 7 8 7 Ref.
Grant C. Tullar, 1898

1. Face to face with Christ my Sav - ior, Face to face—what will it be—
2. On - ly faint - ly now I see Him, With the dark-ling veil be-tween;
3. What re - joic - ing in His pres - ence When are ban-ished grief and pain;
4. Face to face! O bliss-ful mo - ment! Face to face— to see and know;

When with rap - ture I be-hold Him, Je - sus Christ who died for me?
But a bless - ed day is com - ing When His glo - ry shall be seen.
When the crook - ed ways are straight-ened And the dark things shall be plain.
Face to face with my Re-deem - er, Je - sus Christ who loves me so.

Refrain

Face to face I shall be-hold Him, Far be-yond the star - ry sky;

Face to face in all His glo - ry, I shall see Him by and by!

THE LIFE ETERNAL

535 The Sands of Time Are Sinking

Behold, the Bridegroom cometh; go ye out to meet Him. Matt. 25:6

RUTHERFORD 7 6 7 6 7 6 7 5

Chrétien Urhan, 1834
Arr. by Edward F. Rimbault, 1867

Anne R. Cousin, 1857

1. The sands of time are sink - ing, The dawn of heav - en breaks;
2. O Christ! He is the foun - tain, The deep, sweet well of love!
3. O, I am my Be - lov - ed's, And my Be - lov - ed's mine!
4. The Bride eyes not her gar - ment, But her dear Bride-groom's face;

The sum - mer morn I've sighed for, The fair, sweet morn a - wakes:
The streams on earth I've tast - ed, More deep I'll drink a - bove:
He brings a poor vile sin - ner In - to His "house of wine."
I will not gaze at glo - ry But on my King of grace.

Dark, dark hath been the mid - night, But day - spring is at hand,
There to an o - cean ful - ness His mer - cy doth ex - pand,
I stand up - on His mer - it, I know no oth - er stand,
Not at the crown He giv - eth But on His pierc - ed hand,

And glo - ry, glo - ry dwell - eth In Im - man - uel's land.
And glo - ry, glo - ry dwell - eth In Im - man - uel's land.
Not e'en where glo - ry dwell - eth In Im - man - uel's land.
The Lamb is all the glo - ry Of Im - man - uel's land. A - men.

THE LIFE ETERNAL

Jerusalem the Golden 536

...That great city...Jerusalem, descending out of heaven from God. Rev. 21:10

Bernard of Cluny, c. 1145
Trans. by John M. Neale, 1851, and others

EWING 7 6 7 6 D.
Alexander Ewing, 1853

1. Je - ru - sa - lem the gold - en, With milk and hon - ey blest!
2. They stand, those halls of Zi - on, All ju - bi - lant with song,
3. There is the throne of Da - vid; And there, from care re - leased,
4. O sweet and bless - ed coun - try, The home of God's e - lect!

Be - neath thy con - tem - pla - tion Sink heart and voice op - pressed;
And bright with many an an - gel, And all the mar - tyr throng;
The song of them that tri - umph, The shout of them that feast;
O sweet and bless - ed coun - try That ea - ger hearts ex - pect!

I know not, O I know not What joys a - wait me there;
The Prince is ev - er in them, The day - light is se - rene;
And they, who with their Lead - er Have con-quered in the fight,
Je - sus, in mer - cy bring us To that dear land of rest;

What ra - dian - cy of glo - ry, What bliss be - yond com-pare!
The pas - tures of the bless - ed Are decked in glo - rious sheen.
For - ev - er and for - ev - er Are clad in robes of white.
Who art, with God the Fa - ther, And Spir - it, ev - er blest. A - men.

THE LIFE ETERNAL

537 Ten Thousand Times Ten Thousand

Behold, the Lord cometh with ten thousands of His saints. Jude 14

Henry Alford, 1867 and 1870

ALFORD 7 6 8 6 D.
John B. Dykes, 1875

1. Ten thou - sand times ten thou - sand In spark - ling rai - ment bright,
2. What rush of al - le - lu - ias Fills all the earth and sky!
3. O then what rap - tured greet - ings On Ca - naan's hap - py shore!
4. Bring near Thy great sal - va - tion, Thou Lamb for sin - ners slain;

The ar - mies of the ran - somed saints Throng up the steeps of light:
What ring - ing of a thou - sand harps Be - speaks the tri - umph nigh!
What knit - ting sev - ered friend - ships up, Where part - ings are no more!
Fill up the roll of Thine e - lect, Then take Thy pow'r and reign:

Tis fin - ished, all is fin - ished, Their fight with death and sin:
O day, for which cre - a - tion And all its tribes were made;
Then eyes with joy shall spar - kle That brimmed with tears of late,
Ap - pear, De - sire of na - tions, Thine ex - iles long for home;

Fling o - pen wide the gold - en gates, And let the vic - tors in.
O joy, for all its for - mer woes A thou - sand - fold re - paid!
Or - phans no lon - ger fa - ther - less, Nor wid - ows des - o - late.
Show in the heav'ns Thy prom - ised sign; Thou Prince and Sav - ior, come. A - men.

THE LIFE ETERNAL

When All My Labors and Trials Are O'er 538

We shall be like Him; for we shall see Him as He is. I John 3:2

GLORY SONG 10 10 10 10 Ref.

Charles H. Gabriel, 1900

Charles H. Gabriel, 1900

1. When all my la-bors and tri-als are o'er, And I am safe on that
2. When by the gift of His in-fi-nite grace, I am ac-cord-ed in
3. Friends will be there I have loved long a-go; Joy like a riv-er a-

beau-ti-ful shore, Just to be near the dear Lord I a-dore
heav-en a place, Just to be there and to look on His face
round me will flow; Yet, just a smile from my Sav-ior, I know,

Refrain

Will through the a-ges be glo-ry for me. O that will be
O that will

glo-ry for me, Glo-ry for me, glo-ry for me; When by His grace
be glo-ry for me, Glo-ry for me, glo-ry for me;

rit.

I shall look on His face, That will be glo-ry, be glo-ry for me.

THE LIFE ETERNAL

539 Jerusalem, My Happy Home

Our feet shall stand within thy gates. O Jerusalem. Psa. 122:2

"F.B.P.," 16th century
Based on anonymous hymn, 16th century

LAND OF REST C.M.
Traditional American melody
Arr. by Annabel M. Buchanan, 1938

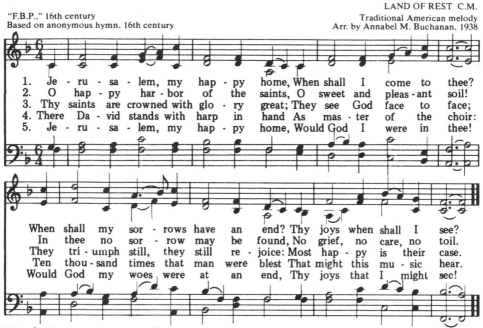

1. Je - ru - sa - lem, my hap - py home, When shall I come to thee?
2. O hap - py har - bor of the saints, O sweet and pleas - ant soil!
3. Thy saints are crowned with glo - ry great; They see God face to face;
4. There Da - vid stands with harp in hand As mas - ter of the choir:
5. Je - ru - sa - lem, my hap - py home, Would God I were in thee!

When shall my sor - rows have an end? Thy joys when shall I see?
In thee no sor - row may be found, No grief, no care, no toil.
They tri - umph still, they still re - joice: Most hap - py is their case.
Ten thou - sand times that man were blest That might this mu - sic hear.
Would God my woes were at an end, Thy joys that I might see!

540 I'm Just a Poor, Wayfaring Stranger

I am a stranger in the earth. Psa. 119:19

American folk hymn

WAYFARING STRANGER Irreg.
Traditional American melody

Unison

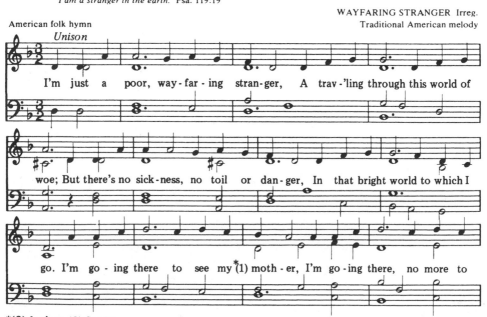

I'm just a poor, way-far-ing stran-ger, A trav-'ling through this world of

woe; But there's no sick-ness, no toil or dan-ger, In that bright world to which I

go. I'm go-ing there to see my (1) moth-er, I'm go-ing there, no more to

*(2) fa-ther, (3) Sav-ior,
THE LIFE ETERNAL

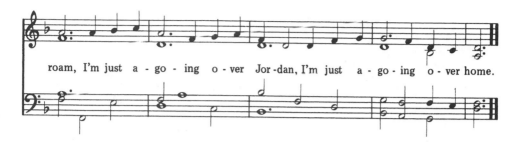

roam, I'm just a - go - ing o - ver Jor-dan, I'm just a - go - ing o - ver home.

Love Divine, So Great and Wondrous 541

They that do His commandments . . . may enter in through the gates into the city. Rev. 22:14

Frederick A. Blom, 1867-1927
Trans. by Nathaniel Carlson, 1879-1957

PEARLY GATES 8 7 8 7 Ref.
Elsie Ahlwén, 1930

1. Love di - vine, so great and won - drous, Deep and might - y, pure, sub - lime;
2. Like a dove when hunt - ed, fright - ened, As a wound-ed fawn was I,
3. Love di - vine, so great and won - drous— All my sins He then for - gave,
4. In life's e - ven - tide, at twi - light, At His door I'll knock and wait;

Com - ing from the heart of Je - sus— Just the same thro' tests of time.
Bro - ken heart - ed, yet He healed me— He will heed the sin - ner's cry.
I will sing His praise for - ev - er, For His blood, His pow'r to save.
By the pre - cious love of Je - sus, I shall en - ter heav - en's gate.

Refrain

He the pearl - y gates will o - pen, So that I may en - ter in;

For He pur-chased my re - demp-tion, And for - gave me all my sin.

THE LIFE ETERNAL

542 In Heaven Above

Mine eyes have seen the King, the Lord of hosts. Isa. 6:5

Laurentius Laurentii Laurinus, 1622
Adapt. by Johan Åström, 1767-1844
Trans. by William Maccall, 1812-1888

HAUGE 8 6 8 6 8 8 6
Traditional Norse melody

1. In heav'n a - bove, in heav'n a - bove, Where God our Fa - ther dwells,
2. In heav'n a - bove, in heav'n a - bove, What glo - ry deep and bright!
3. In heav'n a - bove, in heav'n a - bove, No tears of pain are shed;
4. In heav'n a - bove, in heav'n a - bove, God hath a joy pre - pared,

How bound-less there the bless - ed - ness! No tongue its great - ness tells;
The splen - dor of the noon - day sun Grows pale be - fore its light;
There noth - ing e'er shall fade or die; Life's full - ness 'round is spread,
Which mor - tal ear hath nev - er heard, Nor mor - tal vi - sion shared,

There face to face, and full and free, Ev - er and
That might - y Sun that ne'er goes down, Be - fore whose
And, like an o - cean, joy o'er - flows, And with im -
Which nev - er en - tered mor - tal breast, By mor - tal

ev - er - more we see— We see the Lord of hosts!
face clouds nev - er frown, Is God the Lord of hosts!
mor - tal mer - cy glows Our God the Lord of hosts!
lips was ne'er ex - pressed, 'Tis God the Lord of hosts!

THE LIFE ETERNAL

Then I Saw a New Heaven and Earth 543

And I saw a new heaven and a new earth. Rev. 21:1

Christopher M. Idle, 1972
Based on Revelation 21, 22

NEW HEAVEN Irreg.
Norman L. Warren, 1972

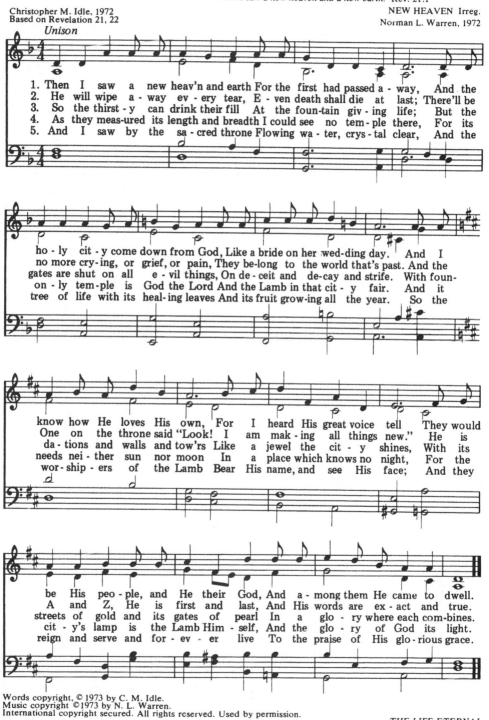

1. Then I saw a new heav'n and earth For the first had passed a - way, And the
2. He will wipe a - way ev - ery tear, E - ven death shall die at last; There'll be
3. So the thirst - y can drink their fill At the foun-tain giv - ing life; But the
4. As they meas-ured its length and breadth I could see no tem - ple there, For its
5. And I saw by the sa - cred throne Flowing wa - ter, crys - tal clear, And the

ho - ly cit - y come down from God, Like a bride on her wed-ding day. And I
no more cry-ing, or grief, or pain, They be-long to the world that's past. And the
gates are shut on all e - vil things, On de - ceit and de-cay and strife. With foun-
on - ly tem-ple is God the Lord And the Lamb in that cit - y fair. And it
tree of life with its heal-ing leaves And its fruit grow-ing all the year. So the

know how He loves His own, For I heard His great voice tell They would
One on the throne said "Look! I am mak - ing all things new." He is
da - tions and walls and tow'rs Like a jewel the cit - y shines, With its
needs nei - ther sun nor moon In a place which knows no night, For the
wor - ship - ers of the Lamb Bear His name, and see His face; And they

be His peo - ple, and He their God, And a - mong them He came to dwell.
A and Z, He is first and last, And His words are ex - act and true.
streets of gold and its gates of pearl In a glo - ry where each com-bines.
cit - y's lamp is the Lamb Him - self, And the glo - ry of God its light.
reign and serve and for - ev - er live To the praise of His glo - rious grace.

THE LIFE ETERNAL

544 When I Can Read My Title Clear

In My Father's house are many mansions. John 14:2

Isaac Watts, 1707

PISGAH 8 6 8 6 6 6 8 6
Traditional American melody
Kentucky Harmony, 1816

1. When I can read my ti - tle clear To man - sions in the skies,
2. Should earth a - gainst my soul en - gage, And fier - y darts be hurled,
3. Let cares like a wild del - uge come, And storms of sor - row fall!
4. There shall I bathe my wea - ry soul In seas of heav'n - ly rest,

I'll bid fare - well to ev - ery fear, And wipe my weep - ing eyes;
Then I can smile at Sa - tan's rage, And face a frown - ing world;
May I but safe - ly reach my home, My God, my heav'n, my all;
And not a wave of trou - ble roll A - cross my peace - ful breast,

And wipe my weep - ing eyes, And wipe my weep - ing eyes,
And face a frown - ing world, And face a frown - ing world,
My God, my heav'n, my all, My God my heav'n, my all,
A - cross my peace - ful breast, A - cross my peace - ful breast,

I'll bid fare - well to ev - ery fear, And wipe my weep - ing eyes.
Then I can smile at Sa - tan's rage, And face a frown - ing world.
May I but safe - ly reach my home, My God, my heav'n, my all.
And not a wave of trou - ble roll A - cross my peace - ful breast.

THE LIFE ETERNAL

On Jordan's Stormy Banks I Stand 545

For He hath prepared for them a city. Heb. 11:16

PROMISED LAND C.M. Ref.

Samuel Stennett, 1787

Traditional American melody
Arr. by Rigdon M. McIntosh, 1895

1. On Jor-dan's storm-y banks I stand, And cast a wish-ful eye
2. All o'er those wide ex-tend-ed plains Shines one e-ter-nal day;
3. No chill-ing winds nor pois'nous breath Can reach that health-ful shore;
4. When shall I reach that hap-py place, And be for-ev-er blest?

To Ca-naan's fair and hap-py land, Where my pos-ses-sions lie.
There God the Son for-ev-er reigns And scat-ters night a-way.
Sick-ness and sor-row, pain and death Are felt and feared no more.
When shall I see my Fa-ther's face, And in His bos-om rest?

Refrain

I am bound for the prom-ised land, I am bound for the prom-ised land;

O who will come and go with me? I am bound for the prom-ised land.

THE LIFE ETERNAL

546 Sing the Wondrous Love of Jesus

. . . At Thy right hand there are pleasures for evermore. Psa. 16:11

Eliza E. Hewitt, 1898

HEAVEN 8 7 8 7 Ref.
Emily D. Wilson, 1898

1. Sing the won-drous love of Je-sus, Sing His mer-cy
2. While we walk the pil-grim path-way Clouds will o-ver-
3. Let us then be true and faith-ful, Trust-ing, serv-ing
4. On-ward to the prize be-fore us! Soon His beau-ty

and His grace; In the man-sions bright and bless-ed He'll pre-
spread the sky; But when trav-'ling days are o-ver, Not a
ev-ery day; Just one glimpse of Him in glo-ry Will the
we'll be-hold; Soon the pearl-y gates will o-pen, We shall

Refrain

pare for us a place.
sha-dow, not a sigh. When we all get to heav-en,
toils of life re-pay. When we all
tread the streets of gold.

What a day of re-joic-ing that will be!
What a day of re-joic-ing that will be! When we

all see Je-sus, We'll sing and shout the vic-to-ry.
When we all and shout the vic-to-ry.

THE LIFE ETERNAL

Jesus, We Want to Meet 547

Where two or three are gathered together in My name, there am I . . . Matt. 18:20

A. T. Olajide Olude, 1949
Trans. by Biodun Adebesin, 1962
Verses by Austin C. Lovelace, 1964

JESU A FE PADE Irreg.
A. T. Olajide Olude, 1949
Arr. by M. O. Ajose, b. 1912

Unison

1. Je - sus, we want to meet On this Thy ho - ly day; We gath - er
2. We kneel in awe and fear On this Thy ho - ly day; Pray God to
3. Thy bless - ing, Lord, we seek On this Thy ho - ly day; Give joy of
4. Our minds we ded - i - cate On this Thy ho - ly day; Heart and soul

round Thy throne On this Thy ho - ly day. Thou art our
teach us here On this Thy ho - ly day; Save us and
Thy vic - to - ry On this Thy ho - ly day. Through grace a - lone
con - se - crate On this Thy ho - ly day. Ho - ly Spir - it,

heav'n - ly Friend, Hear our prayers as they as - cend; Look in - to
cleanse our hearts, Lead and guide our acts of praise, And our faith
are we saved; In Thy flock may we be found; Let the mind
make us whole; Bless the ser - mon in this place; And as

our hearts and minds to - day, On this Thy ho - ly day:
from seed to flow - er raise, On this Thy ho - ly day.
of Christ a - bide in us, On this Thy ho - ly day.
we go, lead us, Lord; We shall be Thine ev - er - more. A - men.

Optional drumbeat patterns

SPECIAL TIMES AND SEASONS: THE LORD'S DAY

548 Safely through Another Week

From one sabbath to another, shall all flesh come to worship before Me . . . Isa. 66:23

John Newton, 1774

SABBATH 7 7 7 7 D.
Lowell Mason, 1824

1. Safe - ly through an - oth - er week God has brought us on our way;
2. While we pray for par - d'ning grace Through the dear Re - deem - er's name,
3. Here we come Thy name to praise; May we feel Thy pres - ence near;
4. May Thy Gos - pel's joy - ful sound Con - quer sin - ners, com - fort saints;

Let us now a bless - ing seek, Wait - ing in His courts to - day:
Show Thy rec - on - cil - ed face, Take a - way our sin and shame;
May Thy glo - ry meet our eyes, While we in Thy house ap - pear;
Make the fruits of grace a - bound, Bring re - lief for all com - plaints;

Day of all the week the best, Em - blem of e - ter - nal rest;
From our world - ly cares set free, May we rest this day in Thee;
Here af - ford us, Lord, a taste Of our ev - er - last - ing feast;
Thus may all our sab - baths prove Till we join the Church a - bove;

Day of all the week the best, Em-blem of e - ter - nal rest.
From our world-ly cares set free, May we rest this day in Thee.
Here af - ford us, Lord, a taste Of our ev - er - last - ing feast.
Thus may all our sab-baths prove Till we join the Church a-bove. A - men.

O Day of Rest and Gladness 549

Upon the first day of the week . . . the disciples came together. Acts 20:7

MENDEBRAS 7 6 7 6 D.

Traditional German melody
Arr. by Lowell Mason, 1839

Christopher Wordsworth, 1862

1. O day of rest and glad-ness, O day of joy and light,
2. On thee, at the cre - a - tion, The light first had its birth;
3. To - day on wea - ry na - tions The heav'n-ly man - na falls;
4. New grac - es ev - er gain-ing From this our day of rest,

O balm of care and sad - ness, Most beau - ti - ful, most bright;
On thee, for our sal - va - tion, Christ rose from depths of earth;
To ho - ly con - vo - ca - tions The sil - ver trump-et calls,
We reach the rest re - main - ing To spir - its of the blest;

On thee the high and low - ly, Through a - ges joined in tune, Sing
On thee our Lord vic - to - rious The Spir - it sent from heav'n; And
Where gos - pel light is glow-ing With pure and ra - diant beams, And
To Ho - ly Ghost be prais - es, To Fa - ther and to Son; The

"Ho - ly, ho - ly, ho - ly," To the great God Tri - une.
thus on thee most glo - rious A tri - ple light was giv'n.
liv - ing wa - ter flow-ing With soul - re - fresh-ing streams.
Church her voice up - rais - es To Thee, blest Three in One. A - men.

THE LORD'S DAY

550 When Morning Gilds the Skies

My voice shalt Thou hear in the morning, O Lord. Psa. 5:3

Katholisches Gesangbuch, Würzburg, 1828
Trans. by Edward Caswall, 1854

LAUDES DOMINI 6 6 6 6 6 6
Joseph Barnby, 1868

1. When morn - ing gilds the skies, My heart a - wak - ing cries:
2. The night be - comes as day When from the heart we say:
3. Sing, suns and stars of space, Sing, ye that see His face,
4. Be this while life is mine My can - ti - cle di - vine:

May Je - sus Christ be praised! A - like at work or prayer
May Je - sus Christ be praised! The pow'rs of dark - ness fear
Sing, Je - sus Christ be praised! Let all the earth a - round
May Je - sus Christ be praised! Be this th' e - ter - nal song,

To Je - sus I re - pair: May Je - sus Christ be praised!
When this sweet chant they hear: May Je - sus Christ be praised!
Ring joy - ous with the sound: May Je - sus Christ be praised!
Through all the a - ges long: May Je - sus Christ be praised! A-men.

551 Awake, My Soul, and with the Sun

I . . . will awake early. I will praise Thee, O Lord. Psa. 108:2, 3

Thomas Ken, 1694

MORNING HYMN L.M.
Francois H. Barthélémon, c. 1789

1. A - wake, my soul, and with the sun Thy dai - ly stage of du - ty run;
2. Wake and lift up thy - self, my heart, And with the an - gels bear thy part,
3. Lord, I my vows to Thee re - new; Dis - perse my sins as morn - ing dew;
4. Di - rect, con - trol, sug - gest this day, All I de - sign or do or say;
5. Praise God from whom all bless-ings flow, Praise Him, all crea - tures here be - low,

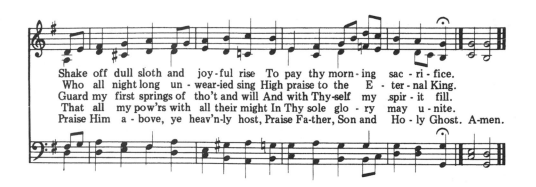

Shake off dull sloth and joy-ful rise To pay thy morn-ing sac-ri-fice.
Who all night long un-wear-ied sing High praise to the E-ter-nal King.
Guard my first springs of tho't and will And with Thy-self my spir-it fill.
That all my pow'rs with all their might In Thy sole glo-ry may u-nite.
Praise Him a-bove, ye heav'n-ly host, Praise Fa-ther, Son and Ho-ly Ghost. A-men.

Still, Still with Thee 552

I will sing aloud of Thy mercy in the morning. Psa. 59:16

CONSOLATION 11 10 11 10

Harriet B. Stowe, 1853

Felix Mendelssohn, 1834

1. Still, still with Thee when pur-ple morn-ing break-eth, When the bird
2. A-lone with Thee a-mid the mys-tic shad-ows, The sol-emn
3. When sinks the soul sub-dued by toil to slum-ber, Its clos-ing
4. So shall it be at last, in that bright morn-ing When the soul

wak-eth and the shad-ows flee; Fair-er than morn-ing, love-lier than the
hush of na-ture new-ly born; A-lone with Thee in breath-less ad-o-
eyes look up to Thee in prayer; Sweet the re-pose be-neath Thy wings o'er-
wak-eth and life's shad-ows flee; O, in that hour, fair-er than day-light

day-light Dawns the sweet con-scious-ness, I am with Thee.
ra-tion, In the calm dew and fresh-ness of the morn.
shad-ing, But sweet-er still to wake and find Thee there.
dawn-ing, Shall rise the glo-rious thought—I am with Thee. A-men.

MORNING

553 Morning Has Broken

In the morning, then ye shall see the glory of the Lord. Exo. 16:7

BUNESSAN 5 5 5 4 D.
Traditional Gaelic melody
Arr. by David Evans, 1927

Eleanor Farjeon, 1931

1. Morn - ing has bro - ken Like the first morn - ing,
2. Sweet the rain's new fall Sun - lit from heav - en,
3. Mine is the sun - light! Mine is the morn - ing

Black - bird has spo - ken Like the first bird.
Like the first dew - fall On the first grass.
Born of the one light E - den saw play!

Praise for the sing - ing! Praise for the morn - ing!
Praise for the sweet - ness Of the wet gar - den,
Praise with e - la - tion, Praise ev - ery morn - ing,

Praise for them, spring - ing Fresh from the Word!
Sprung in com - plete - ness Where His feet pass.
God's re - cre - a - tion Of the new day! A - men.

SPECIAL TIMES AND SEASONS: MORNING

Abide with Me: Fast Falls the Eventide 554

They constrained Him, saying, Abide with us. Luke 24:29

EVENTIDE 10 10 10 10

Henry F. Lyte, 1847

William H. Monk, 1861

1. A - bide with me: fast falls the e - ven - tide;
2. Swift to its close ebbs out life's lit - tle day;
3. I need Thy pres - ence ev - ery pass - ing hour;
4. I fear no foe, with Thee at hand to bless;
5. Hold Thou Thy cross be - fore my clos - ing eyes;

The dark - ness deep - ens; Lord, with me a - bide!
Earth's joys grow dim, its glo - ries pass a - way;
What but Thy grace can foil the tempt - er's power?
Ills have no weight, and tears no bit - ter - ness.
Shine through the gloom and point me to the skies:

When oth - er help - ers fail, and com - forts flee,
Change and de - cay in all a - round I see.
Who, like Thy - self, my guide and stay can be?
Where is death's sting? Where, grave, thy vic - to - ry?
Heav'n's morn - ing breaks, and earth's vain shad - ows flee;

Help of the help - less, O a - bide with me.
O Thou who chang - est not, a - bide with me.
Through cloud and sun - shine, Lord, a - bide with me.
I tri - umph still, if Thou a - bide with me.
In life, in death, O Lord, a - bide with me. A - men.

555 Now the Day Is Over

Thou shalt lie down, and thy sleep shall be sweet. Prov. 3:24

Sabine Baring-Gould, 1865

MERRIAL 6 5 6 5

Joseph Barnby, 1868

1. Now the day is o - ver, Night is draw - ing nigh,
2. Je - sus, give the wea - ry Calm and sweet re - pose;
3. Grant to lit - tle chil - dren Vi - sions bright of Thee;
4. When the morn - ing wak - ens, Then may I a - rise

Shad - ows of the eve - ning Steal a - cross the sky.
With Thy ten - d'rest bless - ing May our eye - lids close.
Guard the sail - ors toss - ing On the deep blue sea.
Pure and fresh and sin - less In Thy ho - ly eyes. A - men.

Copyright, used by permission Gordon Hitchcock, Surrey.

556 Softly Now the Light of Day

Let my prayer be set forth before Thee . . . as the evening sacrifice. Psa. 141:2

George W. Doane, 1824

SEYMOUR 7 7 7 7

Carl Maria von Weber, 1826

1. Soft - ly now the light of day Fades up - on my sight a - way;
2. Thou, whose all - per - vad - ing eye Naught es - capes, with - out, with - in,
3. When for me the light of day Shall for - ev - er pass a - way;
4. Thou who, sin - less, yet hast known All of man's in - firm - i - ty;

Free from care, from la - bor free, Lord, I would com - mune with Thee.
Par - don each in - firm - i - ty, O - pen fault and se - cret sin.
Then from sin and sor - row free, Take me, Lord, to dwell with Thee.
Then from Thine e - ter - nal throne, Je - sus, look with pity - ing eye. A - men.

This tune in a higher key, No. 238

SPECIAL TIMES AND SEASONS

Day Is Dying in the West 557

Holy, holy, holy is the Lord . . . the whole earth is full of His glory. Isa. 6:3

CHAUTAUQUA 7 7 7 7 4 Ref.

Mary A. Lathbury, 1877

William F. Sherwin, 1877

1. Day is dy - ing in the west, Heav'n is touch - ing
2. Lord of life, be - neath the dome Of the u - ni -
3. While the deep - 'ning sha - dows fall, Heart of Love, en -
4. When for - ev - er from our sight Pass the stars, the

earth with rest; Wait and wor - ship while the night Sets her
verse, Thy home, Gath - er us who seek Thy face To the
fold - ing all, Through the glo - ry and the grace Of the
day, the night, Lord of an - gels, on our eyes Let e -

even - ing lamps a - light Through all the sky.
fold of Thy em - brace, For Thou art nigh.
stars that veil Thy face, Our hearts as - cend.
ter - nal morn - ing rise, And shad - ows end.

Refrain

Ho - ly, ho - ly,

ho - ly, Lord God of Hosts! Heav'n and earth are full of Thee!

Heav'n and earth are prais - ing Thee, O Lord most high! A - men.

EVENING

558 Savior, Breathe an Evening Blessing

Thou shalt not be afraid for the terror by night. Psa. 91:5

James Edmeston, 1820

EVENING PRAYER 8 7 8 7
George C. Stebbins, 1878

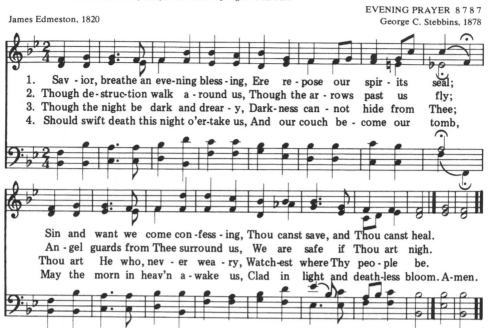

1. Sav - ior, breathe an eve-ning bless-ing, Ere re-pose our spir-its seal;
2. Though de-struc-tion walk a-round us, Though the ar-rows past us fly;
3. Though the night be dark and drear-y, Dark-ness can-not hide from Thee;
4. Should swift death this night o'er-take us, And our couch be-come our tomb,

Sin and want we come con-fess-ing, Thou canst save, and Thou canst heal.
An-gel guards from Thee surround us, We are safe if Thou art nigh.
Thou art He who, nev-er wea-ry, Watch-est where Thy peo-ple be.
May the morn in heav'n a-wake us, Clad in light and death-less bloom. A-men.

559 Sun of My Soul, Thou Savior Dear

The darkness and the light are both alike to Thee. Psa. 139:12

John Keble, 1820

HURSLEY L.M.
Arr. from *Katholisches Gesangbuch*, Vienna, c. 1774

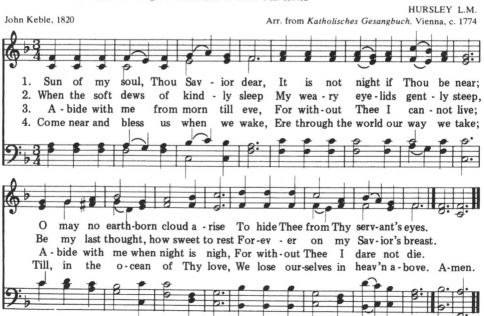

1. Sun of my soul, Thou Sav-ior dear, It is not night if Thou be near;
2. When the soft dews of kind-ly sleep My wea-ry eye-lids gent-ly steep,
3. A-bide with me from morn till eve, For with-out Thee I can-not live;
4. Come near and bless us when we wake, Ere through the world our way we take;

O may no earth-born cloud a-rise To hide Thee from Thy serv-ant's eyes.
Be my last thought, how sweet to rest For-ev-er on my Sav-ior's breast.
A-bide with me when night is nigh, For with-out Thee I dare not die.
Till, in the o-cean of Thy love, We lose our-selves in heav'n a-bove. A-men.

Another Year Is Dawning 560

So teach us to number our days, that we may apply our hearts unto wisdom. Psa. 90:12

AURELIA 7 6 7 6 D.

Frances R. Havergal, 1874

Samuel S. Wesley, 1864

1. An - oth - er year is dawn - ing! Dear Fa - ther, let it be,
2. An - oth - er year of mer - cies, Of faith - ful - ness and grace,
3. An - oth - er year of serv - ice, Of wit - ness for Thy love,

In work - ing or in wait - ing, An - oth - er year with Thee;
An - oth - er year of glad - ness, In the shin - ing of Thy face;
An - oth - er year of train - ing For ho - lier work a - bove;

An - oth - er year of prog - ress, An - oth - er year of praise,
An - oth - er year of lean - ing Up - on Thy lov - ing breast,
An - oth - er year is dawn - ing! Dear Fa - ther, let it be,

An - oth - er year of prov - ing Thy pres - ence all the days.
An - oth - er year of trust - ing, Of qui - et, hap - py rest.
On earth, or else in heav - en, An - oth - er year for Thee. A - men.

This tune in a higher key, No. 247

THE CHANGING YEAR

561 Day by Day and with Each Passing

As thy days, so shall thy strength be. Deut. 33:25

Carolina Sandell Berg, 1865
Trans. by A. L. Skoog, 1856-1934

BLOTT EN DAG Irreg.
Oscar Ahnfelt, 1813-1882

1. Day by day and with each pass-ing mo-ment, Strength I find to meet my tri - als
2. Ev - ery day the Lord Him-self is near me With a spe-cial mer-cy for each
3. Help me then in ev - ery trib - u - la - tion So to trust Thy prom-is - es, O

here; Trust-ing in my Fa-ther's wise be-stow-ment, I've no cause for wor - ry or for
hour; All my cares He fain would bear, and cheer me, He whose name is Coun-sel-lor and
Lord, That I lose not faith's sweet con-so-la-tion Of-fered me with-in Thy ho - ly

fear. He whose heart is kind be-yond all meas-ure Gives un - to each day what He deems
Pow'r. The pro -tec - tion of His child and treas-ure Is a charge that on Him-self He
Word. Help me, Lord, when toil and trouble meeting, E'er to take, as from a fa-ther's

best—Lov-ing - ly, its part of pain and pleas-ure, Min-gling toil with peace and rest.
laid; "As your days, your strength shall be in meas-ure," This the pledge to me He made.
hand, One by one, the days, the mo-ments fleeting, Till I reach the prom-ised land.

SPECIAL TIMES AND SEASONS

Praise to God, Your Praises Bring 562

While the earth remaineth . . . summer and winter . . . shall not cease. Gen. 8:22

SAVANNAH 7 7 7 7

William C. Gannett, 1872

Foundery Collection, 1742

1. Praise to God, your prais - es bring; Hearts, bow down and voic - es, sing
2. Praise Him for His bud - ding green, A - pril's res - ur - rec - tion scene;
3. Praise Him for His sum - mer rain, Feed - ing, day and night, the grain;
4. Praise Him for the win - ter's rest, Snow that falls on na - ture's breast;
5. For His year of won - der done, Praise to the all - glo - rious One!

Prais - es to the glo - rious One, All His year of won - der done.
Praise Him for His shin - ing hours, Star - ring all the land with flowers.
Praise Him for His ti - ny seed, Hold - ing all His world shall need.
Praise for hap - py dreams of birth, Brood - ing in the qui - et earth.
Hearts, bow down and voic - es, sing Praise and love to na - ture's King! A-men.

Great God, We Sing That Mighty Hand 563

Thou hast a mighty arm: strong is Thy hand . . . Psa. 89:13

WAREHAM L.M.

Philip Doddridge, 1755

William Knapp, 1738

1. Great God, we sing that might - y hand By which sup - port - ed still we stand;
2. By day, by night, at home, a - broad, Still are we guard - ed by our God;
3. With grate - ful hearts the past we own; The fu - ture, all to us un - known,
4. In scenes ex - alt - ed or de - pressed, Thou art our Joy, and Thou our Rest;

The o - pening year Thy mer - cy shows; That mer - cy crowns it till it close.
By His in - ces - sant boun - ty fed, By His un - err - ing coun - sel led.
We to Thy guard - ian care com - mit, And peace - ful leave be - fore Thy feet.
Thy good - ness all our hopes shall raise, A - dored thro' all our changing days. A-men.

564 Now Thank We All Our God

Now therefore, our God, we thank Thee, and praise Thy glorious name. I Chron. 29:13

Martin Rinkart, 1636
Trans. by Catherine Winkworth, 1858

NUN DANKET ALLE GOTT 6 7 6 7 6 6 6 6
Johann Crüger, 1647

1. Now thank we all our God With heart and hands and voic - es,
2. O may this boun-teous God Through all our life be near us,
3. All praise and thanks to God The Fa - ther now be giv - en,

Who won-drous things hath done, In whom His world re - joic - es;
With ev - er joy - ful hearts And bless - ed peace to cheer us;
The Son, and Him who reigns With them in high - est heav - en,

Who, from our moth - er's arms, Hath blessed us on our way
And keep us in His grace And guide us when per - plexed,
The one e - ter - nal God Whom earth and heav'n a - dore;

With count-less gifts of love, And still is ours to - day.
And free us from all ills In this world and the next.
For thus it was, is now, And shall be ev - er - more. A - men.

SPECIAL TIMES AND SEASONS

Come, Ye Thankful People, Come 565

The harvest is the end of the world; and the reapers are the angels. Matt. 13:39

ST. GEORGE'S, WINDSOR 7 7 7 7 D.

Henry Alford, 1844

George J. Elvey, 1858

1. Come, ye thank-ful peo - ple, come, Raise the song of har - vest-home:
2. All the world is God's own field, Fruit un - to His praise to yield;
3. For the Lord our God shall come, And shall take His har - vest home;
4. E - ven so, Lord, quick - ly come To Thy fi - nal har - vest-home;

All is safe - ly gath - ered in, Ere the win - ter storms be - gin;
Wheat and tares to - geth - er sown, Un - to joy or sor - row grown;
From His field shall in that day All of - fens - es purge a - way;
Gath - er Thou Thy peo - ple in, Free from sor - row, free from sin;

God, our Ma - ker, doth pro - vide For our wants to be sup - plied:
First the blade, and then the ear, Then the full corn shall ap - pear:
Give His an - gels charge at last In the fire the tares to cast;
There, for - ev - er pu - ri - fied, In Thy pres - ence to a - bide:

Come to God's own tem - ple, come, Raise the song of har - vest-home.
Lord of har - vest, grant that we Whole-some grain and pure may be.
But the fruit - ful ears to store In His gar - ner ev - er - more.
Come, with all Thine an - gels, come, Raise the glo - rious har - vest-home. A-men.

HARVEST AND THANKSGIVING

566 We Plow the Fields, and Scatter

Every good gift and every perfect gift is from above. James 1:17

Matthias Claudius, 1782
Trans. by Jane M. Campbell, 1861

WIR PFLÜGEN 7 6 7 6 D. Ref.
Johann A. P. Schulz, 1800

1. We plow the fields, and scat - ter The good seed on the land, But it is
2. He on - ly is the Mak - er Of all things near and far, He paints the
3. We thank Thee then, O Fa - ther, For all things bright and good, The seed-time

fed and wa - tered By God's al - might - y hand; He sends the snow in
way - side flow - er, He lights the eve - ning star; The winds and waves o -
and the har - vest, Our life, our health, our food; Ac - cept the gifts we

win - ter, The warmth to swell the grain, The breez - es and the sun - shine, And
bey Him, By Him the birds are fed; Much more to us, His chil - dren, He
of - fer For all Thy love im - parts, And what Thou most de - sir - est, Our

Refrain

soft re - fresh - ing rain.
gives our dai - ly bread. All good gifts a - round us Are sent from heav'n a -
hum - ble, thank-ful hearts.

bove; Then thank the Lord, O thank the Lord For all His love. A - men.

God, Who Made the Earth 567

He careth for you. 1 Peter 5:7

CALDWELL CHURCH 5 6 6 4

Sarah B. Rhodes, 1870

David W. Smart, 1965

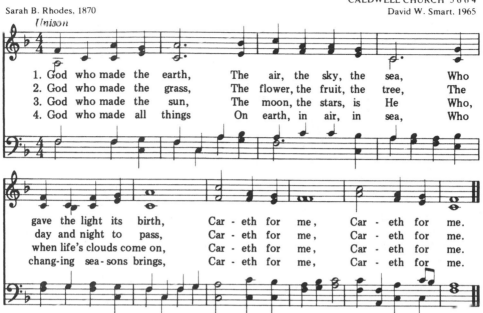

1. God who made the earth, The air, the sky, the sea, Who gave the light its birth, Car - eth for me, Car - eth for me.
2. God who made the grass, The flower, the fruit, the tree, The day and night to pass, Car - eth for me, Car - eth for me.
3. God who made the sun, The moon, the stars, is He Who, when life's clouds come on, Car - eth for me, Car - eth for me.
4. God who made all things On earth, in air, in sea, Who chang-ing sea-sons brings, Car - eth for me, Car - eth for me.

For All the Blessings of the Year 568

Blessed be the Lord, who daily loadeth us with benefits. Psa. 68:19

OLDBRIDGE 8 8 8 4

Albert H. Hutchinson, c. 1909

Robert N. Quaile, 1903

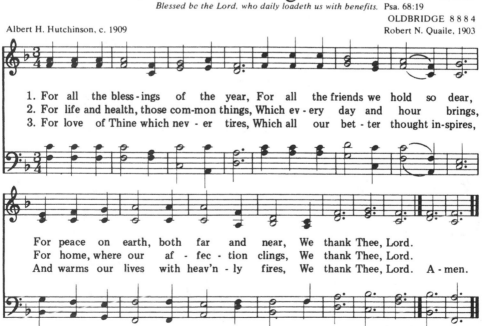

1. For all the bless-ings of the year, For all the friends we hold so dear, For peace on earth, both far and near, We thank Thee, Lord.
2. For life and health, those com-mon things, Which ev - ery day and hour brings, For home, where our af - fec - tion clings, We thank Thee, Lord.
3. For love of Thine which nev - er tires, Which all our bet - ter thought in-spires, And warms our lives with heav'n - ly fires, We thank Thee, Lord. A - men.

HARVEST AND THANKSGIVING

569 When upon Life's Billows

Many, O Lord my God, are Thy wonderful works . . . Psa. 40:5

Johnson Oatman, Jr., 1897

BLESSINGS 11 11 11 11 Ref.
Edwin O. Excell, 1897

1. When up-on life's bil-lows you are tem-pest-tossed, When you are dis-
2. Are you ev-er bur-dened with a load of care? Does the cross seem
3. When you look at oth-ers with their lands and gold, Think that Christ has
4. So a-mid the con-flict, wheth-er great or small, Do not be dis-

cour-aged, think-ing all is lost, Count your man-y bless-ings—name them
heav-y you are called to bear? Count your man-y bless-ings— ev-ery
prom-ised you His wealth un-told; Count your man-y bless-ings—mon-ey
cour-aged—God is o-ver all; Count your man-y bless-ings— an-gels

one by one, And it will sur-prise you what the Lord has done.
doubt will fly, And you will be sing-ing as the days go by.
can-not buy Your re-ward in heav-en nor your home on high.
will at-tend, Help and com-fort give you to your jour-ney's end.

Refrain

Count your bless-ings—name them one by one; Count your
Count your man-y bless-ings— name them one by one; Count your man-y

bless-ings—see what God has done; Count your bless-ings—
bless-ings— see what God has done; Count your man-y bless-ings—

name them one by one; Count your man - y bless - ings—see what God has done.

We Gather Together 570

If God be for us, who can be against us? Rom. 8:31

KREMSER 12 11 12 11

Netherlands folk hymn
Trans. by Theodore Baker, 1917

Nederlandtsch Gedenckelanck. 1626
Arr. by Edward Kremser, 1877

1. We gath - er to - geth - er to ask the Lord's bless - ing;
2. Be - side us to guide us, our God with us join - ing,
3. We all do ex - tol Thee, Thou Lead - er tri - um - phant,

He chas - tens and has - tens His will to make known;
Or - dain - ing, main - tain - ing His king - dom di - vine;
And pray that Thou still our De - fend - er wilt be.

The wick - ed op - press - ing now cease from dis - tress - ing,
So from the be - gin - ning the fight we were win - ning:
Let Thy con - gre - ga - tion es - cape trib - u - la - tion:

Sing prais - es to His name: He for - gets not His own.
Thou, Lord, wast at our side, all glo - ry be Thine!
Thy name be ev - er praised! O Lord, make us free! A - men.

HARVEST AND THANKSGIVING

571 Thanks to God for My Redeemer

In everything give thanks: for this is the will of God . . . I Thess. 5:18

August L. Storm, 1891
Trans. by Carl E. Backstrom, b. 1901

TACK, O GUD 8 7 8 7 D.
John A. Hultman, 1891

1. Thanks to God for my Re-deem-er, Thanks for all Thou dost pro-vide!
2. Thanks for prayers that Thou hast an-swered,Thanks for what Thou dost de-ny!
3. Thanks for ros-es by the way-side,Thanks for thorns their stems con-tain!

Thanks for times now but a mem-'ry, Thanks for Je-sus by my side!
Thanks for storms that I have weath-ered,Thanks for all Thou dost sup-ply!
Thanks for homes and thanks for fire-side, Thanks for hope, that sweet re-frain!

Thanks for pleas-ant, balm-y spring-time, Thanks for dark and drear-y fall!
Thanks for pain and thanks for plea-sure, Thanks for com-fort in de-spair!
Thanks for joy and thanks for sor-row, Thanks for heav'n-ly peace with Thee!

Thanks for tears by now for-got-ten, Thanks for peace with-in my soul!
Thanks for grace that none can meas-ure,Thanks for love be-yond com-pare!
Thanks for hope in the to-mor-row,Thanks thro' all e-ter-ni-ty!

SPECIAL TIMES AND SEASONS: HARVEST AND THANKSGIVING

Praise God from Whom All Blessings 572

Let everything that hath breath praise the Lord. Psa. 150:6

Doxology
Thomas Ken, 1709

OLD 100TH L.M.
Genevan Psalter, 1551

Praise God from whom all bless-ings flow; Praise Him, all crea-tures here be-low;

Praise Him a-bove, ye heav'n-ly host; Praise Fa-ther, Son, and Ho-ly Ghost. A-men.

This tune in another rhythm, No. 20

Praise God from Whom All Blessings 573

Doxology
Thomas Ken, 1709

Richard Avery and
Donald Marsh, 1967

Unison

Praise God from whom all bless-ings flow, Praise Him, all crea-tures here be-low.

Praise Him a-bove, ye heav'n-ly host; praise Fa-ther, Son and Ho-ly Ghost.

A-men. A-men. A-men. A-men. A-men. A-men. A-men.

SERVICE MUSIC: DOXOLOGIES

574 Glory Be to God the Father

Bless the Lord, all His works in all places of His dominion. Psa. 103:22

Gloria Patri
Adapt. by Carlton Young, 1973

Carlton Young, 1973

Glo-ry be to God the Fa-ther, And to Christ His on-ly Son.

Praise we too the Ho-ly Spir-it, Bind-ing all man-

kind as one. As it was in the be-gin-ning, Is for now and

ev-er-more! A - men, A - men!

A - men, A - men!

SERVICE MUSIC: GLORIA PATRI

Glory Be to the Father 575

Give unto the Lord the glory due unto His name. I Chron. 16:29

Gloria Patri
Traditional, 2nd century

GREATOREX Irreg.
Henry W. Greatorex, 1851

Glo - ry be to the Fa - ther, and to the Son, and to the
Ho - ly Ghost; As it was in the be - gin - ning, is
now, and ev - er shall be, world with - out end. A - men, A - men.

Glory Be to the Father 576

Gloria Patri
Traditional, 2nd century

MEINEKE Irreg.
Christoph Meineke, 1844

Glo - ry be to the Fa - ther, and to the Son, and to the
Ho - ly Ghost; As it was in the be - gin - ning, is
now, and ev - er shall be, world with - out end. A - men, A - men.

SERVICE MUSIC: GLORIA PATRI

577 Jesus, Stand Among Us

The same day at evening . . . came Jesus and stood in the midst. John 20:19

William Pennefather, 1873

BEMERTON 6 5 6 5
Friedrich Filitz, 1847

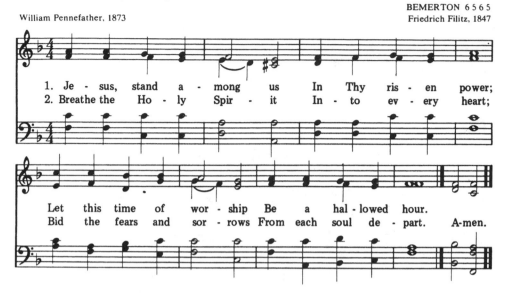

1. Je - sus, stand a - mong us In Thy ris - en power;
2. Breathe the Ho - ly Spir - it In - to ev - ery heart;

Let this time of wor - ship Be a hal - lowed hour.
Bid the fears and sor - rows From each soul de - part. A-men.

578 The Lord Is in His Holy Temple

I will come into Thy house and . . . worship toward Thy holy temple. Psa. 5:7

Habakkuk 2:20

QUAM DILECTA Irreg.
George F. Root, 1820-1895

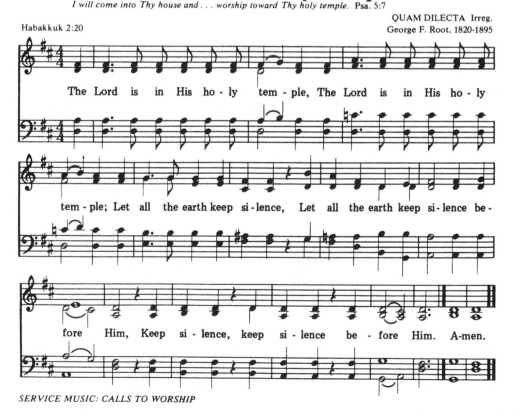

The Lord is in His ho - ly tem - ple, The Lord is in His ho - ly

tem - ple; Let all the earth keep si - lence, Let all the earth keep si - lence be-

fore Him, Keep si - lence, keep si - lence be - fore Him. A-men.

Holy, Holy, Holy, Lord God of Hosts 579

There is none holy as the Lord . . . I Sam. 2:2

Sanctus
Isaiah 6:3

Samuel S. Wesley, c. 1865

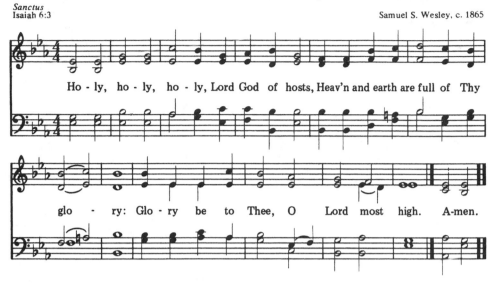

Ho - ly, ho - ly, ho - ly, Lord God of hosts, Heav'n and earth are full of Thy

glo - ry: Glo - ry be to Thee, O Lord most high. A - men.

Now to the King of Heaven 580

Now unto the King eternal . . . be honor and glory forever . . . I Tim. 1:17

Isaac Watts, 1719, and
Philip Doddridge, 1755

ST. JOHN 66.66.88
The Parish Choir, 1851

Now to the King of heav'n Your cheer - ful voic - es raise; To

Him be glo - ry giv'n, Pow'r, maj - es - ty and praise; Wide as He reigns His

name be sung By ev - ery tongue in end - less strains. A - men.

581 There's a Sweet, Sweet Spirit

Behold, how good and how pleasant it is for brethren to dwell together in unity! Psa. 133:1

SWEET, SWEET SPIRIT. Irreg.

Doris Akers, 1963

Doris Akers, 1963

1. There's a sweet, sweet Spir-it in this place, And I
2. There are bless-ings you can-not re-ceive Till you

know that it's the Spir-it of the Lord; There are
know Him in His full-ness, and be-lieve. You're the

sweet ex-pres-sions on each face, And I
one to pro-fit when you say, "I am

know they feel the pres-ence of the Lord.
going to walk with Je-sus all the way."

SERVICE MUSIC: CALLS TO WORSHIP

Sweet Ho - ly Spir - it, Sweet heav-en-ly Dove, Stay right here

with us, Fill - ing us with your love, And for these

bless - ings we lift our hearts in praise; With-out a

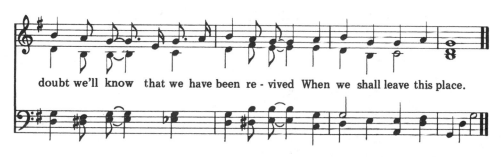

doubt we'll know that we have been re - vived When we shall leave this place.

582 All Things Are Thine

For all things come of Thee . . . I Chron. 29:14

John G. Whittier, 1872

HERR JESU CHRIST L.M.
Pensum Sacrum, Gorlitz, 1648

All things are Thine: no gift have we, Lord of all gifts, to of - fer Thee,

And hence with grate - ful hearts to-day, Thine own be - fore Thy feet we lay.

583 We Give Thee but Thine Own

William W. How, 1858

SCHUMANN S.M.
Mason and Webb's *Cantica Laudis,* 1850

We give Thee but Thine own, What - e'er the gift may be: All

that we have is Thine a - lone, A trust, O Lord, from Thee. A-men.

584 All Things Come of Thee, O Lord

I Chron. 29:14

John F. Wilson, 1967

All things come of Thee, O Lord, And of Thine own have we giv - en Thee. A-men.

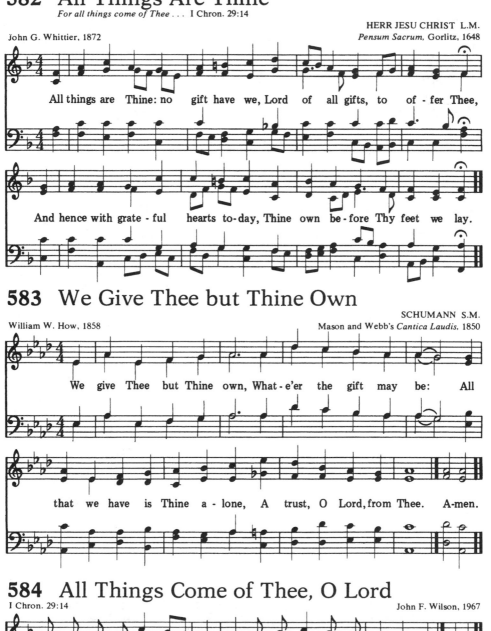

SERVICE MUSIC: OFFERTORY SENTENCES

Hear Our Prayer, O Lord 585

The Lord . . . heareth the prayer of the righteous. Prov. 15:29

Psa. 143:1

George Whelpton, 1897

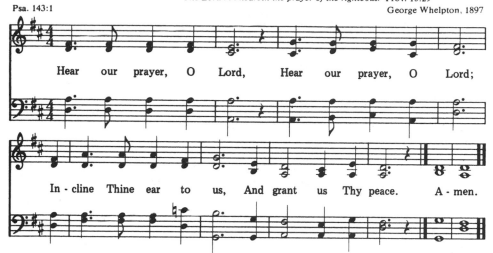

Hear our prayer, O Lord, Hear our prayer, O Lord;

In - cline Thine ear to us, And grant us Thy peace. A - men.

Hear Our Prayer, O Heavenly Father 586

Whatsoever ye shall ask the Father in My name, He will give it you. John 16:23

Traditional

Attr. to Frederic Chopin, 1810-1849

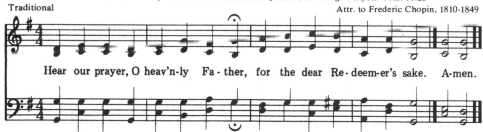

Hear our prayer, O heav'n-ly Fa - ther, for the dear Re - deem-er's sake. A-men.

Let the Words of My Mouth 587

For by thy words thou shalt be justified. Matt. 12:37

Psalm 19:14

Adolph Baumbach, 1862

Let the words of my mouth and the med - i - ta - tion of my heart be ac -

cept - a - ble in Thy sight, O Lord, my strength and my Re-deem - er. A - men.

SERVICE MUSIC: PRAYER RESPONSES

588 Amens

May the Grace of Christ Our Savior 589

The grace of our Lord Jesus Christ be with you all. Rev. 22:21

John Newton, 1779

OMNI DEI 8 7 8 7
Corner's *Gesangbuch*, 1631

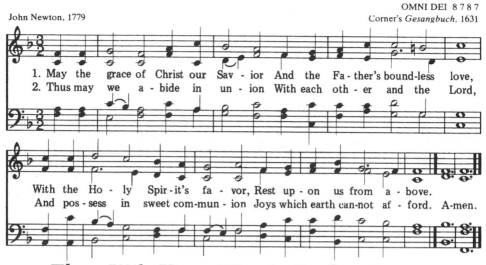

1. May the grace of Christ our Sav - ior And the Fa - ther's bound-less love,
2. Thus may we a - bide in un - ion With each oth - er and the Lord,

With the Ho - ly Spir - it's fa - vor, Rest up - on us from a - bove.
And pos - sess in sweet com-mun - ion Joys which earth can-not af - ford. A-men.

Thou Wilt Keep Him in Perfect Peace 590

Isa. 26:3

DUKE'S TUNE Irreg.
Arr. from *Scottish Psalter*, 1615

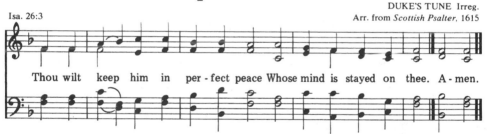

Thou wilt keep him in per - fect peace Whose mind is stayed on thee. A - men.

Lord, Let Us Now Depart in Peace 591

Lord, now lettest Thou Thy servant depart in peace. Luke 2:29

Source unknown

DISMISSAL Irreg.
George Whelpton, 1847-1930

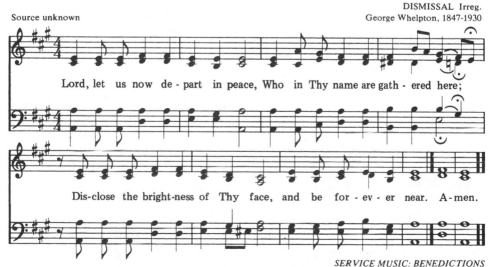

Lord, let us now de - part in peace, Who in Thy name are gath - ered here;

Dis-close the bright-ness of Thy face, and be for - ev - er near. A - men.

SERVICE MUSIC: BENEDICTIONS

SCRIPTURE READINGS (Translations)

Indexes to the Scripture Readings will be found on pages 548 through 550.

592 GOD, THE CREATOR

In the beginning God created the heavens and the earth.

The earth was without form and void, and darkness was upon the face of the deep; and the Spirit of God was moving over the face of the waters.

And God said, "Let there be light"; and there was light. And God saw that the light was good; and God separated the light from the darkness.

God called the light Day, and the darkness he called Night. And there was evening and there was morning, one day.

Then God said, "Let us make man in our image, after our likeness."

So God created man in his own image, in the image of God he created him; male and female he created them.

And God blessed them, and God said to them, "Be fruitful and multiply, and fill the earth and subdue it; and have dominion over the fish of the sea and over the birds of the air and over every living thing that moves upon the earth."

And God saw everything that he had made, and behold, it was very good. And there was evening and there was morning, a sixth day.

Thus the heavens and the earth were finished, and all the host of them.

And on the seventh day God finished his work which he had done, and he rested on the seventh day from all his work which he had done.

Let all the earth fear the Lord, let all the inhabitants of the world stand in awe of him!

For he spoke, and it came to be; he commanded, and it stood forth.
From Genesis 1 and 2, Psalm 33

593 GOD AND THE FAMILY

So God created man in his own image, in the image of God he created him; male and female he created them.

And God blessed them, and God said to them, "Be fruitful and multiply, and fill the earth and subdue it: and have dominion over every living thing that moves upon the earth."

And you shall love the Lord your God with all your heart, and with all your soul, and with all your might.

And these words which I command you this day shall be upon your heart; and you shall teach them diligently to your children, and you shall talk of them when you sit in your house, and when you walk by the way, and when you lie down, and when you rise.

Be subject to one another out of reverence for Christ. Wives, be subject to your husbands, as to the Lord. For the husband is the head of the wife as Christ is the head of the church, his body, and is himself its Savior.

Husbands, love your wives, as Christ loved the church and gave himself up for her, that he might sanctify her, having cleansed her by the washing of water with the word.

Children, obey your parents in the Lord, for this is right.

"Honor your father and mother" (this is the first commandment with a promise), "that it may be well with you and that you may live long on the earth."

Fathers, do not provoke your children to anger, but bring them up in the discipline and instruction of the Lord.

Finally, be strong in the Lord and in the strength of his might.
From Genesis 1, Deuteronomy 6, Ephesians 5 and 6

594 GOD'S COMMANDMENTS

And God spake all these words, saying, I am the Lord thy God, which have brought thee out of the land of Egypt, out of the house of bondage. Thou shalt have no other gods before me.

Thou shalt not make unto thee any graven image, or any likeness of any thing that is in heaven above, or that is in the earth beneath, or that is in the water under the earth: Thou shalt not bow down thyself to them, nor serve them:

Thou shalt not take the name of the Lord thy God in vain; for the Lord will not hold him guiltless that taketh his name in vain.

Remember the sabbath day to keep it holy. Six days shalt thou labour and do all thy work: But the seventh day is the sabbath of the Lord thy God:

Honour thy father and thy mother: that thy days may be long upon the land which the Lord thy God giveth thee.

Thou shalt not kill.

Thou shalt not commit adultery.

Thou shalt not steal.

Thou shalt not bear false witness against thy neighbour.

Thou shalt not covet thy neighbour's house, nor any thing that is thy neighbour's.

Then one of them, which was a lawyer, asked him a question, tempting him, and saying, Master, which is the great commandment in the law?

Jesus said unto him, Thou shalt love the Lord thy God with all thy heart, and with all thy soul, and with all thy mind. This is the first and great commandment.

And the second is like unto it, Thou shalt love thy neighbour as thyself.

On these two commandments hang all the law and the prophets.
From Exodus 20 and Matthew 22

595 GOD AND THE NATION

Righteousness exalts a nation, but sin is a reproach to any people.

So you shall keep the commandments of the Lord your God, by walking in his ways and by fearing him.

For the Lord your God is bringing you into a good land, a land of brooks of water, of fountains and springs, flowing forth in valleys and hills,

A land of wheat and barley, of vines and fig trees and pomegranates, a land of olive trees and honey,

A land in which you will eat bread without scarcity, in which you will lack nothing, a land whose stones are iron, and out of whose hills you can dig copper.

And you shall eat and be full, and you shall bless the Lord your God for the good land he has given you.

"Take heed lest you forget the Lord your God, by not keeping his commandments and his ordinances and his statutes, which I command you this day.

"Lest when you have eaten and are full, and have built goodly houses and live in them, . . . and all that you have is multiplied, then your heart be lifted up and you forget the Lord your God.

"Beware lest you say in your heart, 'My power and the might of my hand have gotten me this wealth.'

"You shall remember the Lord your God, for it is he who gives you power to get wealth:

"And if you forget the Lord your God and go after other gods and serve them and worship them, I solemnly warn you this day that you shall surely perish.

"Like the nations that the Lord makes to perish before you, so shall you perish, because you would not obey the voice of the Lord your God."
From Proverbs 14 and Deuteronomy 8

SCRIPTURE READINGS (TRANSLATIONS)

Blessed is the man that walketh not in the counsel of the ungodly, nor standeth in the way of sinners, nor sitteth in the seat of the scornful.

But his delight is in the law of the Lord: and in his law doth he meditate day and night.

And he shall be like a tree planted by the rivers of water, that bringeth forth his fruit in his season; his leaf also shall not wither; and whatsoever he doeth shall prosper.

The ungodly are not so: but are like the chaff which the wind driveth away.

Therefore the ungodly shall not stand in the judgment, nor sinners in the congregation of the righteous.

For the Lord knoweth the way of the righteous; but the way of the ungodly shall perish.   Psalm 1

*   *   *

Happy is the man who refuses the advice of evil men, who does not follow the example of sinners, or join those who make fun of God.

Instead, he enjoys reading the law of the Lord, and studying it day and night.

He is like a tree that grows beside a stream; it gives fruit at the right time, and its leaves do not dry up. He succeeds in everything he does.

But evil men are not like this at all; they are like straw that the wind blows away.

Evil men will be condemned by God; sinners will be kept apart from the righteous.

The Lord cares for the righteous man, but the evil man will be lost forever.   Psalm 1

SCRIPTURE READINGS (TRANSLATIONS)

The heavens are telling the glory of God; and the firmament proclaims his handiwork.

Day to day pours forth speech, and night to night declares knowledge.

There is no speech, nor are there words; their voice is not heard;

Yet their voice goes out through all the earth, and their words to the end of the world.

The law of the Lord is perfect, reviving the soul;

The testimony of the Lord is sure, making wise the simple;

The precepts of the Lord are right, rejoicing the heart;

The commandment of the Lord is pure, enlightening the eyes;

The fear of the Lord is clean, enduring for ever;

The ordinances of the Lord are true, and righteous altogether.

More to be desired are they than gold, even much fine gold; sweeter also than honey and drippings of the honeycomb.

Moreover by them is thy servant warned; in keeping them there is great reward.

But who can discern his errors? Clear thou me from hidden faults.

Keep back thy servant also from presumptuous sins; let them not have dominion over me!

Then I shall be blameless, and innocent of great transgression.

Let the words of my mouth and the meditation of my heart be acceptable in thy sight, O Lord, my rock and my redeemer.   From Psalm 19

The Lord is my shepherd; I shall not want.

He maketh me to lie down in green pastures: he leadeth me beside the still waters.

He restoreth my soul: he leadeth me in the paths of righteousness for his name's sake.

Yea, though I walk through the valley of the shadow of death, I will fear no evil: for thou art with me; thy rod and thy staff they comfort me.

Thou preparest a table before me in the presence of mine enemies; thou anointest my head with oil; my cup runneth over.

Surely goodness and mercy shall follow me all the days of my life: and I will dwell in the house of the Lord for ever.
Psalm 23

* * *

The Lord is my shepherd; I have everything I need.

He lets me rest in fields of green grass and leads me to quiet pools of fresh water.

He gives me new strength. He guides me in the right way, as he has promised.

Even if that way goes through deepest darkness, I will not be afraid, Lord, because you are with me! Your shepherd's rod and staff keep me safe.

You prepare a banquet for me, where all my enemies can see me; you welcome me by pouring ointment on my head and filling my cup to the brim.

Certainly your goodness and love will be with me as long as I live; and your house will be my home forever.
Psalm 23

The earth is the Lord's and the fulness thereof, the world and those who dwell therein;

For he has founded it upon the seas, and established it upon the rivers.

Who shall ascend the hill of the Lord? And who shall stand in his holy place?

He who has clean hands and a pure heart, who does not lift up his soul to what is false, and does not swear deceitfully.

He will receive blessing from the Lord, and vindication from the God of his salvation.

Such is the generation of those who seek him, who seek the face of the God of Jacob.

Lift up your heads, O gates! and be lifted up, O ancient doors! that the King of glory may come in.

Who is the King of glory?

The Lord, strong and mighty, the Lord, mighty in battle!

Lift up your heads, O gates! and be lifted up, O ancient doors! that the King of glory may come in.

Who is this King of glory?

The Lord of hosts, he is the King of glory!

The Lord reigns; let the earth rejoice; let the many coastlands be glad!

His lightnings lighten the world; the earth sees and trembles.

The mountains melt like wax before the Lord, before the Lord of all the earth.

The heavens proclaim his righteousness; and all the peoples behold his glory.
From Psalm 24 and 97

SCRIPTURE READINGS (TRANSLATIONS)

600 CHRISTIAN STEWARDSHIP

The earth is the Lord's, and the fulness thereof; the world, and they that dwell therein.

The silver is mine, and the gold is mine, saith the Lord of hosts.

For every beast of the forest is mine, and the cattle upon a thousand hills.

And all the tithe of the land, whether of the seed of the land, or of the fruit of the tree, is the Lord's: it is holy unto the Lord.

Honour the Lord with thy substance, and with the firstfruits of all thine increase:

So shall thy barns be filled with plenty, and thy presses shall burst out with new wine.

Bring ye all the tithes into the storehouse... and prove me now herewith, saith the Lord of hosts, if I will not open you the windows of heaven, and pour you out a blessing, that there shall not be room enough to receive it.

Render therefore unto Caesar the things which are Caesar's; and unto God the things that are God's.

But this I say, He which soweth sparingly shall reap also sparingly; and he which soweth bountifully shall reap also bountifully.

Every man according as he purposeth in his heart, so let him give; not grudgingly, or of necessity: for God loveth a cheerful giver.

And God is able to make all grace abound toward you; that ye, always having all sufficiency in all things, may abound to every good work:

As every man hath received the gift, even so minister the same one to another, as good stewards of the manifold grace of God.
From Psalm 24 and 50, Haggai 2, Leviticus 27, Proverbs 3, Malachi 3, Matthew 22, 2 Corinthians 9, 1 Peter 4

SCRIPTURE READINGS (TRANSLATIONS)

601 FAITH AND CONFIDENCE

The Lord is my light and my salvation; whom shall I fear? The Lord is the stronghold of my life; of whom shall I be afraid?

When evildoers assail me, uttering slanders against me, my adversaries and foes, they shall stumble and fall.

Though a host encamp against me, my heart shall not fear; though war arise against me, yet I will be confident.

One thing have I asked of the Lord, that will I seek after; that I may dwell in the house of the Lord all the days of my life, to behold the beauty of the Lord, and to inquire in his temple.

For he will hide me in his shelter in the day of trouble; he will conceal me under the cover of his tent, he will set me high upon a rock.

And now my head shall be lifted up above my enemies round about me; and I will offer in his tent sacrifices with shouts of joy; I will sing and make melody to the Lord.

Hear, O Lord, when I cry aloud, be gracious to me and answer me!

Thou hast said, "Seek ye my face." My heart says to thee, "Thy face, Lord, do I seek." Hide not thy face from me.

Turn not thy servant away in anger, thou who hast been my help. Cast me not off, forsake me not, O God of my salvation!

Teach me thy way, O Lord: and lead me on a level path because of my enemies.

I believe that I shall see the goodness of the Lord in the land of the living!

Wait for the Lord; be strong, and let your heart take courage; yea, wait for the Lord! From Psalm 27

602 DIVINE DELIVERANCE

Rejoice in the Lord, O you righteous! Praise befits the upright.

For the word of the Lord is upright; and all his work is done in faithfulness.

He loves righteousness and justice; the earth is full of the steadfast love of the Lord.

Let all the earth fear the Lord, let all the inhabitants of the world stand in awe of him!

The Lord brings the counsel of the nations to nought; he frustrates the plans of the peoples.

The counsel of the Lord stands for ever, the thoughts of his heart to all generations.

Blessed is the nation whose God is the Lord, the people whom he has chosen as his heritage!

The Lord looks down from heaven, he sees all the sons of men.

From where he sits enthroned he looks forth on all the inhabitants of the earth,

He who fashions the hearts of them all, and observes all their deeds.

A king is not saved by his great army; a warrior is not delivered by his great strength.

The war horse is a vain hope for victory, and by its great might it cannot save.

Behold the eye of the Lord is on those who fear him, on those who hope in his steadfast love,

That he may deliver their soul from death, and keep them alive in famine.

Our soul waits for the Lord; he is our help and shield.

Yea, our heart is glad in him, because we trust in his holy name.
From Psalm 33

603 DIVINE PROVIDENCE

I will bless the Lord at all times; his praise shall continually be in my mouth.

My soul makes its boast in the Lord; let the afflicted hear and be glad.

O magnify the Lord with me, and let us exalt his name together.

I sought the Lord, and he answered me, and delivered me from all my fears.

The angel of the Lord encamps around those who fear him, and delivers them.

O taste and see that the Lord is good! Happy is the man who takes refuge in him!

O fear the Lord, you his saints, for those who fear him have no want!

The young lions suffer want and hunger, but those who seek the Lord lack no good thing.

The eyes of the Lord are toward the righteous, and his ears toward their cry.

The face of the Lord is against evil-doers, to cut off the remembrance of them from the earth.

When the righteous cry for help, the Lord hears, and delivers them out of all their troubles.

The Lord is near to the broken-hearted, and saves the crushed in spirit.

Many are the afflictions of the righteous; but the Lord delivers him out of them all.

The Lord redeems the life of his servants; none of those who take refuge in him will be condemned.
From Psalm 34

SCRIPTURE READINGS (TRANSLATIONS)

604 PATIENCE AND TRUST

Don't be worried on account of the wicked; don't be jealous of those who do wrong;

They will disappear like grass that dries up; they will die like plants that wither.

Trust in the Lord and do good; live in the land and be safe.

Seek your happiness with the Lord, and he will give you what you most desire.

Give yourself to the Lord; trust in him, and he will help you;

He will cause your goodness to shine as the light and your righteousness as the noonday sun.

Be calm before the Lord, and wait patiently for him to act;

Don't be worried about those who prosper or those who succeed in their evil plans.

The Lord guides a man safely in the way he should go and is pleased with his conduct.

If he falls, he will not stay down, because the Lord will help him up.

I am old now and no longer a boy, but I have never seen a good man abandoned by the Lord, or his children begging for food.

At all times he gives freely and lends to others, and his children are a blessing.

The good man's words are wise, and he speaks of what is right.

He keeps the law of his God in his heart and never departs from it.

Put your hope in the Lord and obey his commandments;

He will give you the strength to possess the land, and you will see the wicked driven out. From Psalm 37

SCRIPTURE READINGS (TRANSLATIONS)

605 PRAYER OF PENITENCE

Be merciful to me, God, because of your constant love,

Wipe away my sins, because of your great mercy!

Wash away my evil, and make me clean from my sin!

I recognize my faults; I am always conscious of my sins.

I have sinned against you—only against you, and done what you consider evil.

So you are right in judging me; you are justified in condemning me.

I have been evil from the time I was born; from the day of my birth I have been sinful.

A faithful heart is what you want; fill my mind with your wisdom.

Remove my sin, and I will be clean; wash me, and I will be whiter than snow.

Let me hear the sounds of joy and gladness; and though you have crushed and broken me, I will be happy once again.

Create a pure heart in me, God, and put a new and loyal spirit in me.

Do not banish me from your presence; do not take your holy spirit away from me.

Give me again the joy that comes from your salvation, and make my spirit obedient.

Then I will teach sinners your commands, and they will turn back to you.

You do not want sacrifices, or I would offer them; you are not pleased with burnt offerings.

My sacrifice is a submissive spirit, God; a submissive and obedient heart you will not reject. From Psalm 51

606 BLESSINGS FROM GOD

Bless the Lord, O my soul; and all that is within me, bless his holy name!

Bless the Lord, O my soul, and forget not all his benefits,

Who forgives all your iniquity, who heals all your diseases,

Who redeems your life from the Pit, who crowns you with steadfast love and mercy,

Who satisfies you with good as long as you live so that your youth is renewed like the eagle's.

The Lord works vindication and justice for all who are oppressed.

He made known his ways to Moses, his acts to the people of Israel.

The Lord is merciful and gracious, slow to anger and abounding in steadfast love. He will not always chide, nor will he keep his anger for ever.

He does not deal with us according to our sins, nor requite us according to our iniquities.

For as the heavens are high above the earth, so great is his steadfast love toward those who fear him;

As far as the east is from the west, so far does he remove our transgressions from us.

As a father pities his children, so the Lord pities those who fear him. For he knows our frame; he remembers that we are dust.

As for man, his days are like grass; he flourishes like a flower of the field; for the wind passes over it; and it is gone, and its place knows it no more.

But the steadfast love of the Lord is from everlasting to everlasting upon those who fear him, and his righteousness to children's children.
From Psalm 103

607 CREATOR AND SUSTAINER

Praise the Lord, my soul! Lord, my God, how great you are!

You are clothed with majesty and glory; you cover yourself with light.

You stretched out the heavens like a tent, and built your home on the waters above. You use the clouds as your chariot, and walk on the wings of the wind.

You use the winds as your messengers, and flashes of lightning as your servants. You have set the earth firmly on its foundations, and it will never be moved.

You make springs flow in the valleys, and water run between the hills.

They provide water for the wild animals; the wild donkeys quench their thirst; in the trees near by the birds make their nests and sing.

From heaven you send rain on the mountains, and the earth is filled with your blessings.

You make grass grow for the cattle, and plants for man to use, so he can grow his crops, and produce wine to make him happy, olive oil to make him cheerful, and bread to give him strength.

Lord, you have made so many things! How wisely you made them all! The earth is filled with your creatures.

All of them depend on you to give them food when they need it. You give it to them, and they eat it; you provide food, and they are satisfied.

May the glory of the Lord last forever! May the Lord be happy with what he made!

I will sing to the Lord all my life; I will sing praises to my God as long as I live. Praise the Lord, my soul! Praise the Lord!
From Psalm 104

SCRIPTURE READINGS (TRANSLATIONS)

Lord, you have examined me, and you know me.

You know everything I do; from far away you understand all my thoughts.

You see me, whether I am working or resting; you know all my actions.

Even before I speak you already know what I will say.

You are all around me, on every side; you protect me with your power.

Your knowledge of me is overwhelming; it is too deep for me to understand.

Where could I go to escape from your spirit? Where could I get away from your presence?

If I went up to heaven, you would be there; if I lay down in the world of the dead, you would be there.

If I flew away beyond the east, or lived in the farthest place in the west, you would be there to lead me, you would be there to help me.

I could ask the darkness to hide me, or the light around me to turn into night, but even the darkness is not dark for you, and the night is as bright as the day.

You created every part of me; you put me together in my mother's womb.

I praise you because you are to be feared; all you do is strange and wonderful. I know it with all my heart.

You saw me before I was born. The days that had been created for me had all been recorded in your book, before any of them had ever begun.

Examine me, God, and know my mind; test me, and discover my thoughts. Find out if there is any deceit in me, and guide me in the eternal way. From Psalm 139

SCRIPTURE READINGS (TRANSLATIONS)

The blessing of the Lord, it maketh rich, and he addeth no sorrow with it.

The liberal soul shall be made fat: and he that watereth shall be watered also himself.

There is a way which seemeth right unto a man, but the end thereof are the ways of death.

In the fear of the Lord is strong confidence: and his children shall have a place of refuge.

A soft answer turneth away wrath: but grievous words stir up anger.

A man's heart deviseth his way; but the Lord directeth his steps.

A merry heart doeth good like a medicine: but a broken spirit drieth the bones.

A man that hath friends must shew himself friendly: and there is a friend that sticketh closer than a brother.

He that hath pity upon the poor lendeth unto the Lord: and that which he hath given will he pay him again.

Wine is a mocker, strong drink is raging: and whosoever is deceived thereby is not wise.

A good name is rather to be chosen than great riches, and loving favour rather than silver and gold.

Train up a child in the way he should go: and when he is old, he will not depart from it.

He that covereth his sins shall not prosper: But whoso confesseth and forsaketh them shall have mercy.

The fear of man bringeth a snare: but whoso putteth his trust in the Lord shall be safe. From Proverbs

610 CHRIST IN PROPHECY

There shall come forth a shoot from the stump of Jesse, and a branch shall grow out of his roots,

And the Spirit of the Lord shall rest upon him, the spirit of wisdom and understanding, the spirit of counsel and might, the spirit of knowledge and the fear of the Lord.

And his delight shall be in the fear of the Lord. He shall not judge by what his eyes see, or decide by what his ears hear;

But with righteousness he shall judge the poor, and decide with equity for the meek of the earth;

And he shall smite the earth with the rod of his mouth, and with the breath of his lips he shall slay the wicked.

Righteousness shall be the girdle of his waist, and faithfulness the girdle of his loins.

Behold my servant, whom I uphold, my chosen, in whom my soul delights; I have put my Spirit upon him, he will bring forth justice to the nations.

He will not fail or be discouraged till he has established justice in the earth; and the coastlands wait for his law.

"Behold, the days are coming, says the Lord, when I will raise up for David a righteous Branch, and he shall reign as king and deal wisely, and shall execute justice and righteousness in the land.

"In his days Judah will be saved, and Israel will dwell securely. And this is the name by which he will be called: 'The Lord is our righteousness.'

"For behold, the day comes, burning like an oven, when all the arrogant and all evildoers will be stubble; ...

"But for you who fear my name the sun of righteousness shall rise, with healing in its wings."

From Isaiah 11 and 42, Jeremiah 23, Malachi 4

611 COMFORT FROM GOD

Comfort, comfort my people, says your God.

Speak tenderly to Jerusalem, and cry to her that her warfare is ended, that her iniquity is pardoned, that she has received from the Lord's hand double for all her sins.

A voice cries: "In the wilderness prepare the way of the Lord, make straight in the desert a highway for our God.

"Every valley shall be lifted up, and every mountain and hill be made low;

"The uneven ground shall become level, and the rough places a plain.

"And the glory of the Lord shall be revealed, and all flesh shall see it together, for the mouth of the Lord has spoken."

Get you up to a high mountain, O Zion, herald of good tidings; lift up your voice with strength, O Jerusalem, herald of good tidings, lift it up, fear not;

Say to the cities of Judah, "Behold your God!" Behold, the Lord God comes with might, and his arm rules for him:

The Lord is the everlasting God, the Creator of the ends of the earth. He does not faint or grow weary, his understanding is unsearchable.

He gives power to the faint, and to him who has no might he increases strength.

Even youths shall faint and be weary, and young men shall fall exhausted; but they who wait for the Lord shall renew their strength.

They shall mount up with wings like eagles, they shall run and not be weary, they shall walk and not faint.

From Isaiah 40

SCRIPTURE READINGS (TRANSLATIONS)

Who has believed what we have heard? And to whom has the arm of the Lord been revealed?

For he grew up before him like a young plant, and like a root out of dry ground; he had no form or comeliness that we should look at him, and no beauty that we should desire him.

He was despised and rejected by men; a man of sorrows, and acquainted with grief; and as one from whom men hide their faces he was despised, and we esteemed him not.

Surely he has borne our griefs and carried our sorrows; yet we esteemed him stricken, smitten by God, and afflicted.

But he was wounded for our transgressions, he was bruised for our iniquities; upon him was the chastisement that made us whole, and with his stripes we are healed.

All we like sheep have gone astray; we have turned every one to his own way; and the Lord has laid on him the iniquity of us all.

He was oppressed, and he was afflicted, yet he opened not his mouth; like a lamb that is led to the slaughter, and like a sheep that before its shearers is dumb, so he opened not his mouth.

By oppression and judgment he was taken away; and as for his generation, who considered that he was cut off out of the land of the living, stricken for the transgression of my people?

Yet it was the will of the Lord to bruise him; he has put him to grief: ... Therefore I will divide him a portion with the great, and he shall divide the spoil with the strong;

Because he poured out his soul to death, and was numbered with the transgressors; yet he bore the sin of many, and made intercession for the transgressors. From Isaiah 53

"Ho, every one who thirsts, come to the waters; and he who has no money, come, buy and eat! Come, buy wine and milk without money and without price.

"Why do you spend your money for that which is not bread, and your labor for that which does not satisfy?

"Hearken diligently to me, and eat what is good, and delight yourself in fatness.

"Incline your ear, and come to me; hear, that your soul may live; and I will make with you an everlasting covenant.

"Seek the Lord while he may be found, call upon him while he is near;

"Let the wicked forsake his way, and the unrighteous man his thoughts: let him return to the Lord, that he may have mercy on him, and to our God, for he will abundantly pardon.

"For my thoughts·are not your thoughts, neither are your ways my ways, says the Lord.

"For as the heavens are higher than the earth, so are my ways higher than your ways and my thoughts than your thoughts.

"For as the rain and the snow come down from heaven, and return not thither but water the earth, making it bring forth and sprout, giving seed to the sower and bread to the eater,

"So shall my word be that goes forth from my mouth: it shall not return to me empty, but it shall accomplish that which I purpose, and prosper in the thing for which I sent it.

"For you shall go out in joy, and be led forth in peace;

"The mountains and the hills before you shall break forth into singing, and all the trees of the field shall clap their hands." From Isaiah 55

614 PEACE AND RENEWAL

It shall come to pass in the latter days that the mountain of the house of the Lord shall be established as the highest of the mountains, and shall be raised up above the hills; and peoples shall flow to it,

And many nations shall come, and say: "Come, let us go up to the mountain of the Lord, to the house of the God of Jacob that he may teach us his ways and we may walk in his paths."

For out of Zion shall go forth the law, and the word of the Lord from Jerusalem.

He shall judge between many peoples, and shall decide for strong nations afar off;

For all the peoples walk each in the name of its god, but we will walk in the name of the Lord our God for ever and ever.

In that day, says the Lord, I will assemble the lame and gather those who have been driven away, and those whom I have afflicted;

And the lame I will make the remnant; and those who were cast off, a strong nation;

And the Lord will reign over them in Mount Zion from this time forth and for evermore.

Who is a God like thee, pardoning iniquity and passing over transgression for the remnant of his inheritance?

He does not retain his anger for ever because he delights in steadfast love.

And they shall beat their swords into plowshares, and their spears into pruning hooks; nation shall not lift up sword against nation, neither shall they learn war any more:

But they shall sit every man under his vine and under his fig tree, and none shall make them afraid; for the mouth of the Lord of hosts has spoken.
From Micah 4 and 7

615 ADORATION OF THE MAGI

Now when Jesus was born in Bethlehem of Judea in the days of Herod the king, behold, wise men from the East came to Jerusalem, saying,

"Where is he who has been born king of the Jews? For we have seen his star in the East, and have come to worship him."

When Herod the king heard this, he was troubled, and all Jerusalem with him;

And assembling all the chief priests and scribes of the people, he inquired of them where the Christ was to be born.

They told him, "In Bethlehem of Judea; for so it is written by the prophet:

"'And you, O Bethlehem, in the land of Judah, are by no means least among the rulers of Judah; for from you shall come a ruler who will govern my people Israel.'"

Then Herod summoned the wise men secretly and ascertained from them what time the star appeared;

And he sent them to Bethlehem, saying, "Go and search diligently for the child, and when you have found him bring me word, that I too may come and worship him."

When they had heard the king they went their way; and lo, the star which they had seen in the East went before them, till it came to rest over the place where the child was.

When they saw the star, they rejoiced exceedingly with great joy;

And going into the house they saw the child with Mary his mother, and they fell down and worshiped him.

Then, opening their treasures, they offered him gifts, gold and frankincense and myrrh. From Matthew 2

Then Jesus came from Galilee to the Jordan to John, to be baptized by him. John would have prevented him, saying, "I need to be baptized by you, and do you come to me?"

But Jesus answered him, "Let it be so now; for thus it is fitting for us to fulfill all righteousness." Then he consented.

And when Jesus was baptized, he went up immediately from the water, and behold, the heavens were opened and he saw the Spirit of God descending like a dove, and alighting on him;

And lo, a voice from heaven, saying, "This is my beloved Son, with whom I am well pleased."

And Jesus came and said to them, "All authority in heaven and on earth has been given to me. Go therefore and make disciples of all nations.

Baptizing them in the name of the Father and of the Son and of the Holy Spirit, teaching them to observe all that I have commanded you;

And Peter said to them, "Repent, and be baptized every one of you in the name of Jesus Christ for the forgiveness of your sins; and you shall receive the gift of the Holy Spirit.

"For the promise is to you and to your children and to all that are far off, every one whom the Lord our God calls to him."

So those who received his word were baptized, and there were added that day about three thousand souls. And they devoted themselves to the apostles' teaching and fellowship, to the breaking of bread and the prayers

We were buried therefore with him by baptism into death, so that as Christ was raised from the dead by the glory of the Father, we too might walk in newness of life.
From Matthew 3 and 28, Acts 2, Romans 6

Seeing the crowds, he went up on the mountain, and when he sat down his disciples came to him. And he opened his mouth and taught them, saying: "Blessed are the poor in spirit, for theirs is the kingdom of heaven.

"Blessed are those who mourn, for they shall be comforted.

"Blessed are the meek, for they shall inherit the earth.

"Blessed are those who hunger and thirst for righteousness, for they shall be satisfied.

"Blessed are the merciful, for they shall obtain mercy.

"Blessed are the pure in heart, for they shall see God.

"Blessed are the peacemakers, for they shall be called sons of God.

"Blessed are those who are persecuted for righteousness' sake, for theirs is the kingdom of heaven.

"Blessed are you when men revile you and persecute you and utter all kinds of evil against you falsely on my account.

"Rejoice and be glad, for your reward is great in heaven, for so men persecuted the prophets who were before you.

"You are the salt of the earth; but if salt has lost its taste, how shall its saltness be restored? It is no longer good for anything except to be thrown out and trodden under foot by men.

"You are the light of the world. A city set on a hill cannot be hid.

"Nor do men light a lamp and put it under a bushel, but on a stand, and it gives light to all in the house.

"Let your light so shine before men, that they may see your good works and give glory to your Father who is in heaven." From Matthew 5

"Do not lay up for yourselves treasures on earth, where moth and rust consume and where thieves break in and steal,

"But lay up for yourselves treasures in heaven, where neither moth nor rust consumes and where thieves do not break in and steal. For where your treasure is, there will your heart be also.

"No one can serve two masters; for either he will hate the one and love the other, or he will be devoted to the one and despise the other. You cannot serve God and mammon.

"Therefore I tell you, do not be anxious about your life, what you shall eat or what you shall drink, nor about your body, what you shall put on. Is not life more than food, and the body more than clothing?

"Look at the birds of the air: they neither sow nor reap nor gather into barns, and yet your heavenly Father feeds them. Are you not of more value than they?

"And why are you anxious about clothing? Consider the lilies of the field, how they grow; they neither toil nor spin; yet I tell you, even Solomon in all his glory was not arrayed like one of these.

"But if God so clothes the grass of the field, which today is alive and tomorrow is thrown into the oven, will he not much more clothe you, O men of little faith?

"Therefore do not be anxious, saying, 'What shall we eat?' or 'What shall we drink?' or 'What shall we wear?'

"For the Gentiles seek all these things; and your heavenly Father knows that you need them all.

"But seek first his kingdom and his righteousness, and all these things shall be yours as well." From Matthew 6

And Jesus went about all the cities and villages, teaching in their synagogues and preaching the gospel of the kingdom, and healing every disease and every infirmity.

When he saw the crowds, he had compassion for them, because they were harassed and helpless, like sheep without a shepherd.

Then he said to his disciples, "The harvest is plentiful, but the laborers are few;

"Pray therefore the Lord of the harvest to send out laborers into his harvest."

For there is no distinction between Jew and Greek; the same Lord is Lord of all and bestows his riches upon all who call upon him.

For, "every one who calls upon the name of the Lord will be saved."

But how are men to call upon him in whom they have not believed? And how are they to believe in him of whom they have never heard?

And how are they to hear without a preacher? And how can men preach unless they are sent?

"Do you not say, 'There are yet four months, then comes the harvest?' I tell you, lift up your eyes, and see how the fields are already white for harvest.

"He who reaps receives wages, and gathers fruit for eternal life, so that sower and reaper may rejoice together."

May those who sow in tears reap with shouts of joy!

He that goes forth weeping, bearing the seed for sowing, shall come home with shouts of joy, bringing his sheaves with him.
From Matthew 9, Romans 10, John 4, and Psalm 126

SCRIPTURE READINGS (TRANSLATIONS)

620 THE CHURCH

Now when Jesus came into the district of Caesarea Philippi, he asked his disciples, "Who do men say that the Son of man is?"

And they said, "Some say John the Baptist, others say Elijah, and others Jeremiah or one of the prophets."

He said to them, "But who do you say that I am?"

Simon Peter replied, "You are the Christ, the Son of the living God."

And Jesus answered him, "Blessed are you, Simon Bar-Jona! For flesh and blood has not revealed this to you, but my Father who is in heaven.

"And I tell you, you are Peter, and on this rock I will build my church, and the powers of death shall not prevail against it."

Husbands, love your wives, as Christ loved the church and gave himself up for her, that he might sanctify her, having cleansed her by the washing of water with the word,

That the church might be presented before him in splendor, without spot or wrinkle or any such thing, that she might be holy and without blemish.

So then you are no longer strangers and sojourners, but you are fellow citizens with the saints and members of the household of God,

Built upon the foundation of the apostles and prophets, Christ Jesus himself being the cornerstone . . . .

Now you are the body of Christ and individually members of it.

He is the head of the body, the church; he is the beginning, the first-born from the dead, that in everything he might be preeminent.
From Matthew 16, Ephesians 5 and 2,
1 Corinthians 12, Colossians 1

SCRIPTURE READINGS (TRANSLATIONS)

621 CHRIST AND CHILDREN

At the same time came the disciples unto Jesus, saying, Who is the greatest in the kingdom of heaven?

And Jesus called a little child unto him, and set him in the midst of them, and said,

Verily I say unto you, Except ye be converted, and become as little children, ye shall not enter into the kingdom of heaven.

Whosoever therefore shall humble himself as this little child, the same is greatest in the kingdom of heaven.

And whoso shall receive one such little child in my name receiveth me.

But whoso shall offend one of these little ones which believe in me, it were better for him that a millstone were hanged about his neck, and that he were drowned in the depth of the sea.

Take heed that ye despise not one of these little ones; for I say unto you, that in heaven their angels do always behold the face of my Father which is in heaven.

Whosoever shall receive one of such children in my name, receiveth me: and whosoever shall receive me, receiveth not me, but him that sent me.

And they brought young children to him, that he should touch them: and his disciples rebuked those that brought them.

But when Jesus saw it, he was much displeased, and said unto them, Suffer the little children to come unto me, and forbid them not: for of such is the kingdom of God.

Verily I say unto you, Whosoever shall not receive the kingdom of God as a little child, he shall not enter therein.

And he took them up in his arms, put his hands upon them, and blessed them. From Matthew 18, Mark 9 and 10

"When the Son of Man comes as King, and all the angels with him, he will sit on his royal throne, and all the earth's peoples will be gathered before him.

"Then he will divide them into two groups, just as a shepherd separates the sheep from the goats: he will put the sheep at his right and the goats at his left.

"Then the King will say to the people on his right: 'You who are blessed by my Father: come! Come and receive the kingdom which has been prepared for you ever since the creation of the world.

"'I was hungry and you fed me, thirsty and you gave me drink; I was a stranger and you received me in your homes, naked and you clothed me; I was sick and you took care of me, in prison and you visited me.'

"The righteous will then answer him: 'When, Lord, did we ever see you hungry and feed you, or thirsty and give you drink? When did we ever see you a stranger and welcome you in our homes, or naked and clothe you? When did we ever see you sick or in prison, and visit you?'

"The King will answer back, 'I tell you, indeed, whenever you did this for one of the least important of these brothers of mine, you did it for me!'

"Then he will say to those on his left: 'Away from me, you who are under God's curse! Away to the eternal fire which has been prepared for the Devil and his angels!

"'I was hungry but you would not feed me, thirsty but you would not give me drink;

"'I tell you, indeed, whenever you refused to help one of these least important ones, you refused to help me.'

"These, then, will be sent off to eternal punishment; the righteous will go to eternal life." From Matthew 25

After the Sabbath, as Sunday morning was dawning, Mary Magdalene and the other Mary went to look at the grave.

Suddenly there was a strong earthquake; an angel of the Lord came down from heaven, rolled the stone away, and sat on it.

His appearance was like lightning and his clothes were white as snow.

The guards were so afraid that they trembled and became like dead men.

The angel spoke to the women. "You must not be afraid," he said. "I know you are looking for Jesus, who was nailed to the cross.

"He is not here; he has risen, just as he said. Come here and see the place where he lay.

"Quickly, now, go and tell his disciples: 'He has been raised from death, and now he is going to Galilee ahead of you; there you will see him!' Remember what I have told you."

So they left the grave in a hurry, afraid and yet filled with joy, and ran to tell his disciples.

Suddenly Jesus met them and said, "Peace be with you." They came up to him, took hold of his feet, and worshiped him.

"Do not be afraid," Jesus said to them. "Go and tell my brothers to go to Galilee, and there they will see me."

It was late that Sunday evening, and the disciples were gathered together behind locked doors, because they were afraid of the Jews. Then Jesus came and stood among them. "Peace be with you," he said.

After saying this, he showed them his hands and his side. The disciples were filled with joy at seeing the Lord. From Matthew 28 and John 20

SCRIPTURE READINGS (TRANSLATIONS)

624 THE GREAT COMMISSION

Now the eleven disciples went to Galilee, to the mountain to which Jesus had directed them.

And when they saw him they worshiped him; but some doubted.

And Jesus came and said to them, "All authority in heaven and earth has been given to me. Go therefore and make disciples of all nations, baptizing them in the name of the Father and of the Son and of the Holy Spirit,

"Teaching them to observe all that I have commanded you; and lo, I am with you always, to the close of the age."

Then he opened their minds to understand the scriptures, and said to them, "Thus it is written, that the Christ should suffer and on the third day rise from the dead, and that repentance and forgiveness of sins should be preached in his name to all nations, beginning from Jerusalem.

"You are witnesses of these things. And behold, I send the promise of my Father upon you; but stay in the city, until you are clothed with power from on high."

So when they had come together, they asked him, "Lord, will you at this time restore the kingdom to Israel?"

He said to them, "It is not for you to know times or seasons which the Father has fixed by his own authority.

"But you shall receive power when the Holy Spirit has come upon you; and you shall be my witnesses in Jerusalem and in all Judea and Samaria and to the end of the earth."

And they went forth and preached everywhere, the Lord working with them, and confirming the word with signs following. Amen.
From Matthew 28, Luke 24, Acts 1, and Mark 16

SCRIPTURE READINGS (TRANSLATIONS)

625 THE TRIUMPHAL ENTRY

They were now approaching Jerusalem, and when they reached Bethphage and Bethany, at the Mount of Olives, he sent two of his disciples with these instructions:

'Go to the village opposite, and, just as you enter, you will find tethered there a colt which no one has yet ridden. Untie it and bring it here.

'If anyone asks, "Why are you doing that?", say, "Our Master needs it, and will send it back here without delay."'

So they went off, and found the colt tethered at a door outside in the street.

They were untying it when some of the bystanders asked, 'What are you doing, untying that colt?'

They answered as Jesus had told them, and were then allowed to take it.

So they brought the colt to Jesus and spread their cloaks on it, and he mounted.

And people carpeted the road with their cloaks, while others spread brushwood which they had cut in the fields;

And those who went ahead and the others who came behind shouted, 'Hosanna! Blessings on him who comes in the name of the Lord!

'Blessings on the coming kingdom of our father David! Hosanna in the heavens!'

When he entered Jerusalem the whole city went wild with excitement. 'Who is this?' people asked,

And the crowd replied, 'This is the prophet Jesus, from Nazareth in Galilee.' From Mark 11 and Matthew 21

626 THE LAST SUPPER

Now on the first day of Unleavened Bread, when the Passover lambs were being slaughtered, his disciples said to him, 'Where would you like us to go and prepare for your Passover supper?'

So he sent out two of his disciples with these instructions: 'Go into the city, and a man will meet you carrying a jar of water. Follow him, and when he enters a house give this message to the householder: "The Master says, 'Where is the room reserved for me to eat the Passover with my disciples?'"

'He will show you a large room upstairs, set out in readiness. Make the preparations for us there.'

Then the disciples went off, and when they came into the city they found everything just as he had told them. So they prepared for Passover.

In the evening he came to the house with the Twelve. As they sat at supper Jesus said, 'I tell you this: one of you will betray me—one who is eating with me.'

'The Son of Man is going the way appointed for him in the scriptures; but alas for that man by whom the Son of Man is betrayed! It would be better for that man if he had never been born.'

During supper he took bread, and having said the blessing he broke it and gave it to them, with the words: 'Take this; this is my body.'

Then he took a cup, and having offered thanks to God he gave it to them; and they all drank from it.

And he said, 'This is my blood of the covenant, shed for many. I tell you this: never again shall I drink from the fruit of the vine until that day when I drink it new in the kingdom of God.

After singing the Passover Hymn, they went out to the Mount of Olives.
From Mark 14

627 THE SAVIOR'S ADVENT

In those days a decree went out from Caesar Augustus that all the world should be enrolled. And all went to be enrolled, each to his own city.

And Joseph also went up from Galilee, from the city of Nazareth, to Judea, to the city of David, which is called Bethlehem, . . . to be enrolled with Mary, his betrothed, who was with child.

And while they were there, the time came for her to be delivered.

And she gave birth to her first-born son and wrapped him in swaddling clothes, and laid him in a manger, because there was no place for them in the inn.

And in that region there were shepherds out in the field, keeping watch over their flock by night.

And an angel of the Lord appeared to them, and the glory of the Lord shone around them, and they were filled with fear.

And the angel said to them, "Be not afraid; for behold, I bring you good news of a great joy which will come to all the people;

"For to you is born this day in the city of David a Savior, who is Christ the Lord. And this will be a sign for you: you will find a babe wrapped in swaddling clothes and lying in a manger."

And suddenly there was with the angel a multitude of the heavenly host praising God and saying,

"Glory to God in the highest, and on earth peace among men with whom He is pleased!"

When the angels went away from them into heaven, the shepherds said to one another, "Let us go over to Bethlehem and see this thing that has happened, which the Lord has made known to us."

And they went with haste, and found Mary and Joseph, and the babe lying in a manger.
From Luke 2

SCRIPTURE READINGS (TRANSLATIONS)

The child grew big and strong and full of wisdom; and God's favour was upon him.

Now it was the practice of his parents to go to Jerusalem every year for the Passover festival; and when he was twelve, they made the pilgrimage as usual.

When the festive season was over and they started for home, the boy Jesus stayed behind in Jerusalem.

His parents did not know of this; but thinking that he was with the party they journeyed on for a whole day, and only then did they begin looking for him among their friends and relations.

As they could not find him they returned to Jerusalem to look for him; and after three days they found him sitting in the temple surrounded by the teachers, listening to them and putting questions;

And all who heard him were amazed at his intelligence and the answers he gave.

His parents were astonished to see him there, and his mother said to him, 'My son, why have you treated us like this? Your father and I have been searching for you in great anxiety.'

'What made you search?' he said. 'Did you not know that I was bound to be in my Father's house?' But they did not understand what he meant.

Then he went back with them to Nazareth, and continued to be under their authority; his mother treasured up all these things in her heart.

As Jesus grew up he advanced in wisdom and in favour with God and men. From Luke 2

Then a certain teacher of the Law came up and tried to trap Jesus. "Teacher," he asked, "what must I do to receive eternal life?"

Jesus answered him, "What do the Scriptures say? How do you interpret them?"

The man answered: "'You must love the Lord your God with all your heart, and with all your soul, and with all your strength, and with all your mind;' and, 'You must love your neighbor as yourself.'"

"Your answer is correct," replied Jesus; "do this and you will live."

But the teacher of the Law wanted to put himself in the right, so he asked Jesus, "Who is my neighbor?"

Jesus answered: "A certain man was going down from Jerusalem to Jericho, when robbers attacked him, stripped him and beat him up, leaving him half dead.

"It so happened that a priest was going down that road; when he saw the man he walked on by, on the other side.

"In the same way a Levite also came there, went over and looked at the man, and then walked on by, on the other side.

"But a certain Samaritan who was traveling that way came upon him, and when he saw the man his heart was filled with pity.

"He went over to him, poured oil and wine on his wounds and bandaged them; then he put the man on his own animal and took him to an inn, where he took care of him."

And Jesus concluded, "Which one of these three seems to you to have been a neighbor to the man attacked by the robbers?" The teacher of the Law answered, "The one who was kind to him."

Jesus replied, "You go, then, and do the same." From Luke 10

SCRIPTURE READINGS (TRANSLATIONS)

One time Jesus was praying in a certain place. When he finished, one of his disciples said to him, "Lord, teach us to pray, just as John taught his disciples."

Jesus said to them, "This is what you should pray: 'Father, may your name be kept holy, may your Kingdom come. Give us day by day the food we need.

" 'Forgive us our sins, for we forgive everyone who has done us wrong. And do not bring us to hard testing.' "

And Jesus said to his disciples: "Suppose one of you should go to a friend's house at midnight and tell him, 'Friend, let me borrow three loaves of bread. A friend of mine who is on a trip has just come to my house and I don't have a thing to offer him!'

"And suppose your friend should answer from inside, 'Don't bother me! The door is already locked, my children and I are in bed, and I can't get up to give you anything.' Well, what then?

"I tell you, even if he will not get up and give you the bread because he is your friend, yet he will get up and give you everything you need because you are not ashamed to keep on asking.

"And so I say to you: Ask, and you will receive; seek, and you will find; knock, and the door will be opened to you.

"For everyone who asks will receive, and he who seeks will find, and the door will be opened to him who knocks.

"As bad as you are, you know how to give good things to your children. How much more, then, the Father in heaven will give the Holy Spirit to those who ask him!"

"Until now you have not asked for anything in my name; ask and you will receive, so that your happiness may be complete." From Luke 11 and John 16

In the beginning was the Word, and the Word was with God, and the Word was God.

The same was in the beginning with God.

All things were made by him; and without him was not any thing made that was made.

In him was life; and the life was the light of men.

There was a man sent from God, whose name was John.

The same came for a witness, to bear witness of the Light, that all men through him might believe.

He was not that Light, but was sent to bear witness of that Light.

That was the true Light, which lighteth every man that cometh into the world.

He was in the world, and the world was made by him, and the world knew him not.

He came unto his own, and his own received him not.

But as many as received him, to them gave he power to become the sons of God, even to them that believe on his name:

Which were born, not of blood, nor of the will of the flesh, nor of the will of man, but of God.

And the Word was made flesh, and dwelt among us, and we beheld his glory, the glory as of the only begotten of the Father, full of grace and truth.

No man hath seen God at any time; the only begotten Son, which is in the bosom of the Father, he hath declared him. From John 1

SCRIPTURE READINGS (TRANSLATIONS)

As Moses lifted up the serpent in the wilderness, even so must the Son of man be lifted up: That whosoever believeth in him should not perish, but have eternal life.

For God so loved the world, that he gave his only begotten Son, that whosoever believeth in him should not perish, but have everlasting life.

For God sent not his Son into the world to condemn the world; but that the world through him might be saved.

He that believeth on him is not condemned: but he that believeth not is condemned already, because he hath not believed in the name of the only begotten Son of God.

And this is the condemnation, that light is come into the world, and men loved darkness rather than light, because their deeds were evil.

For every one that doeth evil hateth the light, neither cometh to the light, lest his deeds should be reproved.

But he that doeth truth cometh to the light, that his deeds may be made manifest, that they are wrought in God.

He that believeth on the Son hath everlasting life: and he that believeth not the Son shall not see life; but the wrath of God abideth on him.

In this was manifested the love of God toward us, because that God sent his only begotten Son into the world, that we might live through him.

Herein is love, not that we loved God, but that he loved us, and sent his Son to be the propitiation for our sins.

Beloved, if God so loved us, we ought also to love one another.

We love him, because he first loved us. From John 3 and 1 John 4

SCRIPTURE READINGS (TRANSLATIONS)

"Truly, truly, I say to you, he who does not enter the sheepfold by the door but climbs in by another way, that man is a thief and a robber;

"But he who enters by the door is the shepherd of the sheep.

"To him the gatekeeper opens; the sheep hear his voice, and he calls his own sheep by name and leads them out.

"When he has brought out all his own, he goes before them, and the sheep follow him, for they know his voice.

"I am the door; if any one enters by me, he will be saved, and will go in and out and find pasture.

"The thief comes only to steal and kill and destroy; I came that they might have life, and have it abundantly.

"I am the good shepherd. The good shepherd lays down his life for the sheep.

"He who is a hireling and not a shepherd, whose own the sheep are not, sees the wolf coming and leaves the sheep and flees; and the wolf snatches them and scatters them.

"He flees because he is a hireling and cares nothing for the sheep.

"I am the good shepherd; I know my own and my own know me,

"As the Father knows me and I know the Father;

"And I lay down my life for the sheep.

"And I have other sheep, that are not of this fold; I must bring them also, and they will heed my voice. So there shall be one flock, one shepherd.

"My sheep hear my voice, and I know them, and they follow me; and I give them eternal life, and they shall never perish, and no one shall snatch them out of my hand." From John 10

634 CHRISTIAN UNITY

I am the good shepherd; I know my own and my own know me, as the Father knows me and I know the Father; and I lay down my life for the sheep.

And I have other sheep, that are not of this fold; I must bring them also, and they will heed my voice. So there shall be one flock, one shepherd.

When Jesus had spoken these words, he lifted up his eyes to heaven and said, "Father, the hour has come; glorify thy Son that the Son may glorify thee.

"I have manifested thy name to the men whom thou gavest me out of the world; thine they were, and thou gavest them to me, and they have kept thy word.

"And now I am no more in the world, but they are in the world, and I am coming to thee. Holy Father, keep them in thy name, which thou hast given me, that they may be one, even as we are one.

"That they may all be one; even as thou, Father, art in me, and I in thee, that they also may be in us, so that the world may believe that thou hast sent me."

For just as the body is one and has many members, and all the members of the body, though many, are one body, so it is with Christ.

For by one Spirit we were all baptized into one body—Jews or Greeks, slaves or free—and all were made to drink of one Spirit. For the body does not consist of one member but of many.

There is one body and one Spirit, just as you were called to the one hope that belongs to your call,

One Lord, one faith, one baptism, one God and Father of us all, who is above all and through all and in all.
From John 10 and 17, 1 Corinthians 12, Ephesians 4

635 COMFORT FROM CHRIST

"Let not your hearts be troubled; believe in God, believe also in Me.

"In My Father's house are many dwelling places. If this were not so, I would have told you. For I am going away to prepare a place for you.

"And when I have gone and have prepared a place for you, I will come again, and take you to Myself so that where I am, you also will be.

"And where I am going, you know the way."

Thomas remarked to Him, "Lord, we do not know where you are going. How do we know the way?"

Jesus said to him, "I am the Way and the Truth and the Life; no one comes to the Father except through Me.

"Had you recognized Me, you would have known My Father as well. From now on you do know Him; yes, you have seen Him."

Philip said to Him, "Lord, show us the Father and it is enough for us."

Jesus replied, "How long have I been with you without your knowing Me, Philip? He who has looked on Me has seen the Father. What do you mean by saying, 'Show us the Father'?

"Do you not believe that I am in the Father and the Father in Me? The words that I give to you all, I do not speak just from Myself; the Father, who dwells in Me carries on His works.

"Truly I assure you, the one who believes in Me will himself do the deeds I do and do greater things than these, for I go to the Father.

"And I will bring about whatever you ask in My name, so that the Father may be glorified in the Son.

"I will do whatever you may ask in My name, so that the Father may be glorified in the Son.

"If you love Me, keep My commands."
From John 14

636 THE HOLY SPIRIT PROMISED

"Truly, truly, I say to you, he who believes in me will also do the works that I do; and greater works than these will he do, because I go to the Father.

"**Whatever you ask in my name, I will do it, that the Father may be glorified in the Son; if you ask anything in my name, I will do it.**

"If you love me, you will keep my commandments. And I will pray the Father, and he will give you another Counselor, to be with you for ever,

"**Even the Spirit of truth, whom the world cannot receive, because it neither sees him nor knows him; you know him, for he dwells with you, and will be in you.**"

"But because I have said these things to you, sorrow has filled your hearts. Nevertheless I tell you the truth: it is to your advantage that I go away,

"**For if I do not go away, the Counselor will not come to you; but if I go, I will send him to you.**"

"I have yet many things to say to you, but you cannot bear them now. When the Spirit of truth comes, he will guide you into all the truth;

"**For he will not speak on his own authority; but whatever he hears he will speak, and he will declare to you the things that are to come. He will glorify me, for he will take what is mine and declare it to you.**"

"These things I have spoken to you, while I am still with you. But the Counselor, the Holy Spirit, whom the Father will send in my name, he will teach you all things, and bring to your remembrance all that I have said to you.

"**Peace I leave with you; my peace I give to you; not as the world gives do I give to you. Let not your hearts be troubled, neither let them be afraid.**" From John 14 and 16

637 THE VINE AND BRANCHES

"I am the true vine, and my Father is the vinedresser. Every branch of mine that bears no fruit, he takes away, and every branch that does bear fruit he prunes, that it may bear more fruit.

"**You are already made clean by the word which I have spoken to you. Abide in me, and I in you. As the branch cannot bear fruit by itself, unless it abides in the vine, neither can you, unless you abide in me.**

"I am the vine, you are the branches. He who abides in me, and I in him, he it is that bears much fruit, for apart from me you can do nothing.

"**If a man does not abide in me, he is cast forth as a branch and withers; and the branches are gathered, thrown into the fire and burned.**

"If you abide in me, and my words abide in you, ask whatever you will, and it shall be done for you.

"**By this my Father is glorified, that you bear much fruit, and so prove to be my disciples.**

"As the Father has loved me, so have I loved you; abide in my love.

"**If you keep my commandments, you will abide in my love, just as I have kept my Father's commandments and abide in his love.**

"These things I have spoken to you, that my joy may be in you, and that your joy may be full.

"**This is my commandment, that you love one another as I have loved you.**

"Greater love has no man than this, that a man lay down his life for his friends. You are my friends if you do what I command you.

"**You did not choose me, but I chose you and appointed you that you should go and bear fruit and that your fruit should abide: so that whatever you ask the Father in my name, he may give it to you.**" From John 15

Then Pilate handed Jesus over to them to be nailed to the cross. So they took charge of Jesus.

He went out, carrying his own cross, and came to "The Place of the Skull," as it is called. (In Hebrew it is called "Golgotha.")

There they nailed him to the cross; they also nailed two other men to crosses, one on each side, with Jesus between them.

Pilate wrote a notice and had it put on the cross. "Jesus of Nazareth, the King of the Jews," is what he wrote.

After the soldiers had nailed Jesus to the cross, they took his clothes and divided them into four parts, one part for each soldier.

They also took the robe, which was made of one piece of woven cloth, without any seams in it.

The soldiers said to each other, "Let us not tear it; let us throw dice to see who will get it."

This happened to make the scripture come true: "They divided my clothes among themselves, they gambled for my robe."

Standing close to Jesus' cross were his mother, his mother's sister, Mary the wife of Clopas, and Mary Magdalene. Jesus saw his mother, and the disciple he loved standing there; so he said to his mother, "Woman, here is your son."

Then he said to the disciple, "Here is your mother." And from that time the disciple took her to live in his home.

Jesus knew that by now everything had been completed; and in order to make the scripture come true he said, "I am thirsty." They soaked a sponge in the wine, put it on a branch of hyssop, and lifted it up to his lips.

Jesus took the wine and said, "It is finished!" Then he bowed his head and died. From John 19

When the day of Pentecost had come, they were all together in one place.

And suddenly a sound came from heaven like the rush of a mighty wind, and it filled all the house where they were sitting.

And there appeared to them tongues as of fire, distributed and resting on each one of them.

And they were all filled with the Holy Spirit and began to speak in other tongues, as the Spirit gave them utterance.

Now there were dwelling in Jerusalem Jews, devout men from every nation under heaven.

And all were amazed and perplexed, saying to one another, "What does this mean?" But others mocking said, "They are filled with new wine."

But Peter, standing with the eleven, lifted up his voice and addressed them, "Men of Judea and all who dwell in Jerusalem, let this be known to you, and give ear to my words.

"For these men are not drunk, as you suppose, since it is only the third hour of the day;

"But this is what was spoken by the prophet Joel: 'And in the last days it shall be, God declares, that I will pour out my Spirit upon all flesh.

" 'And your sons and your daughters shall prophesy, and your young men shall see visions, and your old men shall dream dreams:

" 'Yea, and on my menservants and my maidservants in those days I will pour out my Spirit; and they shall prophesy.

" 'And it shall be that whoever calls on the name of the Lord shall be saved.' " From Acts 2

SCRIPTURE READINGS (TRANSLATIONS)

Therefore, since we are justified by faith, we have peace with God through our Lord Jesus Christ.

Through him we have obtained access to this grace in which we stand, and we rejoice in our hope of sharing the glory of God.

More than that, we rejoice in our sufferings, knowing that suffering produces endurance, and endurance produces character, and character produces hope,

And hope does not disappoint us, because God's love has been poured into our hearts through the Holy Spirit which has been given to us.

While we were yet helpless, at the right time Christ died for the ungodly.

Why, one will hardly die for a righteous man—though perhaps for a good man one will dare even to die. But God shows his love for us in that while we were yet sinners Christ died for us.

Since, therefore, we are now justified by his blood, much more shall we be saved by him from the wrath of God.

For if while we were enemies we were reconciled to God by the death of his Son, much more, now that we are reconciled, shall we be saved by his life.

Then as one man's trespass led to condemnation for all men, so one man's act of righteousness leads to acquittal and life for all men.

For as by one man's disobedience many were made sinners, so by one man's obedience many will be made righteous.

Law came in, to increase the trespass; but where sin increased, grace abounded all the more,

So that, as sin reigned in death, grace also might reign through righteousness to eternal life through Jesus Christ our Lord. From Romans 5

For all who are led by the Spirit of God are sons of God.

For you did not receive the spirit of slavery to fall back into fear, but you have received the spirit of sonship.

When we cry, "Abba! Father!" it is the Spirit himself bearing witness with our spirit that we are children of God,

And if children, then heirs, heirs of God and fellow heirs with Christ, provided we suffer with him in order that we may also be glorified with him.

I consider that the sufferings of this present time are not worth comparing with the glory that is to be revealed to us.

We know that in everything God works for good with those who love him, who are called according to his purpose.

What, then shall we say to this? If God is for us, who is against us?

He who did not spare his own Son but gave him up for us all, will he not also give us all things with him?

Who shall separate us from the love of Christ? Shall tribulation, or distress, or persecution, or famine, or nakedness, or peril, or sword?

No, in all these things we are more than conquerors through him who loved us.

For I am sure that neither death, nor life, nor angels, nor principalities, nor things present, nor things to come, nor powers,

Nor height, nor depth, nor anything else in all creation, will be able to separate us from the love of God in Christ Jesus our Lord. From Romans 8

642 CALL TO CONSECRATION

So then, my brothers, because of God's many mercies to us, I make this appeal to you: Offer yourselves as a living sacrifice to God, dedicated to his service and pleasing to him. This is the true worship that you should offer.

Do not conform outwardly to the standards of this world, but let God transform you inwardly by a complete change of your mind. Then you will be able to know the will of God—what is good, and is pleasing to him, and is perfect.

Love must be completely sincere. Hate what is evil, hold on to what is good.

Love one another warmly as brothers in Christ, and be eager to show respect for one another.

Work hard, and do not be lazy. Serve the Lord with a heart full of devotion.

Let your hope keep you joyful, be patient in your troubles, and pray at all times.

Share your belongings with your needy brothers, and open your home to strangers.

Ask God to bless those who persecute you; yes, ask him to bless, not to curse.

Rejoice with those who rejoice, weep with those who weep.

Show the same spirit toward all alike. Do not be proud, but accept humble duties. Do not think of yourselves as wise.

If someone does evil to you, do not pay him back with evil. Try to do what all men consider to be good.

Do everything possible, on your part, to live at peace with all men. Do not let evil defeat you; instead, conquer evil with good. From Romans 12

643 CHRISTIAN LOVE

If I could speak the languages of men, of angels too, and have no love, I am only a rattling pan or a clashing cymbal.

If I should have the gift of prophecy, and know all secret truths, and knowledge in its every form, and have such perfect faith that I could move mountains, but have no love, I am nothing.

If I should dole out everything I have for charity, and give my body up to torture in mere boasting pride, but have no love, I get from it no good at all.

Love is so patient and so kind;

Love never boils with jealousy;

It never boasts, is never puffed with pride; It does not act with rudeness, or insist upon its rights;

It never gets provoked, it never harbors evil thoughts;

Is never glad when wrong is done, but always glad when truth prevails;

It bears up under anything;

It exercises faith in everything,

It keeps up hope in everything,

It gives us power to endure in anything.

Love never fails; If there are prophecies, they will be set aside; If now exist ecstatic speakings, they will cease; If there is knowledge, it will soon be set aside; For what we know is incomplete and what we prophesy is incomplete.

And so these three, faith, hope and love endure, but the greatest of them is love. From 1 Corinthians 13

SCRIPTURE READINGS (TRANSLATIONS)

644 CHRIST AND IMMORTALITY

For I delivered to you as of first importance what I also received, that Christ died for our sins in accordance with the scriptures,

That he was buried, that he was raised on the third day in accordance with the scriptures.

Now if Christ is preached as raised from the dead, how can some of you say that there is no resurrection of the dead?

But if there is no resurrection of the dead, then Christ has not been raised; if Christ has not been raised, then our preaching is in vain and your faith is in vain.

But in fact Christ has been raised from the dead, the first fruits of those who have fallen asleep.

For as by a man came death, by a man has come also the resurrection of the dead.

Lo! I tell you a mystery. We shall not all sleep, but we shall all be changed, in a moment, in the twinkling of an eye, at the last trumpet.

For the trumpet will sound, and the dead will be raised imperishable, and we shall be changed.

For this perishable nature must put on the imperishable, and this mortal nature must put on immortality.

When the perishable puts on the imperishable, and the mortal puts on immortality, then shall come to pass the saying that is written: "Death is swallowed up in victory."

"O death, where is thy victory? O death, where is thy sting?"

The sting of death is sin, and the power of sin is the law. But thanks be to God, who gives us the victory through our Lord Jesus Christ.
From 1 Corinthians 15

SCRIPTURE READINGS (TRANSLATIONS)

645 CHRISTIAN CONDUCT

What human nature does is quite plain. It shows itself in immoral, filthy, and indecent actions; in worship of idols and witchcraft.

People become enemies, they fight, become jealous, angry, and ambitious.

They separate into parties and groups; they are envious, get drunk, have orgies, and do other things like these.

I warn you now as I have before: those who do these things will not receive the Kingdom of God.

But the Spirit produces love, joy, peace, patience, kindness, goodness, faithfulness, humility, and self-control. There is no law against such things as these.

And those who belong to Christ Jesus have put to death their human nature, with all its passions and desires.

My brothers, if someone is caught in any kind of wrongdoing, those of you who are spiritual should set him right; but you must do it in a gentle way.

And keep an eye on yourself, so that you will not be tempted, too. Help carry one another's burdens, and in this way you will obey the law of Christ.

Do not deceive yourselves: no one makes a fool of God. A man will reap exactly what he plants.

If he plants in the field of his natural desires, from it he will gather the harvest of death; if he plants in the field of the Spirit, from the Spirit he will gather the harvest of eternal life.

So let us not become tired of doing good; for if we do not give up, the time will come when we will reap the harvest.
From Galatians 5 and 6

Finally, be strong in the Lord and in the strength of his might.

Put on the whole armor of God, that you may be able to stand against the wiles of the devil.

For we are not contending against flesh and blood, but against the principalities, against the powers, against the world rulers of this present darkness, against the spiritual hosts of wickedness in the heavenly places.

Therefore take the whole armor of God, that you may be able to withstand in the evil day, and having done all, to stand.

Stand therefore, having girded your loins with truth, and having put on the breastplate of righteousness, and having shod your feet with the equipment of the gospel of peace;

Above all taking the shield of faith, with which you can quench all the flaming darts of the evil one.

And take the helmet of salvation, and the sword of the Spirit, which is the word of God.

Pray at all times in the Spirit, with all prayer and supplication.

For though we live in the world we are not carrying on a worldly war, for the weapons of our warfare are not worldly, but have divine power to destroy strongholds.

We destroy arguments and every proud obstacle to the knowledge of God, and take every thought captive to obey Christ.

I have fought the good fight, I have finished the race, I have kept the faith.

Henceforth there is laid up for me the crown of righteousness, which the Lord, the righteous judge, will award to me on that Day, and not only to me but also to all who have loved his appearing.

From Ephesians 6, 2 Corinthians 10, and 2 Timothy 4

Brothers, we want you to know the truth about those who have died, so that you will not be sad, as are those who have no hope.

We believe that Jesus died and rose again; so we believe that God will bring with Jesus those who have died believing in him.

For this is the Lord's teaching we tell you: we who are alive on the day the Lord comes will not go ahead of those who have died.

There will be the shout of command, the archangel's voice, the sound of God's trumpet, and the Lord himself will come down from heaven!

Those who have died believing in Christ will be raised to life first; then we who are living at that time will all be gathered up along with them in the clouds to meet the Lord in the air. And so we will always be with the Lord.

Therefore, cheer each other up with these words.

There is no need to write you, brothers, about the times and occasions when these things will happen. For you yourselves know very well that the Day of the Lord will come like a thief comes at night.

When people say, "Everything is quiet and safe," then suddenly destruction will hit them! They will not escape.

But you, brothers, are not in the darkness, and the Day should not take you by surprise like a thief.

All of you are people who belong to the light, who belong to the day.

God did not choose us to suffer his wrath, but to possess salvation through our Lord Jesus Christ,

Who died for us in order that we might live together with him, whether we are alive or dead when he comes.

From 1 Thessalonians 4 and 5

Now faith is the assurance of things hoped for, the conviction of things not seen. For by it the men of old received divine approval.

By faith Noah, being warned by God concerning events as yet unseen, took heed and constructed an ark for the saving of his household.

By faith Abraham obeyed when he was called to go out to a place which he was to receive as an inheritance; and he went out, not knowing where he was to go.

By faith Moses, when he was grown up, refused to be called the son of Pharaoh's daughter, choosing rather to share ill-treatment with the people of God than to enjoy the fleeting pleasures of sin.

And what more shall I say? For time would fail me to tell of Gideon, Barak, Samson, Jephthah, of David and Samuel and the prophets—

Who through faith conquered kingdoms, enforced justice, received promises, stopped the mouths of lions, quenched raging fire, escaped the edge of the sword.

Others suffered mocking and scourging, and even chains and imprisonment.

They were stoned, they were sawn in two, they were killed with the sword; they went about in skins of sheep and goats, destitute, afflicted, ill-treated— of whom the world was not worthy.

Therefore, since we are surrounded by so great a cloud of witnesses, let us also lay aside every weight, and sin which clings so closely,

And let us run with perseverance the race that is set before us, looking to Jesus the pioneer and perfecter of our faith. From Hebrews 11 and 12

SCRIPTURE READINGS (TRANSLATIONS)

"My son, do not regard lightly the discipline of the Lord, nor lose courage when you are punished by him.

"For the Lord disciplines him whom he loves, and chastises every son whom he receives."

It is for discipline that you have to endure. God is treating you as sons; for what son is there whom his father does not discipline?

If you are left without discipline, in which all have participated, then you are illegitimate children and not sons.

Besides this, we have had earthly fathers to discipline us and we respected them. Shall we not much more be subject to the Father of spirits and live?

For they disciplined us for a short time at their pleasure, but he disciplines us for our good, that we may share his holiness.

For the moment all discipline seems painful rather than pleasant;

Later it yields the peaceful fruit of righteousness to those who have been trained by it.

Therefore lift your drooping hands and strengthen your weak knees, and make straight paths for your feet, so that what is lame may not be put out of joint but rather be healed.

Strive for peace with all men, and for the holiness without which no one will see the Lord.

"Behold, happy is the man whom God reproves; therefore despise not the chastening of the Almighty.

"For he wounds, but he binds up; he smites, but his hands heal."

For this slight momentary affliction is preparing for us an eternal weight of glory beyond all comparison,

Because we look not to the things that are seen but to the things that are unseen; for the things that are seen are transient, but the things that are unseen are eternal. From Hebrews 12, Job 5, 2 Corinthians 4

Count it all joy, my brethren, when you meet various trials, for you know that the testing of your faith produces steadfastness.

And let steadfastness have its full effect, that you may be perfect and complete, lacking in nothing.

Blessed is the man who endures trial, for when he has stood the test he will receive the crown of life which God has promised to those who love him.

Let no one say when he is tempted, "I am tempted by God"; for God cannot be tempted with evil and he himself tempts no one;

But each person is tempted when he is lured and enticed by his own desire.

Then desire when it has conceived gives birth to sin; and sin when it is full-grown brings forth death.

Blessed be the God and Father of our Lord Jesus Christ! By his great mercy we have been born anew to a living hope through the resurrection of Jesus Christ from the dead,

And to an inheritance which is imperishable, undefiled and unfading, kept in heaven for you, who by God's power are guarded through faith for a salvation ready to be revealed in the last time.

In this you rejoice, though now for a little while you may have to suffer various trials, so that the genuineness of your faith, more precious than gold which though perishable is tested by fire, may redound to praise and glory and honor at the revelation of Jesus Christ.

Without having seen him you love him; though you do not now see him you believe in him and rejoice with unutterable and exalted joy. As the outcome of your faith you obtain the salvation of your souls.
From James 1 and 1 Peter 1

First of all you must understand this, that no prophecy of scripture is a matter of one's own interpretation,

Because no prophecy ever came by the impulse of man, but men moved by the Holy Spirit spoke from God.

All scripture is inspired by God and profitable for teaching, for reproof, for correction, and for training in righteousness,

That the man of God may be complete, equipped for every good work.

For the word of God is living and active, sharper than any two edged-sword, piercing to the division of soul and spirit, of joints and marrow, and discerning the thoughts and intentions of the heart.

For whatever was written in former days was written for our instruction, that by steadfastness and by the encouragement of the scriptures we might have hope.

I have laid up thy word in my heart, that I might not sin against thee.

Open my eyes, that I may behold wondrous things out of thy law.

Teach me, O Lord, the way of thy statutes; and I will keep it to the end.

Give me understanding, that I may keep thy law and observe it with my whole heart.

Thy word is a lamp to my feet and a light to my path.

The unfolding of thy words gives light; it imparts understanding to the simple.

Great peace have those who love thy law; nothing can make them stumble.

The grass withers, the flower fades; but the word of our God will stand for ever.
From 2 Peter 1, 2 Timothy 3, Hebrews 4, Romans 15, Psalm 119, Isaiah 40

SCRIPTURE READINGS (TRANSLATIONS)

I want to remind you that in the last days there will come scoffers who will do every wrong they can think of, and laugh at the truth.

This will be their line of argument: "So Jesus promised to come back, did he? Then where is he? He'll never come! Why, as far back as anyone can remember everything has remained exactly as it was since the first day of creation."

They deliberately forget this fact: That God did destroy the world with a mighty flood, long after he had made the heavens by the word of his command, and had used the waters to form the earth and surround it.

And God has commanded that the earth and the heavens be stored away for a great bonfire at the judgment day, when all ungodly men will perish.

The day of the Lord is surely coming, as unexpectedly as a thief, and then the heavens will pass away with a terrible noise and the heavenly bodies will disappear in fire, and the earth and everything on it will be burned up.

And so since everything around us is going to melt away, what holy, godly lives we should be living!

You should look forward to that day and hurry it along—the day when God will set the heavens on fire, and the heavenly bodies will melt and disappear in flames.

But we are looking forward to God's promise of new heavens and a new earth afterwards, where there will be only goodness.

Dear friends, while you are waiting for these things to happen and for him to come, try hard to live without sinning; and be at peace with everyone so that he will be pleased with you when he returns.

And remember why he is waiting. He is giving us time to get his message of salvation out to others.

2 Peter 3

SCRIPTURE READINGS (TRANSLATIONS)

"A new commandment I give to you, that you love one another; even as I have loved you, that you also love one another.

"By this all men will know that you are my disciples, if you have love for one another."

He who says he is in the light and hates his brother is in the darkness still. He who loves his brother abides in the light, and in it there is no cause for stumbling.

But he who hates his brother is in the darkness and walks in the darkness, and does not know where he is going, because the darkness has blinded his eyes.

See what love the Father has given us, that we should be called children of God; and so we are.

The reason why the world does not know us is that it did not know him.

Beloved, we are God's children now; it does not yet appear what we shall be, but we know that when he appears we shall be like him, for we shall see him as he is.

And every one who thus hopes in him purifies himself as he is pure.

We know that we have passed out of death into life, because we love the brethren. He who does not love remains in death.

By this we know love, that he laid down his life for us; and we ought to lay down our lives for the brethren.

But if any one has the world's goods and sees his brother in need, yet closes his heart against him, how does God's love abide in him?

Little children, let us not love in word or speech but in deed and in truth.

From John 13, 1 John 1 and 3

654 THE HOLY CITY

And I saw a new heaven and a new earth: for the first heaven and the first earth were passed away; and there was no more sea.

And I John saw the holy city, new Jerusalem, coming down from God out of heaven, prepared as a bride adorned for her husband.

Having the glory of God: and her light was like unto a stone most precious, even like a jasper stone, clear as crystal;

And had a wall great and high, and had twelve gates, and at the gates twelve angels, and names written thereon, which are the names of the twelve tribes of the children of Israel.

And the wall of the city had twelve foundations, and in them the names of the twelve apostles of the Lamb.

And the building of the wall of it was of jasper: and the city was pure gold, like unto clear glass.

And I saw no temple therein: for the Lord God Almighty and the Lamb are the temple of it.

And the city had no need of the sun, neither of the moon, to shine in it: for the glory of God did lighten it, and the Lamb is the light thereof.

And the nations of them which are saved shall walk in the light of it: and the kings of the earth do bring their glory and honour into it.

And the gates of it shall not be shut at all by day: for there shall be no night there.

And they shall bring the glory and honour of the nations into it. And there shall in no wise enter into it any thing that defileth,

Neither whatsoever worketh abomination, or maketh a lie: but they which are written in the Lamb's book of life.
From Revelation 21

655 THE FINAL WORD

I John am he who heard and saw these things. And when I heard and saw them, I fell down to worship at the feet of the angel who showed them to me;

But he said to me, "You must not do that! I am a fellow servant with you and your brethren the prophets, and with those who keep the words of this book. Worship God."

And he said to me, "Do not seal up the words of the prophecy of this book, for the time is near.

"Let the evildoer still do evil, and the filthy still be filthy, and the righteous still do right, and the holy still be holy.

"Behold, I am coming soon, bringing my recompense, to repay every one for what he has done.

"I am the Alpha and the Omega, the first and the last, the beginning and the end."

Blessed are those who wash their robes, that they may have the right to the tree of life and that they may enter the city by the gates.

The Spirit and the Bride say, "Come." And let him who hears say, "Come." And let him who is thirsty come, let him who desires take the water of life without price.

I warn every one who hears the words of the prophecy of this book: if any one adds to them, God will add to him the plagues described in this book,

And if any one takes away from the words of the book of this prophecy, God will take away his share in the tree of life and in the holy city, which are described in this book.

He who testifies to these things says, "Surely I am coming soon."

Amen. Come, Lord Jesus!
From Revelation 22

SCRIPTURE READINGS (TRANSLATIONS)

SCRIPTURE READINGS (Paraphrases)

Indexes to the Scripture Readings will be found on pages 548 through 550.

656 LIVING PSALMS

Oh, the joys of those who do not follow evil men's advice, who do not hang around with sinners, scoffing at the things of God:

But they delight in doing everything God wants them to, and day and night are always meditating on his laws and thinking about ways to follow him more closely.

They are like trees along a river bank bearing luscious fruit each season without fail. Their leaves shall never wither, and all they do shall prosper.

But for sinners, what a different story! They blow away like chaff before the wind.

They are not safe on Judgment Day; they shall not stand among the godly.

For the Lord watches over all the plans and paths of godly men, but the paths of the godless lead to doom.
Psalm 1

*　　*　　*

Because the Lord is my Shepherd, I have everything I need!

He lets me rest in the meadow grass and leads me beside the quiet streams.

He restores my failing health. He helps me do what honors him the most.

Even when walking through the dark valley of death I will not be afraid, for you are close beside me, guarding, guiding all the way.

You provide delicious food for me in the presence of my enemies. You have welcomed me as your guest; blessings overflow!

Your goodness and unfailing kindness shall be with me all of my life, and afterwards I will live with you forever in your home.
Psalm 23

SCRIPTURE READINGS (PARAPHRASES)

657 GODLY WOMANHOOD

If you can find a truly good wife, she is worth more than precious gems.

Her husband can trust her, and she will richly satisfy his needs. She will not hinder him, but help him all his life.

She finds wool and flax and busily spins it. She buys imported foods, brought by ship from distant ports.

She gets up before dawn to prepare breakfast for her household, and plans the day's work for her servant girls.

She goes out to inspect a field, and buys it; with her own hands she plants a vineyard. She is energetic, a hard worker, and watches for bargains. She works far into the night!

She sews for the poor, and generously gives to the needy. She has no fear of winter for her household, for she has made warm clothes for all of them.

Her husband is well known, for he sits in the council chamber with the other civic leaders.

She is a woman of strength and dignity, and has no fear of old age.

When she speaks, her words are wise, and kindness is the rule for everything she says.

She watches carefully all that goes on throughout her household, and is never lazy.

Her children stand and bless her; so does her husband. He praises her with these words: "There are many fine women in the world, but you are the best of them all."

Charm can be deceptive and beauty doesn't last, but a woman who fears and reverences God shall be greatly praised.
From Proverbs 31

658 CHALLENGE TO YOUTH

Don't let the excitement of being young cause you to forget about your Creator. Honor him in your youth before the evil days come—when you'll no longer enjoy living.

It will be too late then to try to remember him, when the sun and light and moon and stars are dim to your old eyes, and there is no silver lining left among your clouds.

For there will come a time when your limbs will tremble with age, and your strong legs will become weak, and your teeth will be too few to do their work, and there will be blindness too.

And you will waken at dawn with the first note of the birds; but you yourself will be deaf and tuneless, with quavering voice.

You will be afraid of heights and of falling—a white-haired, withered old man, dragging himself along: without sexual desire, standing at death's door, and nearing his everlasting home.

Yes, remember your Creator now while you are young, before the silver cord of life snaps, and the golden bowl is broken, and the pitcher is broken at the fountain, and the wheel is broken at the cistern; and the dust returns to the earth as it was, and the spirit returns to God who gave it.

The wise man's words are like goads that spur to action. They nail down important truths. Students are wise who master what their teachers tell them.

But, my son, be warned: there is no end of opinions ready to be expressed. Studying them can go on forever, and become very exhausting!

Here is my final conclusion: fear God and obey his commandments, for this is the entire duty of man.

For God will judge us for everything we do, including every hidden thing, good or bad. From Ecclesiastes 12

659 FIRST THINGS FIRST

"You cannot serve two masters: God and money. For you will hate one and love the other, or else the other way around.

"So my counsel is: Don't worry about things—food, drink, and clothes. For you already have life and a body—and they are far more important than what to eat and wear.

"Look at the birds! They don't worry about what to eat—they don't need to sow or reap or store up food—for your heavenly Father feeds them. And you are far more valuable to him than they are.

"Will all your worries add a single moment to your life?

"And why worry about your clothes? Look at the field lilies! They don't worry about theirs. Yet King Solomon in all his glory was not clothed as beautifully as they.

"And if God cares so wonderfully for flowers that are here today and gone tomorrow, won't he more surely care for you, O men of little faith?

"So don't worry at all about having enough food and clothing. Why be like the heathen? For they take pride in all these things and are deeply concerned about them.

"But your heavenly Father already knows perfectly well that you need them, and he will give them to you if you give him first place in your life and live as he wants you to.

"So don't be anxious about tomorrow. God will take care of your tomorrow too.

"Live one day at a time."

"For anyone who keeps his life for himself shall lose it; and anyone who loses his life for me shall find it again.

"What profit is there if you gain the whole world—and lose eternal life? What can be compared with the value of eternal life?" From Matthew 6 and 16

SCRIPTURE READINGS (PARAPHRASES)

"Listen, all of you. Love your enemies. Do good to those who hate you.

"Pray for the happiness of those who curse you; implore God's blessing on those who hurt you.

"If someone slaps you on one cheek, let him slap the other too! If someone demands your coat, give him your shirt besides.

"Give what you have to anyone who asks you for it; and when things are taken away from you, don't worry about getting them back. Treat others as you want them to treat you.

"Do you think you deserve credit for merely loving those who love you? Even the godless do that! And if you do good only to those who do you good—is that so wonderful? Even sinners do that much!

"And if you lend money only to those who can repay you, what good is that? Even the most wicked will lend to their own kind for full return!

"Love your enemies! Do good to them! Lend to them! And don't be concerned about the fact that they won't repay.

"Then your reward from heaven will be very great, and you will truly be acting as sons of God: for he is kind to the unthankful and to those who are very wicked.

"Try to show as much compassion as your Father does. Never criticize or condemn—or it will all come back on you.

"Go easy on others; then they will do the same for you. For if you give, you will get!

"Your gift will return to you in full and overflowing measure, pressed down, shaken together to make room for more, and running over.

"Whatever measure you use to give—large or small—will be used to measure what is given back to you."

From Luke 6

SCRIPTURE READINGS (PARAPHRASES)

"Men of Athens, I notice that you are very religious, for as I was out walking I saw your many altars, and one of them had this inscription on it—'To the Unknown God.'

"You have been worshiping him without knowing who he is, and now I wish to tell you about him.

"He made the world and everything in it, and since he is Lord of heaven and earth, he doesn't live in man-made temples; and human hands can't minister to his needs—for he has no needs!

"He himself gives life and breath to everything, and satisfies every need there is.

"He created all the people of the world from one man, Adam, and scattered the nations across the face of the earth.

"He decided beforehand which should rise and fall, and when. He determined their boundaries.

"His purpose in all of this is that they should seek after God, and perhaps feel their way toward him and find him—though he is not far from any one of us.

"For in him we live and move and are! As one of your own poets says it, 'We are the sons of God.' If this is true, we shouldn't think of God as an idol made by men from gold or silver or chipped from stone.

"God tolerated man's past ignorance about these things, but now he commands everyone to put away idols and worship only him.

"For he has set a day for justly judging the world by the man he has appointed, and has pointed him out by bringing him back to life again."

From Acts 17

The Ten Commandments were given so that all could see the extent of their failure to obey God's laws. But the more we see our sinfulness, the more we see God's abounding grace forgiving us.

Well then, shall we keep on sinning so that God can keep on showing us more and more kindness and forgiveness?

Of course not! Should we keep on sinning when we don't have to? For sin's power over us was broken when we became Christians and were baptized to become a part of Jesus Christ;

Your old sin-loving nature was buried with him by baptism when he died, and when God the Father, with glorious power, brought him back to life again, you were given his wonderful new life to enjoy.

For you have become a part of him, and so you died with him, so to speak, when he died; and now you share his new life, and shall rise as he did.

Your old evil desires were nailed to the cross with him; that part of you that loves to sin was crushed and fatally wounded, so that your sin-loving body is no longer under sin's control, no longer needs to be a slave to sin;

For when you are deadened to sin you are freed from all its allure and its power over you.

And since your old sin-loving nature "died" with Christ, we know that you will share his new life.

Christ rose from the dead and will never die again. Death no longer has any power over him. He died once for all to end sin's power, but now he lives forever in unbroken fellowship with God.

So look upon your old sin nature as dead and unresponsive to sin, and instead be alive to God, alert to him, through Jesus Christ our Lord.

From Romans 5 and 6

For this is what the Lord himself has said about his Table, and I have passed it on to you before: That on the night when Judas betrayed him, the Lord Jesus took bread,

And when he had given thanks to God for it, he broke it and gave it to his disciples and said, "Take this and eat it. This is my body, which is given for you. Do this to remember me."

In the same way, he took the cup of wine after supper, saying, "This cup is the new agreement between God and you that has been established and set in motion by my blood. Do this in remembrance of me whenever you drink it."

For every time you eat this bread and drink this cup you are retelling the message of the Lord's death, that he has died for you. Do this until he comes again.

So if anyone eats this bread and drinks from this cup of the Lord in an unworthy manner, he is guilty of sin against the body and the blood of the Lord.

That is why a man should examine himself carefully before eating the bread and drinking from the cup.

For if he eats the bread and drinks from the cup unworthily, not thinking about the body of Christ and what it means, he is eating and drinking God's judgment upon himself; for he is trifling with the death of Christ.

That is why many of you are weak and sick, and some have even died.

But if you carefully examine yourselves before eating you will not need to be judged and punished.

Yet, when we are judged and punished by the Lord, it is so that we will not be condemned with the rest of the world.

From 1 Corinthians 11

SCRIPTURE READINGS (PARAPHRASES)

And now, brothers, I want to write about the special abilities the Holy Spirit gives to each of you; for I don't want any misunderstanding about them.

Now God gives us many kinds of special abilities, but it is the same Holy Spirit who is the source of them all.

There are different kinds of service to God, but it is the same Lord we are serving.

There are many ways in which God works in our lives, but it is the same God who does the work in and through all of us who are his.

The Holy Spirit displays God's power through each of us as a means of helping the entire church.

To one person the Spirit gives the ability to give wise advice; someone else may be especially good at studying and teaching, and this is his gift from the same Spirit.

He gives special faith to another, and to someone else the power to heal the sick.

He gives power for doing miracles to some, and to others power to prophesy and preach.

He gives someone else the power to know whether evil spirits are speaking through those who claim to be giving God's messages—or whether it is really the Spirit of God who is speaking.

Still another person is able to speak in languages he never learned; and others, who do not know the language either, are given power to understand what he is saying.

It is the same and only Holy Spirit who gives all these gifts and powers, deciding which each one of us should have.

All of you together are the one body of Christ and each one of you is a separate and necessary part of it.

From 1 Corinthians 12

SCRIPTURE READINGS (PARAPHRASES)

If I had the gift of being able to speak in other languages without learning them, and could speak in every language there is in all of heaven and earth, but didn't love others, I would only be making noise.

If I had the gift of prophecy and knew all about what is going to happen in the future, knew everything about everything, but didn't love others, what good would it do?

Even if I had the gift of faith so that I could speak to a mountain and make it move, I would still be worth nothing at all without love.

If I gave everything I have to poor people, and if I were burned alive for preaching the Gospel but didn't love others, it would be of no value whatever.

Love is very patient and kind, never jealous or envious, never boastful or proud, never haughty or selfish or rude.

Love does not demand its own way. It is not irritable or touchy.

It does not hold grudges and will hardly even notice when others do it wrong.

It is never glad about injustice, but rejoices whenever truth wins out.

If you love someone you will be loyal to him no matter what the cost.

You will always believe in him, always expect the best of him, and always stand your ground in defending him.

All the special gifts and powers from God will someday come to an end, but love goes on forever.

There are three things that remain—faith, hope, and love—and the greatest of these is love.

From 1 Corinthians 13

Dear Brothers, if a Christian is overcome by some sin, you who are godly should gently and humbly help him back onto the right path, remembering that next time it might be one of you who is in the wrong.

Share each other's troubles and problems, and so obey our Lord's command. If anyone thinks he is too great to stoop to this, he is fooling himself. He is really a nobody.

Let everyone be sure that he is doing his very best, for then he will have the personal satisfaction of work well done, and won't need to compare himself with someone else.

Each of us must bear some faults and burdens of his own. For none of us is perfect!

Those who are taught the Word of God should help their teachers by paying them.

Don't be misled; remember that you can't ignore God and get away with it: a man will always reap just the kind of crop he sows!

If he sows to please his own wrong desires, he will be planting seeds of evil and he will surely reap a harvest of spiritual decay and death;

But if he plants the good things of the Spirit, he will reap the everlasting life which the Holy Spirit gives him.

And let us not get tired of doing what is right, for after a while we will reap a harvest of blessing if we don't get discouraged and give up.

That's why whenever we can we should always be kind to everyone, and especially to our Christian brothers.

As for me, God forbid that I should boast about anything except the cross of our Lord Jesus Christ.

Dear brothers, may the grace of our Lord Jesus Christ be with you all.

From Galatians 6

Is there any such thing as Christians cheering each other up? Do you love me enough to want to help me?

Does it mean anything to you that we are brothers in the Lord, sharing the same Spirit? Are your hearts tender and sympathetic at all?

Then make me truly happy by loving each other and agreeing wholeheartedly with each other, working together with one heart and mind and purpose.

Don't be selfish; don't live to make a good impression on others. Be humble, thinking of others as better than yourself.

Don't just think about your own affairs, but be interested in others, too, and in what they are doing.

Your attitude should be the kind that was shown us by Jesus Christ, who, though he was God, did not demand and cling to his rights as God, but laid aside his mighty power and glory, taking the disguise of a slave and becoming like men.

And he humbled himself even further, going so far as actually to die a criminal's death on a cross.

Yet it was because of this that God raised him up to the heights of heaven and gave him a name which is above every other name,

That at the name of Jesus every knee shall bow in heaven and on earth and under the earth,

And every tongue shall confess that Jesus Christ is Lord, to the glory of God the Father.

"The more lowly your service to others, the greater you are. To be the greatest, be a servant.

"But those who think themselves great shall be disappointed and humbled; and those who humble themselves shall be exalted."

From Philippians 2 and Matthew 23

SCRIPTURE READINGS (PARAPHRASES)

If you are then "risen" with Christ, reach out for the highest gifts of Heaven, where Christ reigns in power. Give your heart to the heavenly things, not to the passing things of earth.

For, as far as this world is concerned, you are already dead, and your true life is a hidden one in God, through Christ. In so far, then, as you have to live upon this earth, consider yourself dead to worldly contacts:

But now, put all these things behind you. No more evil temper or furious rage: no more evil thoughts or words about others, no more evil thoughts or words about God, and no more filthy conversation.

Don't tell one another lies any more, for you have finished with the old man and all he did and have begun life as the new man, who is out to learn what he ought to be, according to the plan of God.

As, therefore, God's picked representatives of the new humanity, purified and beloved of God himself, be merciful in action, kindly in heart, humble in mind.

Accept life, and be most patient and tolerant with one another, always ready to forgive if you have a difference with anyone. Forgive as freely as the Lord has forgiven you.

And, above everything else, be truly loving, for love is the golden chain of all the virtues.

Let the peace of Christ rule in your hearts, remembering that as members of the one body you are called to live in harmony, and never forget to be thankful for what God has done for you.

Teach and help one another along the right road with your psalms and hymns and Christian songs, singing God's praises with joyful hearts.

And whatever work you may have to do, do everything in the name of the Lord Jesus, thanking God the Father through him. From Colossians 3

SCRIPTURE READINGS (PARAPHRASES)

The Lord's servant must not be a man of strife: he must be kind to all, ready and able to teach: he must have patience and the ability gently to correct those who oppose his message.

He must always bear in mind the possibility that God will give them a different outlook, and that they may come to know the truth.

But you must realize that in the last days the times will be full of danger. Men will become utterly self-centered, greedy for money, full of big words.

They will be proud and contemptuous, without any regard for what their parents taught them. They will be utterly lacking in gratitude, purity and normal human affections.

They will be men of unscrupulous speech and have no control of themselves. They will be passionate and unprincipled, treacherous, self-willed and conceited, loving all the time what gives them pleasure instead of loving God.

They will maintain a facade of "religion," but their conduct will deny its validity. You must keep clear of people like this.

Persecution is inevitable for those who are determined to live really Christian lives, while wicked and deceitful men will go from bad to worse, deluding others and deluding themselves.

Yet you must go on steadily in those things that you have learned and which you know are true.

Remember from what sort of people your knowledge has come, and how from early childhood your mind has been familiar with the holy scriptures.

All scripture is inspired by God and is useful for teaching the faith and correcting error, for resetting the direction of a man's life and training him in good living. From 2 Timothy 2 and 3

670 THE DAY OF THE LORD

First of all, you must understand that in the last days some men will appear whose lives are controlled by their own passions.

They will make fun of you and say: "He promised to come, didn't he? Where is he? Our fathers have already died, but everything is still the same as it was since the creation of the world!"

They purposely ignore this fact: long ago God spoke, and the heavens and earth were created. The earth was formed out of water, and by water, and it was by water also, the water of the Flood, that the old world was destroyed.

But the heavens and earth that now exist are being preserved, by the same word of God, for destruction by fire. They are being kept for the day when wicked men will be judged and destroyed.

But the Day of the Lord will come as a thief. On that Day the heavens will disappear with a shrill noise, the heavenly bodies will burn up and be destroyed, and the earth with everything in it will vanish.

Since all these things will be destroyed in this way, what kind of people should you be?

Your lives should be holy and dedicated to God, as you wait for the Day of God, and do your best to make it come soon—

The Day when the heavens will burn up and be destroyed, and the heavenly bodies will be melted by the heat.

But God has promised new heavens and a new earth, where righteousness will be at home, and we wait for these.

And so, my friends, as you wait for that Day, do your best to be pure and faultless in God's sight and to be at peace with him. From 2 Peter 3

671 GOD'S LOVE AND OURS

Dear friends, let us practice loving each other, for love comes from God and those who are loving and kind show that they are the children of God, and that they are getting to know him better.

But if a person isn't loving and kind, it shows that he doesn't know God— for God is love.

God showed how much he loved us by sending his only Son into this wicked world to bring to us eternal life through his death.

In this act we see what real love is: it is not our love for God, but his love for us when he sent his Son to satisfy God's anger against our sins.

Dear friends, since God loved us as much as that, we surely ought to love each other too.

For though we have never yet seen God, when we love each other God lives in us and his love within us grows ever stronger.

We know how much God loves us because we have felt his love and because we believe him when he tells us that he loves us dearly. God is love, and anyone who lives in love is living with God and God is living in him.

And as we live with Christ, our love grows more perfect and complete; so we will not be ashamed and embarrassed at the day of judgment, but can face him with confidence and joy, because he loves us and we love him too.

If anyone says "I love God," but keeps on hating his brother, he is a liar; for if he doesn't love his brother who is right there in front of him, how can he love God whom he has never seen?

And God himself has said that one must love not only God, but his brother too. 1 John 4

SCRIPTURE READINGS (PARAPHRASES)

ALPHABETICAL INDEX OF SCRIPTURE READINGS

Abbreviations (Index) and Credits for Translations and Paraphrases

Ber— from THE HOLY BIBLE, THE BERKELEY VERSION IN MODERN ENGLISH
by Gerrit Verkuyl. Copyright© 1945. Assigned 1958 to Zondervan. Revised 1969.
Used by permission.

KJV— from THE HOLY BIBLE, AUTHORIZED KING JAMES VERSION.

LB— from THE LIVING BIBLE. Copyright© 1971 by Tyndale House Publishers.
Used by permission.

NEB— from THE NEW ENGLISH BIBLE. Copyright© The Delegates of the
Oxford University Press and the Syndics of the Cambridge University Press 1961, 1970.
Reprinted by permission.

Phi— from the NEW TESTAMENT IN MODERN ENGLISH.
Reprinted with Permission of Macmillan Publishing Co., Inc. and Collins Publishers.
Copyright© by J. B. Phillips 1958, 1960, 1972.

RSV— from THE REVISED STANDARD VERSION OF THE BIBLE.
Copyrighted 1946, 1952 and ©1971 by the Division of Christian Education of the
National Council of the Churches of Christ in the USA and used by permission.

TEV— from the TODAY'S ENGLISH VERSION OF THE NEW TESTAMENT.
Copyright© American Bible Society 1966, 1971. Used by permission.

Wms—from NEW TESTAMENT: TRANSLATION IN THE LANGUAGE OF THE PEOPLE
by Charles B. Williams. Copyright© 1966 by Edith S. Williams.
Used by permission, Moody Press, Moody Bible Institute.

SUBJECT INDEX OF SCRIPTURE READINGS

SCRIPTURAL INDEX OF SCRIPTURE READINGS

SCRIPTURAL ALLUSIONS AND QUOTATIONS IN HYMNS

*"Paraphrase" indicates that all or a substantial part of the passage has been versified.

INDEX OF SCRIPTURE ALLUSIONS

INDEX OF SCRIPTURE ALLUSIONS

ALPHABETICAL INDEX OF TUNES

TUNE INDEXES

METRICAL INDEX OF TUNES

Note: This index is commonly used in choosing alternate tunes for a particular hymn text. For this reason only those meters are listed that are represented by at least two tunes. This index also does not include hymns with irregular meters or hymns with refrains. Every tune (with its meter) is listed in the Alphabetical Index of Tunes.

INDEX OF AUTHORS, COMPOSERS AND SOURCES

A

A Missionary Service Book, 1937, w:2
Abelard, Peter (1079-1142) w: 133
Ackley, Alfred Henry (1887-1960) w: 158, 491; m: 158
Ackley, Bentley DeForest (1872-1958) m: 343, 491, 497
Adams, Jessie (1863-1954) w: 449
Adams, Sarah Flower (1805-1848) w: 348
Addison, Joseph (1672-1719) w: 38, 54
Adebesin, Biodun (b. 1928) w: 547
Ahlwén, Elsie (b. 1905) m: 541
Ahnfelt, Oscar (1813-1882) m: 561
Ajose, M. O. (b. 1912) m: 547
Akers, Doris Mae (20th Century) w: 581; m: 581
Alexander, Cecil Frances Humphreys (1818-1895) w: 53, 70
Alford, Henry (1810-1871) w: 537, 565
Alington, Cyril Argentine (1872-1955) w: 170
Allen, Blaine H. (b. 1943) w: 123; m: 123
Allen, Chester G. (1838-1878) m: 96
Allen, George Nelson (1812-1877) m: 495
Ambrose of Milan, St. (c. 340-397) w: 16
American folk hymn, w: 540
American melody, Traditional, m: 15, 28, 181, 224, 230, 250, 269, 288, 304, 325, 413, 429, 494, 498, 522, 539, 540, 544, 545
Antes, John (1740-1811) m: 50
Arne, Thomas Augustus (1710-1778) m: 316, 510
Aström, Johan (1767-1844) w: 542
Atkins, George (19th century) w: 199
Atkinson, Frederick Cook (1841-1896) m: 198
Avery, Richard Kinsey (b. 1934) m: 573

B

Babcock, Maltbie Davenport (1858-1901) w: 58
Bach, Johann Sebastian (1685-1750) m: 136
Backstrom, Carl E. (b. 1901) w: 571
Baker, Henry (1835-1910) m: 5, 91, 357
Baker, Henry Williams (1821-1877) w: 46, 122, 227; m: 259
Baker, Theodore (1851-1934) w: 570
Bakewell, John (1721-1819) w: 95
Barham-Gould, Arthur Cyril (1891-1953) m: 349
Baring-Gould, Sabine (1834-1924) w: 470, 555
Barnard, Charlotte Alington (1830-1869) m: 217, 465
Barnby, Joseph (1838-1896) m: 242, 371, 529, 550, 555
Barraclough, Henry (b. 1891) w: 150; m: 150
Barthelemon, Francois Hippolyte (1741-1808) m: 551
Bartlett, Eugene Monroe, Jr., (b. 1918) w: 479; m: 479
Barton, Bernard (1784-1849) w: 329
Bateman, Christian Henry (1813-1889) w: 60
Bates, Katharine Lee (1859-1929) w: 520
Bathurst, William Hiley (1796-1877) w: 316
Baumbach, Adolph (1830-1880) m: 587
Baxter, Lydia (1809-1874) w: 66
Bayly, Albert Frederick (b. 1901) w: 512
Beethoven, Ludwig van (1770-1827) m: 25, 223
Bennard, George (1873-1958) w: 236; m: 236
Berg, Carolina V. Sandell (1832-1903) w: 41, 561
Bergen, Esther (b. 1921) w: 291
Bernard of Clairvaux (1091-1153) w: 73, 83, 91, 136
Bernard of Cluny (12th century) w: 536
Bethune, George Washington (1805-1862) w: 97
Bevan, Emma Frances (1827-1909) w: 271
Bickersteth, Edward Henry (1825-1906) w: 396
Bilhorn, Peter Philip (1865-1936) m: 296
Blandy, E. W. (19th century) w: 369
Bliss, Philip Paul (1838-1876) w: 155, 222, 231, 254, 261, 390, 408; m: 155, 222, 231, 254, 261, 390, 401, 508
Blom, Frederick A. (1867-1927) w: 541
Boberg, Carl (1859-1940) w: 32
Bode, John Ernest (1816-1874) w: 506
Bohemian Brethren melody, Traditional, m: 474
Bohemian Brethren's *Kirchengesänge*, Berlin, 1566, m: 13
Bonar, Horatius (1808-1889) w: 8, 210, 242, 247, 309, 500
Borthwick, Jane Laurie (1813-1897) w: 324, 450
Bortniansky, Dimitri Stepanovich (1752-1825) m: 523
Bottome, Frank (1823-1894) w: 189
Bourgeois, Louis (c. 1510-c. 1561) m:20
Bourges Breviary, 1734, w: 468
Bowring, John (1792-1872) w: 39, 140
Boyd, William (1845-1928) m: 469
Bradbury, William Batchelder (1816-1868) m: 97, 139, 226, 260, 313, 321, 363, 434, 439
Breck, Carrie E. (1855-1934) w: 534

Bridgers, Luther Burgess (1884-1948) w: 393; m: 393
Bridges, Matthew (1800-1894) w: 85
Bridges, Robert Seymour (1844-1930) w: 152
Briggs, George Wallace (1875-1959) w: 223
Brooke, Stopford Augustus (1832-1916) w: 27
Brooks, Phillips (1835-1893) w: 121
Brownlie, John (1857-1925) w: 181
Bruckner, Herman (1866-1942) w: 444
Buchanan, Annabel M. (b. 1888) m: 15, 539
Budry, Edmond Louis (1854-1932) w: 171
Buell, Harriett Eugenia (1834-1910) w: 323
Bullinger, Ethelbert William (1837-1913) m: 330
Bundes-Lieder, Joachim Neander's, 1680, m: 375
Burke, Christian Caroline Anna (1859-1944) w: 528
Burleigh, Harry T. (1866-1949) m: 513
Burleigh, William Henry (1812-1871) w: 441
Burnap, Uzziah Christopher (1834-1900) m: 73
Burton, John, Sr. (1773-1822) w: 226
Butler, Aubrey Lee (b. 1933) m: 285
Byrne, Mary Elizabeth (1880-1931) w: 344

C

Çaird, George Bradford (b. 1917) w: 118
Caldbeck, George Thomas (1852-1918) m: 396
Caldwell, William (19th century) w: 77
Caldwell's *Union Harmony*, 1837, m: 224
Calkin, John Baptiste (1827-1905) m: 490
Calvin, John (1509-1564) w: 80
Camp, Mabel Johnston (1871-1937) w: 184; m: 92, 184
Campbell, Jane Montgomery (1819-1878) w: 566
Campbell, John D. Sutherland (1845-1914) w: 44
Campbell, Thomas (1777-1844) m: 248
Cantica Laudis, Mason and Webb's, 1850, m: 507, 582
Cantus Diversi, John F. Wade's, 1751, m: 103
Carlson, Nathaniel (1879-1957) w: 541
Carmichael, Ralph Richard (b. 1927) w: 257, 276, 426, 447; m: 257, 276, 426, 447
Carter, Russell Kelso (1849-1928) w: 225; m: 225
Caswall, Edward (1814-1878) w: 73, 83, 143, 550
Cennick, John (1718-1755) w: 185, 445
Chapman, J. Wilbur (1859-1918) w: 99, 128
Charles, Elizabeth Rundle (1828-1896) w: 7
Charlesworth, Vernon J. (1839-1915) w: 322
Chatfield, Allen William (1808-1896) w: 341
Chisholm, Thomas Obediah (1866-1960) w: 37, 135, 319, 333, 380
Chopin, Frederic (1810-1849) m: 586
Chorley, Henry Fothergill (1808-1872) w: 527
Christian Harmony, Ingalls', 1805, m: 87
Christiansen, Avis Marguerite Burgeson (b. 1895) w: 235, 292, 367, 382, 405
Christmas Carols, William Sandys', 1833, m: 108
Clark, John H. (1839-1888) w: 468
Clark, Jeremiah (c. 1669-1707) m: 176
Clark, William H. (19th century) w: 81
Clarke, Harry D. (1888-1957) m: 235
Clarkson, E. Margaret (b. 1915) w: 28, 79, 475, 481
Claudius, Matthias (1740-1815) w: 566
Clayton, Norman J. (b. 1903) w: 277, 308; m: 277, 308
Clayton, William (1814-1879) w: 405
Clement of Alexandria (c.150-c.220) w: 74
Clephane, Elizabeth Cecilia (1830-1869) w: 151
Clough, Samuel O'Malley (1837-1910) w: 436
Cober, Kenneth L. (b. 1902) w: 205
Codner, Elizabeth (1824-1919) w: 363
Coffman, Samuel Frederick (1872-1954) w: 214
Collection, Henry W. Greatorex's, 1851, m: 329
Collins, Henry (1827-1919) w: 335
Columbian Harmony, 1825, m: 199
Conkey, Ithamar (1815-1867) m: 140
Converse, Charles Crozat (1832-1918) m: 435
Cook, John (d. 1948) m: 403
Cook, Joseph Simpson (1859-1933) w: 107
Cooper, Edward (1770-1833) w: 5
Copeland, Roger (b. 1924) w: 501; m: 501
Copenhaver, Laura Scherer (1868-1940) w: 488
Copes, V. Earle (b. 1921) m: 515
Corner's *Gesangbuch*, 1631, m: 588
Cosin, John (1594-1672) w: 188
Cousin, Anne Ross (1824-1906) w: 535
Cowper, William (1731-1800) w: 47, 230, 352
Cox, Frances Elizabeth (1812-1897) w: 13
Coxe, Arthur Cleveland (1818-1896) w: 464
Croft, William (1678-1727) m: 19, 48
Croly, George (1780-1860) w: 198

Crosby, Fanny Jane (1820-1915) w: 40, 96, 130, 251, 272, 285, 317, 334, 354, 361, 402, 433, 440, 480
Crotch, William (1775-1847) m: 22
Cruger, Johann (1598-1662) m: 152, 159, 432, 564
Crum, John Macleod Campbell (1872-1958) w: 162
Cummings, William Hayman (1831-1915) m: 106
Cushing, William Orcutt (1823-1902) w: 310, 400
Cutler, Henry Stephen (1824-1902) m: 467, 485

D

Damon's, William, *Psalms*, 1579, m: 341
Danker, William J. (b. 1914) w: 477
Darwall, John (1731-1789) m: 70, 79, 177
Davison, Fannie Estelle (1851-1887) w: 389
Dearmer, Percy (1867-1936) w: 474
Decius, Nicolaus (c.1490-1541) w: 10; m: 10
Dexter, Henry Martyn (1821-1890) w: 74
Dix, William Chatterton (1837-1898) w: 105, 114, 174
Dixon, Helen Cadbury Alexander (1877-1969) w: 328
Doane, George Washington (1799-1859) w: 490, 556
Doane, William Howard (1832-1915) m: 40, 66, 251, 334, 354, 359, 361, 433, 480
Doddridge, Philip (1702-1751) w: 216, 239, 454, 563, 580
Doudney, Sarah (1841-1926) w: 499
Douglas, Charles Winfred (1867-1944) m: 122
Döving, Carl (1867-1937) w: 201
Draper, William Henry (1855-1933) w: 59
Drese, Adam (1620-1701) m: 450
Duffield, George (1818-1888) w: 455, 456
Dunbar, C. R. (19th century) m: 368
Dunkerly, William Arthur (See pseudonym, Oxenham, John)
Dunlop, Merrill (b. 1905) m: 135, 382
Dwight, Timothy (1752-1817) w: 203
Dyer, Samuel (1785-1835) m: 30, 188
Dyer's, Samuel, *Third Edition of Sacred Music*, 1824, m: 30
Dykes, John Bacchus (1823-1876) m: 1, 2, 46, 83, 197, 202, 309, 352, 414, 442, 511, 531, 537

E

Edgar, Mary Susanne (b. 1889) w: 388
Edmeston, James (1791-1867) w: 558
Edmunds, Lidie H. (19th century) w: 287
Ein Neu Gesengbüchlen, Michael Weisse's, Behmen, 1531, m: 227
Ellerton, John (1826-1893) w: 169, 529
Elliott, Charlotte (1789-1871) w: 260, 315, 427
Elliott, Emily Elizabeth Steele (1836-1897) w: 124
Ellor, James (1819-1899) m: 62
Elvey, George Job (1816-1893) m: 85, 376, 422, 458, 519, 565
Emurian, Ernest K. (b. 1912) w: 517
English carol, Traditional, w: 108
English melody, Traditional, m: 53, 57, 105, 205, 405, 449
Evans, David (1874-1948) m: 60, 327, 553
Everest, Charles William (1814-1877) w: 357
Ewing, Alexander (1830-1895) w: 536
Excell, Edwin Othello (1851-1921) w: 280; m: 146, 280, 288, 569

F

Faber, Frederick William (1814-1863) w: 33, 206, 233
Fallersleben, Heinrich August Hoffmann von (1798-1874) m: 67
Farjeon, Eleanor (1881-1965) w: 553
Fawcett, John (1740-1817) w: 207
Featherstone, William Ralph (1846-1873) w: 72
Fecamp, Jean de (d. 1078) w: 152
Fellers, Foss Luke (1887-1924) m: 471
Ferguson, Manie Payne (19th century) w: 192
Filitz, Friedrich (1804-1876) m: 143, 577
Fillmore, James Henry (1849-1936) m: 157, 389
Findlater, Sarah Borthwick (1823-1907) w: 532
Finnish melody, Traditional, m: 327
Fischer, William Gustavus (1835-1912) m: 270, 302, 386
Flemming, Friedrich Ferdinald (1778-1813) m: 7, 315, 395
Forrest, C. H. (19th century) m: 381
Fortunatus, Venantius Honorius C. (c.530-609) w: 169
Fosdick, Harry Emerson (1878-1969) w: 466
Foster, Myles Birket (1851-1922) m: 468
Foulkes, William Hiram (1877-1962) w: 374
Foundery Collection, 1742, m: 18, 562
Foundling Hospital Collection, 1796, w: 17

Francis of Assisi, St. (1182-1226) w: 59
Francis, Samuel Trevor (1834-1925) w: 229
Franz, Ignace (1719-1790) w: 9
Frazer, George West (1830-1896) w: 3
French carol, Traditional, w: 113
French melody, Traditional, m: 101, 113, 160, 162

G

Gabriel, Charles Hutchinson (1856-1932) w: 294, 299, 362, 538; m: 281, 294, 299, 355, 362, 412, 538
Gaelic melody, Traditional, m: 553
Gannett, William Channing (1840-1923) w: 562
Gardiner, William (1770-1853) m: 21, 38, 241, 514
Gardiner's, William, *Sacred Melodies*, 1812, m: 38
Gardiner's, William, *Sacred Melodies*, 1815, m: 21, 241, 514
Gastoldi, Giovanni Giacomo (c.1556-1622) m: 64
Gauntlett, Henry John (1805-1876) m: 34, 109
Geibel, Adam (1855-1933) m: 455
Geistliche Kirchengesang, Cologne, 1623, m: 59, 166
Gellert, Christian Fürchtegott (1715-1769) w: 159
Genevan Psalter, 1551, w: 20, 22, 80, 572
Gerhardt, Paul (1607-1676) w: 136, 364, 422
German-Latin, w: 118
German melody, Traditional, m: 30, 78, 116, 118, 188, 549
Gesangbuch, Corner's, 1631, m: 588
Gesangbuch, Münster, 1677, w: 67
Gesangbuch, Wirtemberg, 1784, m: 134
Geystliche Lieder, Leipzig, 1539, m: 10, 111
Giardini, Felice de (1716-1796) m: 4, 74
Gibbs, Ada Rose (1865-1905) m: 347
Gilmore, Joseph Henry (1834-1918) w: 439
Gladden, Washington (1836-1918) w: 504
Gläser, Carl Gotthelf (1784-1829) m: 90, 346
Gloria in Excelsis, w: 10
Gordon, Adoniram Judson (1836-1895) m: 72, 300
Goss, John (1800-1880) m: 26, 460
Gottschalk, Louis Moreau (1829-1869) m: 194
Graeff, Frank E. (1860-1919) w: 416
Grant, David (1833-1893) m: 45
Grant, Robert (1779-1838) w: 21
Grape, John Thomas (1835-1915) m: 232
Gray, James Martin (1851-1935) w: 282, 293
Greatorex, Henry Wellington (1813-1858) m: 329, 575
Greek hymn, Early, w: 181, 259
Green, Harold (1871-1930) m: 360
Greenwell, Dora (1821-1882) w: 305
Grimes, E. May (1864-1927) w: 360
Grimes, Katherine A. (b. 1877) w: 370
Griswold, Alexander Viets (1766-1843) w: 6
Grose, Howard Benjamin (1851-1939) w: 465
Grüber, Franz Xaver (1787-1863) m: 117
Grundtvig, Nicolai F. S. (1783-1872) w: 201
Gurney, Dorothy Frances Blomfield (1858-1932) w: 529

H

Hall, Elvina Mabel (1820-1889) w: 232
Hall, J. Lincoln (1866-1930) m: 290, 416
Hammond, Mary Jane (1878-1964) m: 196
Hammontree, Homer (1884-1965) m: 367
Hanby, Benjamin Russell (1833-1867) w: 127; m: 127
Handel, George Frederick (1685-1759) m: 119, 120, 171, 454
Hankey, Arabella Catherine (1834-1911) w: 302
Hanks, Billie, Jr. (b. 1944) w: 482; m: 482
Hansen, Fred C. M. (1888-1965) w: 201
Harkness, Georgia Elma (b. 1891) w: 515
Harkness, Robert (1880-1961) m: 99
Harrison, Ralph (1748-1810) m: 29
Hart, Joseph (1712-1768) w: 269
Hassler, Hans Leo (1564-1612) m: 136
Hastings, Thomas (1784-1872) w: 423; m: 89, 149, 214, 430
Hatch, Edwin (1835-1889) w: 187
Hatton, John (c.1710-1793) m: 489
Hausmann, Julie Katharina (1825-1901) w: 444
Havergal, Frances Ridley (1836-1879) w: 98, 330, 378, 385, 397, 460, 508, 560; m: 169
Havergal, William Henry (1793-1870) m: 16, 132, 221
Hawks, Annie Sherwood (1835-1918) w: 340
Haydn, Franz Joseph (1732-1809) m: 17, 54, 209, 244, 464
Haydn, Johann Michael (1737-1806) m: 21
Head, Bessie Porter (1850-1936) w: 196
Hearn, Marianne (1834-1909) w: 371
Heath, George (1750-1822) w: 462
Heber, Reginald (1783-1826) w: 1, 211, 467, 472
Hedge, Frederick Henry (1805-1890) w: 11

Heermann, Johann (1585-1647) w: 152
Helmore, Thomas (1811-1890) m: 100
Hemmets Koral Bok, 1921, m: 474
Hemy, Henri Frederick (1818-1888) m: 206, 364
Henderson, S. J. (19th century) w: 301
Herbert, George (1593-1632) w: 24
Hewitt, Eliza Edmunds (1851-1920) w: 273, 339, 399, 546
Hickman, Roger M. (1888-1968) m: 298
Hiller, Phillip F. (1699-1769) w: 291
Hindi, Traditional, w: 332
Hine, Stuart K. (b. 1899) w: 32; m: 32
Hodges, John Sebastian Bach (1830-1915) m: 211
Hoffman, Elisha Albright (1839-1929) w: 86, 289, 417, 437; m: 86, 437
Holden, Oliver (1765-1844) m: 63
Holmes, Oliver Wendell (1809-1894) w: 30
Hopper, Edward (1816-1888) w: 446
Housman, Laurence (1865-1959) w: 516
How, William Walsham (1823-1897) w: 219, 262, 507, 533, 583
Howe, Julia Ward (1819-1910) w: 522
Hoyle, Richard Birch (1875-1939) w: 171
Hudson, Ralph E. (1843-1901) w: 81, 279, 368; m: 81, 279, 283
Hugg, George C. (1848-1907) m: 307
Hughes, John (1873-1932) m: 448, 466
Hull, Eleanor Henrietta (1860-1935) w: 344
Hultman, John Alfred (1861-1942) m: 571
Hunter, William (1811-1877) w: 71
Husband, Edward (1843-1908) m: 262
Husband, John Jenkins (1760-1825) m: 358
Hussey, Jennie Evelyn (1874-1958) w: 154
Hustad, Donald Paul (b. 1918) m: 218, 274, 344, 413
Hutchinson, Albert H. (no dates available) w: 568
Hymns for the Young, 1836, w: 321

I

Idle, Christopher Martin (b. 1938) w: 543
India, Folk melody from, m: 451
Ingalls' *Christian Harmony*, 1805, m: 87
Ingalls, Jeremiah (1764-1828) m: 87
Irish hymn (c.8th century) w: 344
Irish melody, Traditional, w: 344
Irvine, Jessie Seymour (1836-1887) m: 45
Italian hymn (18th century) w: 143

J

Jabusch, Willard F. (b. 1930) w: 518; m: 518
Jackson, Robert (1842-1914) m: 187
James, Mary D. (1810-1883) w: 384
Jewish *Doxology*, w: 36
John of Damascus (c.696-c.754) w: 164, 168
Johnson, William (b. 1906) w: 142
Johnston, Julia Harriette (1849-1919) w: 240
Jones, Joseph David (1827-1870) m: 12
Jones, Lewis Edgar (1865-1936) w: 255; m: 255
Jones, Richard G. (b. 1926) w: 52
Jude, William Herbert (1851-1922) m: 503
Judson, Adoniram (1788-1850) w: 215

K

Kaiser, Kurt Frederic (b. 1934) w: 484; m: 484
Katholisches Gesangbuch, Vienna, c. 1774, m: 9, 559
Katholisches Gesangbuch, Würzburg, 1828, w: 550
Keble, John (1792-1866) w: 559
Kelly, Thomas (1769-1855) w: 78, 172, 175, 176
Ken, Thomas (1637-1710) w: 551, 572, 573
Kennedy, Benjamin Hall (1804-1889) w: 144
Kentucky Harmony, 1816, m: 181, 544
Kerr, Hugh Thompson (1872-1950) w: 326
Ketchum, Albert Allen (20th century) w: 93; m: 93
Kethe, William (d. c. 1600) w: 20, 21
Kirchengesänge, Bohemian Brethren's, Berlin, 1566, m: 13
Kirk, James M. (1854-1945) m: 192
Kirkpatrick, William James (1838-1921) m: 81, 112, 154, 189, 273, 287, 305, 312, 333, 402, 486
Kitchin, George W. (1827-1912) w: 141
Knapp, Phoebe Palmer (1839-1908) m: 317
Knapp, William (1698-1768) m: 563
Knecht, Justin Heinrich (1752-1817) m: 262, 445
Kocher, Conrad (1786-1872) m: 55, 114
Kremser, Edward (1838-1914) m: 570

L

Lane, Spencer (1843-1903) m: 418
Langran, James (1835-1909) m: 210, 441
Larcom, Lucy (1826-1893) w: 356
Lathbury, Mary Artemisia (1841-1913) w: 220, 557
Latin carol (14th century) w: 116
Latin hymn, w: 100, 103, 161, 468
Laufer, Calvin Weiss (1874-1938) m: 374
Laurinus, Laurentius Laurentii (1573-1655) w: 542
Leavitt's *The Christian Lyre*, 1831, m: 443, 493
Leddy, Stephen (b. 1944) w: 94; m: 94
Leech, Bryan Jeffery (b. 1931) w: 492
Lemmel, Helen Howarth (1864-1961) w: 252; m: 252
Liljestrand, Paul (b. 1931) m: 492
Lillenas, Haldor (1885-1959) w: 218, 245; m: 245, 292
Lindeman, Ludvig Mathias (1812-1887) m: 201
Lindemann, Johann (c.1550-c.1634) w: 64
Liturgy of St. James (5th century) w: 101
Lloyd, Eva B. (b. 1912) w: 498
Loes, Harry Dixon (1892-1965) w: 82; m: 76, 82
Loizeaux, Alfred Samuel (1877-1962) w: 3
Longstaff, William Dunn (1822-1894) w: 392
Lovelace, Austin Cole (b. 1919) w: 547; m: 511
Loveless, Wendell P. (b. 1892) m: 319
Lowden, Carl Harold (1883-1963) m: 380, 388
Lowell, James Russell (1819-1891) w: 463
Lowry, Robert (1826-1899) w: 165, 237, 275; m: 165, 237, 275, 340, 345, 440
Luther, Charles Carroll (1847-1924) w: 478
Luther, Martin (1483-1546) w: 11, 111; m: 11
Lvov, Alexis Feodorovich (1799-1870) m: 527
Lynch, Thomas Toke (1818-1871) w: 193
Lyon, Meyer (1751-1797) m: 36, 475
Lyra Davidica, London, 1708, m: 163
Lyte, Henry Francis (1793-1847) w: 12, 26, 443, 554

M

Macaulay, Joseph C. (b. 1900) w: 76
Macduff, John Ross (1818-1895) w: 183
Mackay, William Paton (1839-1885) w: 358
Macmillan, Ernest Campbell (1893-1973) m: 107
Macomber, Winfield (1865-1896) w: 186; m: 186
Madan, Martin (1725-1790) w: 95, 185
Main, Hubert Platt (1839-1925) m: 443, 493
Maker, Frederick Charles (1844-1927) m: 151, 256, 407
Malan, Henri Abraham César (1787-1864) m: 144, 385
Mann, Arthur Henry (1850-1929) m: 506
Mant, Richard (1776-1848) w: 34
Maori melody, Traditional, m: 387
March, Daniel (1816-1909) w: 493
Marlatt, Earl (b. 1892) w: 383
Marsh, Charles Howard (1886-1956) m: 128, 179
Marsh, Donald Stuart (b. 1923) m: 573
Marshall, W. S. (19th century) m: 192
Martin, Civilla Durfee (1866-1948) w: 421
Martin, George Clement (1844-1916) m: 335
Martin, W. C. (19th century) w: 311
Martin, Walter Stillman (1862-1935) m: 421
Mason and Webb's *Cantica Laudis*, 1850, m: 507, 582
Mason, Harry Silvernale (1881-1964) m: 383
Mason, Lowell (1792-1872) m: 65, 90, 120, 125, 148, 172, 207, 230, 346, 348, 366, 419, 462, 472, 496, 532, 548, 549
Matheson, George (1842-1906) w: 351, 376
Matthews, Timothy Richard (1826-1910) m: 124
Maxwell, Mary E. (20th century) w: 347
McAfee, Cleland Boyd (1866-1944) w: 342; m: 342
McCutchan, Robert Guy (1877-1958) m: 24, 429
McDaniel, Rufus Henry (1850-1940) w: 281
McDonald, William (1820-1901) w: 270
McGranahan, James (1840-1907) w: 297, 487; m: 178, 249, 271, 295, 297, 306, 459, 487
McIntosh, Rigdon McCoy (1836-1899) m: 545
McKinney, Baylus Benjamin (1886-1952) w: 473; m: 473
Medley, Samuel (1738-1799) w: 65, 77, 166
Meineke, Christoph (1782-1850) m: 576
Melodia Sacra, Weyman's, 1815, m: 119, 454
Mendelssohn, Felix (1809-1847) m: 98, 106, 219, 425, 552
Merrill, William Pierson (1867-1954) w: 461, 521
Messiter, Arthur Henry (1834-1916) m: 14
Miles, C. Austin (1868-1946) w: 398; m: 398
Milman, Henry Hart (1791-1868) w: 132
Milton, John (1608-1674) w: 50
Mohr, Joseph (1792-1848) w: 117
Monk, William Henry (1823-1889) m: 55, 161, 554
Monsell, John Samuel Bewley (1811-1875) w: 469

Montgomery, James (1771-1854) w: 22, 110, 147, 212, 413, 418, 429
Moody, May Whittle (1870-1963) m: 314
Moore, Thomas (1779-1852) w: 423
Moore, William (19th century) m: 199
Morris, Lelia Naylor (1862-1929) w: 180, 268, 353; m: 180, 268, 353
Mote, Edward (1797-1874) w: 313
Moultrie, Gerard (1829-1885) w: 101
Mountain, James (1844-1933) m: 394, 397, 409
Mozart, Wolfgang Amadeus (1756-1791) m: 443, 493
Mühlenberg, William Augustus (1796-1877) w: 217
Murphy, Anne S. (d. 1942) w: 406; m: 406
Musicalisch Handbuch, Georg Rebenlein's, Hamburg, 1690, m: 16, 132, 221

N

Nägeli, Johann Hans Georg (1768-1836) m: 207, 419
Neale, John Mason (1818-1866) w: 100, 116, 122, 131, 160, 164, 168, 259, 536
Neander, Joachim (1650-1680) w: 43; m: 183, 375
Neander's, Joachim, *Bundes-lieder*, 1680, m: 375
Nederlandtsch Gedenckelanck, 1626, m: 570
Netherlands Folk hymn, m: 570
Netherlands melody, Traditional, m: 95
Neumark, Georg (1621-1681) w: 420; m: 420
Neumeister, Erdmann (1671-1756) w: 271
Neuvermehrtes Gesangbuch, Meiningen, 1693, m: 98, 219, 530
Newbolt, Michael R. (1874-1956) w: 141
Newell, William Reed (1868-1956) w: 286
Newman, John Henry (1801-1890) w: 442
Newton, John (1725-1807) w: 68, 146, 209, 288, 431, 548, 589
Nichol, Henry Ernest (1862-1926) w: 483; m: 483
Nicholson, James L. (c.1828-1876) w: 386
Nicholson, Sydney Hugo (1875-1947) m: 141
Noel, Caroline Maria (1817-1877) w: 61
Norris, John Samuel (1844-1907) m: 369
Norse melody, Traditional, m: 287, 542
North, Frank Mason (1850-1935) w: 514

O

Oakeley, Frederick (1802-1880) w: 103
Oatman, Johnson, Jr. (1856-1922) w: 307, 355, 569
Ogden, William Augustus (1841-1897) w: 265; m: 265
Olivers, Thomas (1725-1799) w: 36
Olson, Ernest William (1870-1958) w: 41
Olude, A. T. Olajide (b. 1908) w: 547; m: 547
Orr, J. Edwin (b. 1912) w: 387
Ortlund, Anne (b. 1923) w: 485
Osler, Edward (1798-1863) w: 17
Ostrom, Henry (19th century) w: 179
Owens, Priscilla Jane (1829-1907) w: 486
Oxenham, John (1852-1941) w: 414, 513, 519

P

Palestrina, Giovanni Pierluigi da (1525-1594) m: 161
Palmer, Ray (1808-1887) w: 91, 366
Park, John Edgar (1879-1956) w: 125
Parker, Edwin Pond (1836-1925) w: 502; m: 194, 502
Parry, Joseph (1841-1903) m: 246
Peace, Albert Lister (1844-1912) m: 351
Peek, Joseph Yates (1843-1911) m: 337
Pennefather, William (1816-1873) w: 577
Pensum Sacrum, Gorlitz, 1648, m: 581
Perronet, Edward (1726-1792) w: 62, 63
Perry, Jean (1865-1935) w: 92
Peterson, John W. (b. 1921) w: 49, 56, 69, 182, 410; m: 49, 56, 69, 182, 410, 481
Phelps, Sylvanus Dryden (1816-1895) w: 345
Piae Cantiones, 1582, m: 107
Pierpoint, Folliott Sanford (1835-1917) w: 55
Pigott, Jean Sophia (1845-1882) w: 394
Plainsong melody, m: 100, 122, 148
Plumptre, Edward Hayes (1821-1891) w: 14
Pollard, Adelaide Addison (1862-1934) w: 372
Pollock, Thomas Benson (1836-1896) w: 202
Poole, William Clement (1875-1949) w: 412
Pott, Francis (1832-1909) w: 161
Pounds, Jessie Brown (1861-1921) w: 157, 328
Praxis Pietatis Melica, Berlin, 1653, m: 432
Prentiss, Elizabeth Payson (1818-1878) w: 359
Prichard, Rowland Hugh (1811-1887) w: 99, 102, 174, 408, 512, 521
Prudentius, Aurelius Clemens (348-c.413) w: 122
Psalmes, Thomas Ravenscroft's, 1621, m: 33, 47

Psalmodia Evangelica, Thomas Williams', 1789, m: 500
Psalmody, Tattersall's, 1794, m: 528
Psalms, William Damon's, 1579, m: 341
Purday, Charles Henry (1799-1885) m: 44, 326
Pusey, Philip (1799-1855) w: 395

Q

Quaile, Robert Newton (1867-1927) m: 568

R

Rabanus Maurus (c. 776-856) w: 188
Rader, Paul (1879-1938) w: 190; m: 190
Ramsey, Benjamin Mansell (1849-1923) w: 379; m: 379
Rankin, Jeremiah Eames (1828-1904) w: 42
Ravenscroft, Thomas (c.1592-c.1635) m: 33, 47
Ravenscroft's *Psalmes*, 1621, m: 33, 47
Rebenlein's, Georg, *Musicalisch Handbuch*, Hamburg, 1690, m: 16, 132, 221
Redhead, Richard (1820-1901) m: 147, 193
Redner, Lewis Henry (1830-1908) m: 121
Reed, Andrew (1787-1862) w: 194
Reichardt, C. Luise (c.1780-1826) m: 460
Reinagle, Alexander Robert (1799-1877) m: 68
Reitz, Albert Simpson (b. 1879) w: 438; m: 438
Repository of Sacred Music, John Wyeth's, 1813, m: 28
Reynolds, Mary Lou (b. 1924) w: 31
Reynolds, William Jensen (b. 1920) m: 31
Rhodes, Sarah Betts (1829-1904) w: 567
Rimbault, Edward Francis (1816-1876) m: 239, 535
Rinkart, Martin (1586-1649) w: 564
Rippon, John (1751-1836) w: 62, 63, 224
Rippon's *Selection of Hymns*, 1787, w: 224
Roberts, Daniel Crane (1841-1907) w: 526
Roberts, John (1822-1877) m: 173
Robinson, George Wade (1838-1877) w: 409
Robinson, Robert (1735-1790) w: 28
Röntgen, Julius (1855-1932) m: 95
Root, George Frederick (1820-1895) m: 578
Roth, Elton Menno (1891-1951) w: 404; m: 404
Rousseau, Jean Jacques (1712-1778) m: 291
Rowe, James (1865-1933) w: 343
Rowley, Francis Harold (1854-1952) w: 296
Runyan, William Marion (1870-1957) w: 428; m: 37, 370, 428

S

Sacred Harp, 1844, m: 205, 405, 413, 498
Sacred Melodies, William Gardiner's, 1812, m: 38
Sacred Melodies, William Gardiner's, 1815, m: 21, 241, 514
Sammis, John H. (1846-1919) w: 318
Sandys' *Christmas Carols*, 1833, m: 108
Sandys, William (1792-1874) m: 108
Sankey, Ira David (1840-1908) w: 322; m: 310, 320, 322, 400, 436, 453
Sateren, Leland B. (b. 1913) m: 142
Saward, Michael (b. 1932) w: 234
Schlegel, Katharina Amalia von (1697-?) w: 324
Schlesische Volkslieder, H. A. Hoffmann von Fallersleben's, 1842, m: 67
Schneider, Kent (b. 1946) w: 208; m: 208
Schuler, George S. (1882-1973) m: 505
Schulz, Johann Abraham Peter (1747-1800) m: 566
Schumann, Robert Alexander (1810-1856) m: 378
Schütz, Johann Jakob (1640-1690) w: 13
Schwedler, Johann Christoph (1672-1730) w: 144
Scott, Clara H. (1841-1897) w: 350; m: 350
Scottish Psalter, 1615, m: 589
Scottish Psalter, 1650, w: 45
Scriven, Joseph Medlicott (1819-1886) w: 435
Sears, Edmund Hamilton (1810-1876) w: 104
Seiss, Joseph Augustus (1823-1904) w: 67
Selection of Hymns, Rippon's, 1787, w: 224
Shaw, Geoffrey Turton (1879-1943) m: 516
Shaw, Martin Edward Fallas (1875-1958) m: 162
Shepherd, Thomas (1665-1739) w: 495
Sheppard, Franklin Lawrence (1852-1930) m: 58
Sherwin, William Fiske (1826-1888) w: 220, 557
Shirreff, Emily L. (1814-1897) w: 530
Showalter, Anthony Johnson (1858-1924) m: 417
Shrubsole, William (1760-1806) m: 63
Shurtleff, Ernest Warburton (1862-1917) w: 457
Sibelius, Jean (1865-1957) m: 324
Silcher, Friedrich (1789-1860) m: 444
Skoog, Andrew L. (1856-1934) w: 561

TOPICAL INDEX OF HYMNS

TOPICAL INDEX

ALPHABETICAL INDEX OF HYMNS

The basic listing is of first lines;
common titles are in *Italics*.

ALPHABETICAL INDEX